THE RIVER OF GOLDEN SAND

BEING THE NARRATIVE OF A JOURNEY THROUGH CHINA AND EASTERN TIBET TO BURMAH

WILLIAM JOHN GILL,
EDWARD COLBORNE BABER,
HENRY YULE

GYAN

Published by

Gyan Publishing House
5, Ansari Road
Daryaganj, New Delhi-110002
Phone: 011-47034999, 9811692060
E-mail: books@gyanbooks.com

Distribution Network
gyanbooks.com
India, USA, Canada, UK, Australia

ISBN: 978-93-7169-348-6 (HB)

First Published, 1883

2nd Impression 2026

Printed at: Gyan Press, Delhi.

THE RIVER OF GOLDEN SAND

Author: WILLIAM JOHN GILL, EDWARD COLBORNE BABER, HENRY YULE

Yours very sincerely
William Gill

THE RIVER OF GOLDEN SAND:

BEING THE NARRATIVE OF

A JOURNEY THROUGH CHINA AND EASTERN TIBET TO BURMAH;

BY THE LATE

CAPTAIN WILLIAM GILL, R.E.

CONDENSED

BY EDWARD COLBORNE BABER,

CHINESE SECRETARY TO H. M.'S LEGATION AT PEKING.

EDITED, WITH A MEMOIR AND INTRODUCTORY ESSAY,

BY COLONEL HENRY YULE, C.B., R.E.

With Portrait, Map, and Woodcuts.

LONDON:
JOHN MURRAY, ALBEMARLE STREET.
1883.

TREADMILL—IRRIGATION WHEEL.

PREFATORY NOTE.

Miss F. E. M. Gill, desiring that an illustrated edition of 'The River of Golden Sand' should be prepared as a memorial of her deeply lamented brother, requested me to undertake the superintendence of the work.

It was felt that the bulk of the original book had been too great, and it seemed essential that the error should not be repeated. But abridgment of such a narrative is a difficult matter, especially when the task can no longer be supervised by the author. The difficulty was got over when it was found that Mr. E. Colborne Baber, Chinese Secretary to H.M.'s Legation at Peking, and now in England, was willing to undertake this abridgment. Mr. Baber, by the fact of his being one of Captain Gill's most intimate and valued friends, combined with that of his having been the traveller's companion on the ascent of the Yang-Tzŭ, and by his unique knowledge of Western China and the adjoining hill-country, was qualified for this task as no one else could be.

It was Miss Gill's wish that the Introductory Essay which was issued with the original edition should not be omitted. I have modified it somewhat, and endeavoured to bring it up to a recent date.

The memoir of Captain Gill is based on a sketch, also by the present writer, which was printed in December last in the 'Royal Engineers' Journal,' a paper circulating privately among the officers of the Corps. This has now been expanded, chiefly by additional extracts from my friend's diaries.

The illustrations, in addition to the few which appeared in 1880, are derived mainly from drawings which Captain Gill caused to be made under his own supervision from his very rough sketches. A few have been added (*clichés*) from Lieutenant G. Kreitner's narrative of Count Széchenyi's expedition (*Im Fernen Osten*, Vienna 1881). The portrait which forms the frontispiece has been etched by Mr. T. Blake Wirgman from a photograph; and the group engraved by Mr. Cooper is from the last likeness of Captain Gill, taken at Malta in the beginning of 1882.

H. YULE.

LONDON: *Oct. 26th*, 1883.

CONTENTS.

BRIEF MEMOIR OF CAPTAIN GILL.

GEOGRAPHICAL INTRODUCTION.

CHAPTER I.

CATHAY, AND THE WAY THITHER.

CHAPTER II.

THE CITY OF CAMBALUC.

CHAPTER III.

A CYCLE OF CATHAY.

CHAPTER IV.

THE OCEAN RIVER.

CHAPTER V.

THE GORGES OF THE GREAT RIVER.

CHAPTER VI.

CH'UNG-CH'ING TO CH'ÊNG-TU-FU.

CHAPTER VII.

A LOOP-CAST TOWARDS THE NORTHERN ALPS.

Ch'êng-Tu to Sung-P'an-T'ing.

CHAPTER VIII.

CH'ÊNG-TU, AND THE ROAD TO TIBET.

CHAPTER IX.

TA-CHIEN-LU.

CHAPTER X.

THE GREAT PLATEAU.

1. Ta-Chien-Lu to Lit'ang.

CHAPTER XI.

THE GREAT PLATEAU.

2. Lit'ang to Bat'ang.

CHAPTER XII.

REGION OF THE RIVER OF GOLDEN SAND.

1. Bat'ang to Sha-Lu.

CHAPTER XIII.

REGION OF THE RIVER OF GOLDEN SAND.

2. Sha-Lu to Ta-Li-Fu.

CHAPTER XIV.

IN THE FOOTSTEPS OF MARCO POLO AND OF AUGUSTUS MARGARY.

1. 'The Land of the Gold Teeth.'

CHAPTER XV.

IN THE FOOTSTEPS OF MARCO POLO AND OF AUGUSTUS MARGARY.

2. The Marches of the Kingdom of Mien.

LIST OF ILLUSTRATIONS.

PLATES.

WOODCUTS.

[1] All the cuts not otherwise specified are by Mr. Cooper.

MEMOIR OF WILLIAM GILL

Und zu mir selber sprach ich dann:
Was schmückt den Jüngling, ehrt den Mann?
Was leisteten die tapfern Helden
Von denen uns die Lieder melden,
Die zu der Götter Glanz und Ruhm
Erhub das blinde Heidenthum?
Sie reinigten von Ungeheuern
Die Welt in kühnen Abentheuern,
Begegneten in Kampf dem Leu'n
Und rangen mit dem Minotauren
Die armen Opfer zu befrein,
Und liessen sich das Blut nicht dauren.

SCHILLER.

A BRIEF MEMOIR

OF

CAPTAIN WILLIAM JOHN GILL, R.E.

WILLIAM JOHN GILL was born in 1843 at Bangalore, where his father, the late Major Robert Gill, of the Madras Army, then held a temporary staff appointment. Major Gill, an accomplished artist, was the author of those remarkable copies of ancient paintings on the walls of the Ajanta cave-temples which used to adorn the Crystal Palace at Sydenham, to which they had been lent by the Court of East India Directors, and the destruction of which by the fire there, some fourteen or fifteen years ago, was not the least of the losses caused by that calamity.

William Gill was educated at Brighton College, where one of his contemporaries was Augustus Margary, his precursor in travel from China to the Irawadi, and also in the nature of his death.

His character, even in those early days, was resolute, serious, as well as pure; he was bent on doing his duty and making the best use of his time. His sister writes :—

> . . . When quite a young boy at Brighton College, he asked me to illuminate on a large card the words *England expects every man to do his duty*. This he had hanging on the wall of his bedroom.

She mentions also that he had arranged an alarum with mechanism to pull the clothes off him at a very early hour, and he was habitually at work long before breakfast.

He obtained an entrance into the Royal Military Academy, passing out with his commission in the Royal Engineers in 1864. In September, 1869, he went to India, and served there till March, 1871. Just before his return, a distant relation of his mother, who had no family of his own, left Lieutenant Gill a very handsome fortune. Handsome fortunes do not abound in the Corps, and this circumstance was the subject of various stories more or less mythical.[1] It enabled Gill for the rest of his too brief career to give scope to the intense desire for exploration and adventure which was born with him, but which was on every opportunity turned by him into that channel which seemed best calculated to serve the need of England at the time.

The first occasion of his becoming known as a traveller was when he joined Colonel V. Baker in that journey to Persia of which an account was published by the latter, early in 1876, under the title of 'Clouds in the East.' The journey occupied from April, 1873, to the end of that year. The party travelled to Tiflis and Baku, and thence across the Caspian to Ashurada and Astrabad. Finding no possibility of exploring the Atrek valley, as they desired, from this quarter, they proceeded to Teheran, visiting on the way that famous palace of Shah Abbas at Ashraf, regarding whose Court there we have such interesting details from Pietro della Valle (1618), that rare phenomenon among travellers, and, indeed, among writers of any kind, who is

[1] Mr. G. H. Sawtell, Captain Gill's executor, has kindly furnished the following note at my request: 'Alison Maclellan, a daughter of the then Lord Kirkcudbright, about 1732 married John Rutherford, a son of the then Lord Rutherford. Among their grandchildren in one branch was John Rutherford, a merchant, who died 60 years ago, leaving a considerable fortune. In another branch were many daughters, one of whom married Mr. Heusch, a Dutch merchant, while another married a Mr. Lefevre, whose daughter was Mrs. Gill's mother. Frederick Heusch of Wimbledon, the grandson of the Mr. Heusch just mentioned, was the testator under whose will Captain Gill benefited. Frederick Heusch's mother had inherited from her cousin, John Rutherford, about half of *his* property. There was, as far as I can ascertain, no male relative of Mr. Heusch, when he died, nearer than Captain Gill. The peerage books do not clearly bear out the statement of Mrs. Gill's mother. The peerages both of Kirkcudbright and Rutherford were contested by many claimants in last century.'

always long—as long as Richardson's novels—but never wearisome. The first course of their travels from Teheran was among the Elburz mountains north of that city, crossing the range by a pass 12,000 feet in height, in search of ibex and moufflon.

Here is a passage from Gill's account referred to below—

The tops of these mountains are covered with loose stones. In the winter the cold is of course intense at these immense altitudes, the water in the numerous courses freezes, and the expansion bursts the rock into innumerable fragments. In these solitudes (where down below lies the vast and arid plain stretching towards the horizon, invisible in the dim haze of the desert) is the home of the ibex and moufflon; and often, when no other sound is to be heard but the scream of an eagle astonished at the unwonted sight of a human being, the metallic ring of the loose stones rolling down the mountain-side attracts the sportsman's notice to a herd of these animals, dashing up what would appear an almost impassable precipice.

Then, skirting the great mountain Demavend, they descended again into the dense forests of Mazanderan, and recrossing the mountains to Damghan, followed that line of road along the northern border of the Desert of Khorasan, which has been traced by many a traveller from Marco Polo to Baillie Fraser, and in later years. After visiting Meshhed they struck north to Kila't, the famous stronghold of Nadir Shah.

Kila't (says Gill) is one of the most remarkable places in the world; it is a natural fortress, and if anything in the world can be impregnable it is certainly Kila't. The description of the Happy Valley in the romance of 'Rasselas' might almost be taken for it. It is a large valley, surrounded on all sides by mountains absolutely inaccessible from the outside. At the tops of these mountains can be seen perpendicular cliffs, some 200 or 300 feet high. There are five entrances to the valley, through narrow gorges only two or three yards wide, the cliffs on each side towering up like walls. The valley, besides a stream that runs through it, is plentifully supplied with water from springs. . . . The inhabitants have their herds, and cultivate their corn all in the valley, and consequently they could not be starved out.

From this they passed on to the Darah-gaz district, a fertile tract on the northern skirt of the mountains that look down on the Turcoman steppes, inhabited by an old colony of Kurds, and then flourishing under the wise and vigorous rule of their hereditary chief Ilayar Khan. Here Gill was obliged to rest to recover from a strange gun accident which had nearly cut short his career.

The hillside was broken by steep and rocky ravines, and one had to descend very carefully, creeping down over sloping slabs of rock. G——, it appears, was making his way down one of these places with his gun loaded, but on half-cock, and he had rested it for a moment on a projecting ledge, when, to his horror, it suddenly slipped, and, sliding down muzzle upwards, went off, the discharge being straight at him within three yards. . . . One of his boots (high brown leather riding boots), was cut all to pieces by the shot, and it was an anxious time until we got them off and examined the injury. . . . Neither vein nor artery had been injured. It was a most merciful escape.—*Clouds in the East*, pp. 200–201.

In the same work (p. 224) the author bears testimony to his companion's habitual diligence in survey :—

G—— was most careful and hardworking in his observations, and for many hundreds of miles never missed an angle in the road he followed, ever marching on, compass and note-book in hand.

Recrossing the great frontier range (Kuren-dagh) the travellers explored the upper course of the Atrek, and thence went south-west by Jájirm to Shahrúd, and rejoined the high road from Meshhed to Teheran.

Lieutenant Gill read a short but interesting paper on this journey at the Belfast meeting of the British Association in 1874. This was published in that valuable but now defunct periodical, the 'Geographical Magazine' (October of that year), accompanied by a map which embodied Lieutenant Gill's own route-surveys. These surveys, though rough and made under great difficulties, embraced valuable additions to correct geographical knowledge. Major (now Sir Oliver) St. John was at the time of the traveller's return engaged at the India Office in compiling a new map of Persia, and he has testified warmly to the great advantage he derived from Gill's MS. routes. Nadir's Kila't had been visited apparently by Sir John M'Neill, in 1838, by the late Colonel Beake,[2] and some others; but so little had been ascertained about its true position that till Gill's return it appeared in duplicate—not a very uncommon phenomenon in tentative geography—and in two different positions on our maps. Darah-gaz, too, if laid down at all in previous maps, was entered as a town or village, instead of an extensive and flourishing district forming a separate Government.[3] The corrections which Baker and Gill made as to the true position and course of the Atrek were still more important in their political bearing. This matter is summarised in a note from Sir Oliver St. John as follows:—

About 1869–70 the Russians obtained from the Shah a recognition of their claim to all territory on the eastern shore of the Caspian north of the Atrek river. The Persians (no doubt with truth) affirmed subsequently that their recognition was confined to the littoral, while the Russians contended that their right to all districts north of the Atrek *throughout its course* had been acknowledged.

Previous to Gill's journey the Atrek had been represented on our maps as a stream of the orthodox type with numerous affluents on both banks; or as a stream with few affluents on the north and many on the south. Inhabited Persian districts were all placed on the south bank; and taking the Russian definition of their treaty, it looked as if nothing but bare mountain and barren desert had been given them. But Gill and

[2] Colonel Beake was a gentleman whose personal history, if written down, would have made a book of very uncommon interest. Originally a subaltern in the Bengal Army, he afterwards served under Abbas Mirza, in Khorasan. That prince made him a grant of the famous turquoise mines of Nishapur, but the grantee never was able to realise the concession! In his latter years Colonel Beake was engaged in various mining projects in the Kingdom of Naples, and in Sicily. The p esent writer once travelled with him from Palermo to London, and was entertained the whole way by his personal reminiscences, told with extraordinary vivacity. Colonel Beake was a brother of the late well-known Dr. Beke, but they differed about many things, including even the spelling of their names.

[3] Baillie Fraser on both his journeys to Khorasan was prevented from visiting Kila't. On his second journey (1833) he reached Darah-gaz, but on this journey he carried no instruments.

Baker found that the main stream of the Atrek had no southern affluents, but many northern ones, and that its north bank for a considerable distance from its source was lined with Persian towns and villages. One entire district, Darah-Gaz, lying quite clear of the river to the north, was practically discovered by them. The result was that we were able to back up the Persians in their interpretation of the understanding about the Atrek by appealing to facts, and that the Russians at last modified their claim.

The next enterprise on which the young officer embarked was of a very different character. In the spring of 1874, after the Chief Engineer of the State had laid that unexpected petard of dissolution by which himself and all his crew were hoist, Lieutenant Gill presented himself to the metropolitan borough of Hackney as a Conservative candidate. He was at the bottom of the poll, which ran: Reed, 6,968; Holms, 6,893; Gill, 6,310. But in consequence of mismanagement in the ballot, then first introduced, the election was invalidated. When the new election took place three months later, Gill stood again against Mr. Fawcett and Mr. Holms, and was again defeated, though carrying the respectable number of 8,994 votes. Captain Gill stood for Nottingham at the general election six years later, with similar bad success; and the whole process on that occasion so wearied and disgusted him that he said he would never try the experiment again.

He has not been forgotten at Hackney, and after the announcement of his loss, eight years later, a letter reached his family from that borough, expressing this in a very kindly way.

Gill's name as that of a brother officer was well known to me, through the travels in Persia and the Hackney rejection, but we had never met till one day, in May 1876, when he visited me at the India Office, and announced that he was meditating an expedition by way of Western China into either Tibet or Eastern Turkestan, and wished to consult me. One of the suggestions made was to make Marco Polo his bosom friend, and this he cherished and acted upon throughout his travels; but I also introduced him to two men who could advise him from singular practical experience—I mean Baron Ferdinand v. Richthofen and Mr. T. T. Cooper.

Of Baron Richthofen I will venture to quote words written on another occasion :—

> It is true that the announcement of his presence at the evening meetings (of the Royal Geographical Society) would draw no crowds to the doors ; no extra police would be required to keep the access ; no great nobles would interest themselves about engaging St. James's Hall for his reception, . . . but it is a fact that in his person are combined the great traveller, the great physical geographer, and the accomplished writer, in a degree unknown since Humboldt's best days. In the actual extent of his journeys in China, he has covered more ground than any other traveller of note, and he has mapped as he went. His faculty of applying his geological knowledge to the physical geography of the country he traverses is very remarkable, but not more so than his power of lucid and interesting exposition.

Gill went to Berlin to visit him, and the fullness and cordiality with which his advice and information were communicated are recorded by Gill near the beginning of the narrative of his own travels in China :—

> Hour after hour he gave up his valuable time to me, and opened volumes from his rich store of information. . . . Baron von Richthofen possesses in a remarkable manner the faculty of gathering up the details presented to his view ; putting them together and generalising on them with rare judgment ; forming out of what would be to a lesser genius but scattered and unintelligible fragments, a uniform and comprehensive whole. . . . not one hint was given me that did not subsequently prove its value ; his kind thoughts for my comfort and amusement were never ceasing, and his refined and cultivated intellect and genial manner rendered the recollections of my stay in the German capital some of the most pleasant in my life.—Vol. i. p. 3.

T. T. Cooper was far from any pretension to be classed as a traveller with Richthofen, but he was one of the most adventurous explorers of our time ; he was the first, with the exception of the French missionary priests, to penetrate the mountains west of Szechuen ; and had indeed made two bold attempts, one from that side and a second from the side of Assam, to force that Tibetan barrier which remains yet unpierced between India and China. It is curious that whilst Mr. Cooper was one of the last persons with whom Lieutenant Gill took counsel (it was in my room at the India Office) regarding his journey, before quitting England, it was the same Cooper who received the traveller with open arms and hearty hospitality at Bhamò on the Irawadi, when he emerged from the wilds of the Chinese frontier in November, 1877. A few months later (April 24, 1878) poor Cooper, in his solitary residence at Bhamò, was murdered by a soldier of his sepoy guard.

Gill reached Peking September 21, 1876, and wasted no time there, for on the 25th he had already entered on his first journey in China. This, which was made in the north of Pechili to the borders of Liaotung and the sea-terminus of the Great Wall, was but a trial of his pinions ; the next journey was one of far larger scope. It began with the ascent of the Yang-Tzŭ as far as Ch'ung-Ch'ing in Ssŭ-Ch'uan, and so far he had the best companion probably that he could have found in all China, Mr. Edward Colborne Baber, now Chinese Secretary to our Embassy. From Ch'ung-Ch'ing he travelled to Ch'êng-Tu-Fu, the famous capital of Ssŭ-Ch'uan. Here he had to delay his advance some time, in hope of being joined by Mr. Mesny, a Jerseyman, who had spent many years in the interior of China in the service of the Chinese Government. The delay was spent in an excursion from Ch'êng-Tu to the Alps in the north of Ssŭ-Ch'uan, those 'Min Mountains' of the ancient Yü-Kung, from which the great Kiang of the Chinese, 'the River' *par excellence* (for this, and not the Kinsha from Tibet and Yun-nan, they regard as the main stream), flows down into Ssŭ-Ch'uan. So far as I know, no traveller had preceded Gill in that part of China. The journey formed a loop of some 400 miles, and occupied a month or more. On the day after his return to Ch'êng-Tu Mr. Mesny appeared.

Hitherto Gill's aspirations had been directed to a journey through North-West China to Kashgaria and so to Europe. But the troubled aspect of affairs between

Russia and England now threatened to render this issue impracticable; while at a time of possible war, when duty might be calling him to quite another field in the west, he felt especially unwilling to risk seclusion in some Asiatic *cul de sac.* He was forced to the conclusion that his steps must be directed homeward; but this homeward route might still be one which no European had yet achieved. So he started from Ch'êng-Tu for England *viâ* Eastern Tibet and the Irawadi.

Ta-Chien-Lu, Gill's first place of halt after leaving Ch'êng-Tu, is the Chinese Gate of Tibet on the Ssŭ-Ch'uan frontier. Politically speaking, it is more correctly the gate between what we should call, in Anglo-Indian phrase, the Chinese 'regulation province' of Ssŭ-Ch'uan and the Chinese 'non-regulation province' of the Tibetan Marches. It was also the residence of the late Bishop Chauveau, of the French Missions, an old man whose noble presence and benign character seem to have deeply impressed every traveller who came in contact with him.[4] Captain Gill has told the story of the Chinese etymology of Ta-Chien-Lu ('the Arrow Forge'), but it is a Chinese fancy. The name is really Tibetan—Tartsendo—'confluence of the Tar and Tsen,' as Mr. Baber states, in that admirable and delightful narrative, published in the spring of 1882 by the Royal Geographical Society, which the periodical Press has allowed to pass almost absolutely unnoticed—taking it, I suppose, for a Blue-book, because it is blue!

From Ta-Chien-Lu (8,340 ft.) Gill mounted at once to the

[4] See the *River of Golden Sand*, original edition, vol. ii. pp. 111, 112, and the present volume, p. 185. Mr. Cooper says: 'I perceived a venerable old man, dressed in Chinese costume, with a long snow-white beard. I shall never forget him as long as I live. He was sixty years of age, forty of which he had spent in China as a missionary—his long illness made him look older; his countenance was very beautiful in its benignity; his eye, undimmed by age and suffering, lighted on me with a kindly expression, and he bade me welcome in English, which he had learned from his mother, an English lady, with a tremulous but musical voice.' And again: 'The kindness of the people of Ta-tsian-loo had made a deep impression on me, and in taking leave of the kind old bishop, who with tears in his eyes invoked a blessing upon me, my emotion checked all utterance.'—*Travels*, pp. 181, 222.

summit level of the great Tibetan tableland, on which, with the exception of one or two dips into the gorges of great rivers, he might have continued his way, should lamas and such-like have withdrawn opposition, without ever descending below 11,000 ft., until he hailed the Russian outposts on the northern skirts of Pamir, 1,800 miles away. He continued his journey by Lit'ang (13,280 ft.) to Bat'ang (8,546 ft.) in a tributary valley of the great Kin-sha, and then crossing that river, the real parent stream of the Yang-Tzŭ according to our notions, he turned south, travelling parallel to the river, and frequently along its banks, for twenty-four marches, on his way to Ta-Li-Fu. At this city, the western capital of Yunnan, and the Carajan of Marco Polo, he may be said to have emerged from *terra incognita*, and there the most laborious part of his daily task ceased; for the route thence to the Irawadi had been already surveyed by Mr. Baber when accompanying the Grosvenor mission to inquire into the murder of Margary.

The region north of Ta-Li-Fu traversed by Gill and Mesny presents a singular congeries of tribes. Two of the most prominent, the Músús and the Lísús, are not without claims to civilisation, and their women wear picturesque and graceful costumes bearing a strong analogy to those old fashions of Swiss or Pyrenean valleys, popular types for fancy balls.

The Músús, who call themselves *Náshi*, are said formerly to have possessed a kingdom, the capital of which was Li-Kiang-Fu, which the Tibetans, and the hill-people generally, call Sadam. Their king bore the Chinese style of Mu-tien-wang, and M. Desgodins, from whose authority these facts are derived, says that frequently during his journeys on the banks of the Lan-T'sang and the Lu-Kiang he has come upon the ruins of Músú forts and dwellings, 'as far north as Yerkalo and further,' therefore as far north as Kiangka (about lat. 30°), or nearly so.

Gill met with some Músús at or near Kudeu on the Kin-sha, and he was much struck by the European aspect of a lama (or quasi-lama) who visited him, 'more like a Frenchman than a Tibetan.' This recalled to him what Mr. Baber says of two women, called 'of Kutung,' whom he met near

Tali. These Kutung people were also encountered on their travels further south, in the later journey of Mr. A. R. Colquhoun.

The Lísús, or Lissaus, again, are described by Dr. Anderson as 'a small hill-people, with fair, round, flat faces, high cheek-bones, and some little obliquity of the eye. The men adopt the Shan dress, and the women, like those of the Músús, a picturesque costume of their own. In the upper parts of the great valleys, the Lísús seem intermixed with the Músús, but they have a wide and sparse distribution further to the west, and further to the south.

The onward track from Tali was no longer new. The Irawadi was reached and descended, and Captain Gill, after a short stay in Calcutta, reached England again, after twenty months of travel.

His journal was eventually (1880) published by Mr. Murray in two volumes, under the title of 'The River of Golden Sand' (the real translation of 'Kin-Sha-Kiang'), and it had with the public a fair, though hardly a brilliant success, being certainly too bulky, though free from anything like padding.

The present volume is an endeavour to do more justice to the essential merits of the book, by presenting it in a shorter form. It was thought that no one was more capable of accomplishing the abridgment judiciously than Gill's attached friend and fellow-traveller, Mr. Baber; and happily he has been able to accept the task to which he was invited.

Before the book appeared the merits of Gill's enterprise were recognised by one of the two gold medals of the Royal Geographical Society (May 26, 1879).

The award declared this to be assigned on account

Of the admirable geographical work performed during two long journeys of exploration, voluntarily undertaken along the northern frontier of Persia in 1873, and over previously untravelled ground in Western China and Tibet in 1877, and especially for the careful series of hypsometrical observations and the traverse-survey made during the latter journey, by which we have for the first time the means of constructing with considerable accuracy profile sections of those elevated and little-known regions. Also for the elaborate Memoir contributed to the Journal of the Society on the subject of his expedition, and for the maps of his route in 42 sheets, on a scale of two miles to the inch.

The Paris Geographical Society also in the following year bestowed one of their gold medals on him. It is right to remind readers that the bright personal narrative in his book, as has been indicated by the award just quoted, does not represent Captain Gill's scientific results. Any one who desires to appreciate the real character of his labours must look at the memoir just referred to ('Journal of the Royal Geographical Society,' vol. xlviii. pp. 57, *seqq.*). From his first departure to the north from Ch'êng-Tu, till his arrival at Ta-Li-Fu, a route survey was constantly kept up, while observations for altitude with aneroids and with Casella's hypsometric thermometer were taken daily at frequent intervals. The itinerary appended to the report in the memoir contains a mass of minute detail, filling between Ch'êng-Tu and Momien (near the Burmese frontier) 46 pages of very close print.

Here it may be well to repeat part of a passage quoted by the present writer, in the original issue of his introductory essay to 'The River of Golden Sand,' from a letter of Baron von Richthofen, which carries great weight :—

Captain Gill's results have been of the highest interest to me, particularly those of his journey north of Ch'êng-Tu, and of his route between Ta-tsien-lu and Atentzĕ. He is an acute observer of men and nature, and stands very high indeed by the accuracy and persistency with which he has carried through his surveying work. . . . Many a famous traveller might learn in this respect from Captain Gill. The determination of so many altitudes is, too, a very important part of his work. . . . I regret however that he did not put down on the map all that he was able to see. . . . I presume that Captain Gill wished, ... by the tendency to the utmost possible exactness, to abstain from laying down on his map whatever was lying at some distance from the road. I think it would be well if he could be induced to supply this want.

The regret expressed in these last words has seemed to me well founded, as well as the praise in those that precede them. But Mr. Baber alleges that it is hardly ever possible to get a view of the run of the mountain ranges.

Not long after his return from China, and whilst the negotiations at Santo Stefano were going on, Captain Gill went off with a friend, rather suddenly, to the Danube, with the view of visiting the scenes of recent war in the provinces about to be detached from Turkey. But the Russian officials were too much for Gill and his companion, who did not succeed in getting beyond Giurgevo. They took their revenge by making fun of the Muscovites in 'Vanity Fair.'[5] This escapade dwells in my recollection from the circumstance that an invitation which had been sent to his rooms in Westminster was answered by a telegram from Bucharest.

In the spring of 1878 Captain Gill was sent to Constantinople on duty, in association with Major Clarke, R.A., as assistant in the commission on the settlement of the new Asiatic boundary between Turkey and Russia, consequent on the Treaty of Berlin. Owing to differences of opinion between the English and Russian members as to a portion of the line to be followed, the commission did not that year leave Constantinople; and Gill, after kicking his heels between Constantinople and Therapia for many months, came home. In the following year a fresh commission was appointed of which Sir E. Hamley was the head, and the work was accomplished.

I extract a passage or two from his journal during the stay on the Bosphorus:—

April 12.—As he (B——) remarks, this is a wonderful country. He has no money and no transports; there are absolutely no means for doing anything, and yet, he says, the things will get done somehow, as they always do. H—— says the same thing; sometimes they come to him, and tell him that there is no rice for the men, none to be had anywhere, none to

[5] 'Arrested by the Russians'—in the numbers of that paper for June 1, 8, and 15, 1878.

be bought, no money to pay for any, and the prospect of the whole fleet starving is opened up, but just at the last moment a week's supply turns up from somewhere, no one knows where, and no one knows how. The astounding way in which this country lives from hand to mouth is almost beyond belief.

April 14.—Scobeleff says that no sane being in Russia imagines for a moment that the Russian policy is not *India*, and he said to B——: 'We shall get there—we shall creep on and on, for there will always be plenty of fools in England who will believe that we are *not* doing so; and then some day when you English are unprepared we shall strike the blow. Why of course we all want India! . . . We can't touch you anywhere, thanks to your silver streak. But by advancing towards India we obliterate that silver streak, and at last when we are near enough you will become vulnerable.'

Again, in the summer of 1880, when the news of the defeat of Maiwand reached England, Captain Gill obtained some months' leave and hurried to the scene of expected action in retrieval of that disaster. But Roberts had made yet better haste, and Gill did not reach Quetta till Candahar had been relieved and Ayúb beaten. Eager for some active employment, he was allowed to join Sir Charles Macgregor in his well-conducted but almost bloodless expedition against the Maris, with the duty of a survey-officer. I shall make a few extracts from his diaries again.[6]

August 20 (in the train on his way to Brindisi).—The lamps are lit, beds made up and everyone turned in but me. I sat long looking at the moon rising over the calm blue sea; then, as to my mind all earthly sounds were hushed—hushed the rattle of the train, the hum of human voices, the murmur of the waves—in the spirit I seemed to look with the moon and stars at my own land with all that it contained—all the strifes, passions, loves, struggles, jealousies, hates—and, looked at from that distance, from the serene depths of the heavens, where all is order, all is regularity, how petty, mean, and miserable seemed the aims of all earthly creatures.

September 12 (on the railway in Sind crossing the Desert to Sibi).—I awoke in the Desert. As far as eye can range, nothing

[6] The italicising of a few characteristic passages in the journals is editorial.

but an absolute plain of sand as flat as a billiard table, with not a blade of grass. The Desert of Persia and the Desert in Egypt are nothing to this of Sinde, and the railway was laid across it at the rate of two miles a day. Water-trains for the thousands of labourers had to be sent up, I think, twice a day, and they only broke down once. The labourers were then without water for sixteen hours, which must have been hours of actual torment. For a stretch of 80 miles, there is not one drop of water in the blazing sun of almost the hottest place in the world. Arrived at Sibi. Trains are continually coming in, hundreds of coolies always shouting, piles upon piles of bales of commissariat stores lying about; everything looks like overwork in the blazing sun.

September 15 (after passing up the Bolan).—There is something in mountain air quite different to anything else, it seems so elastic and invigorating, it has such a distinct individuality that you recognise it at once; it is like the Chinaman—exactly the same wherever you meet it; and as you get to a height of about 6,000 feet, you suddenly recollect the feelings you have experienced before, and in a moment what pictures memory conjures up! The Alps, the Caucasus, Persia, China, and Tibet, where the same feeling has been experienced,—you find it at about 6,000 feet above the sea, but not much lower,—and once having felt the exhilaration, you never forget it and always long for it.

September 17 (in the Desert called Dasht-i-Bedaulat).—We got on cheerily enough, meeting every here and there a string of camels. Now that Ayub Khan has been so thoroughly beaten the people are very civil and make profound salaams, with every expression of friendship, but would cut one's throat with the greatest pleasure all the same; that is prestige amongst Asiatics! People at home sometimes sneer at prestige, but if they had marched over this road a month ago and again now, they would go home wiser and give up sneering at prestige.

September 25.—They say that the defeat of Khushk-i-Nakhud (Maiwand) was all but a victory. Ayub Khan wrote a letter to the Khan of Kelat describing it. D—— saw this letter, and it said it was the most desperate battle ever fought in Afghanistan; the letter was far from being boastful. There is no doubt that if —— had not kept the cavalry under fire for hours doing nothing, and thus demoralised them, they would have been able to charge, and so counteract the attack of the Ghazis on our left flank.

September 26.—It seems as if in some terrible convulsion of nature one end of the valley had suddenly sunk and broken the mountain ridges on each side, as you would snap a piece of wood, thus forming what are called rifts; these are simply cracks, going from the top to the bottom of the mountain, quite narrow and with huge perpendicular walls. This rift is not 10 yards wide, and the cliffs rise perpendicularly on either side some 1,500 feet.

He gives a most painful picture of the sudden abandonment of the railway line on the hills between Sibi and Quetta, which had been ordered on the arrival of the news of Maiwand :—

October 6 (at Kotali).—There is about a mile of railway laid here, and a locomotive stands on it which the Maris tried to destroy. They have, however, burnt all the woodwork of it, and the few carriages that were there. The scene of desolation is really shameful. Here is a photograph book, there a dozen or so of novels, the remains of a printing press, the telescope of a theodolite, half a box of cigars (spoilt); a packet of letters was picked up by St. V—— ; Col. L——'s chest of drawers, or rather the remains of it, lie on the ground; broken wheelbarrows, chairs, tables, washhand-stands, strew the ground. The General looted a pewter pot. *And the amount of stationery and printed forms everywhere is astonishing; they fairly litter the road for miles.*

The last feature is strikingly characteristic of Anglo-India!

October 7.—We continue our march down the river, the scene of wreck and ruin being more apparent than ever; broken carts and wheelbarrows; broken-open cartridge-boxes and cash-boxes, old portmanteaus, quantities of books—novels, books of poetry, the Polite Letter Writer (! !), mathematical tables, engineers' books—and then the scene of the fight with a couple of grinning skulls to remind one of the disgraceful disaster. . . . It has been a mistake, I think, bringing the Bengal Sepoys down this way, for they open their eyes in astonishment, and say that they could not have believed that such a disaster could have occurred to the Government. I suppose that —— could never have received or even asked for the sanction of the Government. It seems impossible to believe that the Government would thus have madly sacrificed such a vast amount of valuable property for nothing.

October 12.—I always remember what I do on October 12 [a family aniversary]. Once I was at Kalat-i-Nadiri, in Persia (vide 'Clouds in the East'), once I was at Shan-hai-Kuan; the next year I remember drinking Robert's health when I was with Mesny, though exactly where I do not know.[7] *Now* I shall be at the camp two miles south of Kalat-i-Kila.

I now discovered that M'C——'s syce had bolted (his servant had disappeared some days before with 40 rupees)—, and that all of C——'s and St. V——'s mules had vanished. Naturally I felt for them;—as my box had to be carried by their mules! If I had not had that box, no doubt the misfortunes of my good friends would have given me great satisfaction. MacGregor, however, appeared like the good fairy, and supplied some animals, but these did not start till about 7. I found a table lying about;—everyone had gone, and all their property. It was a table I did not recognise, and was smaller than most. This was a sore temptation. Good people say you should resist temptation. I did not even try. I am a bold bad man! I bid the muleteer put the table on the top of my box. It is a beautiful table; it does not weigh a couple of pounds. I stole that table; I am a thief and I feel no remorse whatever. I took the table to camp: I asked several people if it was theirs (carefully selecting those who would I knew reply in the negative). Then I felt my bosom swell with pride at the excess of my honesty! Anyhow, I've got the table and intend to stick to it. If anyone claims it I shall swear he's a liar. I shall ask him if he wants to impugn my honour; I shall look fierce and draw my sword!

October 16 (Camp at Kwat).—The Goorkhas are wonderful little fellows on the mountain side; they are just like goats, and hop and skip about where I am obliged to go mincingly holding on by hands and feet; they are certainly the best soldiers we have in India, and perhaps out of it.

October 21 (Camp, Biland Well).—The Bombay troops deserve everything that has been said about them; their arrangements are miserable, their commissariat and transport inefficient, their sepoys weak, sickly and useless; they never kept together, never lent a hand to anyone else, but directly a

[7] At Yung-Chang-Fu (Vochan of Marco Polo) on the Chino-Burman frontier (see *River of Golden Sand*, orig. ed. ii. 337).

load came off one of their animals, they laid themselves down to sleep and expected some one else to do their work.

October 22.—The march we made yesterday was really a very remarkable one, and in all probability the most difficult accomplished during the whole Afghan war; the want of water was the most terrible thing, and it was lucky it was not hot; if it had been and we had been opposed, I really don't believe the march would have been possible. As it was we lost about 60 animals and the Bombay troops lost about 100.

October 29.—The Goorkhas, B—— said, worked like bricks, always cheerful; they crack their jokes under the most dismal circumstances, have no sense of fear, and can run up hills and mountains like goats.

October 30 (after reaching Karam Khan).—I can't make out yet whether these people are friends or foes. Some are Pathans—these are friends; some are Maris—these are enemies. Affairs are complicated because the Maris have driven out the Pathans, taken their fields, and then let the Pathans come back as tenants.

Query, then, are the crops the crops of the Mari robber proprietors, or of the Pathan tenants (not at will, but much against their will)? The difference between this place and Ireland is, that in Ireland tenants kill their landlords, here the landlords kill the tenants.

November 2 (near Mamand).—The General had intended (if a peaceful arrangement had not been attained) to have sent half his force to Kahan, to have taken the other half to Safid Tok; he had made arrangements for both the forces from Thull and from Kwat Mandai to have converged at the same time, and if it had been fighting it would simply have been slaughter. *One cannot help feeling glad that this has been avoided, even though we lose the medal we might have got if the Maris had been pitched into.*

November 4 (at Khanki).—I am always much amused at the discussion of heights and distances. Says someone to me (I am, I believe, the only man in the force with a barometer), 'Well, Gill, what did we come down to-day?' I observe 530 feet. 'Oh,' says my interlocutor, 'we came down double that.' I always now expect this answer, so say nothing; *he* generally finishes by writing down the height I gave him.

November 15 (between Fatehpur and Rajanpur).—What a treat to see an avenue of acacias and babul trees, not scrubby bushes! How our eyes revelled in the cultivated fields and gardens! This is peace; these are the effects of a few years of wise rule. This place was a desert a few years ago, now there is prosperity and safety for everyone.

November 17.—Got up at 6 and started about 7. The air was fresh but very damp, owing to the proximity of the mighty stream of Indus. . . . We determined to ride straight in and breakfast at the Railway Station, Kahnpur. I never enjoyed a ride more. Of course it was over the perfectly flat plain, bu after the dreary deserts of Baluchistan, the plain of Bhawalpur looked a very garden, though people from India look on it more or less as a howling wilderness. There were nice villages ensconced in trees, large ber trees, babuls, and date-palms; plains of rich green grass; sugar-cane khets, and rice fields spoke of peace and a peaceful quiet rule. It was indeed refreshing, and quite raised our spirits to see the fine large villages, the ryots at work with their ploughs, the many travellers on the roads, all of whom salaam, or give a pleasant answer to the usual inquiry of 'How far off?' *The very droning of the Persian wheels, monotonous noise though it be, was pleasant enough, for it spoke of irrigation and fruitful fields, industry and prosperity.*

Of Gill's employment on the Mari Expedition, its leader, Sir Charles Macgregor, writes to me thus:—

Gill came out to Quetta, just as my brigade was going off, and I was very glad to take him with me. He undertook and carried out in the most conscientious manner a survey of the country we went over, and though this was of itself a sufficiently laborious task for any man, he was always ready to lend a hand where he could be useful; he did many times prove of great assistance to me, and in my despatch I mentioned being specially indebted to him. After we got back, without any rest he started off for Merv, by way of Bandar Abbass.

He was a great favourite with the whole force, and I am sure I have met few men of whom I have had such a high opinion. As a subordinate I know how reliable he was, and I always felt that if his day ever came he would not shine less as a commander.

I cannot conclude these few remarks better than by transcribing what Col. Brackenbury writes to me of him: 'There are few men like him; few who have ever combined such a gallant spirit with such unassuming modesty;' every word of which I can heartily endorse.

In Gill's personal journal for his family, he notes under November 3 :—

As for my march, is it not written in the book of Chronicles of my official Diary, where an accurate description of every yard is written ?

Gill had leave still available when he reached the coast, and determined to make use of it in a bold attempt to reach Merv. He embarked at Karáchi on December 4, for Bandar Abbás, and travelled by Sirján, Kírmán, Yezd, and Teheran to Meshhed. His original intention had been to go direct from Kermán to Meshhed, but this was impracticable on account of the snow in the high tracts to be passed. At Meshhed he found the expedition to Merv impossible, without permission from home and extension of leave. He would have been certain to overstay his leave, and had therefore to return (riding *chappa*) to Teheran, to meet the reply, which was, as he had feared, a refusal. The complaints of M. de Giers about 'the English officers who haunted the frontier' were recent. Gill returned from Teheran, crossing the Caspian from Enzeli to Baku, and thence by Tiflis and across the Caucasus, and so home by Moscow and Berlin. At Tiflis, where he stopped a few days, he made a variety of acquaintances, and met many whom he had known at Constantinople. By somewhat desperate efforts he reached Moscow on March 28, and London on April 1, 1881, the day his leave expired. His sister writes : 'William telegraphed to us at home to dine with him on his arrival that evening, tired though he must have been.' Tired enough surely ! He had been just nine days travelling from Tiflis to his chambers in Edinburgh Mansions, Victoria Street. We give a few extracts from the journal of this Persian episode :—

December 13 (at mouth of Pass above Bandar Abbas).—The moon was still well up and the stars shone brightly, so that it was easy to see to pack up. We turned up a narrow and quite dry gorge ; in this light it had a most weird aspect ; the light was no doubt deceptive, but it looked as if the rocks were going to precipitate themselves into the valley. The precipices seemed to rise straight up and overhang the road, the lights and shadows were quite startling, and the effect was heightened by the abominable nitrous smell that pervaded the place. The gorge twisted and turned like some horrid snake, between great masses of bare rock.

December 21 (at Saidabad, on the way to Kirmán).—I am somewhat dismal at the prospect of a complete failure, which it seems I must look forward to—and I fancy my writing, disjointed and disconnected, reflects my dismal frame of mind.

Thought my plans well over and determined to abandon the enterprise (of getting to Merv), which now appears hopeless. The direct road to Meshhed was said to be blocked with snow, and they will not undertake the journey to Kirmán under five days. I am also met with the pleasing intelligence that the road beyond Kirmán is impassable even for the post messengers —and what that means in these countries where post messengers are supposed to go through anything, can be imagined.

I could not leave Kirmán before January 1, and I should have 50 days only at the outside to do at least 1,000 miles, and in all probability less time to do much more. I am therefore determined to go to Kirmán without baggage animals, get my letters, &c., and come back here as quickly as possible, and so on to Shiraz, whence I shall ride post to Teheran and so home.

December 23.—Munshi, who had never seen snow, remarked that it was the funniest sort of rain he had ever seen in his life.

December 25 (Caravanserai at Akhar-abad, between Măshis and Kirmán).—Looking back there was a splendid panorama of snowy mountains, nearly all round, Kuh-Kala-Asker rising grandly above them all; but somehow I find that snow-mountains, much as I love to feast my eyes on the sight, when one knows the snow is not perpetual, seem to impress one very differently to those grand giants whose heads never know the loss of their glorious crowns. However, it was a splendid sight, and worth coming a long way to see.

My Christmas dinner was excellent, but without plum pudding.

My heart was lightened by the thought that to-day my letter would be a welcome Christmas gift; for I calculate that my first from Karachi will be received to-day.

His sister notes here :—

He never failed to send letters to reach home as nearly as possible on any special days or seasons *besides* the regular letters.

December 31 (on way from Kirmán to Yezd).—Heavy clouds everywhere, a sea of mud before us and the telegraph posts stretching away into the dim distance, the only signs of civilisation, seeming, too, a link between me and home, inviting me to abandon these desolate places and asking me what was the good of giving up everything that makes life worth living ; and as the prospects of success in the enterprise I have undertaken seem more and more dim, it requires all the resolution I have to continue in the uncomfortable task.

January 12 (1881).—As we approached Yezd, a number of riders, some on exceedingly good horses, and with two led horses, gaily caparisoned with bridles covered with gold lace, appeared. Here, I thought, is the Shahzada on his way to Kirmán ; but no, these were people whom the Governor of Yezd had sent out to meet me and welcome me ; they were officers, some in a high position. I had almost forgotten the custom of sending out led horses, and it brought to my mind my previous travels in Persia, for in this country, instead of coming out yourself, you send your best horses in their best clothing. The two chief of these officers were sober, stately gentlemen. Some of the others now went through their games. One man stood on his head on the saddle, and put both legs straight up in the air. Many of them dashed backwards and forwards, and round and round, firing off their rifles. Another dashed off at full gallop, threw his rifle in the air and caught it again, then, dropping the reins on the animal's neck, fired at an imaginary foe. As we neared the city others came to meet me, and when inside a number of farashes (domestic servants) of the Governor joined the procession, now a formidable array. We descended at the door of a magnificent house that had been prepared for us, with an unlimited number of servants and guard ; then the Governor sent to inquire after my health, which he did about every ten minutes ; in the evening he came himself, and his talk was chiefly of sport, of which he seems very fond. He treats me magnificently, feeds my horses, finds all materials for my food, and sends the Munshi a very fine dinner. I really don't like taking all this, but of course there will be presents to make when I go away, &c.

The whole business is very amusing, that, coming into Persia utterly unknown, without a letter, or credentials, or passport of any form or kind, except my own statement that I am an English officer, I should receive such hospitality. The Governor complained that he had done nothing for me, and apologised for not doing more.

I always feel suspicious when such protestations, almost servile from our point of view, are made.

January 17.—Persia is like a filled-up basin, there is no drainage to the sea, and in the course of many ages the *débris* and sand washed down from the mountains have filled up this basin, for nothing can be carried away except by dust storms—thus these everlasting plains have been formed; they of course get higher and higher, and the mountains get lower. The gaps between these get filled up.[8]

January 19.—Somewhere in the sandy waste we crossed to-day, we passed the boundary of Isfahan and entered the province of Khorasan, the garden of Persia; but what a garden and what a hopeless country!—nothing but dreary wastes of salt sand and salt water, with a few salt streams.

While at Yezd talking with the Governor, a man who was sitting by said he had heard of a prophet having arisen in America, and wanted to know something about it. I told him of the Mormons and Salt Lake City, of Brigham Young and his 100 wives. I told him the American Government did not approve of all this, but up to now had been unable to put it down; to which he replied, he hoped that God would help that Government in its attempts.

January 20.—As usual, there is a marked contrast between this country and China. China is a country that is drained to the sea; there everything tends to get steeper and steeper, while here everything gets shallower and less steep. The time is of course the time of geological ages, but the effects of the work of time plainly show what is still going on. In China you travel through deep ravines, and the mountain passes are crossed by desperately steep ascents. Here, to cross a 'godar,' as they style them, you ascend a gentle and easy slope, and scarcely know when you are at the top. There the summits are like the edge of a knife.

January 26 (at Sang-gird).—We went up the Sir Valley, which in spring or autumn must be delightful—extensive gardens of vines, figs, pomegranates, peaches, apricots, walnuts, and cherries. A stream of real fresh water ripples over a pebbly

[8] During his travels in China, and since, he had often discussed Richthofen's speculations on steppe-formation. I find in a letter of his, dated May 12 (1881): 'I often used to think of Richthofen's remarks about Central Asia being "filled up," when travelling through Persia. The latter is regularly a "filled-up country"—all filled up, except the tops of the mountains, which stick up out of the sand like rocky islands out of a sea.'

bed, overhung by plane and walnut trees. At other times we passed rows of mulberry trees. It certainly was a treat to ride through this, after the dreary and desolate wastes to which we have been accustomed; and I could well appreciate Ferrier's ecstasy at Dehrud, which (when we were there eight years ago) we were much disappointed with, because we had been travelling in comparatively fertile places. I saw here the first magpies to-day that I have seen on this journey. I like the sight of magpies, they always seem to me homely friendly birds.

January 27.—We marched $37\frac{1}{4}$ miles to Kăfgīr, thus completing upwards of 1,000 miles from Bandar Abbas.

January 29 (Măshhăd or Meshhed. After meeting different people there he writes): Now what chance have I in doing in a few days what they have failed in doing in months (speaking of Napier, O'Donovan, and Stewart)? I might of course manage it if I could stay here some time, but travelling as I am, without Government sanction, I cannot possibly overstay my leave, nor even run the risk of it. There is only one course for me to pursue—that is, to get permission from the Minister. It is the only way not tried by S——. It is altogether a very forlorn hope, for I feel certain that the answer to my telegram will be a decided refusal.

January 30.—My people and horses were glad enough to have finished this march of upwards of 500 miles, in 15 days, for we left Yezd on the 15th, and from Yezd to Meshhed is, at my computation, just 505 miles; and my distances compared with those of Smith from Kirmán to Yezd, or with those of McGregor from Yezd, and those of Stewart from Yezd, as far as they came my road, are all too short; so that is not bad marching.

February 8.—S—— and I rode out to the Mosque of Khája-Rabbi, about four miles out from the city—a pretty place with gilt minarets and a garden that would be delightful in spring or summer; the gardener gave us some violets, but I have come to the conclusion that from one end of Persia to the other there is absolutely nothing worth coming to see, and the way in which people in old days used to talk about the glories and beauties of Persian cities is simply ridiculous.

February 18 (from Meshhed to Teheran).—Average distance (from Meshhed) $68\frac{3}{4}$ miles a day. From 10th to 18th we came $549\frac{1}{2}$ miles; for the first and last days can count as one only—making eight days.

Very easy going for *chappa* riding.

March 2 (in Ghilan).—To-day's ride would be lovely anywhere—through beautiful forests, woods of olives, tumbling streams, green park-like bits; banks with quantities of violets and primroses in blossom; picturesque huts, with high thatched roofs; everything to remind one that we are now in a wet climate.

March 3.—The climate of Ghilan is rife with a poisonous fever. I was offered hospitality in the kindest way by Monsieur Schwaabe.

March 24 (on way from Tiflis to Kazbek).—Our things were soon transferred into a sleigh, which easily carried Gerome, myself, and our luggage, and we went off with two horses tandem. The road was very narrow, between walls of snow, sometimes twelve feet high. Under is any depth of snow up to twenty or thirty feet. For the great avalanche that fell the other day came down from a valley and buried nearly the whole of *this stage*, and in it twelve men were lost.

In October of the same year Captain Gill again obtained leave. This time the transactions of the French in Tunis had drawn his attention to North Africa, and it appeared to him that there was great need of detailed knowledge of the provinces between Tunis and Egypt. On his way he made a short tour in Sicily, climbing Etna to the foot of the cone, but hindered by rough weather from completing the ascent. At Malta (October 31) he was joined by a dragoman whom he had summoned, a Syrian from Beyrut, by name Khalíl-Atík. This man seems to have won much of his master's regard; rejoining him on the last fatal expedition, and perishing with him.[9] Gill's first experience of the new dragoman's *aplomb* (to say the least) rather startled him.

November 1.—I gave Khalíl a circular note and told him to ask the landlord if he could change it. He brought me back 25 napoleons. 'But,' I said, 'I must sign it.' 'Oh!' replied Khalíl, 'I've done that for you.' I made him bring back the note and found he had forged my name with the most complete *sang-froid*, though hardly in a way my bankers would recognise.

On November 7 he writes at Tripoli:—

Here I am again in my old style, writing my diary as of old in many a Chinese inn. Of all, I think the one that is brought

[9] This faithful servant was the son of Nimja Atík, a widow in the employment of the British School Mission (Mrs. Bowen Thomson's) at Beyrút.

most forcibly to my recollection is one, a day or two beyond Ch'êng-Tu. It was the hottest night I ever remember, the city was fearfully closed in, the heat and sleepiness were awful, the bugs were plentiful; though I sat nearly naked, I think I drowned one or two in the perspiration that dropped from me.[1] I remember Mesny's wonder, not unmixed with admiration, at my being able to sit down and write. However, recollections crowd upon me, so that if I once begin I shall never leave off.

His sojourn in Tripoli extended from the first week of November, 1881, to the first week in April following. Three-fifths of this time was wasted in waiting for a permission from Constantinople to travel, which never came, and, after it became necessary to dispense with that, much also in waiting for the execution of promises which never were kept. But Gill brought to bear the same patience and persistence that had carried him through difficulties on the frontier of China, Tibet, and Burma; several interesting journeys were accomplished, and a large mass of information collected. His first journey was, parallel to the coast, westward to Zuara and Farwa (105 m. from Tripoli); a second to Nalut in the hill country, W.S.W. of Tripoli, and thence eastward along the hill country itself to Yifrín, and then N. by E. to Tripoli; lastly from Tripoli S. into the hill country by Wádi Mijinín, then east to Homs upon the coast, and back along the coast by Lebda to the capital. He had desired to travel by land from Tripoli to Benghazi, and it was in the hope of obtaining an opportunity for this that he waited long in vain. At last, when this hope failed, he proceeded to Benghazi by steamer, leaving Tripoli April 3.

I extract a few passages from his journals during his sojourn in Tripoli:—

November 26.—Of course a load fell off one of the camels immediately after starting, but that I had naturally looked forward to. Khalîl says he never knew what patience meant before he came here, but he is rapidly learning it now. *All delays come to me now as a matter of course. I take them like the rain or the sun.*

December 6.—The 'Times' correspondent has been here,

[1] Apparently at Hsin-Chin-Hsien, July 11, 1877.

and spent a week in one of my rooms; he is coming back again next month. I wish *I* had come out as a special correspondent—I could easily have managed it—and then I should have been able to go where I liked; for they would never dare to incur the displeasure of the great English newspapers.

December 20.—*It is strange*—at least it seems so to me—*that people whose lives are little better than miserable should set such value on them, while people who have everything they want in this world care nothing at all about their lives.*

The journal abounds in characteristics of Turkish ways and modes of government.

Under February 4 we find more than one such :—

There is no telegraph from this to Malta, and telegrams go therefore to Malta by steamer, and thence are wired by an English company.

It appears that the Ferik (General) here has been sending great numbers of telegrams to Constantinople, but as there is a difficulty about prepayment (for the telegraph company have no agent here) the company, taking into consideration his high position and the fact that his messages were for his Government, allowed the Ferik to run up a bill. But having run it up he declined to pay it, and as he is to be deposed immediately, he is quite indifferent about the results. The consequence is, that the company now refuse to send any telegrams for the military authorities here, who are thus cut off from all communication with Constantinople.

. . . . Of one thing I am quite sure from conversation with Khalîl, and that is, that at no very distant day there will be a terrible reckoning for the Turks in Syria, when the Christians in that country, assisted by some outside power (or without such assistance, should the Turks be driven in a war with another Power to withdraw all their troops from Syria), shall unlock the floodgates of bitter hatred which have been shut for so many years, and let loose the torrent of wild revenge which, having been held back for so long, has been constantly growing and increasing in volume, till now it is ready to sweep in a vast flood over the whole country—revenge for years of insult and oppression—revenge for the death of fathers, mothers, sisters, and brothers—revenge for the deprivation of those liberties which make life worth living—and more than all, revenge for religious persecution.

Under March 18 Gill relates the story of John Brown, and how he was hanged by Governor Wise, of Virginia, as it was told him by Colonel Robeson, the American Consul-General at Tripoli. Gill was a boy, I fancy, of thirteen or fourteen when the thing happened, and was evidently not familiar with the history, which older men remember well. But Colonel Robeson's story had a continuation worth extracting :—

All this occurred before the war, and Governor Wise was at that time a very wealthy, powerful, and opulent person. After the war he was nearly penniless, and in one of the border states it so happened that Colonel Robeson was in the Quarter-Master-General's office, when a shabby mean-looking person came in and asked for assistance. 'Who are you?' said the Quarter-Master-General. 'I was Governor Wise,' said the stranger; 'I am absolutely penniless now, and have come to ask you for assistance to help me back to Virginia.' The Quarter-Master-General paused. It was just time for guard-mounting, and during the pause the band marched by the window, playing 'John Brown!' It was a mere chance, but a very remarkable one. The Quarter-Master-General gave the late Governor all he could, and sent him on his way.

March 24.—Took a ride in the afternoon by myself.

Out at the gate by the seashore, where the rising westerly wind sends little wavelets even here into the sheltered harbour to break on the sandy shore skirting the grim old battlemented wall, we pass with difficulty through a busy crowd. Here are dozens of hucksters with little tables spread selling bread, white, brown, and black. An Arab, wrapt up in a *barakan* so that he can only see right in front of him, like a horse with blinkers, drives a donkey among my horse's legs. But I know the spot and go cautiously. My horse, fresh with big feeds of barley and little work, puts his ears back and prepares to dance. But I know *him* too by this time, and I check him just in time to prevent him upsetting half-a-dozen tables. Successfully we thread the intricacies of the crowd, and here, in a wide sandy road between low mud walls that enclose barley-fields, now green and fresh, are hucksters sitting in a row with bundles of lucerne grass and carrots, their donkeys, camels, and horses tethered hard by out of the way, or lying provokingly in the way in the middle of the road. Masaud out of pure joyousness of heart tries to snatch a carrot or a mouthful of corn, and when hindered looks round reproachfully at me. So we pass the throng on to the quiet road, where a quarter of a mile onward a white mosque with a picturesque minaret stands at the beginning of the palms. Through these we ride for a couple of miles, the bare rough stems of the trees rising from fields of green barley, glowing red with poppies ; the fig trees and the pomegranates just putting forth their leaves, exulting in the early spring, which here indeed is radiant ; almond trees covered with blossoms rest lovingly against the more sombre olives ; oranges and lemons laden with their golden fruit would tempt the passer-by to pluck one here and there were they not so common, and the air is laden with the scent of the orange flowers, &c. . . . .

And as the sun sets we again pass through the gates with a fervent prayer that this may be the last time, and that the steamer may come to-morrow. Then to the stables, where we see our horses fed, and sit for half-an-hour with old Taylor, while his tongue runs on continually, as we silently smoke a cigarette, and so home to the solitary dinner !

Benghazi was reached by steamer on April 6. It was reached *à la Turc*, however, from the *eastward*, the Captain having overshot the mark some 50 miles in the night. Gill was told after landing that a Turkish steamer expected from the west always appeared from the east and *vice versâ*.

He writes under date April 8, in a letter to a friend :—

The vessel belongs partly to a company, but I don't exactly know the ins and outs. She used to be commanded by an Austrian, but recently the government have put Turkish naval officers into her, as part of their policy of exciting all Mussulmans against all Christians. That this is their policy now I am certain ; I have no doubt that the Egyptian troubles are a part of it ; and it is a fact that the officers of the Turkish army have been ordered to associate as little as possible with Christians. * * * The officers of the ship were fortunately exceedingly polite and good natured (as Turks always are) and allowed the three first-class passengers to use the bridge. One of them was a young Italian, who belongs to a pseudo-geographico-scientifico-meteorologico-commercial society. This society has a station at Benghazi, and another at Derna ; but heaven knows what they do, unless you omit all the other o's, and substitute 'politico.'

One of his objects was to travel from Benghazi through the Cyrenaica by land to Egypt. Having failed to obtain any Turkish permission to travel, but understanding that the Vali would not make any opposition to his going without leave, he made a start at night (April 21), having first sent most of his things out of the town to a garden-house two miles distant. But the last despatch of luggage was intercepted by an officious *Zaptieh*; a party were sent after them; they were turned back, and his camel-men, &c., were thrown into prison.

It was a costly and vexatious failure, and Gill felt it much. He writes on April 26:—

Alas, alas! spilt milk, spilt milk, in huge cans full! It's no use crying over it, but it's uncommonly hard to help it.

.... Though Tripoli is badly governed, this Vilayat is infinitely worse. The present Vali was at one time Pasha at Tripoli, but D—— H—— got him kicked out, after a reign of forty days only, for indulging too openly in the traffic of slaves. Here he can do this with less trouble, for although the people in England may not know it, the slave-trade flourishes exceedingly. ... He was once turned out of this place also. He went away with a large retinue of slaves in a steamer, touching at Crete. The Consul here managed to apprise the Consul at Crete of the affair; the latter boarded the ship, but all the slaves were found with passports, and declared themselves free and willing servants of the Pasha, who, partly by threats, and partly by telling them the foreigners would come and make them Christians by force, had made them deny their slavery. Of course, directly they left Crete, the passports were taken away and burnt.

On May 8, he left Benghazi by steamer for Malta; and thence on the 15th for Catania, where he caught the steamer for Constantinople. I believe his efforts to obtain any redress, or the release of his men arrested at Benghazi, were unsuccessful. He started from Constantinople by rail on May 29. I give a few more extracts:—

May 29.—I think there was a little malice mixed up in my determination to travel without a *teskere*, that is, without leave; for the Ambassador wigged me so severely (in S——'s presence) for travelling without leave in Tripoli, that I confess I take some

CAPTAIN W. J. GILL,

WITH THE COMPANIONS OF HIS JOURNEYS IN TRIPOLI.

pleasure in doing the same thing here, with the knowledge of the Ambassador himself, and by the advice of his private secretary (S——).

. . . This man (X——) got a contract for the railway from Constantinople to —— and onwards through the mountains, and he arranged it so as to be paid at so much a kilomètre, the same price per kilomètre in the mountains as in the plains, a sort of medium rate having been chosen; accordingly he set to work and made the line in the plain as long as he could, winding about instead of going straight, for in the plains where the line costs much less per mile than he was paid by his contract, the longer he could make it the better for himself. Then as soon as he reached the mountains he employed agents who went to the Minister of Public Works, and by his (X——'s) instructions abused it, pointed out that the line had purposely been made longer than necessary, and advised the Minister to break the concession. The Minister fell into the trap, and wanted to break off the engagement. X—— pretended to be angry and demanded compensation, which was given him by allowing him to cut, in perpetuity apparently, as much timber as he liked in the Forest of Y——, but which in the somewhat curious wording of the concession he was to treat *en bon père de famille*. . . . Thus have the wretched Turks been spoiled by the Christian *entrepreneurs*. Of course it is their own fault, as they will do nothing without bribes, and thus respectable men are driven away.

May 30 (at Philippopolis).—The German (agent of a water company) made one very significant remark. He said, 'Everything is safe here, that is why my company comes here. We know that if we get our concession our money will be paid regularly, and that our investment is a safe one; whereas in Turkey everything is different and nothing is secure.'

He reached London on June 16. On the 21st of the following month he was again on the move; starting on what was to be his last expedition. He was directed to proceed to Egypt on special service, with rank as Deputy-Assistant-Adjutant-General and Deputy-Assistant-Quarter-Master-General. I had no opportunity of personally wishing him God-speed, being out of town at the moment, but I may be forgiven if I transcribe here the words, now so greatly valued, in which he told me of the orders :—

1 Edinburgh Mansions, 20-7.

Just one line to wish my kindest friend good-bye. I received orders last night to start to-morrow for Alexandria. The very short peeps I have had of you have been the pleasantest half-hours of my short stay at home.

The circumstances of Captain Gill's deputation to Egypt were first publicly stated in a speech delivered by Lord Northbrook at the Royal Geographical Society on November 13, 1882. Gill had been employed, under Lord Northbrook's instructions, in association with Colonel Bradford, a distinguished officer of the Indian service, in collecting information as to the Bedouin tribes adjoining the Canal. Such an inquiry soon brought them into communication with Professor E. H. Palmer as the person best able to assist them, and before long it led to the despatch of Professor Palmer to the desert.[2] Lord Northbrook, seeing Gill's character and value, proposed to send him also out to join Admiral Hoskins at Port Said as an officer of the Intelligence Department. The charge of cutting the telegraph wire from Cairo, which crossed the Desert to El-Arish and Syria, and so to Constantinople, by which Arábi (in rebellion against the Porte !) obtained information and support from that capital, eventually devolved on him.

More than once indications have been manifested of a supposition that Gill's despatch on this last fatal expedition had originated somehow on his own motion. There was no ground for this idea except the voluntary character of some of his former journeys, in which, though travelling at his own cost, he procured information of great public value ; and it is quite dispelled by the following passages (over which one might fancy some presentiment to hover), gathered from the torn and stained fragments of diary which were recovered from the surface of the Desert many weeks after his death, and pieced together by his sister's pious care:—

Wednesday, July 19.— * * East, who told me I was to go to-morrow to Egypt. Found a memo. from Sir Garnet Wolseley to that effect when I got home. Two lines only * * *

[2] Professor Palmer left London June 30 ; left Jaffa July 12 ; left Gaza for Suez through the Desert about July 14.

Friday, 21st.— * * I have this consolation, that whatever happens I never asked any one to send me, or to let me go to Egypt. When G. Wolseley * * to go, I was quite prepared, until Lord [Northbrook] expressly sent for me, and asked me to go to Admiral Hoskins. *Personally I would rather have been with* [* * Wolseley (?)] * *but now whatever turns up I shall feel that I have simply done what I was told.*

On another torn scrap, on which no date remains, but which seems to have been written at this time, we find these touching and suggestive words:—

* * *chance for which* * * *come at last. I do I have spent my life* * * *the earth in search of information* * * *by way of fitting myself for active* [*service*] * * *but the latter I have always missed by ill-luck.*

I volunteered for Abyssinia when a boy * *

He reached Alexandria on July 27, and next day proceeded to Port Said in the 'Decoy' to report himself to Admiral Hoskins. Here he became an official guest of Captain Dennistoun of the 'Tourmaline' till August 5, when he left for Suez, arriving there on the 6th at 4 A.M.

Before going further I will here cite a few passages from the last pages of his journal.[3]

July 27 (Alexandria).—There is not much to say about the streets of Alexandria. Some of them are in hideous ruins, others fairly intact, but the impression of driving down a street which is not ruined is almost more melancholy than driving in one that is, because all the houses and shops are shut up, the streets are quite deserted, and the place has the appearance of a city of the dead ; it almost puts one in mind of Pompeii.

July 29 (Port Said).—Met B., 'Standard' correspondent, to-day. Met him at dinner about three weeks ago at Sir Oliver St. John's. How one does meet people one has met elsewhere ! Wandering about the world one meets a certain lot of people that one meets everywhere else out of England. It always

[3] Some fragments of the diary retained by himself were picked up, as already mentioned, in the Desert, and a few additional extracts from these (sometimes deciphered with difficulty) are introduced further on. The remainder, and much the larger part, are taken from the somewhat fuller and more explanatory journal which he transmitted to his mother from Suez before the fatal start of August 8.

seems to me that I know more people in every foreign capital than I do in London. This is not, of course, really the case, but it is true that abroad I am certain to stumble casually on lots of people I know—that in foreign places I always find an *entrée* at once into the whole society, so that I know everyone in a very short time—while, at home, London is so immense, that though one keeps on increasing one's acquaintance, there are always hundreds, not to say thousands, of whom one knows nothing.

August 1.—The position of affairs here is most extraordinary; we are living nominally and apparently at peace with everyone—no military precautions are anywhere taken—no preparations made, and yet we are at war. We cannot buy a camel, nor a sheep, nor a donkey, nor a sack of straw, because we have no place to put anything in. We cannot collect animals at Suez until we take it. The same is the case at Ismailia. Thus we are apparently friendly with everyone, and liable at the same time to have the water cut off at any moment; we cannot even begin to get into relations with the Arab Sheikhs, who, in the meantime, are gradually going over to Arabi.

During his stay at Port Said, he wrote a memorandum to the Admiral (now before me) 'On the Position of Affairs at Port Said and Ismailia,' but his chief occupation seems to have been making arrangements for a supply of fresh water, in case the existing supply should be cut off, which was threatened. In this he was associated with Captain Seymour of the 'Iris.' On the 3rd, he writes :—

Saw a man named D——, an Englishman, an engineer, who has the ice factory here. He is employed by us to buy from the Canal Company six steam tugs, old and useless for their proper purpose. . . . If he gets them we can turn them into condensers, condensing 200 tons a day. We then propose to moor two or three big iron lighters in the corner of the Commercial Basin—holding about sixty tons between them—and to moor the 'N. Briton' (refugee ship) close by; to make her small engines of use for condensing, and her tanks for storage, and to keep the iron lighters always full of water. The people can then come and get what they want out of the lighter.

Friday, August 4.—On board the 'Penelope;' learnt that the Admiral had gone to Ismailia last night about 10. He has not seen my memo. on Palmer's report, which has gone straight to Beauchamp Seymour. It does not matter except that I should have asked Hoskins whether he had the money for Palmer, before writing the memo., if I had known it would go straight to B. S. £25,000 will, according to Palmer, buy over 50,000 Arabs on the east of the Canal. I intend to urge that this money should be straightway sent down to him at Suez. . . . I hear that most of the policemen here will join our side when the time comes, and carry on the ordinary and usual police work. This will be a great blessing, and saving of difficulties, though it will offend the European population. The Europeans at Alexandria are furious that we employ the native policemen, and write as if we were the lords and masters of Egypt already. It is the continually employing Europeans instead of natives which has been the root of all the evils in Egypt, and now this miserable European population howl because we don't exercise a most arbitrary authority, to which we have no right whatever, and turn out the police of the Khedive.

. . . ——, the —— correspondent, went to Suez to-day—a good riddance, for it is a nuisance to have a man always pumping you. I wish I had known it in time enough to write to Palmer, and warn him to keep out of his way ! . . . X—— here amused me the other day. I was talking about the water being cut off, and he said : 'Ah, it really does not matter to me if they cut it off, for I always drink soda-water.' I mentally added, 'with plenty of B.'

From this forward I print the journal entire, omitting only some statements as to speed, &c., of the boat that carried him to Suez.

August 5.—Got a message from the Admiral that he wanted to see me, and found that he had received orders to cut the telegraph wire between Kantara and El-Arish.[4] This is to be done without breaking the neutrality of the Suez Canal, so we cannot simply pick up the cable where it crosses the Canal, and take it away, nor can we land at Kantara.

To land at or near El-Arish would be very risky, unless we were in communication with the Bedouins near.

So I decided to go and consult —— and Palmer.

I was given a picket boat, which is a large steam-launch

[4] Kantara is on the Suez Canal, and El-Arish on the Mediterranean coast, nearly one hundred miles east of Port Said.

supposed to go 12 knots, but in fact not averaging more than 9½. There was a Lieut. Grove and a middy with me, and we took a pilot. We left at 3h. 20m. . . . Between the nineteenth and twentieth mile-posts saw people working on the western bank. It did not look like fortifying the place, but fresh earth was being thrown over the bank. I could not make out what they were doing, but I was too low down to see.

We arrived alongside the 'Orion' at Ismailia at about 8 P.M. The senior officer, Captain Fitzroy, was not on his ship, but was dining with Stevenson on the 'Carysfort,' and thither I went. Found them half through dinner; they gave me to eat, and then, having sent for —— we discussed matters. —— was of opinion that we could not depend on landing near El-Arish, which was also my very strong opinion. He wants himself to go to Gaza, where he says he knows the Governor. . . . I did not think the proposal hopeful, but did not say so. Fitzroy told me that there were 3,000 men at Nifish, with their front facing the Canal to Ismailia, their right resting on the railway station, and their left towards the desert on the north; and that the railway bridge to Suez over the Freshwater Canal, on their extreme right, was still intact; four guns were counted, and horses were seen. This morning two battalions were seen at drill, and this evening a larger number. There was a picket in the Arab town of Ismailia, and Lesseps himself was stopped by this picket. There is also constant communication between Nifish and Ismailia.

The old Governor of Ismailia, Gaver Bey, being afraid of Arábi, is on board one of the English men-of-war. The new Governor is Ari Effendi Zulf Agha, or some such name. He was some years ago cashier in the Custom House at Alexandria. —— knows him and thinks he could buy him, but he thinks that of everybody!

After about an hour we went on again. I slept a good deal between 10 and 2. After this we met another man-of-war launch, in which was Helsham Jones, going up to Ismailia to have a look round.

We reached the flag-ship of Sir W. Hewett, V.C., K.C.B., at about 4 A.M. Stopped here to take in water, and then went ashore, as Hewett is living at the Suez Hotel.

We had been carrying 20,000*l.* in gold, and I was not sorry to get rid of it. There was scarcely anyone on board the flag-ship besides the first lieutenant, who gave us sailors' coffee. I do think the coffee you get on a man-of-war for nastiness beats even that on board a P. and O.

All the sailors are landed, as there was a scare the other night—last night, I think—which ended in nothing. It turns out that the water is not cut off from Suez.

Sunday, August 6.—Found Hewett at the hotel; also Tanner, who was my fellow-passenger from London to Alexandria. Saw Palmer also. He is the professor of Arabic at Cambridge, and has travelled much in the Sinaitic Peninsula, and knows all the Arab Sheikhs. He has just come from among them, and is hopeful of buying about 50,000 over to us for about 25,000*l.* Had a long talk with him and determined to go and cut the wire myself; this will help to show me how far Palmer's rather hopeful opinions are true. Palmer has arranged for a great meeting of Sheikhs in a few days, and if he were to go north to cut the cable he would miss this meeting, which might do incalculable injury. There is no one here to send except military and naval officers, who have never travelled among this sort of people; and for every reason it is best for me to go.

. . . . I brought Palmer down authority to spend 20,000*l.* amongst the Bedouins.[5]

We are in a very curious position now, but I do not think that Arábi will break the neutrality of the Canal as long as we don't; and as all Europe is against any one doing anything to affect its neutrality, I don't suppose our Government will dare to do it, so that we shall probably have to march on Cairo from Suez direct, and, without using the fertile and well-watered *waadi*, we shall have to go straight across the Desert. Then I believe we shall find ourselves at war with Turkey, if not with Russia also, and several of the other Powers.

Of course I had to set to work to buy an outfit, Arab clothes, pillows, cooking-pots, meat, flour, &c. &c. Then I got hold of Lieut. Brant, gunnery lieutenant, and got from him all the things necessary, gun-cotton, Bickford's fuse, detonators, axes,

[5] Captain Gill was mistaken in supposing, as he appears to have done (or, at any rate, as has been concluded from this passage in connection with a preceding paragraph), that the money which Lieutenant Grove, R.N., brought down in the picket-boat in which Gill travelled was an advance for Palmer. It was for the Admiral's chest, and to meet all demands thereon that might arise (inclusive doubtless of any advances to Palmer that might be authorised). See Lord Northbrook's statements in the House of Lords, March 16, 1883. See also Mr. Besant's Memoir of Palmer, p. 301.

&c., and am ready now to destroy one of the greatest works of civilisation—a telegraph line. Suez is not altogether or by any means deserted; still it is empty. War is always melancholy to me. The sad side of it always forces itself on my attention somehow. *The newspaper correspondent, who lives in an atmosphere of gunpowder, and does not know what it is to travel in an uncivilised country in a state of profound peace, does not feel it like one who has travelled about a good deal and lived amongst a poor and uncivilised people in a state of peace.*

Many laughable incidents occurred at the capture of Suez. Colonel Tanner, with a dozen marines, trying to catch the train, in which the Governor was being carried off, and Arabi's soldiers looking at them out of window. How Palmer impressed Captain C—— (the oldest resident Englishman's) favourite donkey, on which Helsham Jones mounted, tumbled into the Freshwater Canal, and spoilt the saddle. C—— does not see the point of the landing now, at all! How the only two soldiers who stopped behind did not like giving up their arms. Poor fellows! I believe there was something good about those two! They stayed behind, and they almost cried when they had their rifles taken from them.

I went out to the Camp, as it is now called—Victoria Hospital it was in 1869, when Dick Roberts lived there, with whom I spent a day. Suez was quite a gay place in those days. The table d'hôte of this hotel was always crowded, and there were plenty of ladies. My next visit here was on returning from China, and the Drummonds were here too.

—— My watch has come to grief. I usually travel with about half-a-dozen timepieces altogether; hitherto my watch has never stopped. For the first time I believe in all my travels I have only one watch; now something has gone wrong with the catch of the winding gear, and it won't wind up.

These words are the last in William Gill's journal sent home, as his habit was, to his mother and sister. One of the torn and partly obliterated fragments picked up in the Desert by Sir Charles Warren goes further :—

Monday, August 7.—The Admiral would not let us start today, and indeed it won't make much delay, for Palmer is expecting Emtaiyarr, chief of the Hawetât.[6] If we miss him it will

[6] This is the man better known as Meter Âbu Sofiah, on whose

delay us, as he has all the country close to Suez. A steam-launch went up to-day to reconnoitre. I went with it. Charrington, the flag-lieutenant of the Admiral, was with us, and a middy of course (Gore Brown). Gordon, of the —— (an officer waiting for his regiment), came too. . . . Helsham Jones rode out with a naval officer; he also saw them, but being on the Cairo side of the Canal, they levelled their rifles at him. This shows that Arabi will respect the Canal as long as we do. Our party came from Canal, or Canal land, and his soldiers did not notice us. Jones came on the other side, or land not belonging to Canal, and he was threatened.

In the evening Emtaiyarr arrived, much to our relief. This man has never seen a house before. Arabi has sent to him many times, and he has always refused to go; but a word from Palmer brought him in. The Admiral gave him a sword. He was immensely proud.

Tuesday, August 8.—A ship arrived with the late 72nd this morning.

These are his last written words.

Professor Palmer had reached Suez on August 1, after that venturesome journey from Gaza, described in Mr. Besant's biography of his friend, in the chapter entitled 'The Great Ride of the Sheikh Abdulla.' On his way he had met Mislah, the Sheikh of the Teyahah Bedouins, who introduced him to Meter Âbu Sofîah already mentioned, as the head Sheikh of the Lehewât, occupying all the country east of Suez.

According to Sir Charles Warren's report, both statements were deceptions. Meter Âbu Sofîah was *not* a Sheikh of the Lehewât, and that tribe does *not* occupy the position alleged. And it was principally, he considers, owing to the difficulties arising from these deceptions that Palmer and his companions fell into the hands of the Bedouins who murdered them.

Professor Palmer had made arrangements for certain Sheikhs of the Desert tribes to meet him on the 12th, at Nakhl, which is a fort in the Desert about half-way between Suez and Akaba. And at his request Lieutenant Harold Charrington, Admiral Hewett's flag-lieutenant, was to ac-

duplicity and avarice the chief blame of the catastrophe seems to rest. His tribe is called Lehewât.

company him as a guarantee to the chiefs that Palmer was acting on the part of the Queen's Government. Palmer took with him 3,000*l.* in sovereigns, received from the 'Euryalus.' And this, there is no just ground for questioning, was intended mainly to procure camels; though there is no need to ignore the perfectly legitimate object of the expedition, which was the chief duty which Palmer had taken upon him, viz. to secure the adhesion of the sheikhs.

Gill, it would appear, arranged to keep them company, and afterwards to proceed to destroy the wire. The party, consisting of the three English gentlemen, with Gill's dragoman, Khalíl Atík, Palmer's cook (a Hebrew, Bokhor Hassûn), Meter Âbu Sofîah and his nephew, left Suez, in Arab clothing, on the 8th for the Well of Moses, where they picked up camels and camelmen. They started from the Wells next morning. Admiral Hewett does not appear to have expected to hear from them before the 18th. Even some days before this date disquieting rumours began to spread, but no serious alarm was taken, and on the 27th Admiral Hoskins reported that Gill was stated to be safe, and was expected to reach Suez the day after.

This report appears to be connected with what was heard and repeated by Mr. ——, who had been sent about the middle of August to Gaza. His people brought him news that Gill had been at an encampment of the Terabin Arabs in that neighbourhood recently, and had started for Suez;[7] a mystification which has not been explained. But —— also heard a rumour that two white men had been murdered.

In England, though much reticence was observed, just anxiety seems to have been awakened at the Admiralty, earlier than at Suez; and Colonel (now Sir Charles) Warren, R.E., whose experience and qualifications for dealing with an inquiry among Arabs were estimated highly, and not more highly than the result has shown that they deserved, was sent out in the end of August to advise and assist

[7] These lines are part of the original memoir as printed in the *Royal Engineers' Journal* for December 1882. They are quite corroborated by Colonel Warren's letter to Lord Alcester dated February 16, 1883, and published in the 'Supplementary Correspondence' presented to Parliament.

Admiral Hewett in this matter. Warren proceeded to Tor, and at a later date to Akaba, by steamer. He found the Arabs at both places singularly indisposed to enter into any communication ; but up to the end of September, and even later, he did not despair of the travellers being still alive, and it was not till October 20 that he could report the story of their having been attacked on August 10, and put to death.

Four days later (October 24) Colonel Warren was on the scene of the murder, and all doubt was at an end.

I shall not dwell on the complex and painful details of the last scenes. All that could be derived from a comparison of the evidence and confessions has been detailed by Colonel Warren in his letter to the Admiralty of April 10 ('Supp. Corres.' pp. 24, *seqq.*), and reprinted by Mr. Besant in his Life of Palmer. On the night of the 9th the party encamped at Wâdi Kahalin (which I do not find on any map, but which must lie somewhat less than 30 miles S.S.E. of Suez). Here they were detained a great part of the next day by the search for two camels that had been stolen during the night, and they did not quit the ground until 3 P.M. After midnight, at a place called Maharib, in Wâdi Sadr,[8] they were attacked and fired on by Bedouins in ambuscade, some twenty-five in number. Nothing certain is known of what passed in the capture, but it is probable (says Colonel Warren) that the Bedouins, finding they were so few in number, rushed in upon them and disarmed them. Meter Âbu Sofîah had escaped to his own camp, and on the 11th brought down a few of his tribesmen, ostensibly for the rescue of the travellers. He found them stripped but unguarded, and at this time an escape seems to have been possible, had the guide been true. But the enemy returned ; Âbu Sofîah went through some attempt, or pretext, of negotiation for ransom, which was rejected, and they were left to their fates ; 'it being understood by the Meter and those who accompanied him that the party were to be killed.' They were driven, stripped to their shirts and bareheaded,

[8] This has generally been written Wady *Sudr* ; but I gather that the vowel is the *fatḥa* or short *ă*, and the name in systematic spelling would be written *Sadr*, possibly *Ṣadr*.

under an August sun, to a ravine in the Wadi Sadr, and there the murder was accomplished.

They died, let it be distinctly said, honourably engaged in their country's service. But whether the murder was the act of greedy ruffians, or was ordered from a distance, we see as yet no absolutely clear ground for judgment. Indeed, Sir Charles Warren himself, though tending to the former view, evidently has doubts. I incline to the other, and to assent to all the grounds for doubt in that direction, which are so well stated by Mr. Besant.[9] Indeed, cold-blooded murder of this kind is not usual with Bedouins.

A question which has frequently been asked is why Admiral Hewett allowed the party to go on such an expedition, and with such a sum of money, without escort? I believe that there were no means of supplying escort, and that the question therefore for Sir W. Hewett's decision really was, whether in such circumstances the party was to go without escort or not to go at all. Palmer certainly impressed him with the view that there was no serious danger. The real danger, which almost certainly produced the catastrophe—that is, the agency of the Shedid Sheikhs at Cairo in stirring up Bedouins in their allegiance—seems not to have been present to any one's mind. It will also be seen from Warren's letter (in the 'Supp. Corres.' p. 16) that Palmer had written on the 4th to Meter Âbu Sofîah desiring him to come to Moses' Wells with twenty armed men to escort him to Nakhl. We do not know whether Palmer had agreed with Âbu Sofîah, to dispense with these, or, on finding that they were not forthcoming, still decided to go on, in order to keep the appointment at Nakhl, trusting to the safeguard of Âbu Sofîah.

The tragedy occurred on August 11, apparently in the afternoon.

Colonel Warren, when he reached the scene more than ten weeks later (October 24), collected the very scanty relics of the victims and of their clothing, &c. He then proceeded to Nakhl, where he succeeded, without resistance, in installing the new Governor who had accompanied him from Suez. The old Governor was arrested.

[9] *Life of E. H. Palmer*, pp. 320, *seqq.*

Meter Âbu Sofîah on November 6 gave himself up to Captain Stephenson, R.N., at Suez. He was examined by Colonel Warren, but died in the native hospital at Suez, January 6, so that he never was tried.

By the extraordinary and prolonged exertions of Colonel Warren, involving not only much hardship and considerable danger, but the exercise of great tact, judgment, and patience, the story was traced out, evidence collected, and the majority of the chief participators in the crime brought to justice. These were tried in his presence by the Egyptian commission at Tantah, February 6 to 14, and five of the principal culprits condemned to death; eight others (including the ex-governor of Nakhl) to various terms of imprisonment; capital sentence being also pronounced against five who were still at large. The execution was carried out at Zagazig on March 1.

The three victims of this memorable calamity might all be called young men, and full of promise, but two of them were also men who had given such proofs of their great qualities, 'that their loss might have dimmed a victory.'[1] They will not, I trust, be forgotten by the country for whose service they gave their lives. And in regard to this subject, I venture to quote here words of my own used at the Royal Geographical Society on November 13—words which also give briefly my impression of my friend's character:—

. . . . What a singular Nemesis has brooded over the fate of those travellers who were the earliest in our day to take part in rending the veil which hung over these Indo-Chinese frontier lands! Francis Garnier, Cooper, Margary, and now poor Gill—all perishing by violence. Three of the four I knew; two of these, Garnier and Gill, did me the honour to call me friend.

It was surely, my Lord, a sad and strange lot that fell to me, under Providence, twice within ten days last month, to be called on, through no action of my own, to furnish notices to the public press of the careers of friends of mine, each eminent for what he had accomplished—both still greater in promise for the future—and each of them young enough to have been my son!—one, Arthur Burnell, a scholar, and a ripe and good one, the

[1] Words of Lord Dalhousie, in a G. O., regarding the murder of Colonel Mackeson at Peshâwar in 1853.

most eminent scholar, indeed, on the lists of the modern Indian Services; a man of many high qualities, but eminently a man of books. The other, William Gill, a man to whom action—action—action—was everything; reserved, often taciturn in company, but having beneath that undemonstrative exterior a soul of fire!

Look at his constant eagerness to devote himself to useful enterprise; to take on himself any amount of toil; to face any amount of danger and hardship—and, still harder to bear, any amount of weary waiting, and the monotony of temporary failure, when his country seemed to need it at his hands; and all this at his own charges—literally spending and spent in the public service.

Lately, by favour of his family, a vast mass of his journals, which he kept in great detail, and regularly forwarded for his mother's perusal (for he was a good son as well as a good servant of his country), have passed under my eye. Reviewing through these his brief career, and the vast amount of toilsome enterprise crowded into it, it seems to me that his ardent and loyal soul had wrested from the enemy the pet adage of treason, and bound as a cognisance round his gallant brow, '*England's necessity is my opportunity.*'

Let me, before I sit down, add a word more regarding this good soldier and his companions. It was no common occasion on which they were sent forth into the Desert of the Wanderings, from which their footsteps were never to emerge; it was by no common tragedy that their bright career was quenched; they were no common men! Let England show that she feels it!

In one of those journals of which I have spoken, to which my friend used to commit his thoughts in his wanderings, he one day wrote thus:—

'I have been considering what I should give as the definition of a Great Power, and I have come to the conclusion that a Great Power is one which can best protect its subjects wherever they may be.'

It must needs be that disasters should sometimes come. England cannot everywhere anticipate them. But when they come from crime and treachery, surely, in spite of all that is come and gone, England may still say with truth, 'Woe to him from whom they come!' And she will, we may gather from a late reply of Mr. Gladstone's, make provision for those of the families left behind who may require such provision. But more than that! She is bound to see that, if their mortal part lay for weeks and months dishonoured and bleaching beneath the desert sun, at least no honour shall now be grudged to their memory, but that a tablet in St. Paul's or Westminster shall commemorate their names, their career, and their common fate.

But yet again. My Lord Aberdare, you referred in your Address to those thousands of rock-inscriptions on Sinai, which Palmer had interpreted. I would fain see another rock-inscription added! I would fain see that, aloft on that fatal cliff in Paran, a panel should be hewn, and on it cut, large and deep, so as to show black in the mid-day sun, and to be legible for miles across the waste, such words as these: '*Go, Traveller, and tell in England that we three died here in obedience to her behests.*'

The desire expressed in the foregoing sentences for the erection of some public memorial in honour of these three gallant gentlemen is now, thanks to the generous zeal with which the object has been promoted by Lord Northbrook, in process of fulfilment. The scanty relics of the murdered men collected by Colonel Warren were solemnly interred in the crypt of St. Paul's on April 6, 1883, in presence of Lord Northbrook and many friends of the deceased, including a great many officers of Engineers. A granite slab marked with their initials and ages will cover the tomb, whilst a brass tablet on the wall will briefly record the circumstances. And arrangements, I understand, are being made to cut an inscription on the rocks in Wâdi Sadr.[2]

I would, with entire adoption, add to what has been said a few words written to me, when the positive news of Gill's fate was received, by his friend and mine, Mr. Edward Colborne Baber:—

I know he was a good son, a good friend, and a good soldier, and a most accomplished traveller.

Mr. Baber wrote also:—

I was engaged in defending his remarkable and minute accuracy as a traveller against a very kindly critic, on the very

[2] A painted window in memory of Captain Gill has been put up by his brother officers of the corps in Rochester Cathedral; a tablet also in Brighton College chapel by subscription of those connected with that institution; and three 'Gill Scholarships' for the sons of officers of the army have been founded at the same college, by subscription largely aided by the family.

day when the sad calamity of his death was made known; and what is strange enough, on the same day I received a letter from him which had been delayed, bearing date July 14, and containing these almost prescient words:—

'I am tearing my hair that I am not in Egypt, but if there is any sort of military expedition I shall go there either on duty or on leave, and I think that, peace having been concluded, my next wanderings will be in Asia Minor or in Syria. *But God knows I seldom go to a place that I have thought much about.*'

He would often tell me that he had a horror of old age; and in answer to the argument that age is the period of literary enjoyment, and that there is pleasure in watching the labour of others, which is only the continuation and completion of our own, he would reply: 'No; life is worthless without activity. I do not wish to live long.'

Colonel Frederick Burnaby wrote in the 'Times' of October 30, among other things, of Captain Gill:—

In the age in which we live, men like this unfortunate officer are seldom seen. Unfortunate officer! Yet why should I have written those words? He died not in battle, it is true, but was slain after having been employed upon the most dangerous duty which he could perform—that of cutting a telegraph wire in a hostile country.[3] Certain death would naturally have been the lot of any one if discovered. He knew full well his risk, but danger to him was nothing new. He played his life as he had played it on many other occasions. This time was once too often. He died, as he would have wished, for England.

Of fine-weather friends there are enough and to spare; but friends such as Captain Gill, whose first thought was for others and how best to lend them a helping hand, are few and far between. Only accident made us aware of his numerous acts of generosity, and many people who have been aided by him will feel acutely the death of their benefactor. His good deeds were done secretly—his right hand did not know what his left gave away in charity. The poor have lost a friend, the profession to which he belonged has been deprived of one of its brightest ornaments.

The Rev. Dr. Macduff, who had known Gill from boyhood, writes of him in a work called 'Early Graves':—

All that was allied to, or had connivance with what was

It was then supposed that this duty had been accomplished before the disaster.

base, or mean, or impure, ignoble or unworthy, was simply with him impossible and repugnant to his whole nature. I firmly believe no one more truly than he has been now served heir to the legacy bequeathed by Divine lips in that lofty beatitude—'Blessed are the pure in heart, for they shall see God.'

We have seen how often Captain Gill's adventurous journeys were made when on leave from his regular duties, and strangers might not unreasonably ask how such frequent leave from these could be given to any officer. But it is not often that burning energy, abundant means, and the desire to employ them in the public service are combined, at least to such a degree as they were in this young engineer officer; and we may conceive how unwillingly the Department would have lost the aid of an officer so devoted, and so ready on every occasion to undertake the acquisition of knowledge useful to his country, provided it had a spice of difficulty and danger, at his own charges. Indeed most hearty and generous testimony has been borne to his value, in a paragraph published by the 'Times' on November 2, which I can hardly err in attributing to Colonel East, his immediate superior in his Department of the War Office :—

It will be no easy matter to replace him in the Intelligence Department, where he had been employed for the last six years, and for the duties of which he possessed special qualifications. Owing to the confidential nature of the work on which he was employed, it is not possible that the great value of the information he has at various times, and at great risks, collected, can ever be known to the public, but it has been fully appreciated by those for whom he worked so zealously. One of his most hazardous journeys was undertaken last winter, and the graphic and modest manner in which he narrated the many dangerous adventures he then encountered elicited on several occasions the strongest expressions of approval and admiration from his Royal Highness the Field-Marshal Commanding-in-Chief, from Sir Garnet Wolseley, and from General Herbert, the Quartermaster-General. Not only will his untimely death be grievously felt by his many personal friends, but the State has lost in him an experienced, able, and trusted servant, whose services could ill be spared at any time, but the loss of which will be particularly felt during the present unsettled state of affairs in the East.

Baron von Richthofen's testimony to the value of Gill's journeys in Western China and Tibet has been already quoted. I extract a few more words of a recent letter from the same great traveller and geographer :—

I have only twice seen Gill for a few days, but I deplore his death as that of a friend. Reserved on the surface, but ardent below ; these words render fully his character. I like to recall in my mind the first impression which I got of him before he went to China, and which satisfied me at once that he was unusually qualified for carrying out successfully his great plans.

I then saw him again after his return, calm and modest as before, but just as ardent and ready to engage in new enterprises. He has deserved a better fate, . . . although, in either case, he lost his life honourably for his country, engaged in a brave and daring enterprise. . . . Gill was at the commencement of his career : his boldness and enterprise might have conducted him to deeds of importance. However, his travels in China, of which the excursion to Sung-pan-ting shows best his eminent personal qualifications as a traveller, will secure them a lasting and very honourable memory beyond his native conntry.

Fame is the ſpurre that the clear ſpirit doth raise
(That last infirmitie of noble mind)
To ſcorn delights, and live laborious dayes ;
But the fair guerdon when we hope to find,
And think to burſt out into ſudden blaze,
Comes the blind Furie with the abhorred ſhears
And ſlits the thin-ſpun life.

William Gill was indeed one who scorned delights and lived laborious days, nor need we contest that the infirmity of which Milton speaks in those magnificent lines had some hold on him ; but it was far from being the leading motive of his acts. That lay in the burning desire to put to some good use the internal force of which he was conscious, to make some sacrifice for the Country which he loved, and for whose honour and greatness he was very jealous. She has lost that loving and ungrudging service all too early, as it seems to our mortal and partial vision ; not, however, through the movement of a 'blind Fury' or stolid Atropos, but by the Will of Him who sees and guides the Whole.

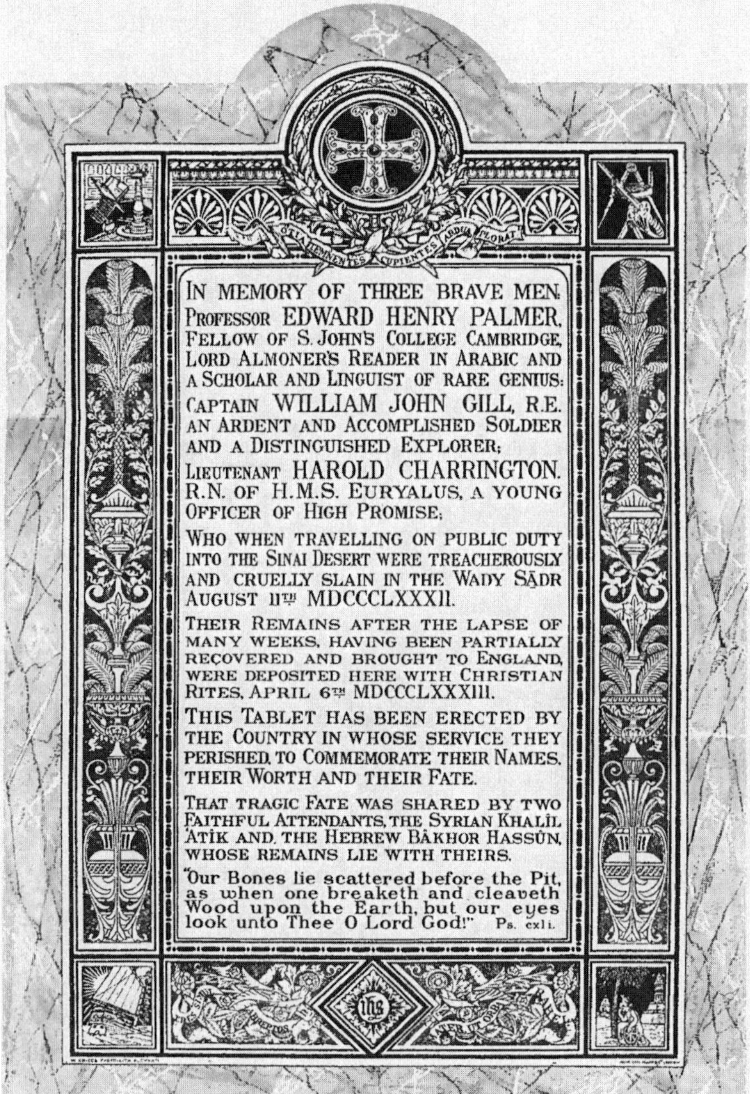
IN MEMORY OF THREE BRAVE MEN:
PROFESSOR EDWARD HENRY PALMER,
FELLOW OF S. JOHN'S COLLEGE CAMBRIDGE,
LORD ALMONER'S READER IN ARABIC AND
A SCHOLAR AND LINGUIST OF RARE GENIUS:
CAPTAIN WILLIAM JOHN GILL, R.E.
AN ARDENT AND ACCOMPLISHED SOLDIER
AND A DISTINGUISHED EXPLORER;
LIEUTENANT HAROLD CHARRINGTON.
R.N. OF H.M.S. EURYALUS, A YOUNG
OFFICER OF HIGH PROMISE;
WHO WHEN TRAVELLING ON PUBLIC DUTY
INTO THE SINAI DESERT WERE TREACHEROUSLY
AND CRUELLY SLAIN IN THE WADY SĀDR
AUGUST 11TH MDCCCLXXXII.
THEIR REMAINS AFTER THE LAPSE OF
MANY WEEKS, HAVING BEEN PARTIALLY
RECOVERED AND BROUGHT TO ENGLAND,
WERE DEPOSITED HERE WITH CHRISTIAN
RITES, APRIL 6TH MDCCCLXXXIII.
THIS TABLET HAS BEEN ERECTED BY
THE COUNTRY IN WHOSE SERVICE THEY
PERISHED, TO COMMEMORATE THEIR NAMES,
THEIR WORTH AND THEIR FATE.
THAT TRAGIC FATE WAS SHARED BY TWO
FAITHFUL ATTENDANTS, THE SYRIAN KHALÎL
'ATÎK AND, THE HEBREW BÂKHOR HASSÛN,
WHOSE REMAINS LIE WITH THEIRS.
"Our Bones lie scattered before the Pit,
as when one breaketh and cleaveth
Wood upon the Earth, but our eyes
look unto Thee O Lord God!" Ps. cxli.

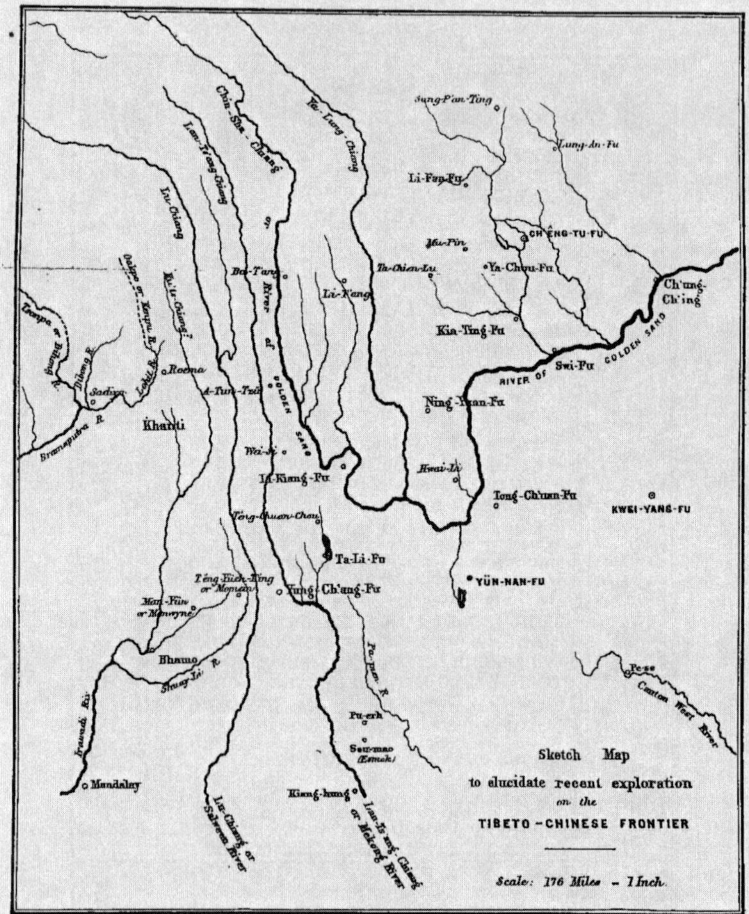

W. & A. K. Johnston, Edinburgh.

London John Murray, Albemarle Street, 1883.

GEOGRAPHICAL INTRODUCTION.

(*Originally written* 1879; *Recast* 1883.)

§ 1. 'The River of Golden Sand' was printed during the absence of its author at Constantinople in 1879 (see p. [31]), and we had been so much in communication on the subject of his intended book that the business of seeing it through the press in his absence seemed naturally to devolve on me. On Gill's return he and my friend Mr. Murray asked me to write a preface to the book; and out of this request arose the somewhat lengthy essay which is now reproduced, with a few modifications, including some passages intended to bring it up to the date of the present republication.

§ 2. The 'general reader,' whose eye may be caught by the title of this work, will not, we trust, be misled by the familiar melody of Bishop Heber to suppose that the traveller will conduct him to 'Afric's sunny fountains.' The 'River of Golden Sand' is a translation of the name *Kin-Sha-Kiang*, or (in the new orthography, in which I find it hard to follow my author) *Chin-Sha-Chiang* (Gold-Sand-River), by which the Chinese, or at least Chinese geographers, style the great Tibetan branch of the Yang-tzŭ, down to its junction, at Sü-chau (or Swi-Fu, as it is now called), with the Wen or Min River, descending from Ssŭ-Ch'uan. Of other names we shall speak a little below.

It is proposed now to indicate some of the points of geographical interest in the little-known region of which the River of Golden Sand is as it were the axis—that region of Eastern Tibet which intervenes between the two great historic continents of India and China—and to sketch the history of explorations in this tract previous to that of Captain Gill. If in this task I sometimes use words that I have used before, on one or other of the somewhat frequent occasions that this dark region, from which the veil lifts but slowly, has attracted me,[1] let me be forgiven. And all the more one may overcome scruples at such repetition in seeing how persistent error is. I recently read of 'an able argument' (I certainly did not read the argument itself) to prove the identity of the Tibetan Tsanpu and the Irawadi. Life seems too short for the study of able demonstrations that the moon is made of green cheese, but, if these are still to be proffered, there can be no harm in stating the facts again.[2]

I do not forget the pungent words with which Abbé Huc concludes his sparkling *Souvenirs d'un Voyage*: 'Quoiqu'il soit arrivé au savant Orientaliste, J. Klaproth, de trouver *l'Archipel Potocki*, sans sortir de son cabinet, il est en général assez difficile de faire des découvertes dans un pays sans y avoir pénétré.'[3] But as regards a large part of the country of which I am going to speak we are all on a level, for no one has seen it, not even the clever Abbé himself and his companion; and of *geographical* information regarding the region in question, they can hardly be said to have brought anything back.

[1] E.g., in a review of Huc and Gabet in *Blackwood*, 1852; in connection with the *Narrative of Major Phayre's Mission to Ava* (Calcutta 1856, London 1858); in the *Journal of the Asiatic Society of Bengal for* 1861, p. 367; in the notes to *Marco Polo*; and in various papers in *Ocean Highways* and the *Geographical Magazine*, and discussions in the *Proceedings of the Royal Geographical Society* (the last occasion reported in the number for May 1882, pp. 269–271).

[2] Since the first publication of this essay I have seen the work in question; and I desire to say that I mean no disparagement to its author, Mr. R. Gordon, a most diligent observer, and valued public servant; though I do regret the time and ingenuity expended on the maintenance (as I judge) of an untenable theory.

[3] The name of Potocki Islands was given by Klaproth in honour of Count Potocki, under whom he had served on a Russian mission to Peking, to a group of eighteen islands in the Gulf of Corea. This sheet of the Jesuit map of China had been mislaid or omitted when D'Anville engraved it. Klaproth afterwards became owner of the missing tracing, and on it, *sans sortir de son cabinet*, found these islands, and claimed their discovery.

§ 3. Everyone who has looked at a map of Asia with his eyes open must have been struck by the remarkable aspect of the country between Assam and China, as represented, where a number of great rivers rush southward in parallel courses, within a very narrow span of longitude, their delineation on the map recalling the fascis of thunderbolts in the clutch of Jove, or (let us say, less poetically) the aggregation of parallel railway lines at Clapham Junction.

Reckoning these rivers from the westward, the first of importance (i.) is the Subanshiri, which breaks through the Himálaya, and enters the valley of Assam in long. 94° 9′. This is a great river, and undoubtedly comes from Tibet, i.e. from Lhassa territory. Some good geographers have started the hypothesis that the Subanshiri, rather than the Dihong, is the outflow of the Tsanpu; but recent information shows this to be next to impossible.

§ 4. The next of these great rivers (ii.) is the Dihong, which enters Assam in long. 95° 17′, and joins the Lohit—or proper Brahmaputra—near Sadiya. Though the identity of this river with the great river of Central Tibet, the Yaru Tsanpu, has never yet been continuously traced as a fact of experience, every new piece of evidence brings us nearer to assurance of the identity, and one might be justified in saying that no reasonable person now doubts it. Instead of being a new and heterodox theory invented by a European geographer, as its latest opponents have imagined, it is the old belief of the natives on both sides of the mountains. It was indeed the belief of the illustrious Rennell, who first recognised the magnitude of the Brahmaputra, long before we had any knowledge of the Dihong, or of the manner and volume of its emergence from the Mishmi Hills.[4] Many

[4] 'On tracing this river in 1765, I was no less surprised at finding it rather larger than the Ganges than at its course previous to its entering Bengal. This I found to be from the east; although all the former accounts represented it as from the north; and this unexpected discovery soon led to inquiries, which furnished me with an account of its general course to within 100 miles of the place where Du Halde left the Sanpoo. I could no longer doubt that the Burrampooter and Sanpoo were one and the same river, and to this was added the positive assurances of the Assamers "that *their* river came from the north-west,

years, however, before Rennell's work was published, in fact, twelve years before Rennell was born, P. Orazio della Penna, writing in Tibet (1730), had stated that the river was then believed to join the Ganges, explaining (from such maps as were available to him in those days) 'towards Rangamatti and Chittagong.' A conjecture to the same effect occurs in the memoir on the map of Tibet, by Père Regis, at the end of du Halde. Giorgi, in his *Alphabetum Tibetanum* (Rome 1762), says the like.[5] The same view is distinctly set forth in the geography of Tibet which is translated in the 14th volume of the great French collection of *Mémoires concernant les Chinois*, a document compiled by order of the Emperor K'ang-hi, and issued, with others of like character, in 1696. This represents the Yaru Tsanpu as rising to the west of Tsang (West Central Tibet), passing to the north-east of Jigar-Kungkar (south of Lhassa), flowing south-east some 400 miles, and then issuing at the south of Wei (or U, East Central Tibet) into the region of the *Lokh'aptra*, 'tattooed people' (*i.e.* Mishmis *et hoc genus omne*); then turning south-west it enters India, and discharges into the southern sea (pp. 177-178). Mr. David Scott, the first British commissioner of Assam after the first Burmese War (about 1826), met with Lhassa merchants in that province, who told him that the Brahmaputra was their own river, that it passed Lhassa, penetrated the frontier mountains, and there received an additional supply from the Brahmakund. Wilcox heard the same from a Mishmi chief.

§ 5. The Pundit Nain Singh, on the journey to Lhassa which first made him famous (1865), was told by Nepalese, Newars, and Kashmiris at that city, that the great river of

through the Bootan Mountains."'—*Mem. of a Map of Hindoostan*, 3rd edition, pp. 356–7, see also p. 259. Rennell's actual knowledge of the Brahmaputra extended only to long. 91°, a few miles above Goalpara, but his sketch of the probable entrance of the river from Tibet is very like the truth. On the other hand, it is curious how he was misled as to the source of the Ganges, which he identified with what are really the upper waters of the Indus and Sutlej. The importance of the Dihong was first pointed out by Lieutenant Wilcox in 1826, in the *Calcutta Gazette*. (See *As. Res.* vol. xvii.)

[5] '*Sese tandem in Gangem exonerat.*' But Giorgi's information was derived from della Penna and the other Capuchins.

Tibet was the Brahmaputra; whilst all the natives who were questioned also declared that, after flowing east for a considerable distance, it flowed down into India. The Pundit's information on his last great journey, when he crossed the river somewhat further to the eastward, before striking south into Assam, did not add much, but it was all in corroboration of the same view.[6] And this has been still further confirmed by the report of exploration from the Chief of the Indian surveys for 1878–9.

The explorer (N—m—g) took up the examination of the Tsanpu at Chetang, where it was crossed by Nain Singh on his way from Lhassa to Assam (in about long. 91° 43′, lat. 29° 15′), and followed it a long way to the eastward. He found that the river, before turning south, flows much further east than had been supposed, and even north-east. It reaches its most northerly point in about long. 94°, and lat. 30°, some 12 m. to the north-east of Chamkar. The river then turns due south-east, but the explorer was not able to follow it beyond a place, 15 miles from the great bend, called *Gya-la Sindong*. There, however, he saw that it flowed on for a great distance, passing through a considerable opening in the mountain ranges, to the west of a high peak called *Jung-la*. Chamkar appears in D'Anville's map as Tchamka, and in one of Klaproth's[7] as *Temple Djamga*, in a similar position with regard to the river. And Gya-la Sindong seems to be the *Temp. Sengdam* of the latter map, standing just at the head of the '*défilé Sing-ghian Khial*,' by which Klaproth carried off the waters of the Tsanpu into the Irawadi. If the position of Gya-la Sindong as determined by the explorer is correct, its direct distance from the highest point hitherto fixed on the Dihong river, from the Assam side, is only about 100 miles.[8]

[6] See *Journal of Royal Geographical Society*, xlvii. p. 116. It is remarkable that the information collected by the Pundit on his first journey was most accurate as to the position where the river turns to the south, which he placed in about long. 94°. (See Montgomerie, in *J. R. G. S.*, xxxviii. p. 218, *note*.) His later conclusion was less accurate.

[7] In vol. iii. of his *Mémoires Relatifs à l'Asie*.

[8] This is just the space at which Rennell, 100 years ago, estimated the unknown gap. (See p. [69] *note*, above.)

§ 6. Evidence more recent and more positive has been adduced, in the end of 1882, by the return of another of Gen. Walker's explorers after an absence of four years in Tibet and Mongolia. Omitting the greater part of his travels, which are not relevant to the present question, we may state briefly that after visiting Ta-Chien-Lu and Bat'ang, he got as far as *Sama* (or Samé, see pp. [77–78] *infra*) in an attempt to reach Assam by the direct route. Here he was stopped, and had to take the circuitous route by Alanto and Gyamdo, whence he turned to Chetang on the Tsanpu, and thence by Giangze Long and Phari to Darjiling. Now, as General Walker justly observes, if the Tsanpu river passes into the Irawadi, the traveller must have crossed it between Bat'ang and Sama, between Sama and Gyamdo, and again at Chetang. But he is positive that he crossed the Tsanpu only once, viz. at Chetang; and that on the way from Sama to Gyamdo there is a great range to the west separating the basin of the affluents of the Tsanpu from that of the streams flowing to the east. One of these latter may possibly fall into the Irawadi, but the Tsanpu assuredly cannot do so.

We have mentioned above that some have supposed the Subanshiri to be the real continuation of the Tsanpu. The idea seems to have been grounded in part on an exaggerated estimate of the volume of the Subanshiri, and partly on Nain Singh's indications (in 1874) of the course of the Tsanpu, which seemed to bring it in such close juxtaposition to the Subanshiri as to allow no room for the development of another river of such volume as was attributed to the latter. The last of these foundations for the theory has been removed by the explorer N—m—g's extended journey, carrying the south-eastern bend of the Tsanpu so much further to the east; and the first also was erroneous. Careful and detailed observations by Lieut. Harman in 1877–78 give the comparative volumes of the Assam rivers with which we have to do, at their mean low level, as follows :—

	Cubic feet per second		Cubic feet per second
Dihong . . .	55,400	Dihong and Dibong before union with Brahmaputra ('Lohit') .	82,652
Brahmaputra ('Lohit') above Sadiya . .	33,832	The combined (Brahmaputra) river at Dibrúgarh . . .	116,115
Ditto at the Brahmah-Kund . . .	25,000	The Subanshiri . .	16,945
Dibong . . .	27,202		

We see here how the Dihong vastly surpasses in discharge not only the Subanshiri, but also the Lohit Brahmaputra and the Dibong, while both greatly exceed the Subanshiri.[9]

§ 7. Very eminent geographers have, however, not been content to accept the view of the identity of the Tsanpu and the Brahmaputra, and several have contended that the Irawadi of Burma was the true continuation of the great Tibetan river. D'Anville, I believe, was the first to start this idea.[1] It was repeated by our countryman Alexander Dalrymple, the compiler of the 'Oriental Repertory' and much else, the founder of the Hydrographic Department of the Admiralty, and a very able geographer, in a map on a small scale which he put together for the illustration of Symes's 'Mission to Ava' (1800). The idea was maintained at a later date with great force and insistence by that remarkable and erratic

[9] It is of some interest to compare these measurements with those made by Bedford and Wilcox in 1825-26. They were as follows (see *Asiatic Researches*, vol. xvii., but I take them from J. A. S. B. xxix. p. 182):—

	December 26, 1825	March 29, 1826
Dihong (after a correction) .	(*a*) 56,000 ft.	
Brahmaputra at Sadiya . .	(*b*) 19,058 ft.	(*a*) 33,965 ft.
Dibong	(*b*) 13,100 ft.	
Dihong and Dibong . .	69,664 ft.	(*a*) 86,211 ft.
Subanshiri, 'in dry season' .	(*a*) 16,000 ft.	

The close approximation in those marked (*a*) to Lieutenant Harman's recent measurements is remarkable; whilst in (*b*) the discrepancy is great. All Lieut. Harman's measurements were taken in March. In some the rivers had risen, and the low level discharge was arrived at by calculation. But it is a pity that no notice is taken of the older measurements in the publication of the recent ones. The suggestion of the facts, on the surface, is that the recent observations do not represent the lowest level, or that the rivers in December 1825 were unusually low.

[1] *Éclaircissements Géographiques sur la Carte de l'Inde*, Paris, 1753, p. 146.

genius Julius Klaproth, who in demonstration played fast and loose on a great scale with latitudes and longitudes, and produced Chinese documents from the days of the T'ang dynasty to those of K'ang-hi in corroboration. His dissertation in its latest form[2] is, like almost everything that Klaproth wrote, of high interest. We need not, as some other things in his career suggest, doubt the genuineness of the Chinese documents. Some of them at least are to be found translated in independent works before his time. But everything is not necessarily true that is written in Chinese, any more than everything that is written in Persian—or even in Pushtu! Chinese writers have found leisure to speculate on geographical questions, as well as Europeans. And some of them, finding, on the one hand, the Tsanpu flowing through Tibet, and disappearing they knew not whither, and finding, on the other, the Irawadi coming down into Burma from the north, issuing they knew not whence, adopted a practice well known to geographers (to Ptolemy, be it said, *pace tanti viri*, not least) long before Dickens humorously attributed it to one of the characters in 'Pickwick'—they 'combined the information,' and concluded that the Tsanpu and the Irawadi were one. Klaproth's view that this was so, and that the actual influx took place near Bhamò, was adopted by many Continental geographers, and staggered even the judicious Ritter. Maps were published in accordance with the theory, some bringing the waters of Tibet into the Irawadi by the Bhamò River (down which Captain Gill floated in Mr. Cooper's boat on the last day's journey which he has recorded), and others through the Shwéli, which enters the Irawadi some eighty miles below Bhamò.

§ 8. It seems hardly worth while now to slay this hypothesis, which was moribund before, but must be quite dead since the reports of General Walker's two last explorers in those regions. Its existence was somewhat prolonged, especially in France, by the fact that some of the missionaries in Eastern Tibet, of whom we shall speak presently, had carried out with them elaborate maps, compiled under the influence of Klaproth's theory; and the ideas derived from these had

[2] *Mémoires relatifs à l'Asie*, vol. iii.

so impregnated their minds that, in communicating geographical information which they had collected on the scene of their labours, it was confused and tinged by the errors of Klaproth.

The main bases for what we may style the orthodox theory of the Irawadi are found in the constant belief of natives above and below the Tibetan passes, and in the evidence of direction and volume. The lamented Col. T. G. Montgomerie, in his most able analysis of the Pundit Nain Singh's first journey, deduced from the particulars recorded by the latter, and a careful oral catechisation, that the discharge of the Tsanpu, where crossed below Jigatze (or Jigarchi), could hardly be less than 35,000 feet per second. We see that the discharge of the Dihong, on its emergence from the hills of Assam into the plains of Assam, is 55,400 feet. These are in reasonable ratio. Now the discharge of the Irawadi, so far down as the head of the Delta, is not more than 75,000 feet, and at Amarapura it cannot, on the best data available, be much more than the 35,000 feet attributed to the Tsanpu on the table-land of Tibet, at a point which would be at least 1,200 miles above Ava along the banks, if the theory of identity were true.[3]

§ 9. The third river (iii.) is the Dibong, which joins the Dihong before its confluence with the Brahmaputra. This has, on Mr. Saunders's map of Tibet accompanying Mr. Markham's book, been identified with the Ken-pu, one of the rivers of Tibet delineated on D'Anville's map. The Kenpu, however, we shall see strong evidence for identifying with a different river, whilst there is positive reason to believe that the Dibong, in spite of its large discharge, does *not* come from Tibet. At a meeting of the Asiatic Society of Bengal in 1861, at which I read a paper connected with this subject, Major (the late Major-General) Dalton stated that the people of Upper Assam admitted only two of their rivers to come from Tibet, viz. the Dihong and the (Lohita) Brahmaputra. An attempt was made in 1878 by Captain (now Lieut.-

[3] See Appendix to *Narrative of Mission to the Court of Ava* (Major Phayre's), pp. 356 *seq.*; and a paper by Major-General A. Cunningham in the *Journal of the Asiatic Society of Bengal*, vol. xxix. pp. 175 *seq.*

Colonel) Woodthorpe, R.E., who has done much excellent work in the survey of the Eastern Frontier, to explore the sources of the Dibong. He was not successful in penetrating far up the river, but he considered himself to have derived, from extensive views, and native information in connection with them, 'a fairly accurate knowledge of the sources of the Dibong, and the course of its main stream in the hills;'[4] and in the map representing this knowledge the river is indicated as having no source further north than about 28° 52′.

§ 10. We next come to the (iv.) true Brahmaputra, or Lohit, which enters Assam at the Brahmakund, or Sacred Pool of Brahma. This I believe to be identical with the Gak-bo of the Tibetan geographies, and the Ken-pu, or Kang-pu, of D'Anville and the Chinese.

Granted, as we may now assume, that the Tsanpu is the Dihong, the Ken-pu can hardly be other than either the Dibong or the Lohit. We have seen that the Dibong does not come from Tibet. But there is a very curious piece of evidence that the Ken-pu is the Lohit.

I have just alluded to a paper connected with our present subject which was read at Calcutta in 1861. This was a letter from Monseigneur Thomine des Mazures, 'Vicar Apostolic of Tibet,' and then actually residing at Bonga in Eastern Tibet, to Bishop Bigandet of Rangoon (himself well known for his works on Burmese Buddhism, &c., and who had been very desirous to establish direct communication with his brethren in the north),' and which contained some interesting geographical notices, though they were, as has been already indicated, impaired in value by the erroneous ideas as to the Tsanpu, gathered from Klaproth, with which French maps were then affected.[5] The paper was read with a comment by the present writer.[6]

[4] Letter of Captain Woodthorpe, dated Shillong, August 10, 1878 forwarded by the Government of India, in their letter of October 31, ia

[5] Particularly the map, on which Bishop Thomine relied, of *Andriveau Goujon*, Paris, 1841.

[6] See *Journal of the Asiatic Society of Bengal*, vol. xxx. pp. 367 *seq.* The Bishop's letter as sent to the Society had been done into English, and not always lucid English. In my present quotations I have corrected this.

Now in this letter Bishop des Mazures spoke of the series of rivers in question, beginning with the Lant'sang, or Mekong, and travelling westward. Next to the Lant'sang was the Lu-ts' Kiang (Lu-Kiang or Salwen). Beyond that the Ku-ts' Kiang, of which we shall speak presently, and then the *Gak-bo Tsanpu*, 'called by the Chinese *Kan-pu-tsangbo*.' The Bishop, influenced by his Klaprothian map, stated this to join the Irawadi. And this would only have made confusion double but for a circumstance which he proceeded to mention. 'In that district,' he wrote, 'according to the Tibetans, is the village of Sâmé, where our two priests, MM. Krick and Boury, were murdered.' Here was a fact that no theories could affect. These two gentlemen were, in the autumn of 1854, endeavouring to make their way to Tibet from Upper Assam, by the route up the Lohit, attempted fourteen years later by Mr. T. T. Cooper, when they were attacked and murdered by a Mishmi chief called Kaiïsa. On the receipt of this intelligence, and after a detailed account of the circumstances had been obtained from the servant of the priests, a party was despatched by the British authorities of Assam into the Mishmi country to capture the criminal chief. This was very dexterously and successfully effected by Lieutenant Eden, who was in command. In the beginning of March, Kaiïsa and some of his party were taken, and were tried and convicted by Major Dalton. Dr. Carew, the Roman Catholic Archbishop, interceded with the Governor-General for a mitigation. But Kaiïsa was hanged. It is an old story, but so creditable to several concerned that it has seemed well worth being briefly told here.

Now the place at which these two travellers were murdered was *Simé, on the banks of the* (Lohit) *Brahmaputra*, a place entered from native information in Wilcox's map some thirty years before, and some fifteen or sixteen miles above the place where Cooper was turned back in 1869.

I can hardly conceive of better evidence than this regarding a country unexplored by European travellers, and I have repeatedly adduced it in proof that the Gak-bo or

Ken-pu is identical with the Lohit, and that the latter comes from Tibet. This, too, being established, there remains no possibility of communication between the Tsanpu and the Irawadi, unless the Tsanpu pass athwart the basin of the Brahmaputra.[7]

Thus, singular to say, from the blood of those two missionary priests, spilt on the banks of the Lohita (the 'Blood-red'), is moulded the one firm link that we as yet possess, binding together the Indian and the Chinese geography of those obscure regions. And once more has this Simé, Samé, or Sama on the Lohit, become an important point in reference to the same subject, as we have seen in the notice of the last native explorations at p. [72].

§ 11. (v.) In the Chinese maps, and in Bishop Thomine des Mazures' list of rivers, there comes next a river variously called *Tchitom* (D'Anville), *Tchod-teng*, or *Schété* (Des Mazures)-Chu, all probably variations of the same name, and also *Ku-ts' Kiang* (Des Mazures), and in Klaproth's map the *Khiu-shi-Ho*. This river, which he calls 'rather inconsiderable,' the Bishop identifies with the Lung-Kiang or Lung-ch'wan Kiang of the Chinese, or Shwé-li of the Burmese, which flows a little east of Momien (called by the Chinese Teng-yueh-chau), and which eventually joins the Irawadi 80 or 90 miles below Bhamò. The Shwé-li does, according to Captain Gill's report, appear to bring down when in flood a vast body of water,[8] but it has not been seen by any European north of where he crossed it. Dr. Anderson, however, who accompanied Major Sladen's expedition, states that he was positively informed that its sources were only 40 or 50 miles north-east of Momien.[9] Bishop T. des Mazures, in his identification of the Schété or Ku-ts' with the Shwé-li, was perhaps again unduly biassed by maps

[7] The only possible doubt is that of the identity of the Gak-bo and the Ken-pu or Kang-pu, but I think there is no room for this. It is asserted by Bishop des Mazures, and a comparison of the course of the *Ken-pou* of D'Anville's map with the *Kakbo Dzanbotsiou* of the Chinese map given by Klaproth in his edition of the *Description du Tübet*, entirely corroborates this.

[8] See the *River of Golden Sand*, vol. ii. p. 357; *infra*, p. 276.

[9] *Report on Expedition to Western Yunan*, Calcutta, 1871, p. 188.

founded on Klaproth's theories, and thus we cannot feel confidence that his statement on this point was derived from native information. Chinese geographical speculators have identified more than one river of Tibet with the Shwé-li, some of them supposing it to be the same with the Gak-bo or Ken-pu.[1] I have long been inclined to the belief that the Ku-ts' Kiang of the Bishop, the Tchitom-chu of D'Anville, represents the unseen eastern source of the Irawadi, which has been the subject of so much controversy. Dr. Anderson's Shan informants gave the unvisited eastern branch of the Irawadi the name of *Kew* (Kiu) *Hom*, a name possibly identical both with the *Khiu-shi* of Klaproth and with the Ku-ts' of Bishop Thomine des Mazures. In any case, judging from D'Anville's map, the best authority we as yet have, the sources of this river, and therefore under my present hypothesis the remotest sources of the Irawadi, will not lie further north than 30° at the most. If so, the extreme length of the Irawadi's course will still fall far short of that assigned to the Lu-Kiang, or Salwen, and to the Lant'sang, or Mekong, to say nothing of our 'River of Golden Sand.' And this will be consistent enough with the calculations regarding the discharge of the Irawadi, which will be found in the places quoted at p. [73] above.

§ 12. (vi.) The Lung-Ch'uan Kiang, Lung-Ch'iang of Captain Gill, and Shwé-li of the Burmese. Of this we have spoken under No. v.

The next of the parallel rivers (vii.) is the Lu-Kiang or Nu-Kiang of Chinese maps, the Lu-ts' Kiang of Bishop des Mazures, the Salwen of Burma, under which name it enters the Gulf of Martaban. Rennell thought that the Nou-Kian (or Lu-Kiang) of the Jesuit maps must be the upper Irawadi. And since then doubts have been thrown on the identity of the Salwen and the Lu-Kiang of Tibetan geography, by myself many years ago, and more recently by Dr. Anderson ; but I am satisfied that the evidence had not been duly considered. The chief ground for discrediting its length of course and its Tibetan origin was its comparatively small body of water as reported. This may, however,

[1] See Ritter, iv. 225.

be due mainly to a restricted basin—and as far as we know the river from Yun-nan downwards, the basin is very restricted;—but also we see, not only how various the relations between the length and the discharge of considerable rivers may be, but how deceptive, as in the case of the Subanshiri, comparative impressions of discharge are apt to be, in the absence of measurements. The French missionaries who were for some years stationed near the Lu-Kiang, about lat. 28° 20,′ speak of it as a great river. Abbé Durand, June 1863, describing a society of heretical lamas who had invited his instructions, and who were willing to consign the paraphernalia of their worship to the waters, writes, 'What will become of it all? The *Great River*, whose waves roll to Martaban, is not more than 200 or 300 paces distant.'[2] . . . A river so spoken of in lat. 28° 20′, or thereabouts, may easily have come from a remote Tibetan source. It is hard to say more as yet, amid the uncertainties of the geography of Tibetan steppes, and the difficulty of discerning between the tributaries of this river and that of the next; but the Lu-Kiang, or a main branch of it, under the name of Suk-chu, appears to be crossed by a bridge on the high road between Ssŭ-Ch'uan and Lhassa,[3] four stations west of Tsiamdo on the Lant'sang.

§ 13. (viii.) The Lant'sang, or Mekong, the great river of Camboja, which rivals the Yang-Tzŭ itself in length, has its sources far north in Tibet, but attended with the uncertainties that we have spoken of under No. vii. Its lower course has long been known in a general way, but only accurately since the French expedition, from its mouth up into Yun-nan, in 1866–67. The town of Tsiamdo, capital of the province of Kham, which stands between the two main branches that form the Mekong, in about lat. 30° 45′, was visited by Huc and Gabet, on their return under arrest from Lhassa; but whatever quasi-geographical particulars Huc gives seem to have been taken, after the manner of

[2] *Ann. de la Prop. de la Foi*, tom. xxxvii.

[3] See *Description du Tübet*, translated by Klaproth, p. 222, and compare Ritter iv. 252, and 225–6; also Huc, ii. 445. The bridge is his Kia-Yu-Kiao, and had fallen just before his arrival.

travellers of his sort, from the Chinese itineraries published in Klaproth's 'Description du Tübet.' Kiepert, in his great map of Asia of 1864, had apparently so little faith in Huc's statements of this kind, that he makes the two branch rivers of Tsiamdo, after their union, form the source of the (Lohit) Brahmaputra. This was a somewhat wild idea even then; but now, when Tsiamdo has been visited by later missionaries (as by Bishop des Mazures and Abbé Desgodins in 1866[4]), travelling from and returning to the Chinese frontier, and following at no great distance the course of the Lan-t'sang, there can hardly be a reasonable doubt as to the course of this river as far north as Tsiamdo; and this is shown roughly in M. Desgodins' map.

§ 14. (ix.) The Kin-sha (or Chin-Sha), 'Golden Sand,' is that which gave a title to Captain Gill's book, a title justified by the fact that he followed its banks, with occasional deviations, during four-and-twenty marches on his way from Bat'ang to Ta-Li-Fu. This river is probably the greatest in Asia, as it is certainly the longest,[5] and one of the most famous; but it would be excelled even in length were the Klaprothian view of the identity of the Tsanpu and the Irawadi correct; and far excelled by the Hoang-Ho, if we could view that river with the eyes of a puzzle-headed ecclesiastical traveller of the middle ages, who traversed all Asia, from Astrakhan to Peking, and who seems to have regarded as one river, which was constantly 'turning up' on his route (and *that* identical with the Phison of Paradise), the Volga, the Oxus, the Hoang-Ho and the Yang-Tzŭ. Well might he say with pride: 'I believe it to be the biggest river of fresh water in the world, and I have crossed it myself!'[6]

The sources of the Kin-sha are really, according to the best of our knowledge, in or about long. 90°, *i.e.* almost as

[4] Desgodins, *La Mission du Thibet*, pp. 80–83. The missionaries call the place *Tcha-mou-to*.

[5] In length the order of the rivers of the world seems to be given: (1) Mississippi (including Missouri), (2) Nile, (3) Amazon, (4) Yangtsze Kiang (or Kin-Sha-K.), (5) Yenesei. But probably the Congo ought, as now known, to take a high place in this list.

[6] John Marignolli, in *Cathay*, &c. p. 350.

far west as Calcutta. Its upper course, though far below the source, was crossed by Huc and Gabet in the winter of 1845; and reached, though not crossed, by Colonel Prejevalsky in January 1873, about long. 90° 40′, lat. 35° 50′. Huc crossed the river on the ice, and says nothing of dimensions, though he leaves on our memories that famous picture of the frozen herd of yaks. But from Prejevalsky we have information as to the great size of the river even in this remote portion of its course: the channel, when seen, 750 feet wide, and flowing with a rapid current, but the whole river-bed from bank to bank upwards of a mile wide, and, in the summer floods, entirely covered to the banks, and sometimes beyond.[7] It must have been in this flooded state that it was crossed by a Dutch traveller, Samuel Van de Putte (who has left singularly little trace of his extraordinary journeys), some time about the year 1730.[8]

The name given to the river in this part of its course is (Mong.) *Murui-ussu*, or *Murus-ussu*, the 'Winding Water,' and (Tib.) *Di-chu*, or *Bhri-chu*, the 'River of the (tame) Yak-Cow,'[9] from one or other of which Marco Polo seems to have taken the name Brius which he gives to the river in Yun-nan.

In leaving the steppes, and approaching the jurisdiction of the Chinese, it seems to receive from them the name of Kin-sha Kiang, and this name is applied, at least as far as Swi-fu, where it is joined by the Min River coming down from Ssŭ-Ch'uan. Here the Great River becomes navigable to the sea, though the navigation is impeded, as Captain Gill's narrative forcibly depicts, by numerous rapids and gorges hard to pass.[1]

[7] *Prejevalsky*, ii. 221.

[8] 'After traversing this country one reaches a very large river called Bi-chu, which, as Signor Samuel Van der, a native of Fleshinghe, in the province of Zeland, in Holland, has written of it, is so large that to cross it in boats of skins he embarked in the morning, and landed on an island in the evening, and could not complete the passage across till the middle of the following day.'—*P. Horace della Penna*, in Appendix to Markham's *Tibet*, p. 312.

[9] These are Klaproth's interpretations, in his notes to *Horace della Penna*. See also Prejevalsky, u.s.

[1] Geographical names are largely names given, or at least defined in

Of all the Tibetan and Yun-nan part of the river, excepting in D'Anville's maps, of which the value in this part has always been a little doubtful, we have had, previous to Captain Gill's journey, nothing of actual survey; of still more recent correction of our knowledge we shall speak below.

§ 15. The next great river (x.) belonging to this series is the Ya-Lung Kiang of the Chinese, a corruption of the Tibetan Jar-lung, or Yar-lung.[2] It rises in the mountains called Baian-Kara, on the south of the Koko-nur basin, about lat. 34°, and flows with a course generally southerly, and parallel to the Kin-sha, till it joins that river in the middle of its great southerly elbow, about lat. 26° 30′. In its upper course it is called, according to Klaproth's authority, Gnia-mtso, which seems to be the same as the Nia-chu of Captain Gill (ii. 135). The Jar-lung valley was the traditional cradle of the Tibetan monarchy,[3] which only at a later time moved into the western highlands of Lhassa. The river was passed, some 260 miles north of the mouth, by Captain Gill on his way from Ta-Chien-Lu to Lit'ang, by a coracle ferry (ii. 139; *infra*, p. 197); near this the width varied from 50 to 120 yards, with a rapid broken current. Baggage animals had to be swum across.

The confluence of the two great rivers Yar-lung and Kin-sha was visited by Lieutenant Garnier and his party in 1868. Garnier thus describes the junction:—

The Kin-sha is here by no means shut in as it is at Mong-kou—(where they had crossed the eastern limb of the great

---

their application, by geographers, and one should always speak cautiously as to how a river or mountain-chain in Asia is called by natives on the spot. Blakiston, at the furthest point of the river ascended by him, found it only known as the 'River of Yun-nan.' So streams are, or used to be, locally known in Scotland only as '*the* watter,' or perhaps the 'watter of —' such a place. In one part, Captain Gill tells, the great river is known as 'the River of Dregs and Lees.'

[2] Ritter gives the meaning of this as 'White River' (iv. 190); Klaproth as 'Vaste Rivière' (*Description du Tübet*, 190). The Tibetan vocabulary in Klaproth gives *ghiar*, 'ample, vaste' (p. 145). *dkar*, 'white,' is perhaps the word; and it will be seen that in its lower course the Chinese do call it Pe-shui, or 'White Water.'

[3] See Sanang Setzen in Schmidt's *Ost-Mongolen*, p. 23 and *passim*.

bend);—and it is reached by a hardly sensible declivity. Little naked hills line the banks. The river comes from the south-west, then describes a curve inclining to 10° south of east; and it is at the apex of this curve that it receives the Ya-long Kiang. The latter arrives from the north, shut in closely by two walls of rock absolutely perpendicular, so that no passage along the banks is possible. Its breadth is nearly equal to that of the Blue River;[4] and its current, at least when we saw it, was somewhat stronger. I could not measure the depth of either, but it seemed considerable. As at Mong-kou the flood-rise was 10 mètres. I was surprised to learn that the country people here gave the name of Kin-sha Kiang to the Ya-long—i.e. to the tributary—and that of Pe-shui Kiang, 'White-Water River,' to the principal stream. If, as regards volume, there was, at first sight, some room for doubt between the two, the aspect of the two valleys showed at once which was entitled to keep the name of Kin-sha Kiang. The mouth of the Ya-long is a sort of accidental gap in the chain of hills that lines the Blue River, and the orographic configuration of the country indicates clearly that the latter river comes from the west and not from the north. . . . This anomaly in their nomenclature will seem less surprising if we remember that in China river-names are always local, and change every 60 miles. About Li-kiang you again find that the Kin-sha has got its proper name, and it is the Ya-long that is there called Pe-shui Kiang.[5]

§ 16. The last of these great parallel rivers with which we have to deal is that great branch (xi.), called on our maps Wen and Min Kiang, which we regard geographically as a tributary of the Kin-sha or Yang-Tzŭ, but which the Chinese hydrographers have been accustomed to regard rather as the principal stream. We find this view distinctly indicated in that oldest of Chinese documents, the Yü-Kung.[6] It comes out again prominently in Marco Polo's account of Sin-da-fu (or Ch'êng-Tu-Fu), which is quoted by Captain Gill at the beginning of his second volume (*infra*, p. 141). . . . 'The

[4] So the French term the Yang-Tzŭ.

[5] *Voyage d'Exploration*, i. 503. Garnier gives a view of the confluence.

[6] See Richthofen's *China*, i. 325: 'On the Min-shan begins the course of the Kiang. Branching eastward it forms the To . . . . &c.' The Min-shan is the mountain country north-west of Ssŭ-Ch'uan.

name of the river is *Kiansuy*,' *i.e.*, as the late M. Pauthier explains, *Kiang-Shui*, 'Waters of the Kiang' (or River Kiang, see *He-Shui*, a little below). The same view appears in Padre Martini's 'Atlas Sinensis' (1655); [7] and very distinctly in a paper professedly (and probably in reality) indited in 1721 by the great Emperor K'ang-hi, which Klaproth has translated in that dissertation of his already spoken of regarding the course of the river of Tibet:—

> From my youth up (says the Emperor), I have been greatly interested in geography; and for such purposes I sent officers to the Kuen-Luen mountains, and into Si-fan. All the great rivers, such as the Great Kiang, the Hwang-Ho (Yellow River), the He-Shui (Black River, the Kara-Ussu of the Mongols), the Kin-Sha Kiang, and the Lan-t'sang Kiang, have their sources in those regions. My emissaries examined everything with their own eyes; they made accurate inquiries, and have embodied their observations in a map. From this it is clear that all the great rivers of China issue from south-eastern slopes of the great chain of *Nom-Khún-ubashi*, which separates the interior from the exterior system of waters. The Hwang-Ho has its source beyond the frontier of Sining, on the east of the Kulkun mountains. . . . The Min-Kiang has its origin to the west of the Hwang-Ho, on the mountains of *Baian-Kara-tsit-sir-khana*, which is called in Tibetan *Miniak-thsuo*; and in the Chinese books *Min-Shan*; it is outside of the western frontier of China; the waters of the Kiang issue from it. . . . According to the Yü-Kung the Kiang comes from the Min-Shan. This is not correct; it only passes through that range; this is ascertained. This river runs to Kuon-hien,[8] and there divides into half a score of branches, which reunite again on reaching Sin-tsin-hien; thence it flows south-east to Sü-chau-fu [or Swi-Fu] where it joins the Kin-sha Kiang.[9]

Captain Gill, so far as we are aware, was the first traveller to trace this river above Ch'êng-Tu, to the alpine highlands, doubtless the Min-Shan of the Yü-Kung, from which it emerges. This he did on that excursion from

[7] To this remarkable work I tried to do some justice in an article in the *Geographical Magazine* for 1874, pp. 147–8.

[8] The Kuan-hsien of Captain Gill, vol. i. p. 330; *infra*, p. 107.

[9] Klaproth, *Mémoires relatifs à l'Asie*, iii. 392.

Ch'êng-Tu to the north, in the months of May and June, 1877, which is described in the last two chapters of the first volume, entitled, 'A Loop-cast towards the Northern Alps.'

§ 17. Captain Gill has pointed out that, of the many branches of the river which ramify through the plain of Ch'êng-Tu, no one now passes through the city at all corresponding in magnitude to that which Marco Polo describes, about 1283, as running through the midst of Sindafu, 'a good half-mile wide, and very deep withal.' The largest branch adjoining the city now runs on the south side, but does not exceed a hundred yards in width; and though it is crossed by a covered bridge with huxters' booths, more or less in the style described by Polo, it necessarily falls far short of his great bridge of half a mile in length. Captain Gill suggests that a change may have taken place in the last five (this should be *six*) centuries, owing to the deepening of the river-bed at its exit from the plain, and consequent draining of the latter. But I should think it more probable that the ramification of channels round Ch'êng-Tu, which is so conspicuous even on a small general map of China, like that which accompanies this work, is in great part due to art; that the mass of the river has been drawn off to irrigate the plain; and that thus the wide river, which in the thirteenth century may have passed through the city, no unworthy representative of the mighty Kiang, has long since ceased, on that scale, to flow. And I have pointed out briefly (ii. 6; *infra*, p. 144) that the fact, which Baron Richthofen attests, of an actual bifurcation of waters on a large scale taking place in the plain of Ch'êng-Tu—one arm 'branching east to form the To'—(as in the terse indication of the Yü-Kung) viz. the To-Kiang or Chung-Kiang flowing south-east to join the great river at Lu-Chau, whilst another flows south to Sü-chau or Swi-Fu, does render change in the distribution of the waters about the city highly credible.[1]

[1] A short but interesting notice of the irrigation and drainage of the plain of Ch'êng-Tu is given by Richthofen in his seventh letter to the Shanghai Chambers, p. 64. He mentions that the existing channels, though not those close to the city, reach in some instances to a width of 1,000 feet.

The various branches, except those that diverge, as just said, to the Ch'ung-Kiang, reunite above Hsin-Chin-Hsien (Sin-tsin-hien of Richthofen, Sing-chin of the general map), which was Captain Gill's second station in leaving Ch'êng-Tu for Tibet. Up to this point the main stream of the Min is navigable, whilst boats also ascend the easternmost branch to the capital. Indeed, vessels with 100 tons of freight reach Ch'êng-Tu by this channel when the river is high.[2] At Kia-ting-fu the Min receives a large river from the mountains on the west, the Tung-Ho, which brings with it both the waters of the Ya-Ho, from Ya-Chou (see vol. ii. p. 47; *infra*, p. 159), and those of the river of Ta-Chien-Lu. Kia-ting is an important trading place, the centre of the produce in silk and white-wax, and situated in a lovely and fertile country. Below this the Min-Kiang is a fine, broad, and deep stream, with a swift but regular current,[3] and obstructed by only one rapid, at Kien-wei, but that a dangerous one. It joins the Kin-sha, as so often mentioned, at Sü-Chau or Swi-Fu.

§ 18. We have spoken, perhaps at too great length, of the great parallel rivers which form the most striking physical characteristic of the region between India and China. Let us now say something of the history of a problem that many attempts have been made to solve: that of opening direct communication between these two great countries.

How difficult a problem this is will be, perhaps, most forcibly expressed by the circumstance that in all the complex history of Asiatic conquest—and in spite of the fact that you can hardly lay your finger on an ordinary atlas-map of Asia without covering a spot that has at one time or other been the focus of a power whose conquests have spread far and wide over that continent—at no time did a conqueror from India ever pass to China, nor (unless with one obscure and transient exception, which will be noticed below) a conqueror from China to India, nor at any time, omitting the brief passage of Chinghiz, who barely touched

[2] Richthofen, p. 71.

[3] Cooper says, 'often a mile wide;' but the river was unusually high, for it was, he says, 'unbroken by a single rapid.' Richthofen specifies the frequent wrecks in the rapid at Kien-wei.

the Punjab, did the conquests of any conqueror embrace any part of both countries.

Moreover, Chinese history seems to establish the fact that India first became known to China, not across these lofty highlands and the vast fissures in which the rivers flow of which we have spoken, but by the huge circuit of Bactria and Kabul. The idea that there was a more ancient intercourse between the two great countries, and that the Chinas of the Laws of Menu and of the Mahabharat were Chinese, must, I now believe, be abandoned. The *Chinas*, as Vivien de St. Martin and Sir H. Rawlinson have indicated, are rather to be regarded as a hill-race of the Himálaya, probably identical with the *Shinas* of Dardistan. The first report of India was brought to China in the year B.C. 127, in the reign of Hsia-wu-ti of the Han dynasty, when Chang-Kien, a military leader who had been exploring the country about the Oxus, returned after an absence of twelve years, and, among many other notices of Western Asia, reported of a land called *Shin-Tu—i.e.* Sindu, Hindu, India—of which he had heard in Tahia, or Bactria, a land lying to the south-east, moist and flat and very hot, the people civilised, and accustomed to train elephants. From its position, and from the fact that stuffs of *Shu* (*i.e.* Ssŭ-Ch'uan, see vol. ii. pp. 17, 35) arrived in the bazaars of Bactria through Shin-Tu, Chang-Kien deduced that this country must lie not far from the western provinces of China. Several efforts were in consequence made to penetrate by the Ssŭ-Ch'uan frontier to India; one got as far as Tiën (now a part of Yun-nan), but others not even so far. The King of Tiën stopped the envoys of the Han, and would not allow them to explore the routes by which India was reached. When communication opened with India some 200 years later, it was by the circuitous route of Bactria, and so it continued for centuries.

§ 19. If the acute general of the Han was right about the stuffs of Shu, the trade that brought these stuffs must have been of an obscure hand-to-hand kind, probably through Tibet, analogous in character to the trade which in prehistoric Europe brought amber, tin, or jade from vast distances. But it is curious to set alongside of these

Chinese notices of obscure trade reaching to India that remarkable passage in the 'Periplus,' a work of the first century A.D., which speaks of *Thin*, and of its great city *Thinae*, 'from which raw silk, and silk thread, and silk stuffs were brought overland through Bactria to Barygaza (Bhrōch), as they were on the *other hand by the Ganges River to Limyrike*' (*Dimyrike*, the Tamul country, Malabar). Ptolemy, too, a century later, says that there was not only a road from the countries of the Seres and of the Sinae to Bactriana by the Stone Tower (*i.e.* by Kashgar and Pamir), but also a road to India which came through Palibothra (or Patna). It is probable that this traffic was still only of that second- and third-hand kind of which we have spoken, and the mention of Palibothra recalls the fact that Patna is the Indian terminus at which the Fathers Grueber and D'Orville arrived after their unique journey from Northern China by Tibet.

Returning to the 'Periplus,' the passage that we have referred to is followed by another speaking of a rude mongoloïd people (it is the shortest abridgment of the description) who frequented the frontier of *Thin*, bringing *malabathrum* or cassia leaves. These, I think, may undoubtedly be regarded as some one or other of the hill tribes on the Assam frontier, and I should in this case regard the mention of *Thin* as vaguely indicating the knowledge, as already popular in India, that there was a great land bearing a name like that beyond the vast barrier of mountains. In a like way we find the name of Mahāchín applied in the fifteenth century by Nicolo Conti, and in the sixteenth century by Abu'l-Fazl, to the countries on the Irawadi; and I remember, many years ago, seeing a Tibetan pilgrim at Hardwár, whose only intelligible indication of where he came from was 'Mahāchín.'

§ 20. As our subject is the history not of communication generally between China and India, but only of that communication across their common highland barrier, we are bound, so far as our knowledge goes, to stride at once from pseudo-Arrian to Marco Polo. There is in the interval, indeed, an obscure record of a Chinese invasion of India, which should perhaps constitute an exception.

In 641, the King of Magadha (Behar, &c) sent an ambassador with a letter to the Chinese court. The Emperor, who was then Tai-tsung of the T'ang dynasty, probably the greatest monarch in Chinese history, in return sent one of his officers to go to the King with an imperial patent, and to invite his submission. The King *Shiloyto* (Siladitya)[4] was all astonishment. 'Since time immemorial,' he asked his courtiers, 'did ever an ambassador come from Mahachina?' 'Never,' they replied. The Chinese author remarks here, that in the tongue of the barbarians, the Middle Kingdom is called 'Mohochintan' (*Maháchínasthâná*). A further exchange of civilities continued for some years. But the usurping successor of Siladitya did not maintain these amicable relations, and war ensued, in the course of which the Chinese, assisted by the kings of Tibet and Nepal, invaded India. Other Indian kings lent aid and sent supplies; and after the capture of the usurper *Alanashan* (?), and the defeat of the army commanded by his queen on the banks of the *Khien-to-wei*, 580 cities surrendered to the arms of China, and the king himself was carried prisoner to that country.

Chinese annals colour things, but they are not given to invention, and one can hardly reject this story.[5] It is probable, however, even from the story as it is told, that this

[4] This Siladitya is a king of whom much mention is made in the Memoirs of Hwen-T'sang. He was a devout Buddhist, and a great conqueror, having his capital at Kanauj, and a dominion extending over the whole of the present Bengal Presidency, from the sea to the frontier of Kashmir.

[5] The account is found in Stanis. Julien's papers from Mat-wan-lin, in the *Jour. Asiat.* ser. iv. tom. x. See also *Cathay, and the Way Thither*, p. lxviii., and Richthofen's *China*, pp. 523. 536-7. It is stated that Wang-hwen-tse, the envoy who went on the mission that resulted in this war, wrote a history of all the transactions in twelve books, but it is unfortunately lost. The Life of Hwen T'sang states that that worthy, when in India, prophesied that, after the death of Siladitya, India would be a prey to dreadful calamities, and that perverse men would stir up a desperate war. The same work mentions as the fulfilment that Siladitya died towards the end of the period *Yung-hwei* (A.D. 650-655), and that in conformity with the prediction, India 'became a prey to the horrors of famine,' of which the envoy Wang-hwen-tse, just mentioned, was an eye-witness. But no mention is made of the Chinese invasion.

was rather a Nepalese and Tibetan invasion, promoted and perhaps led by Chinese, than a Chinese invasion of India. Lassen, as far as I can discover, does not deal with the subject at all. The name of the river on which the Indian defeat took place, *Khien-to-wei*, would according to the usual system of metamorphosis represent *Gandhava*; *qu.* the Gandhak? (Sansk *Gandakavatī*).

§ 21. The story, told by Firishta and others, of an invasion of Bengal by the Mongols, 'by way of Cathay and Tibet,' during the reign of 'Alá-ud-dín Musa'úd, King of Delhi (A.D. 1244), has been shown by my friend Mr. Edward Thomas to have arisen out of a clerical error in MSS. of the contemporary history called *Tabakát-i-Násirí*.[6] But two preposterous attempts were made in the thirteenth and fourteenth centuries, at the counter-project, the invasion of the countries above the Himálaya from Gangetic India.

The first of these (A.D. 1204) was the adventure of Mahommed Bakhtiyár Khilji, the first Mussulman conqueror of Bengal, and ruler of Gaur, of whom the historian just quoted says, that 'the ambition of seizing the country of Turkestan and Tibet began to torment his brain.' The route taken is very obscure; the older interpretations carried it up into Assam, but Major Raverty's conclusion that it ascended the Tísta valley is perhaps preferable. The Khilji leader is stated to have reached the open country of Tibet, a tract entirely under cultivation, and garnished with tribes of people and populous villages. The strenuous resistance met with, the loss in battle with the natives, and the distress of the troops from such a march, compelled a retreat; they were sorely harassed by the men of the Raja of Kamrud (apparently *Kámrúp*, of which Assam was the heart), and Mahommed Bakhtiyár finally escaped with but a hundred horsemen or thereabouts, and soon after fell ill and died.

The second attempt was one of the insane projects of Mahommed Tughlak, which took place in 1337. It was, according to Firishta, directed against China, but it must be said that there is no mention of China as the object in

[6] See Thomas's *Pathán Kings of Dehli*, p. 121.

the earlier accounts. The account given by the historia Ziá-ud-din Barní, who wrote in the next generation, is a follows :—

The sixth project, which inflicted a heavy loss upon th army, was the design which he formed of capturing the moun tain of Karájal. His conception was that, as he had undeı taken the conquest of Khurásán, he would (first) bring unde the dominion of Islam this mountain, which lies between th territories of Hind and those of China, so that the passage fo horses and soldiers, and the march of the army, might be ren dered easy. To effect this, a large force, under distinguishe *amírs* and generals, was sent to the mountains of Karájal, witl orders to subdue the whole mountain. In obedience to order it marched into the mountains, and encamped in various places but the Hindus closed the passes, and cut off its retreat. Th whole force was thus destroyed at one stroke, and out of al this chosen body of men only ten horsemen returned to Dehl to spread the news of its discomfiture.[7]

The account given by the traveller Ibn Batuta, who wa then at the court of Mahommed Tughlak, is to the sam effect ; and though he mentions the names of two place that were taken by the troops, *Jidíya* before entering th mountains, and *Warangal* in the hill-country, Ibn Batut does not aid us by these (the last of which is altogethe anomalous) in fixing the locality, any more than he helps u to understand the object, of the enterprise.

§ 22. Coming now to Marco Polo, whose steps it woulc be hard for any traveller in a little-known region of Asi altogether to avoid, we may briefly say that on the firs important mission to which he was designated by the Grea Khan Kublai, in making his way to the frontier of Burm (*Mien*), he travelled from Ch'êng-Tu (*Sindafu*), by the rout which Captain Gill followed, as far probably as Ch'ing-Chi-Hsien. This was Captain Gill's ninth march from Ch'êng-Tu We do not know the length of Marco's daily journeys, bu after five such from Ch'êng-Tu, he was already in Tibet Probably the country which was counted as Tibet, in thos days, began immediately on passing Ya-Chou and enterin

[7] Elliot's *History of India*, &c. (by Dowson), iii. 241-2.

the mountains. From Ch'ing-Chi-Hsien the routes diverge. Captain Gill, bound for Ta-Chien-Lu and Bat'ang, strikes north-west; Marco Polo's route continued to bear south-south-east, towards the city of Ning-Yuan-Fu, the existing capital of the beautiful valley of Kien-Chang, the Caindu or Ghiendu of the Venetian. This is the route on which Baron Richthofen's journey met with an unfortunate interruption (see p. [112]), and which has since been travelled by Mr. Baber. It is the road by which the greater part of the goods for Bhamò and Ava used to travel from Ch'êng-Tu, before the Mahommedan troubles in Western Yun-nan. Those goods went on by a direct road from Kien-Chang to Ta-Li-Fu. But Marco Polo's road led him south, and across the great elbow of the Kin-sha to the city of Yun-Nan Fu (his *Yachi*). From this he travelled to Ta-Li-Fu (*Carajan*), and thence to Yung-Chang-Fu (*Vochan* or *Unchan*). Beyond this there are difficulties as to the exact extent and direction of his travels, concerning which some discussion occurs in vol. ii. chap. viii. of Captain Gill's book, as well as in my own commentary on the book of Marco. It would hardly profit to enter here on a detailed recapitulation of a discussion which as yet has confessedly received no satisfactory determination.

§ 23. Ta-Li-Fu, which is so often spoken of in these pages, and is so prominent a point in Captain Gill's narrative, is indeed a focal point on this frontier at which many routes converge; and for ages it has been the base of all operations, military or commercial, from the side of China towards Burma. It may still be regarded as the capital of Western Yun-nan, as it was in the days of Marco Polo. Ta-Li-Fu, for some centuries before Kublai Khan, the master whom Marco served, conquered it (A.D. 1253), had been the seat of a considerable Shán kingdom, called by the Chinese Nan (or Southern)- Chao: this latter term being a Shan word for 'prince,' which still figures among the titles of the kings of Siam, and of all the other states of that wide-spread race. During the recent brief independence of the Mahommedans or *Panthés* (probably themselves as much Shan as Chinese in blood), Ta-Li again became a seat of royalty, and here reigned Tu-wen-hsiu, alias Sultan Sulimán, from about 1860 to 1873, when the city was captured by the Imperialists, and the Mahommedans were massacred. The king himself took poison, but his head was sent in honey to Peking.[8]

Mr. Baber, quoted at p. 303 of vol. ii. (*infra*, p. 251), says that the terms *Sultan* and *Suliman* were quite unknown on the spot. The fact is that in Indo-Chinese countries Islam has never assimilated the nationality of those who profess it, as in Western Asia. This is the case in some degree in Java, as it is in greater degree in Burma, and no doubt more than all in China. The people, in these countries, professing Islam, are to be compared with Abyssinian professors of Christianity. At the court of the Mussulman Sultan of Djokjokarta, in Java, I have had the honour of being introduced to half a dozen comely sultanas, and of shaking hands with them; whilst I have seen the Sultan and his Court taking part in a banquet at the Dutch Residency, and in drinking a number of toasts, of which a printed programme in Dutch and Javanese was distributed. In the capital of Burma, where professing Mahommedans are much less secluded from the influence of more orthodox Moslems than those of Yun-nan are, they have been characterised in passages of which I extract the following: 'As might be expected, they are very ignorant sons of the Faith, and, in the indiscriminating character of their diet, are said to be no better than their neighbours; so that our strict Mussulmans from India were not willing to partake of their hospitalities.' And as regards names: 'Every indigenous Mussulman has two names. Like the Irishman's dog, though his true name is *Turk*, he is always called *Toby*. As a son of Islam, he is probably Abdul Kureem; but as a native of Burma, and for all practical purposes, he is Moung-yo, or Shwé-po.'[9] The style of 'Sultan Sulimán,' &c., was no doubt confined to the few Hajjis or Mollahs that were at Ta-li. That there were such is proved by the Arabic circular which was issued, and which reached the Government of India in the way mentioned at page [99] *note* 5, below. The following is an extract from

[8] Tu-Wen-Hsiu, or, as Cooper calls him phonetically, Dow-win-sheow. had been a wealthy merchant in Tali.

[9] *Mission to the Court of Ava in* 1855, pp. 151–152.

that document: 'O Followers of Mahommed! in telling you how it fared with us, we offer grateful thanks to the Almighty. It behoves you to rejoice in the grace that God hath shown to us. . . . God gave us courage and created fear in the hearts of the Idolaters, so we, by the decree of God, did defeat them. . . . Therefore we have set up a Mahommedan Sultan; he is prudent, just, and generous. . . . His name is *Sádik*, otherwise called *Sulimán.* He has now established Mahommedan law. . . . Since we have made him our Imam we have been, by the decree of God, very victorious. . . . The metropolis of infidelity has become a city of Islam.'

Bhamò, again, a small stockaded town, in lat. 24° 16′, stands on a high bank over the Irawadi, on its eastern side, about two miles below the entrance of a considerable stream, which we have been used to call, from the Burmese side, the Ta-peng River, but which Captain Gill, who followed its course almost the whole way from Têng-Yuëh-Chau (or Momien) to its confluence with the Irawadi, calls the Ta-Ying Ho, or T'êng-Yuëh River. Here, or hereabouts, has long been the terminus of the land-commerce from China; and as early as the middle of the fifteenth century we find at Venice, on the famous world-map of Frà Mauro (who no doubt got his information from Nicolo Conti, who had wandered to Burma earlier in that century), on the upper part of the river of Ava, a rubric which runs: *Qui le marchatantie se translata da fiume a fiume per andar in Chataio.* 'Here goods are transferred from river to river, and so pass on to Cathay.' And in the first half of the seventeenth century there is some evidence of the maintenance here of an English factory for the East India Company.

§ 24. The right to travel in the interior of China was first conceded by Article IX. of the Treaty of Tien-Tsin [1]

[1] Art. IX.—British subjects are hereby authorised to travel, for their pleasure or for purposes of trade, to all parts of the interior, under passports which will be issued by their Consuls, and countersigned by the local authorities. These passports, if demanded, must he produced for examination in the localities passed through. . . . If he (the traveller) be without a passport, or if he commit an offence against the law, he shall be handed over to the nearest Consul for punishment, but

which conferred it on all Englishmen. And this treaty undoubtedly constitutes a landmark from which we are to date the commencement of modern exploration, and of a more exact knowledge, only now being slowly built up, of the physical geography of the country, of its natural resources, and of the true characteristics of the cities and populations of China. But here it is necessary to interpose a caveat. When we speak of the commencement of modern exploration in China and Tibet, or allude to any modern traveller as being the first to visit this or that secluded locality in those regions, it must always be understood that we begin by assuming a large exception in favour of the missionaries of the Roman Church : for those regions have to a great extent, and for many years past, been habitually traversed by the devoted labourers who have been extending the cords of their Church in the interior, and on the inland frontier of China. Geographical research is not their object, and for a long period publicity was only adverse to their purpose ; and thus their labours and their journeys in those remote regions, which long preceded the treaty of Tien-Tsin, though often recorded in the *Annales de la Propagation de la Foi* and similar journals for those who seek them there, have only occasionally come before the notice of geographical societies, or of the public in Europe. There are, indeed, notable exceptions, of which we shall presently take account ; but apart from these, in hardly any instance has a traveller penetrated in this region to a point where he has not found a member of these Roman Catholic missions to have been before him.

§ 25. We have already alluded to the letter written from Tibetan territory by an eminent member of these missions, which reached the Asiatic Society of Bengal, to their no small surprise, in 1861. When Lieutenant Garnier and his party made their rapid and venturesome visit to Ta-Li-Fu, in 1868, their guide and helper was their countryman M. Leguilcher, of the same mission, whom they found in his seclusion near the north end of the Lake of Ta-Li-Fu, and with whom

he must not be subjected to any ill-usage in excess of personal restraint. . .

Captain Gill made acquaintance nine years later at the city itself. Not only at Ch'ung-Ch'ing and at Ch'êng-Tu did Captain Gill find kindly aid among the members of these missions, but at Ta-Chien-Lu, on the acclivity of the great Tibetan plateau, like Mr. Cooper before him, he found, as we have mentioned in his Memoir, cordial welcome from the venerable Bishop Chauveau.

Members of the same body were found by both travellers also at Bat'ang, in the basin of the Kin-sha, and on both occasions, at nine years' interval, the Abbé Desgodins was one of their number.

Bat'ang appears to be at present the furthest station of the missionaries towards Tibet; nor have they any now within the actual Lhassa dominions. But at one time they had for some years establishments within the political, as well as the ethnical, boundary of Tibet. Abbé Renou, the first of the body to make an advance in this direction, obtained in 1854 a perpetual lease of Bonga, a small valley in the hills adjoining the Lu-Kiang on its eastern bank, for a rent of 16 or 17 taels. This is under the Government of Kiang-ka, where officials both Chinese and Tibetan reside. The missionaries of Bonga cleared a good deal of land, erected buildings, and began to have considerable success in making converts, both among the wilder tribes of the hills and among the Tibetan villagers around them. But in 1858 they were violently ejected by the person who had given the lease, aided by an armed party. No redress was got till 1862, when the Treaty of Tien-tsin began to take actual effect; the suit of the missionaries was heard in the Court at Kiang-ka, and they were reinstated at Bonga. Three years later, however, the neighbouring Lamas, who, as Captain Gill several times explains, are very unpopular themselves, and who were all the more disposed to view with jealousy whatever success the missionaries had among the people, took advantage of disorders in the province, and expelled the missionaries from Bonga and other settlements outside the Chinese political frontier. MM. Desgodins and F. Biet, who were at Bonga, after a good deal of violence on one side, and some administration of presents on the other, were allowed to carry off their flock into Chinese territory, but their establishment was sacked and burnt (September 29, 1865). MM. Durand and A. Biet, who directed an out-station at a place called Kie-na-tong (among the Lu-tse), on the Salwen, just within the Yun-nan boundary, were driven away, and the former was shot in crossing a swing bridge.

Monseigneur Chauveau, who had at this time succeeded to the government of the mission, established his head-quarters at Ta-Chien-Lu, on the borders of what we should in India call the Regulation and the Non-Regulation Provinces, and out-stations were still maintained at Tseku and Yerkalo on the Lant'sang; the former under Yun-nan, the latter in the Bat'ang territory, but none in Tibet proper.

§ 26. In January 1867 the Kájí Jagat Sher, an envoy from Maharaja Jung Bahadur to the Court of China,[2] was passing through Bat'ang, and made the acquaintance of the missionaries there. Their communications were in English, which was probably indifferent on both sides; but what the Nepalese envoy said led the French fathers to suppose that the British Government in India had heard of their sufferings at the hands of the Tibetans, and had requested the Nepal Government to make inquiry.[3] M. Desgodins accordingly sent by the hands of Jagat Sher a very interesting letter, written in very imperfect English, and addressed to the Resident at Katmandu (then Colonel George Ramsay), with a full account of their circumstances, of the violent treatment they had met with, and of the murder of M. Durand. The Governor-General, in replying to Colonel Ramsay's communication of this letter, expressed the deep interest with which he had read it, but intimated that the only intervention in their favour possible would be through the Maharaja of Nepal, and through our Minister at Peking. The Government letter went on :—

[2] Cooper met Jagat Sher both at Ch'êng-Tu and near Bat'ang in returning. The Envoy had met with very bad treatment from the Chinese, and was not allowed to proceed beyond Ch'êng-Tu. (See *Cooper*, pp. 158 *seq.*, 398 *seq.*)

[3] It does not seem to have been the fact that any news of the kind had reached India.

You will, at the same time, however, observe that if the Government may be permitted to offer an opinion to men animated by higher considerations than those of mere personal security or success, these reverend gentlemen would do well to abandon the country in which their sufferings have been so great, and settle in British India, where there are extensive and peaceful tracts, such as Lahoul, Spiti, and Kulu, containing a semi-Thibetan population, likely to receive Christianity with favour.

Copies of the correspondence were sent to our Minister at Peking, and of the letter intended for the missionaries, not only thither, and to Nepal, but to Ladák and Upper Assam. This shows how difficult any communication is across the iron wall that separates British India from the Chinese frontier;[4] and it is greatly to be questioned if any one of the four copies ever reached its destination. That sent by Nepal was suppressed by the Chinese Amban at Lhassa; the messenger *viâ* Assam failed in making his way, and after going fifteen days' journey from Sadiya, returned; the copy from Ladák was forwarded by Dr. Cayley through the inauspicious medium of a monsignore of the Tibetan Curia, who was returning to Lhassa. Of that sent by Peking the fate has not reached us; it is doubtful, from the allusion to the subject in a collection of notices on Tibet by M. Desgodins, whether it ever was received.[5]

[4] There are but three cases in our time that I can recall in which the iron wall was pierced by a piece of intelligence. The first was the murder of MM. Krick and Boury, of which we have spoken above. The second was this communication from the priests at Bat'ang to the Resident at Katmandu. The third was the Arabic proclamation or circular, issued in the name of the Panthé rulers at Ta-Li-Fu, for the information of the Mahommedan world, which also reached Colonel Ramsay at Katmandu. A copy of it was given me by the lamented Mr. J. W. Wyllie, and it was printed by my late friend Lieutenant Fr. Garnier (to whom I gave it) in the appendix to his *Voyage d'Exploration*, vol. i. p. 564.

[5] See that work (*La Mission du Thibet de* 1855 *à* 1870, Verdun, 1872), pp. 115, 116. The facts in the text are gathered from a correspondence in the India Office After Lord Lawrence's death I read a Roman Catholic article which, while doing him noble justice in most respects, spoke regretfully of the narrow Ulster type of religion in which he had been educated, or words to that effect. I will only say that the Viceroy who despatched the letter quoted above, and

§ 27. This is, however, anticipating in chronological order. The first picture of Eastern Tibet in modern times was that set forth by the Abbé Huc in the famous narrative of his journey with Gabet, which astonished the world in 1850. It is true that occasional letters from both Huc and Gabet had appeared in various numbers of the *Annales de la Propagation de la Foi* in 1847–1850, but the circle to which that publication speaks was then probably even more limited and exclusive than it is now; and I cannot find that practically anything was known to the public of their remarkable journey prior to the publication of the work. Sir John Davis, indeed, has told us how he furnished Lord Palmerston, as early as 1847, with some particulars of the journey, which his secretary, Mr. Johnstone, had obtained from Gabet, who was his fellow-passenger to Europe, and these appear to have been printed, for there are most curiously confused allusions to them in the article 'Asia,' in the eighth edition of the Encyclopædia Britannica,' published in 1853.[6] And up to 1855 there is absolutely, so far as I can discover, no notice of Huc or his companion in the Journals of the Royal Geographical Society, or in the annual discourses of its Presidents, except a singularly meagre one in Captain (afterwards Admiral) W. H. Smyth's address of 1851, a reference which is certainly a notable example of scientific puritanism, true though it be that Huc does not belong in any sense or measure to the scientific category.[7] Just as little was he

took all this trouble for these remote French Roman Catholic priests, was Sir John Lawrence, whilst the signature to the letter is that of Sir William Muir.

[6] 'Our scanty knowledge of Tibet has lately received a valuable addition in the journal of the *Rev. Mr. Puch*, a French missionary, who proceeded from Peking, through Mongolia and Tangut, to L'Hassa, the capital of Tibet, which he left for China by the road through Kham. An English translation of his MS. journal was recently published under the auspices of Lord Palmerston.' The final redactor of the article was evidently unable to make anything of the 'Rev. Mr. Puch,' and at the same time unwilling to disturb the references of his predecessor, so he tells us that 'the travels of Huc, Gabet, and *Fuch* have made some additions to our knowledge of Tartary and Tibet.' (8th edit. vol. i. p. 754.)

[7] 'The Narrative of a Residence in the Capital of Thibet, by M. Huc, a Lazarist missionary, contains some corroborative details

entitled to be ranked, as he is by a late pretentious French writer on Chinese matters, with Pauthier (who with all his faults was a genuine and enthusiastic student), and with that modest and indefatigable scholar Mr. Alexander Wylie, lumping all three together, as this writer does, as 'excellents sinologues.'[8] That Huc was, as a 'sinologue,' next door to an impostor, and that his brilliant and, in the main, truthful sketches of travel in Tartary and Tibet were followed by later works of a greatly degenerated character, is undeniable. But it is equally undeniable that Huc was a daring and distinguished traveller, and the author of one of the most delightful books of travel ever written.[9]

§ 28. Many years before Huc's book appeared, we had, indeed, in the immortal work of Carl Ritter—at once a quarry and an edifice—a full, and, as far as all our subsequent information goes, an accurate account of the great road from Ch'êng-Tu to Lhassa, by Ta-Chien-Lu, Bat'ang, Tsiamdo, &c., with the detail of its daily stages. This is taken from Klaproth's French edition of the Chinese *Description du Tübet*, as rendered into Russian by the priest Hyacinth Bichurin (Paris, 1831). Huc makes a good deal of use of this itinerary, which describes the road which he followed on his return from Lhassa, in the very scanty contributions to geography which his narrative contains; but had it been printed as an appendix to his book, we should have followed his journey with more intelligence. In judging of his work from a geographer's point of view, however, it is fair to remember that, on this half of the journey at least, he and Gabet were travelling under arrest.

At the time of Huc's return the Roman Catholic missions had apparently no outpost beyond Ch'êng-Tu. It was, as we

respecting a country imperfectly known to Europeans.'—*Jour. R. Geog. Soc.* xx. p. lxx.

[8] See the *Athenæum*, August 18, 1877, in which there is a review by the present writer of the work referred to.

[9] I have spoken more fully regarding Huc in the Introductory Essay to my friend Mr. Delmar Morgan's translation of Colonel Prejevalsky's travels, and have there defended the substantial truth of his 'Souvenirs' against the Russian traveller's charges. That Huc embellished, and especially in his dramatic reports of conversations, no one can question.

have seen, about eight years afterwards that they began to establish themselves on the Tibetan frontier and beyond it. And apart from their little known movements, it was not till 1861 that any new endeavour occurred to penetrate those regions.

§ 29. The first attempt to act in this direction upon the concessions of the treaty of Tien-Tsin was the voyage of Captain Blakiston, Lieutenant-Colonel Sarel, and Dr. Barton, accompanied by Mr. (since Bishop) Schereschewsky of an American mission, up the Yang-Tzŭ. Their object was to penetrate by Tibet, and across the Himálaya, into India. That was a bold aim, which even at this date, eighteen years later, has never been accomplished. But they were the first to ascend the Great River above Hankow, and penetrated to some fifty miles above the confluence of the Min River at Sü-chau (Swi-Fu), reaching the town of Ping-shan. Here it was found impossible to go on, for their boatmen refused to advance any further on the river, and a land attempt was impracticable in the then disturbed state of the country. Captain Blakiston was a diligent surveyor, and brought back a detailed chart of the river for 840 miles.[1] Blakiston and Sarel left Hankow in March 1861, and reached it again at the end of June. The work which Captain Blakiston published on the subject of this voyage [2] contains much of interest, and the excellent woodcuts from Dr. Barton's sketches. Turning to another side of the geographical territory of which we are speaking, we should mention here an attempt made by two members of the Government service in Pegu (Captain C. E. Watson, and Mr. Fedden of the Geological Survey) to penetrate northward to Thein-ni, on the direct road between the Burmese capital and Ta-Li-Fu.[3] They reached a point with-

[1] A comparison of Blakiston's chart with the old Jesuit representation of the river as given in D'Anville's maps is very favourable to the general correctness of the latter. Captain Gill, who made the comparison at my request, wrote: 'Generally the agreement is very remarkable. The greatest difference in general conformation is between I-tu and the entrance to the Tung-ting Lake.'

[2] *Five Months on the Yangtsze*, &c. London, J. Murray, 1862.

[3] *Selections from the Records of the Government of India in Foreign Department.* No. xlix. 1865.

in little more than a march of Thein-ni, but the place was then in the hands of an insurgent chief, and they were obliged to turn back. The road is thus one which remains unexplored. It runs through the secluded Shan principality of Kaingma, in about latitude 23° 32′, and thence to the Chinese city of Shun-Ning-Fu, called by the Burmese Shwen-lĭ, and by the Shans Muangchan. At one part of this road, between Thein-ni and Shun-ning, it enters a tract partaking of the excessively unhealthy character ascribed by Marco Polo and by Captain Gill (ii. 345–6; *infra*, pp. 272–4) to the same region a little further north, and the road then crosses the Mekong by an iron suspension bridge.

§ 30. In 1868, no less than three attempts from three different points were made to penetrate the obscurities of the region of which we are treating: one by the French expedition which started from Saigon; a second by Mr. Cooper, from Ssŭ-ch'uan; the third by an English expedition from Bhamò on the Irawadi.

The great effort of the French party under Captain Doudart de la Grée of the navy, had been the exploration of the Mekong, which they ascended and surveyed from the delta, as far as Kiang-Hung, in lat. 22° 0′ (a place that had been reached by Lieutenant, afterwards General, W. C. McLeod of the Madras army, on his solitary journey from Maulmain in 1837).[4] From this point they travelled through Southern Yun-nan, to the provincial capital, Yun-Nan-Fu, which they reached at the end of 1867, the first time in our knowledge that any European traveller (not being a missionary priest) had seen the Yachi of Marco Polo, since he himself was there, *circa* 1283.

In view to examining the upper waters of the Mekong, and to other objects not very clear, but of which one perhaps was merely that of penetrating to a place which had been the subject of so much speculation, and the scene of such a singular revolution, the leaders of the party were very desirous to reach Ta-Li-Fu, then the capital of the chosen sovereign of the Mahommedan, or quasi-Mahommedan, rebels

[4] The latitude of McLeod agrees perfectly with that of the French; there is a difference of 9′ in their longitudes.

of Yun-nan, whom we, after the Burmese, call *Panthés.* The Chinese imperialist authorities at Yun-Nan-Fu received with laughter and amazement the proposal of the Frenchmen that they should be allowed to pass direct from the capital to the rebel outposts; but they were bent on success, and achieved it at a later date, starting from Tong-ch'uan-fu, in the northern part of the province (lat. 26° 25½'). Captain Doudart was too ill to take part in the expedition, though

Lieutenant Francis Garnier, of the French Navy.

his danger was not then suspected; and the conduct of this digression fell to Lieutenant Francis Garnier. Starting from Tong-Ch'uan, January 30, 1868, they crossed and recrossed the River of Golden Sand on the eastern and southern limbs of its great southward curve, passing near Hwai-Li, and crossing on the second occasion near the confluence of the Yarlung with the Kin-sha. In the advance nearer Ta-Li the party owed much (as has been already noticed) to the patriotic aid of M. Leguilcher. The meeting of the party with this gentleman in his remote parsonage at Tu-Tui-Tse, near the northern end of the Lake of Ta-Li, is not unlike the famous meeting of Stanley and Livingstone :—

> One of our guides pointed out to me, some hundred mètres below, a little platform, hung as it were in mid-air against the flank of the mountain; there were a few trees planted in rows, and a group of houses surmounted by a cross. I began running down the break-neck winding path, and before long I came in sight of a man with a long beard standing on the edge of the platform, who was attentively regarding me. In a few minutes more I was by his side: 'Are not you Père Leguilcher?' I said. 'Yes, sir,' he answered with a little hesitation, 'and no doubt you are come to announce Lieutenant Garnier, from whom I have just had a letter?' My dress, my unkempt look, my rifle and revolver, no doubt gave me in the Father's eyes the look of a buccaneer; it was evidently not at all what he expected in an officer of the Navy!—'I am the man who wrote the letter, mon père,' I said, laughing, 'and I see you take me for my own servant. . . .' We exchanged a cordial grasp of the hand, and I introduced the members of the expedition as they came up in succession.[5]

Accompanied by M. Leguilcher the party reached Ta-Li-Fu, but they had to leave it in hot haste (March 4) within thirty-six hours of their arrival. The success of their retreat was due to the tact and boldness of Garnier. They returned to Tong-ch'uan by the route they had come, and on their arrival found that their gallant leader, Captain Doudart de la Grée, had died in their absence.

§ 31. Some years later, after having completed a splendid and valuable book, and after taking an active part in the defence of Paris in 1871, Garnier returned to China, bent on fresh exploration. What he accomplished before he was called away to another field, on which he fell, was chiefly in the detailed examination of the navigation of the Upper Yang-tzŭ, and of some of the scarcely known tributaries of the great river in Kwei-chau and Hu-nan.

But the object which he had made specially his own aim

[5] *Voyage d'Exploratiun*, p. 510.

was the exploration of the virgin field of Tibet. Indeed, in this direction he had, like my other friend, Captain Gill, aimed very high :—

I am come to China (he wrote), as you conjecture, to endeavour to penetrate Tibet. My object is to reconnoitre that part of the Yárú-tsang-pu which lies between Lhassa and Sadiya. If I am able—but I doubt it sorely—I should wish to return by the west, i.e. by Turkestan. I have just returned from Peking, where I have been to ask for passports, and letters of recommendation to the Chinese ambassador at Lhassa. I have seen reason to think, however, that these passports will have no great value, and that the difficulties to be encountered in penetrating Tibet will be very great. And they will be enhanced by this, that instead of aiming at Lhassa by the usual road, I wish to adopt a more southerly line (about the 29th degree of latitude) so as to cross the sources of the Camboja and the Salwen, and to make an attempt to explore the sources of the Irawadi. The Brahmaputra-Irawadi question is, in my judgment, far from being absolutely settled ; and you have yourself, in the maps attached to Marco Polo, prolonged the Irawadi hypothetically beyond the limit assigned to it in your map of 1855. . . .[6]

In another letter, one of the last received from him, he recurred to the subject :—

I thank you much for the paper you sent me on the hydrography of Eastern Tibet. I must have said more than I intended, if in my last letter I led you to suppose that I inclined to the identity of the Irawadi and Tsang-pu. All chances and probabilities seem to me the other way, and in favour of the Brahmaputra, and my general map expresses this sufficiently. But we have to do with a country so singular, and so little like any other, that what would elsewhere amount to proof positive, leaves us here still in doubt. Like you I have no doubt that the continuation of the Irawadi is to be sought in some river of Tibet. The reasons which you assign for identifying this river with the Kuts' Kiang or Chété Kiang of Monsgr. des Mazures are very forcible. Did I tell you that we were informed in Burmese Laos that the Irawadi continued northward as a great river, which the Laotians call the Nam-mao, and which they distinguish from the Nam-Búm and the Nam-Kiú (Myit-ngè

[6] Letter, dated April 17, 1873, to the present writer.

and Myit-gyi).[7] The Nam-mao appears to be the Kuts' Kiang. . . . . I desire to avoid forming a theory, even in my own mind, for nothing hoodwinks a traveller like the adoption of a preconceived idea, ... but I repeat as regards the Brahmaputra the probabilities require to be corroborated by material demonstration.

The south-eastern region of Tibet, as far as we could judge on our approach to Li-kiang-fu and Tali, is a country full of surprises. The rivers vanish and appear again. A stream will bifurcate, and, by help of the caverns which abound in that limestone formation, the two branches will sometimes change from one basin into another, discharging into two different rivers. My *impression*—you will think it a strange one—is that, as regards the Brahmaputra and the Irawadi, or, in more general terms, at some point of the connection of the fluvial system of Tibet with that of India and Indo-China, there is a *perte du fleuve*—a phenomenon in fact analogous to that of the Rhone, but on a larger scale. We have seen this happen in Yun-nan with small rivers. And I am just returned from a journey to the frontiers of Szechuan and Kweichau, where I have been eye-witness of some ten varieties of this very phenomenon—rivers passing over one another, splitting in two, and changing from one basin to another. Nothing could be more curious, or more difficult to determine geographically, than the bydrographic network in the basin of the U-Kiang (the river of Kwei-yang—that river which some have assigned as the line of Marco Polo's return to Szechuan). Now there is a striking analogy of geological formation and orographical character between this tract and the south-east of Tibet. It is altogether on a much smaller scale, that is all. Might not we expect to find in the course of the great rivers, of which we have been speaking, some such solution of continuity, which would explain the obscurity which actually hangs over them? This, I repeat, is no more than impression; I take good care to keep from making it into a theory. . . . Pray make me useful in every way that can help your work. I read it carefully whenever I pass over any fraction of Marco Polo's itinerary. As yet I have found nothing of interest to say, unless it be that it seems to me the most exact and faithful impression of all that can be known at this day of the acts and deeds of the traveller, and of the state of the countries which he traversed. . . . . As soon as

[7] These are the Burmese terms for 'Little River' and 'Great River.'

I shall have conferred with Admiral Dupré, and have definitively settled my plans, I will write again. I should of course be very glad of the support of the English authorities, should I succeed in emerging by Assam or Nepal.[8]

§ 32. The second enterprise of 1868 to which we have made reference was that of Mr. Cooper. He left Hankow on January 4, 1868, Ch'êng-Tu on March 7, and Ta-Chien-Lu on April 30, following, to Lit'ang and Bat'ang, the road over the high plateau, afterwards traversed by Captain Gill. Mr. Cooper's hopes were raised at Bat'ang by the information he received that the town or village of Roemah (on the Lohit

T. T. Cooper.

Brahmaputra), from which Assam was not far, could be reached from that point in eighteen days. These hopes were, however, speedily extinguished by the prohibition of the Chinese authorities. Mr. Cooper then decided on travelling to Ta-Li-Fu and Bhamò. His route beyond Bat'ang diverged from that since followed by Captain Gill. Instead of following the River of Golden Sand he chiefly followed the valley of the Lant'sang. He spent a night at Tse-ku, within the Yun-nan boundary, on the western bank of that

[8] Letter dated Saigon, August 28, 1873.

river, where the French missionaries had an out-station among the aboriginal tribes, and an estate which they had purchased from one of the chiefs, occupied chiefly by converts from those tribes, Lu-tse (from whom the name Lu-ts'-Kiang, by which the river Salwen is known on this frontier, is taken), Lu-sus or Lísús, Mossos or Mú-sús, and what not. This is the most westerly point that has been reached by any traveller from China in the region of the great rivers north of Bhamò. And Mr. Cooper appears to be almost justified in stating that he was here within 80 miles of Manché (on the Upper Irawadi), in the Khamti country, which was visited by Wilcox from India in 1827. The distance is, however, apparently nearly 100 miles. South of this Mr. Cooper reached the Chinese town of Wei-Si-Fu, nearly due west of Li-Kiang-Fu, and there obtained passports from the military commandant to go on to Ta-Li. He advanced three days further, but a local chief of a tribe whom Mr. Cooper calls Tzefan, on the border of the Ta-Li territory (then under the 'Panthé' Sultan), refused to let him proceed, and on his return to Wei-si he was imprisoned and threatened with death by the civil officer in charge, who apparently believed him to be in communication with the Ta-Li rebels. After five weeks' imprisonment he was allowed to depart (August 6), and returned by the way he had come as far as Ya-Chou. Thence he diverged to the south, travelling through a beautiful country of tea-gardens, and of the white-wax cultivation, to Kia-Ting-Fu, a famous river-port and *entrepôt* upon the Min River. This he descended to Swi-fu, where the two great contributories of the Yang-Tzŭ unite. Thence he descended the Great River to Hankow, which he reached November 11, 1868.[9]

In the following year Mr. Cooper made an attempt from the side of Assam to penetrate to Bat'ang. He started from Sadiya October, 1869, and passing up the line of the (Lohit) Brahmaputra, through the Mishmi country, reached Prun, a village about 20 miles from Roemah, the first Tibetan post, and half that distance from Samé, where MM. Krick and Boury were murdered. From this he was turned back.

[9] This is called 1869 in Mr. Cooper's book, p. 450.

§ 33. Major Sladen's expedition, sent under the authority of the Government of India, left Bhamò February 26, 1868. After long detentions on the way, by want of carriage and other obstacles, placed in the way of the party, it was supposed, by the influence of Chinese merchants afraid of injury to their commercial monoply, they reached Momien (Teng-Yueh-Chou of the Chinese), then the frontier city towards the west of the Mahommedan Government of Western Yun-nan. The Governor received and entertained the party with great courtesy and hospitality, but entirely objected to their proceeding further, on the professed ground of danger to themselves from the disturbed state of the country. They reached Momien on May 25, left it July 13, and arrived again at Bhamò on September 5, 1868.

Major Sladen gave an account of the journey before the Royal Geographical Society, June 26, 1871,[1] and Dr. Anderson, the medical attendant of the party, and a good naturalist, has recorded all the proceedings and observations of the expedition in a work which contains much of interest. But there was not much geographical information collected, and an officer who had been specially attached to the party as surveyor was allowed, for reasons which it is not easy to understand, to quit it and return to Burma, when they were about half-way to Momien.[2]

Sir R. Alcock has pointed out how inevitably the friendly intercourse into which we entered, on this occasion, with the representatives of a body in revolt against China must have created distrust in the Imperial Government and its partisans in Yun-nan, and not improbably led, more or less directly, to a tragical catastrophe, when the attempt to explore the trade routes of the Yun-nan frontier was renewed six years later. The suspicion of foreign interference had perhaps another effect, in stimulating the Chinese Government to

[1] *Proceedings of Royal Geographical Society*, xv. pp. 363 *seq.*

[2] Dr. Anderson's account was printed by Government at Calcutta, 1871, *Report of an Expedition to Western Yunan*, large 8vo. In another work, published in London, 1876, *Mandalay to Momien*, he gives an account both of this and of Colonel Browne's expedition, of which also he was a member. And his scientific collections have been separately published in 4to.

effective measures for the extinction of the Mahommedan revolt.

§ 34. We pass now to 1872, in the March of which year Baron Richthofen was at Ch'êng-Tu, engaged on the last of those important journeys which formed the basis of his great work on China. The expedition which he projected and commenced from Ch'êng-Tu brings him within the category of explorers in the region which is our subject, though it

Baron Ferdinand v. Richthofen.

came to an untimely end. His project will be best explained in his own words :—

Although my journey . . . as originally contemplated ended at Ching-tu-fu, I could not resist the temptation of trying to add to it a trip through the south-westernmost portions of China, and to explore the mountains of Western Sz'chwan, as well as the provinces of Yün-nan and Kwei-chau. Besides hoping to contribute to the general knowledge of the geography, geology, and resources of these unknown regions, I wished to examine the metalliferous deposits that are widely spread through them, and to gather some information respecting the many independent tribes inhabiting South-Western China, and their languages. My final object, however, was to explore the road from Ta-li-fu to Burma. I had some difficulty in collecting the necessary information, but finally settled upon the plan to travel by way of Ning-yuen-fu to Ta-li-fu, a journey of about five days, and thence to go to Teng-yuè-chau [Momien], the last place reached by Major Sladen on his way from Bamo to Yün-nan. From that city I intended to go again eastward, by Yün-nan-fu and Kwei-yang-fu, the capitals of the provinces of Yün-nan and Kwei-chau, to Chung-king-fu on the Yangtze.[3]

The traveller had accomplished half his journey to Ning-yuan-fu when, on the high Siang-ling pass, he was involved in a collision with a body of Chinese troops, whose outrageous aggression on his party, and its consequences, compelled him to retrace his steps, and to give up a journey from which a richer harvest might perhaps have been expected than even from any that had preceded it.

The journey has since been made, and Ning-yuan has been visited by Mr. Baber, as we shall see. The details of his journey are of great interest, for the country is secluded, and otherwise entirely unexplored; and to me and some others the interest is of a still more special kind, because Ning-yuan is the capital of the valley and district of Kien-chang, which has been demonstrated (as I think), by Richthofen, to be the Gheindu or Caindu of Marco Polo, a country of which, with its cassia-buds and other spices, its strange Massagetic customs, its currency of gold rods and salt-loaves, the old traveller gives so remarkable an account.[4]

§ 35. In speaking of the labours and incidental journeys of the Roman Catholic missionaries, we have mentioned Abbé Desgodins, a gentleman of great intelligence, and who has shown much interest in geography. A book was published at Verdun in 1872,[5] professedly based upon his letters to his family. It contains a good deal of information for those

[3] *Letters to the Shanghai Chambers*, No. VII. p. 3.
[4] See book ii. chap. 47, and the notes to the second edition (vol. ii. p. 57).
[5] *La Mission du Thibet*, de 1835 à 1870.

who bring to its perusal some previous knowledge, to serve as amalgam in the process of extracting what is valuable; but it has been compiled by a relative of the missionary without much clear acquaintance with the subject, and contains a good deal of matter of a kind which appears to be due to this circumstance. The history of the Abbé Desgodins is not a little remarkable, and shows the persistent character of the man.

When first he quitted France as a recruit for the missions, in 1855, he was directed to proceed by way of British India, and to attempt to make his way to the mission establishments across the Tibetan highlands, in order to avoid the great *détour* and expense of the usual journey by the ports and broad interior of China. His first attempt was made by Darjeeling, where, as might have been expected, he had kindly relations with Mr. Bryan Hodgson, who was then living there. After various endeavours to negotiate admission to Tibet by the Sikkim frontier, he was obliged to give it up, and, accompanied by M. Bernard, an older member of the fraternity, proceeded to the North-West Provinces, in order to attempt an entrance by Simla and the Sutlej. The priests were at Agra when the mutiny of 1857 broke out, and spent the summer in the fort there, with the rest of the 'sahib-lōg.' After the relief, they were able to proceed to Simla, and went on by Rampúr to Chini on the Upper Sutlej. Here M. Desgodins was summoned back, and ordered to proceed by the more usual route to join his mission. We find him again at Agra in the hot weather of 1858, and then doing duty as Roman Catholic chaplain to a British force at Jhansi. From this he writes to his parents:—

You will think I am going to become a regular Crœsus when I tell you that the Government of John Bull gives me for my services as Military Chaplain 800 francs a month, or, as they say here, 320 rupees. . . . However, when you know the state of things in India, and the prices, it is no small matter to make both ends meet; so my dear nephew must not count on a fortune from my savings. Moreover, I hope not to be long in John Bull's service; but soon to be able to join my mission;

I shall feel richer there with next to nothing, than here with my 800 francs.—*La Mission du Thibet*, p. 36.

Receiving a fresh summons from Bishop des Mazures, he took his departure (after drawing at Agra a sum of about 1,000 rupees for his services with the army). During his journey to the interior he was arrested, imprisoned, and sent back to Canton. Starting again under a new disguise, he finally reached the residence of the Bishop, near the frontier of Tibet, in June, 1860, five years after his departure from France.

§ 36. We now come to the journey of the gallant young traveller who, after being the first to open the way from China to the Irawadi, had hardly taken the first step on his return when his blood was left upon the path.

In the spring of 1873 the Imperial Government in Yun-nan succeeded, as has already been noticed, in finally crushing the insurgents who had maintained their independence for some seventeen years.

The Government of India decided on now renewing the attempt to explore the road, and the facilities for trade between the Irawadi and China, which Major Sladen had been unable to carry out, owing to the state of political affairs when he visited Momien. Colonel Horace Browne, of the Pegu Commission, was appointed to lead the mission; and it was settled that an officer of the consular service should be sent across China to Bhamò to meet the mission there, and to accompany them back to China as interpreter and Chinese adviser.

The officer appointed to this duty was Augustus Raymond Margary, a young man of high character and promise. It is needless to detail a story still fresh in the public mind. His journey led him from Hankow across the Tung-Ting Lake, and by the regions, hardly known to Europeans, of Western Hu-Nan and Kwei-Chou to Yun-Nan-Fu, and thence to Ta-Li and Bhamò—the first of Englishmen to accomplish the feat that had been the object of so many ambitions, and to pass from the Yang-Tzŭ to the Irawadi.

Margary reached Yun-Nan-Fu on November 27, 1874,

and writing home from this point he says: 'I quite enjoyed the journey; everywhere the people were charming, and the mandarins extremely civil, so that I had quite a triumphal progress.' The same good treatment was continued through Yun-nan. He started again on December 2, and on the 14th or 15th reached Chao-Chou, 20 miles from Ta-Li (which, as the map will show, lies about ten miles off the direct road from Yun-Nan-Fu to the Burmese frontier). There was some unwillingness to let him visit that city, from a dread, probably real, of popular turbulence; but this was overcome; and he writes home, on returning to his quarters at Chao-Chou:—

I visited the mandarins in turn, and had a most successful interview with all, but especially with the Tartar General, who treated me with extreme civility, very much in the style of a polished English gentleman receiving a younger man. I was perfectly delighted with his reception. He complimented me over and over again on my knowledge of Chinese, and . . . said he hoped on my return I would spend a few days with him. . . . 'I should naturally wish to see everything, if I visited your country,' said he, 'and I shall have a house ready for you and your honoured officials when you return.[6]'

The General gave Margary the place of honour beside him. The Tao-tai, a young man, had omitted this courtesy.

He reached Momien on January 4, 1875, and Manwain, the place where he met his death seven weeks later, on the 11th. Here he was visited by 'a furious ex-brigand called Li-Hsieh-Tai, who attacked our last expedition in 1867, and has been rewarded lately for his services against the rebels with a military command all over the country.' This is the man who was afterwards charged with the murder of Margary. On this occasion, to the traveller's great surprise, he prostrated himself, and paid him the highest honour.

On January 17 Margary reached Bhamò, safe and triumphant. 'You may imagine,' he writes, 'how full of delight

[6] *Margary's Journals*, pp. 236, 278.

I am at the happy results of my journey, and the glowing prospect ahead.'[7]

§ 37. After an unsuccessful attempt to proceed by a more southerly line from Bhamò, through Sawadi, Colonel Browne had to revert to the route by which Margary had come, and a start was made from Tsit-kau on the Bhamò river (Ma-mou or Sicaw of Captain Gill, ii. p. 384; *infra*, p. 312) on February 16. The rest is best told in the words of the editor of his journals :—

Early on the morning of February 19 Margary crossed the frontier with no escort but his Chinese secretary and servants, who had been with him through his whole journey, and a few Burmese muleteers. The next morning brought letters from him, reporting all safe up to Seray. He had been well received there, and had passed on to Manwyne. The mission followed slowly, reaching Seray on the 21st. . . . On the 22nd, in the early morning, the storm broke. The mission camp was almost surrounded by armed bands, while letters from the Burmese agent at Manwyne to the chief in command of their escort told that Margary had been brutally murdered at Manwyne on the previous day. But for the staunchness of the Burmese escort —who resisted all offers of their assailants of heavy bribes if they would draw off and allow them only to kill the 'foreign devils'—and the gallantry of the fifteen Sikhs who formed their body-guard, the whole mission must have shared the fate of their comrade. . . . At Bhamô they eagerly sought for all particulars of the murder, but without much success. The most trustworthy account was that of a Burmese who had seen Margary walking about Manwyne, sometimes with Chinese, sometimes alone, on the morning of the 21st. This man reported that he had left the town on his pony, to visit a hot spring at the invitation of some Chinese, who, as soon as they were outside the town, had knocked him off his pony and speared him.

§ 38. Then followed Sir T. Wade's unwearied negotiations with the Chinese Ministers, and the deputation of the Hon. T. G. Grosvenor, accompanied by Messrs. Baber and Davenport, to be present at the Chinese investigation at Yun-Nan-Fu.

The Chinese Government had given the strongest assur-

[7] Page 308.

ances that the investigation should be conducted with a view to the production of trustworthy witnesses, and the punishment of the real offenders. But the fact was far otherwise. No witness of the murder was allowed to be produced. The story which Mr. Grosvenor was pressed to accept was that Margary had been murdered by savages; that Li-Hsieh-Tai (or Li-Chên-Kou, as he was officially designated in China) had organised the attack on Colonel Browne; that the Momien train-bands had not been moved out of Momien, but had stood there only on the defensive.

The manner in which the affair had been dealt with showed that what had happened in Yun-nan had been done, if not by the direct order, at least with the approval after the fact, of the Central Government, and our Minister could only express his entire disbelief in the case put forward, and decline to agree to the execution of any of the persons whom the Chinese investigation professed to incriminate.

§ 39. The termination of the affair was one of the matters embraced in the 'Agreement of Chefoo,' signed September 13, 1876. This provided, among other things (Sect. I. ii.), that a proclamation should be issued by the Chinese Government, embodying a memorial of the Grand Secretary Li with an imperial decree in reply. These documents embraced a statement of the facts of the deputation and murder of Mr. Margary, a recognition of the gravity of the outrage, of the necessity of observing treaties, of the anxiety of the Imperial Court to maintain friendly relations with foreign powers, and of its regret for what had occurred, with an injunction on local authorities to give protection to foreign travellers, and to study the treaty of Tien-Tsin. It was also agreed that for two years to come officers should be sent by the British Minister to different places in the provinces to see that this proclamation was posted.

This is the *Margary Proclamation*, referred to by Captain Gill in the remoter part of his travels.

The agreement also provided (*ib.* iii.) that an imperial decree should be issued directing that whenever the British Government should send officers to Yun-nan the authorities of that province should select an officer of rank to confer with them, and to conclude a satisfactory arrangement regarding trade.

The British Government was also (*ib.* iv.) to be at liberty for five years to station officers at Ta-Li-Fu, or other suitable place in Yun-nan, to observe the conditions of trade.

Passports having been obtained the preceding year for a mission from India to Yun-nan (Colonel Browne's), it would be open to the Viceroy of India to send such mission when he should see fit.

An indemnity (*ib.* v.) was to be paid on account of the families of those killed in Yun-nan, on account of the expenses occasioned by the Yun-nan affair, and on account of claims of British merchants arising out of the action of officers of the Chinese Government; and this indemnity was fixed at 200,000 taels.

When the case should be closed, an imperial letter of regret was to be carried by a mission to England (vi.).

Under Sect. III. i., several free ports, including I-chang, on the Upper Yang-Tzŭ, were added to those already constituted, and the British Government were authorised to establish a consular officer at Ch'ung-Ch'ing, to watch the trade in Ssŭ-Ch'uan.

Also by a separate article it was provided that the Tsung-Li Yamen should, at the proper time, issue passports for a British mission of exploration, either by way of Peking through Kan-Su and Koko Nor, or by way of Ssŭ-Ch'uan to Tibet. Or, if the mission should proceed by the Indian frontier to Tibet, the Yamen should write to the Chinese resident in Tibet, who should send officers to take due care of the mission, whilst passports also should be issued for the latter.

It is hardly necessary to say that no residents in Yun-nan have been appointed under this agreement; nor has any mission again entered Yun-nan, nor any official mission of exploration been sent to Tibet.

§ 40. Going back a little, I may record that Mr. Grosvenor's mission to Yun-nan left Hankow November 5, 1875, reached Yun-Nan-Fu on March 6, 1876; Ta-Li-Fu on April 11; Momien on May 3; and Bhamò I don't know when, for I have searched the reports, as published, of all the members of the mission without being able to find the date.

Mr. Arthur Davenport, one of the members, has made an interesting report on the trading capabilities of the country traversed by it, forwarded by Sir T. Wade to the Foreign Office, October 9, 1876.

Another of the officers attached to Mr. Grosvenor's mission was fortunately Mr. E. Colborne Baber, a gentleman who seems thoroughly imbued with the true genius of travel,

Edward Colborne Baber.

a spirit which has led him apparently to spend his holidays in exploring fresh fields and gathering fresh stores of knowledge.

On another expedition accomplished in solitude in the autumn of 1877 from his consulate at Ch'ung-Ch'ing, he succeeded in completing the journey which Richthofen was compelled to abandon, making his way from Ya-Chou to Ning-Yuan-Fu.

His notes on the latter part of the route followed by the Grosvenor mission (that between Ta-Li and Momien), published by command, first made the English public, though we fear only a very limited portion of it, acquainted with his name. But these notes, and the maps which accompanied them, have given Mr. Baber *per saltum* a very high place among travellers capable of seeing, of surveying, and of describing with extraordinary vivacity and force.

Considering, however, how intimately I have been associated with Mr. Baber in preparing the present volume for the press, I shall do well, instead of saying more of my own view of what we owe him, to quote what was said by Lord Aberdare as President of the Royal Geographical Society, when presenting him with one of their gold medals on May 28, 1883 :—

If the Royal Geographical Society were asked to justify their choice of you, among several distinguished competitors, for the honour of receiving our Patron's—the Queen's—Gold Medal, we should confidently refer to that first part of our first volume of 'Supplementary Papers,' published by the Society, and containing your 'Travels and Researches in Western China.'

The first of these travels—not in the order of printing, but in date—was the narrative of your mission under the Hon. T. Grosvenor in 1876, sent across Yun-nan to Bhamò, to investigate the murder of Mr. Margary. This narrative, in spite of the disadvantage of making its appearance as a blue-book, and therefore obtaining but a limited circulation, yet 'a fit audience found though few,' and made European geographers acquainted with the fact that a geographical observer and narrator of remarkable power had appeared in the Far East. The map accompanying this blue-book was from your survey.

This narrative was speedily followed by a Journey of Exploration in Western Ssŭ-Ch'uan in 1877, upon which perhaps rest your highest claims as a traveller and explorer. This journey, which completed much that was attempted by our eminent medallist, Baron Ferdinand von Richthofen in 1872, who was baffled in his enterprise by native hostility, and which extended largely the knowledge of that vast district acquired by the distinguished French traveller Francis Garnier in 1868, was in great part over entirely new ground, and introduced us to the knowledge of several objects of the highest interest, such as, among many others, Mount Omi, a notable place of Buddhist pilgrimage, of which and its unique antiquities you gave a most graphic description ; and as the little-known people, the Lolos, from whom you brought back copious specimens of their books, written in an alphabetic character which still remains undeciphered. But perhaps its greatest value depends upon the many important corrections of the Jesuit surveys in those parts, made in the time of the Emperor Kang-Hi, which for more than a century and a half have been the basis of all our maps of China.

Another journey in 1878 in the same province, when, following the earlier part of your former route westward from Kia-ting-fu, you turned northward by a new line of mountain country occupied by the Sifan tribes, to the now well-known town of Tachien-lu on the great Lhassa road, made a considerable addition to the accurate knowledge of those regions.

The same 'Supplementary Papers' also contain a most interesting and valuable monograph by you on the Chinese tea-trade with Tibet.

In all these journeys you made careful route surveys, checked by observations for latitude and longitude. The maps which have been published in our volume, embrace, on your principal journey alone, 121 astronomical determinations of latitude and seven of longitude, and the care and neatness with which these surveys were drawn by you excited general admiration.

Of these great services to geography I have given only the dry outlines. It is the merest justice to you to add that your journeys have been exceptionally productive, because of the exceptional store of various and accurate knowledge with which you started on your travels. Your mastery of the Chinese language, and of Chinese customs and habits of thought, enabled you to collect a great amount of miscellaneous information, which has been conveyed in narratives full of novelty, vivacity, and sustained interest. Altogether, both in these journeys and the report of their results, you have displayed the qualities of an accomplished traveller in a degree of which we have had few examples, and which fully justify our choice of you for sharing with Sir Joseph Hooker our highest distinction, even although you have, we firmly believe, only given the first-fruits of that rich harvest which we expect from your matured powers and enlarged experience.

§ 41. The following passage, describing the first transition from a Chinese to a Tibetan atmosphere, is a fair specimen of the style which makes Mr. Baber's reports, whilst abounding in valuable information, almost as unique among blue-books as the autobiography of his illustrious namesake—I suppose we cannot say ancestor—is among Asiatic volumes :—

The remainder of the journey was impeded by nothing worse than natural difficulties, such as fevers and the extreme ruggedness of the mountain ranges. We quitted cultivation at the foot of a pine-forest, through which we travelled three days, ascending continually until we came to a snowy pass—the only pass in the country which, as the natives say, 'hang-jên,' stops people's breathing. Descending its northern slope, we soon found that we had left China behind. There were no Chinese to be seen. The valley was nearly all pasture-land, on which were grazing herds of hairy animals, resembling immense goats. These I rightly conjectured to be yaks. On entering a hut, I found it impossible to communicate with the family, even a Sifan, whom I had brought with me, being unintelligible to them; but they were polite enough to rescue me from the attack of the largest dogs I have ever seen, and to regale me with barleymeal in a wooden bowl, which I had to wash down with a broth made of butter, salt, and tea-twigs. Further on we met a company of cavaliers, armed with match-lock and sabre, and decorated with profuse ornaments in silver, coral, and turquoise; a troop of women followed on foot, making merry at my expense. A mile or two further, and I came to a great heap of slates, inscribed with Sanskrit characters, whereupon I began to understand that we were in Thibet; for although Thibet proper is many hundred miles west of this point, yet traces of Thibetan race and language extend right up to the bank of the Tatu River—a fact which I had not been led to expect.

§ 42. In this review we have had occasion to speak frequently and largely of the enterprising devotion of the Roman Catholic missionary priests in the obscure regions with which we have had to do. It has been the fortune of the present writer to spend many years in a Roman Catholic country without feeling in the least degree that attraction to the Roman Church which influences some—indeed, he might speak much more strongly. But it is with pleasure and reverence that one contemplates their labour and devotion in fields where these are exercised so much to the side of good, and where there is no provocation to intolerance or to controversy except with the heathen; no room for the display of that spirit which in some regions has led the priests of this Church to take advantage of openings made by others to step in and mar results to the best of their power. The recognition of the labours and devotion of which we spoke just now has often led to sarcastic contrast of their work with that of Protestant missionaries, to the disparagement of the latter—such as occurs not unfrequently in the narrative of Mr. Cooper; in this I have no sympathy. There may be much which the members of Protestant missions should carefully study (and which some of them probably have often studied) in the results that provoke such comparisons, but it is a shallow judgment that condemns them on a superficial view of those results. In any case, the discussion would here be out of place, and I have no intention of entering on it. Though it is only of late years comparatively that Protestant missionaries in China have contributed to our geographical knowledge of the western frontier, we must not overlook what they have done. Mr. Williamson's excellent work [8] does not reach our limits, as he was not nearer than Si-Ngan-Fu. But my valued friend Mr. Alexander Wylie, long agent at Shanghai of the Bible Society, was one of the earliest in our day to visit Ssŭ-Ch'uan, and to give us an account of its highly civilised capital, Ch'êng-Tu. His visit occurred in 1868.[9] More recently, some of the numerous agents of the society called the China Inland Mission have been active in the reconnaissance of these outlying regions.

Mr. McCarthy, one of the agents of this society, was the first non-official traveller to accomplish the journey to Bhamò. This he did from Ch'ung-Ch'ing on foot, travelling south to Kwei-Yang-Fu, and then onwards to Yun-Nan-Fu, and Ta-Li, and so forth, reaching Bhamò on August 26, 1877, a little more than two months before Captain Gill's arrival at

[8] *Journeys in North China, Manchuria, &c.* London, 1870.

[9] See *Proceedings of the Royal Geographical Society*, vol. xiv. p. 168 *seq.* Mr. Wylie has now been visited with total blindness. Few have used their eyes so well and disinterestedly.

that place. Mr. McCarthy wore the Chinese dress, as the members of his mission appear frequently to do, but made the character and object of his journey generally known. He was nearly everywhere treated with civility, often with kindness. 'Throughout the whole journey,' he says, 'I have not once had to appeal to an officer for help of any kind, and in no case has any officer put an obstacle in my way.'[1]

Mr. Cameron, another agent of the same society, followed Captain Gill not long after that officer, leaving Ch'êng-Tu on September 13, 1877, and after an unsuccessful attempt to make the directer road to Ta-Chien-Lu, had to adopt the usual and more circuitous line by Ya-Chou, taken by Captain Gill. He also followed in Captain Gill's traces to Lit'ang, Bat'ang, and A-tun-tzŭ. He was kindly and courteously received by the French priest at Bat'ang (M. Desgodins). At A-tun-tzŭ the solitary traveller was laid up for many days with a bad attack of fever. On his recovery his further route deviated from Captain Gill's, as he went further to the west, by Wei-si, where Cooper was imprisoned in 1868. He reached Ta-Li-Fu on December 23, and Bhamò at the end of January, 1878. Mr. Cameron's journal is that of a simple and zealous man, and from his being without a companion, and thus seeing the more of the people, has many interesting passages. But there is hardly any recognition of geography in it; less a good deal than in Huc's narrative. For example, the passage of the famous Yarlung Kiang is only noticed as that of 'a small river' below a place called Hok'eo.[2]

§ 43. The long passage through which we have conducted our readers—or some of them at least, we trust—in this Geographical Introduction must not close without a brief section devoted to Captain Gill's own journeys; avoiding as far as possible repetition of what has been said in the Memoir.

[1] Letter from the traveller to Mr. T. T. Cooper, British Agent at Bhamò, dated September 4, 1877, in *China's Millions*, the periodical of Mr. McCarthy's Society, for 1878, p. 61. Mr. McCarthy also read an account of his journey before the Royal Geographical Society; see the *Proceedings* (August), 1879, pp. 489 *seq.*

[2] See Captain Gill, vol. ii. p. 137; *infra*, p. 197. Mr. Cameron's journal is published in *China's Millions* for 1879, pp. 65 *seq.*, 97 *seq.*, 109 *seq.*

His first journey, in the north of Pe-Chih-Li, was but a trial of his powers. His ascent of the Yang-Tzŭ, though full of interesting detail, is on a line that has been described by several predecessors since Blakiston. The more important and novel itinerary begins with his excursion from Ch'êng-Tu to the Northern Alps.

Captain Gill on this occasion came into the land of the highland races whom the Chinese call Man-Tzŭ and Si-Fan. It is difficult to grasp the Chinese ethnological distinctions, though doubtless there is some principle at the bottom of those distinctions. The races generally along the western frontier are, as Richthofen tells us,[3] classed by the Chinese as *Lolo, Man-Tzŭ, Si-Fan* and *Tibetan.*

The Lolo are furthest to the south, and occupy the mountains west of the Min, and west of the north-running section of the Kin-sha—fiercely independent, but not ignoble, caterans, a barrier to all direct intercourse across their hills, and frequent in their raids on the Chinese population below. Captain Gill did not come in contact with them, but Mr. Baber has since supplied us with a valuable amount of information regarding their manners, language, and condition.

The *Man-Tzŭ* are regarded by the Chinese as the descendants of the ancient occupants of the province of Ssŭ-Ch'uan, and Mr. Wylie has drawn attention to the numerous cave dwellings which are ascribed to them in the valley of the Min River. The name is applied to the tribes which occupy the high mountains on the west of the province up to about 32° lat. North of that parallel, beginning a little south of Sung-Pan-Ting, the extreme point of Captain Gill's excursion in this direction, are the Si-Fan ('western aliens'), who extend into the Koko-Nur basin, through an alpine country which remains virgin as regards all European exploration.

§ 44. Both terms, Man-Tzŭ and Si-Fan, seem, however, to be used somewhat loosely or ambiguously.

Thus, Man-Tzŭ is applied to some tribes which are not

[3] *Letters to Shanghai Chamber of Commerce,* No. vii. p. 67. Shanghai, 1872.

Tibetan, whilst it is also applied to people, like those on the Ta-Chien-Lu road, who are distinctly Tibetan.[4]

Thus, also, Si-Fan appears to be sometimes applied to the whole body of tribes, of differing languages, who occupy the alpine country between Koko-Nur and the Lolo mountain country, and sometimes distinctively to a Tibetan-speaking race who form a large part of the occupants of that country on the north-east of Tibet, and in the Koko-Nur basin, the *Tangutans* of Colonel Prejevalsky.[5] And in this sense it is used in Captain Gill's book; for the Si-Fan of whom he speaks use a Tibetan dialect, as will presently be manifest, and also (from specimens that he brought away with him) use the Tibetan character. They seem to correspond to the *Amdoans* of Mr. Bryan Hodgson, in the passage which I am about to quote.

This passage exemplifies the wider sense of the term Si-fan[6]:—

From Khokho-Núr to Yúnnán, the conterminous frontier of China and Tibet is successively and continuously occupied (going from north to south) by the Sókpa; . . . by the Amdoans, who for the most part now speak Tibetan; by the Thóchú; by the Gyárúng; and by the Mányák. . . . The people of Sókyúl, of Amdo, of Thóchú, of Gyárúng, and of Mányák, who are under chiefs of their own, styled *Gyábo* or King, *sinicè* 'Wang,' bear among the Chinese the common designation of Sifán, or Western aliens; and the Tibetans frequently denominate the whole of them *Gyárúng-bo*, from the superior importance of the special tribe of Gyarung. . . . The word *Gyá*, in the language of Tibet, is equivalent to that of *Fan* (*alienus*, *barbaros*) in the language of China.[7]

[4] The *Description du Tübet*, translated by Klaproth, says expressly that the people about Ta-Chien-Lu belong to the same *souche* as the Tibetans, and have the same manners (p. 266). Cooper, on this road, uses *Man-Tzŭ* as the Chinese synonym of Tibetan (see p. 174, *et passim*). But ethnologically *Tibetan* is analogous in value to *Latin*.

[5] *Prejevalsky's Travels*, translated by Mr. Delmar Morgan, vol. ii. *passim*, and note at p. 301.

[6] Mr. Baber again, in his printed letter, quoted from in § 40, calls the tribal chief with whom he had to do, a long way south of Ta-Chien-Lu, a *Si-Fan*.

[7] *Hodgson's Essays*, 1874, part ii. pp. 66, 67.

The fact mentioned in the last lines of the extract, if correct (and no one's statements are more full of knowledge or more carefully weighed in general than Mr. Hodgson's), would imply that the Tibetans proper do not regard these Si-Fan tribes as of their own blood, even those of them who now speak Tibetan; and possibly we may have to apply this to the Man-Tzŭ also adjoining the Ta-Chien-Lu road. Mr. Hodgson, in speaking of some of the authorities for the vocabularies which he gives of the Si-Fan languages, tells us that his *Gyárûng* came from Tazar, north of Tachindo (*i.e.* of Ta-Chien-Lu), whilst his *Mányaker* was a mendicant friar (of the heretical Bonpa sect), a native of Ra'kho, six days south of Tachindo. These are the only data I find as to the position of the two tribes named. We shall presently find a third as to the position of the Thochu, which also will fall into its proper place in Hodgson's series, and confirm his accuracy.

I proceed now to insert the numerals of three of the tribes as collected orally by Captain Gill (A, B, C);[8] to which I add for comparison the spoken Tibetan (D), and the Thochu (E), from Hodgson's comparative vocabularies. To these I have now adjoined (F) Mr. Baber's Lolo from the left bank of the T'ung River:—

	A	B	C	D	E	F
1	chek	ár-gú	kí	chĭk	ári	ts'u
2	nyĭ	ner-gú	nyĕ	nyi	gnárí	nĭ
3	sĕ	ksir-gú	song	sum	khshíri	su *or* soa
4	zhĕ	sáir-gú	hgherh	zhyi	gzháré	erh
5	knā	wár-gú	hná	gná	wáré	ngu
6	trŭ	shtúr-gú	dru	thú (druk)	khatáré	fó
7	dăn	shner-gú	ten	dún	stáré	shih
8	gyot	kshár-gú	gyĕ	gyé	khráré	shie
9	guh	rber-gú	kăr	gúh	rgúré	gu
10	pchĕ	khád-gú	chĭ-thomba	chúh *or* chú-thámbá	hadúré	tch'ie *or* ts'e
11	pchĕ-chek	khát-yi	ki-tze	. . .	. . .	tch'i-tsu
12	pchĕ-nyĕ	khá-ner	chu-nye	. . .	. . .	tch'i-nĭ
20	nyĕ-shĕ	ner-sá *or* ne-sá	nye-ka-thomba	nyi-shú	. . .	ni-ts'e.

Now the first thing apparent here is that A and C—*i.e.*

[8] A is the language of the 'Man-Tzŭ' at Li-Fan-Fu; B that of the 'Outer Man-Tzŭ' there—or people further west; C that of the 'Si-Fan' about Sung-Pan-Ting.

the so-called 'Man-Tzŭ' of Li-Fan-Fu, and the 'Si-Fan,' are both Tibetan dialects. The Lolo numerals also show an unexpected amount of similarity to the Tibetan.

Next, a comparison with E shows that the 'outer Man-Tzŭ' of Li-Fan-Fu are the race which Hodgson calls Tho-chu, and that their language is not Tibetan. They will be near Li-Fan-Fu, in their place according to Hodgson's series from north to south, the 'Si-Fan' being assumed to be his *Amdoans*, whilst his *Gyarung*, north of Ta-Chien-Lu, are probably the Man-Tzŭ of Abbé David at Mou-Pin ; and his *Manyak* are Mr. Baber's 'Meniak,' south of Ta-Chien-Lu.

Again, we observe that though the essential parts of the numerals in B and E are identical, the persistent affixes (or, as Hodgson calls them, 'servile' affixes) are different—*gú* in the one, *re* or *ri* in the other. In his comparative table we find the servile affix *ku* in the numerals of another language —a Chinese dialect which he called *Gyami* ; and in the Meniak, or *Manyak*, we find a similar affix, *bu* or *bi*.[9]

§ 45. On his return to Ch'êng-Tu Captain Gill was joined by Mr. Mesny, a gentleman from Jersey, who has passed a good many years in the interior of China, and particularly at Kwei-Yang-Fu, in the service of the Chinese Government.[1]

Captain Gill had intended in his preface to render his thanks and a tribute of praise to his companion for the assistance which was derived from him during the journey from Ch'êng-Tu to Bhamò. And when circumstances caused

[9] Thus 1, tábí ; 2, nabí ; 3, síbi ; 4, rêbi ; 5, gnábi ; 6, trúbi ; 7, skwibí (*qu.* shwibi ?) ; 8 zibi ; 9, gubi ; 10, chêchibi. These from Hodgson correspond fairly with Baber's Meniak (see p. 73 of his papers published by the Royal Geographical Society). Here, comparing with D, the essential part of 2, 3, 5, 6, 9, and 10 is evidently Tibetan ; the others diverge. These 'servile' affixes perhaps correspond to the numeral affixes or co-efficients which are necessary to the use of numerals in Chinese, Burmese, Malay, Mexican, &c., and which change with the class of objects indicated. This would account for the variation between B and E. China 'Pigeon English' replaces the whole of these co-efficients by the universal 'piecey.'

[1] Mr. Mesny has been honoured with the ancient Manchu title of *Baturu*, identical with the *bahādur* of India. Some of Mr. Mesny's itineraries in untravelled, or little travelled, parts of China were prepared for publication at Captain Gill's expense, and will be eventually published by the Royal Geographical Society.

this prefatory essay to be written by another hand, he still desired that the following words of his own should be introduced :—

If Mr. Mesny's name occurs but rarely in my book, it is but because he was so thoroughly and completely identified with myself that it seldom occurred to me to refer to my companion otherwise than as included in the pronoun 'we.' But I should be loth to let slip this opportunity of thanking the companion of so many long and weary marches for the persistence with which he seconded my efforts to achieve a rapid and successful journey; for his patience under difficulties and some real trials, and for the courage he showed when it was called for. Above all, I desire to say how much I feel that, in our dealings with the Chinese officials, the friendly relations we were able to maintain with them, and the aid we were able to obtain from them, were in large measure due to Mr. Mesny. Especially in the negotiation for our passage between Yün-Nan and Burma was Mr. Mesny's help invaluable. And I feel that whatever credit may attach to the successful accomplishment of the journey, a very large share of it is due to Mr. Mesny, who, for the love of travel alone, gave up a remunerative employment under the Chinese Government to become my companion. As long as the events of those sixteen weeks shall have a place in my memory, so long will the kindly support of my companion be among the freshest and pleasantest of them all.

§ 46. The first place of importance reached after leaving Ch'êng-Tu was Ya-Chou, the *entrepôt* and starting-point of the trade with Tibet. The staple of this trade is the brick-tea, or rather cake-tea (afterwards broken up into brick-tea). Captain Gill has given some interesting particulars of this (ii. 47; *infra*, 159); as he has in a previous part of his book (i. 176 *seq.*; *infra*, 47) regarding a similar manufacture carried on by the Russians established at Hankow, for the market of Mongolia.

Whilst I was writing these paragraphs a report was put into my hands, in which Mr. Baber gives most curious details respecting this Tibetan tea-trade.[2] The tea grown for it is

[2] In supplement to *Calcutta Gazette*, November 8, 1879. This has been reprinted with Mr. Baber's Journeys in the *Supplementary Papers of the Royal Geographical Society*, 1882, pp. 192 *seq.*

peculiar. It is not derived from the carefully manipulated leaves of carefully tended gardens, but from scrubby, straggling, and uncared-for trees, allowed to attain a height of nine or ten feet and more. Even of these plants only the inferior produce is devoted to the use of the barbarian: in fact, what is mere refuse. 'I saw great quantities of this,' writes Mr. Baber, 'being brought in from the country on the backs of coolies, in bundles eight feet long by nearly a yard broad, and supposed it to be fuel; it looks like brushwood, and is, in fact, merely branches broken off the trees and dried in the sun, without any pretence at picking. It sells in Yung-Ching for 2,000 cash a pecul at the outside, and its quality may be judged from a comparison of this price with that of the common tea drunk by the poorer classes in the neighbourhood, which is about 20,000 cash a pecul.'

Mr. Baber then describes the process of pressing this stuff into the cakes or *pao* spoken of by Captain Gill. At Ta-Chien-Lu these cakes are cut into the portions—about nine inches by seven by three—which the Chinese call *ch'uan*, or 'bricks,' 'containing a good deal more stick than leaf.' Mr. Baber corroborates Captain Gill's estimate of the extraordinary weights carried by the porters of these *pao* up to Ta-Chien-Lu, mentioning a case in which he overtook a somewhat slenderly built carrier freighted with 22 of the Ya-Chou packages, which must at the lowest computation have exceeded 400 lbs. in weight![3]

The quantity which annually paid duty at Ta-Chien-Lu he calculated on good comparative data at about 10,000,000 lbs., worth at that place £160,000.

A good deal besides is smuggled in by Chinese officials, for it is by means of this tea that those gentlemen feather their nests. Of these administrators and their gains the Tibetans say, 'They come to our country without breeks, and go away with a thousand baggage-yaks.'

§ 47. Mr. Baber, like Captain Gill, speaks of the remarkable manner in which the British-Indian rupee has become

[3] The *pao* purport to weigh each 18 catties, or 24 lbs., as Captain Gill states. But this, according to Mr. Baber, is when saturated. The theoretical weight is a good deal reduced when they are dry.

the currency of Tibet—a circumstance of which my friend General Hyde was probably not aware in his endeavours to estimate the existing amount of current rupees for the Silver Committee of 1876. 'Those (rupees) which bear a crowned presentment of Her Majesty are named *Lama tob-du* or "vagabond Lama," the crown having been mistaken for the head-gear of a religious mendicant.'

Before the introduction of the rupee, tea-bricks were used as currency (just as Marco Polo tells us that in an adjoining region loaves of salt were used in his time), and 'even now in Bat'ang a brick of ordinary tea is not merely worth a rupee, but in a certain sense *is* a rupee, being accepted without minute regard to weight, just like the silver coin, as a legal tender. Since the influx of rupees this tea-coinage has been very seriously debased, having now lost 25 per cent. of its original weight. The system of double monetary[4] standard is approaching its end, at any rate in Tibet; for in May last the Lamas of the Bat'ang monastery, having hoarded a great treasure of bricks, found it impossible to exchange them at par, and had to put up with a loss of 30 per cent.'

Mr. Baber has some judicious remarks as to the outlet for Indian tea into Western Tibet. The obstacle to this, as well as to the admission of European travellers, is the jealous hostility of the Lamas, jealous of power, jealous of enlightenment, jealous, above all, of their monopoly of trade. It is evidently a mistake to suppose that the main difficulty lies in Chinese aversion to open the landward frontier, real as that probably is. The feeling among the Lama hierarchy is evidently very different from what it was in the days of Turner and Bogle; and judging from the

[4] Is it of any use to protest against the silly and ignorant use of this word in the sense of *pecuniary*? We constantly of late see a payment of cash called 'a monetary transaction!' I have seen it so used, within these few weeks, by a clever daily paper, by a literary weekly paper of repute, by a respectable M.P., and in a despatch from the Government of India! *Monetary* surely belongs to matters of *currency* and *minting*, not to money payments. Both money and monetary no doubt come from *moneta*, but by different roads, and carrying different meanings.

reports of both Captain Gill and Mr. Cooper, their rule over the people is now become intolerably oppressive.

We must not lengthen this too long discourse, but the temptation is great to draw upon Mr. Baber, whose reports, whilst they convey a remarkable amount of information, are full of good sense, and as diverting as any story-book !

One fact more, however, we must borrow, before bidding him a reluctant adieu ; and that is his discovery (Fortuna favet fortibus !) upon his last journey—see § 40 above—of two singular local qualities of tea, one of which is naturally provided with sugar, and the other with a flavour of milk or, more exactly, of butter !

§ 48. Ta-Chien-Lu, Captain Gill's first place of halt after leaving Ch'êng-Tu, is a name that is becoming familiar to the public ear, as the Chinese gate of Tibet, on the Ssŭ-Ch'uan frontier. Politically speaking, it is more correctly the gate between the 'regulation Province' of Ssŭ-Ch'uan, and the Chinese 'non-regulation Province' of the Tibetan marches. Captain Gill has told the story of the Chinese etymology of the name (ii. 76, 77), quite fanciful, like many other Chinese (and many other non-Chinese) etymologies that find currency. The name appears from the Tibetan side as *Tarchenton*, *Tazedo* or *Tazedeu*, *Darchando*, and *Tachindo*, and is purely Tibetan,[5] meaning the confluence of the Tar and the Tsen, two streams which unite near the town.

The place itself stands at a height of 8,340 feet above the sea-level, but the second march westward carries the traveller to the summit-level of the great Tibetan table-land. This great plateau here droops southward as far as lat. 29°,

[5] The termination *do* is common in Tibetan names—as Ghiamdo, Tsiamdo—and means a confluence. For the forms above see P. Horace della Penna in *Markham*, 2nd edit. p. 314 : Pundit Nain Singh in *J. R. Geog. Soc.*, vol. xxxviii. p. 172 ; the Nepalese itineraries given by Mr. Hodgson in the *J. A. S. Bengal*, vol. xxv. pp. 488 and 495 ; and another itinerary from Katmandu, given by him at an earlier date in the *Asiatic Researches*, vol. xvii. p. 513 *seq.* This last itinerary is obviously not genuine beyond Lhassa, from which it makes 'Tázédó' only thirteen stages distant, in a beautifully cultivated plain, producing not only peas and potatoes, but rice and mangoes ! But it gives us the Tibetan *name.*

and below that sends out a great buttress or lower terrace, still ranging 6,000 feet and upwards above the sea, which embraces, roughly speaking, nearly the whole of Yun-nan.[6] In the descent from the higher to the lower terrace, and for a long distance both above and below the zone of most sudden declivity, this region of the earth's crust seems in a remote age to have been cracked and split by huge rents or fissures, all running parallel to one another from north to south; for not only the valleys of those great rivers, of which we have said so much, but the gorges of their tributary streams, exhibit this parallelism.[7]

§ 49. The ethnography of the manifold tribes on the mountain frontier of China, Burma, and Tibet, is a subject of great interest, and respecting which very little is yet known. We have touched it already in a loose way in a preceding paragraph regarding the tribes that look down upon Ssŭ-ch'uan, and we should be tempted to do so again in the region of the great rivers descending from Tibet into Yun-nan and Burma, but for the great scarcity of material. Something has been said of the Músús and Lísús, two of the most prominent of these tribes, in the Memoir of Captain Gill, pp. [28–29].

Vocabularies of their languages have been sent home by M. Desgodins, and, though I have not seen these, M. Terrien de la Couperie, who has paid much attention to the philology of the Chinese and bordering tribes, tells me that the two vocabularies have 70 per cent. of words common to both, and show a manifest connection both with some of the Miao-tzŭ tribes and with the Burmese. The last point is corroborated by the statement of Dr. Anderson regarding the Lísús, that the similarity of the Lísú and Burmese languages is so great that it is hardly possible to avoid the conclusion that the two peoples have sprung from one stock.[8]

[6] Height of TaLli-Fn, 6,955 feet; height of Yun-Nan-Fu, 6,397 feet; height of Tong-ch'uan, 7,152 feet, and height of Hui-li, 6,234 feet. These heights were erroneously given in the first edition of this essay.

[7] Gill, vol. ii. p. 228; *infra*, p. 234.

[8] Anderson, u.s.

§ 50. Captain Gill, when at Kudeu, obtained a remarkable manuscript, which he has presented to the British Museum.[9] I have seen the manuscript, but I derive the following account of it from M. Terrien de la Couperie, who is engaged in systematic study of the origin and relations of the Chinese characters, and is deeply interested in this document. It is written in an unknown hieroglyphic character, and consists of eighteen pages, measuring about 9½ inches by 3½. The characters read from left to right; there are three lines on a page; the successive phrases or groups of characters being divided by vertical lines. Among the characters are many of an ideographic kind, which have a strong resemblance to the ancient Chinese characters called *chuen-tzŭ*. With these are mixed numerous Buddhistic emblems.

M. Terrien possesses another document in similar character, but less mixed with Buddhistic symbols, which was traced by M. Desgodins from the book of a *tomba*, or sorcerer, among the Náshi or Músú, a kind of writing which that missionary states to have become obsolete.[1] He considers Captain Gill's manuscript to be probably much older. It is not possible to say whence it came, because it may have been an object plundered in the long disorders of the Yunnan frontier. But M. Terrien is inclined to regard it as a survival of a very ancient ideographic system, perhaps connected with that of the Chinese in very remote times. The late Francis Garnier, during one of his later journeys in Hu-nan, was assured[2] that in certain caves in that province there were found chests containing books written in *European* characters, and judiciously suggests that these may have been books of the extinct aborigines, in some phonetic character. M. Terrien recalls this passage in connection with Captain Gill's manuscript. And he observes that a thorough study of the character, and of the dialects, for which we have as yet very little material, may be most important in its bearing on the ethnographic and linguistic

[9] Additional MSS. No. 2162.

[1] There is a bare allusion to the subject in the book *La Mission du Thibet*, where M. Desgodins speaks 'des livres de sorciers que j'ai eus entre les mains, mais dont je n'ai pu avoir la traduction' (p. 333).

[2] *Bull. de la Soc. de Géog.*, January, 1874, p. 19.

history of ancient China. Very ancient Chinese traditions speak of these races as possessing written documents.[3] Some further material has since been obtained for the investigation of written characters among the tribes west of Ssŭ-Ch'uan.

In the transcript which we have given of Lord Aberdare's address mention is made of one of the most novel and interesting results of Mr. Baber's journeys, viz., his bringing back specimens of documents in the written character of the Lolo people, with two or three imperfect vocabularies of their language, and the bi-script text of a Lolo song in Lolo and Chinese characters. These documents were published by the Royal Geographical Society with the collection of Mr. Baber's papers referred to previously. In 1881 Mr. Baber was good enough to send home as a gift to the present writer a Lolo MS. of more elaborate character than had yet been available, a document probably still unique in Europe. When Mr. Baber was in the Lolo country, a chief had asked his aid in procuring a revolver. The traveller consented, and requested in return a Lolo book, which was promised. Immediately on Mr. Baber's arrival at Ch'ung-Ch'ing the revolver was purchased and despatched, but for three years nothing was heard from Lolodom, and expectation had died away, when this book arrived. The MS. is written with the Chinese hair-pencil on doubled satin, blue on one side and red on the other, of folio size, and consisting of eight panels folded like a screen. It has been ascertained that the work is in a syllabic character and that it partly consists of rhyming stanzas; but little more is known as yet. A short account of the book was read at the Royal Asiatic Society on December 19, 1881, by M. Terrien de la Couperie, who has since been giving some further attention to its interpretation.

A further and still more important contribution to the collection of Lolo MSS. was recently mentioned by Mr. Baber at the Royal Geographical Society (see 'Proceedings' for 1883, p. 447). This, a book bound in goatskin with the hair on, and containing illustrations, was obtained by Mr.

[3] One recalls the tradition of the Karens, that they too once had a book, but a dog ate it!

Mesny in Kwei-Chou, and is deposited in the rooms of the China Branch, R.A.S. at Shanghai.

§ 51. There must be an end to this commentary. I have become through circumstances, and especially through the traveller's friendly confidence in me, too closely associated with his work to put myself forward as a judge of its merits. But I am bound to call attention to some facts.

Captain Gill was weighted with serious disadvantage as a traveller in China by his unacquaintance with the language. No one could be more sensible of what he lost by this than he was. Yet he was singularly fortunate, during two large sections of his travels, in his interpreters—having the aid of Mr. Baber in the voyage up the Yang-Tzŭ, and that of Mr. Mesny across the Tibetan and Burmese frontier. And his success on a journey in which he has had no forerunner, and had no companion—that from Ch'êng-Tu to the north—shows that he carried in his own person the elements of that success—patience, temper, tact, and sympathy.

The first edition of this Essay concluded with the following words :—

'The anonymous writer who edited the journals of Augustus Margary, with so much judgment and good feeling, concludes his biographical sketch of the young man in words from which I extract the following :—

'Whether, and how soon, his countrymen will be able to travel in honour and safety the route which he was the first to explore, will depend upon the faithfulness with which they copy his example. As soon as Englishmen shall be able, as he did, to find "the people everywhere charming, and the mandarins extremely civil" (p. 134)—in spite of all the serious and petty vexations, discomforts, and discourtesies which met him day after day, and which he had to brush aside with a firm hand, but without losing temper—the route will open out and become as safe to them as it proved to him on his lonely westward journey. For his short story, if read aright, and in spite of its violent ending, adds yet another testimony that a little genuine liking and sympathy for them, combined with firmness, will go further and do more with races of a different civilisation from our own, than treaties, gunboats, and grapeshot, without it. If the route is ever to be a durable and worthy monument of the man, it must be opened and used in his spirit, by fair means, and for beneficent ends.

'These are just and admirable words, and I think all candid readers of this narrative will recognise that my friend its author has been not unworthy, tested as those words would have him tested, to do his part in keeping open the track which Margary first explored. He has done that, and more. And I am happy to think that he also is still young, and thus, as this has not been his first adventure in the conquest of knowledge in distant regions, neither will it, I trust, be his last.'

It was not indeed his last, nor even his second last, of such adventures in the conquest of knowledge, though within little more than three years and a half after those words were written, William Gill had laid down his young and precious life on a last adventure in his country's service.

Two journeys that have been made since Captain Gill's are of an importance to call for mention in this Essay, so as to give it more completeness up to the date of its being remoulded for the present edition. These are Count Széchenyi's and Mr. Colquhoun's. We can give but a very brief account of their journeys.

§ 52. Count Bela Széchenyi, a young Hungarian noble, the son of a very distinguished father, after the death of his wife resolved on devoting himself to a journey of exploration and scientific investigation in Eastern or Central Asia. He took with him apparatus of every kind likely to be useful, and was accompanied by a geologist (Herr Ludwig v. Loczy), a surveyor (Lieutenant Gustaf Kreitner), and a linguist (Herr Gabriel Balint).[4] The last, however, was compelled by illness to return from Shanghai, where the party arrived April 12, 1878. After an excursion to Japan, including a visit to Hakodade and some examination of the Aino people of Yesso, and another excursion to Peking, Count Széchenyi's party started on his main expedition, by proceeding up the

[4] Count Széchenyi is understood to be still engaged in preparing the scientific results of his journeys. The only publication which I know of regarding them is a narrative in popular form by Lieutenant Kreitner under the name of *Im Fernen Osten* (Vienna, 1881).

Yang-Tzŭ to Hankow, and thence up the Han River and its tributary the Siĕ-ho, to Tin-Tze-Kwan, whence they went by land to the ancient and celebrated city of Si-Ngan-Fu. They were able here to visit the famous Nestorian tablet, and it appears from their account that it had not been at all injured by the Mahommedan insurgents, as was once reported. An inscription on the back records that more than twenty years before (presumably before the visit of the

Count Bela Széchenyi.

Hungarian party) a pious mandarin had caused the monument to be 'renovated,' and erected in the conspicuous position which it now occupies.

Leaving Si-Ngan-Fu, February 1, 1879, Count Széchenyi travelled to Lan-Chou-Fu on the Yellow River, and thence through Kansu, by the cities of Liang-Chou and of Kan-Chou and Su-Chou, so famous in the early travels to China from the landward side—*e.g.* those of Marco Polo (whose

Campichu and Sukchur those cities are), of Shah Rukh's ambassadors, and of Benedict Goës.

Their hopes of being allowed to penetrate into Tibet this way were baffled, but they were permitted to visit Tung-Hwan-Hsien, the most advanced Chinese station in that direction (south of the Gobi desert), and close to which formerly stood Sha-Chou, the Sachiu of Marco Polo. Returning to Lan-Chou-Fu and visiting Si-Ning-Fu, they were equally unsuccessful in their desire to take the Lhassa road from Koko-Nor. The Chinese officials and the Lamas alike assured them that the only way they could enter Tibet was from Szü-Ch'uan. It is not easy to discover from Lieutenant Kreitner's narrative whether the party got near the shores of the Koko-Nor, but, if so, they merely got within sight of it. They, however, visited the great Convent of Kunbum where Huc and Gabet spent some time, and saw the sacred tree of which Huc tells such wonderful things. It is this tree, in fact (*sKu-bum*, pron. *Ku-bum*, or *Kün-bum*, 'the 100,000 images'), which gives its name to the convent. The Austrian party were not so fortunate as Huc.

Ascending some steps we reached the chief temple. In front of it, protected by a railing, stood the tree of which Abbé Huc relates that it is the nature of its leaves to produce the image of Buddha and the letters of the Tibetan alphabet. We sought for such phenomena in vain. No image of Buddha, no letter was forthcoming; only a sarcastic smile at the corners of the mouth of the old priest who acted as our guide!

In answer to our questions as to the story of the tree, he told us that long ago the tree really used to bear leaves with the likeness of Buddha, but now the miracle appeared very seldom. . . . The last fortunate person was a pious mandarin who visited the convent seven or eight years before.

Next day it was Count Széchenyi's luck to find a leaf on the tree, bearing a rude figure of Buddha—apparently etched with some acid. To pluck leaves or flowers from the tree is permitted by the Lamas to nobody. The fallen leaves are carefully gathered and sold to the pilgrims as a tea good for affections of the throat. The tree has four stems, of six or eight mètres high, and at the time of our visit was thickly clothed with oblong, rounded, dark green leaves. The umbellated flowers were already in bud. Anyhow, the tree belongs to the *Oleaceæ*. I take it for the Syringa of L. (*i.e.* lilac).[5]

Turning south from Lan-Chou-Fu, the party travelled through southern Kan-su, by a route in large part not hitherto described, till at Mien-Chou, about thirty miles from Ch'êng-Tu-Fu, they fell into the route followed by Captain Gill on his return from his excursion from that city to Sung-Pang-Ting.

On October 12, 1879, two years and three months after Gill, they started from Ch'êng-Tu, and followed in his footsteps as far as Bat'ang. Here, like him, they found unconquerable opposition to their taking the Lhassa road. In order to break new ground they travelled from Bat'ang on the east instead of the west side of the River of Golden Sand, rejoining Gill's track again near Li-Kiang-Fu, and following the usual route from Ta-Li-Fu to Bhamò, which was reached on February 13, 1880.

§ 53. Mr. A. R. Colquhoun is an engineer of the Indian Public Works Department, whose zeal for travel seems to have been kindled by a journey to the Siamese-Shan State of Zimmé, to which he accompanied a Mission from British Burma in 1879. Thenceforward his heart was set on more extensive exploration over untrodden ground; and, after much consideration, he determined on an endeavour to make his way from South-West China across the Shan States to Pegu. With his companion Mr. Wahab (who, on the return voyage to England, poor fellow, sank under ailments produced by the fatigues of the journey), Colquhoun ascended the West River of Canton by boat as far as Pesè, where the navigation ceases, and then travelled through Southern Yun-nan to the frontier town of Ssu-Mao (the 'Esmok' of Macleod, and of Captain Spry's persistent agitation of twelve to twenty years ago). Here their wish to penetrate the frontier was baffled in the usual Chinese fashion, and the travellers were compelled to turn northward in order to reach the Irawadi by the road from Ta-Li to Bhamò, so familiar to us in this Essay. They, however, successfully resisted the pressure put upon them by the mandarins to

[5] Kreitner, *Im Fernen Osten*, p. 708.

take the route travelled by Doudart de la Grée and his party to Yun-Nan-Fu, and followed a line of entirely new country, leading up the vàlley of the Papien River, directly upon Ta-Li.

Mr. Colquhoun surveyed the whole of his route, but at the present moment his surveys have not been completely mapped. They will certainly be of great value, and his enterprising journey is of much interest as the first that has been made from sea to sea through Indo-China, in that latitude. The narrative has been published in two volumes, under the name of 'Across Chrysê,' 1883. Mr. Colquhoun keenly advocates further exploration from Pegu in the direction of the southern frontier of Yun-nan and the Shan States, in view to testing the practicability of a railway project in that direction; and it is to be hoped that he may be enabled to conduct such a survey. Mr. Colquhoun's letters to the 'Times' from Hong-Kong and Tonquin, respecting the march of events in the latter region during the summer of 1883, have been of great ability and value.

Indeed these paragraphs are closed for the press at a time when the eyes of the world are turned to China and Indo-China in connection with the ambition of the French Republic, which, not content with an enterprise (so hard to understand, so impossible to justify) aiming, so far as we can see, at the extirpation in Madagascar of the most promising shoot of new civilization and Christianity that the world can show, is fully resolved also (it would seem) to seize Tonquin. One thing we may safely prophesy, and that is, that the veil will never again descend on the geography of Indo-China, and that the game of conquest and politics in that region, the vicissitudes of which have been heretofore almost confined to the struggles of the obscure States within its bounds, will henceforth be played by powers from afar, and will probably influence the future of old European Governments.

Cart crossing Ferry, near Peking.

CHAPTER I.

CATHAY, AND THE WAY THITHER.

China resolved on—Preliminary Visit to Berlin—Baron Ferdinand v Richthofen—Marseilles, and Voyage in the 'Ava'—The Straits—Chinese Practices first realised—Approach to Saigon—The City—Hong Kong reached and quitted—Shanghai and its peculiar Conveyances—The Chinaman's Plait—Voyage to Chi-Fu—The Chi-Fu Convention—The Minister Li-Hung-Chang—Voyage to the Pei-Ho—Difficulties of Navigation up that River—Scenery—Arrival at Tien-Tsin—Carts of Northern China—'Boy' found—Scenes on the Tien-Tsin Bund—Suspicious Wares.

'WHY not China?'

Such were the words addressed to me by a friend I met in Trafalgar Square early in May 1876.

Up to this moment I had never thought of China, and my notions regarding it were crude in the extreme: dim ideas of pigtails, eternal plains, and willow trees; vague conceptions of bird's-nest soup and puppy pies. I had never been particularly attracted to the country, and naturally replied, 'Why should I go to China?'

At the time I gave the matter no further consideration, and it was with some surprise that, a fortnight later, I was met with the same question; this time, however, my friend had some reasons to adduce, the result of which was that, on the 26th of June, a fine breezy morning, I stood on the deck of the Ostend steamer lying in Dover harbour.

A fresh north-easterly breeze just crisped the tops of the waves, and a bright sun lighted up the Dover cliffs as they gradually merged into the mist. For the first time for many days, I had leisure to think, and when at last the cliffs were lost to view, I seemed to have launched into a new and unknown sea; for whither fate would lead my steps I could not say: all that was definite was, that I was going to Peking.

Through the kindness of Colonel Yule I was furnished with a letter of introduction to Baron von Richthofen, the greatest of modern explorers and geographers, whose long travels in China had made him the first authority on the country; and it was to make his acquaintance that I now bent my steps to Berlin, where I esteemed myself fortunate in finding him. The week that I spent in his society passed only too quickly. Hour after hour he gave up his valuable time to me, and opened volumes from his rich store of information; day by day I grew wiser; and little by little true pictures of China and Chinese life formed themselves in my mind. During all my conversation with Baron von Richthofen, not one word passed his lips that was not gold seven times refined, not one hint was given me that did not subsequently prove its value; his kind thoughts for my comfort or amusement were never ceasing, and his refined and cultivated intellect and genial manner rendered the recollections of my stay in the German capital some of the most pleasant of my life.

Leaving Berlin, I journeyed leisurely to Marseilles, and on the 30th of July steamed out of harbour on board the 'Ava,' one of the fleet of the Messageries Maritimes Company. On a sea like glass we glided through the Straits of Bonifacio, steamed into the Bay of Naples, and left it again before the town was well awake. That morning's sun set like a ball of fire behind Stromboli. Scylla frowned, and Charybdis hissed, as if in impotent rage that coal and iron had robbed them of their terrors, and the lights of Messina shone awhile over the summer sea; but one by one even these faded, and the last glimpse of Europe was gone from our view.

A voyage is always rather tedious, and during August the Red Sea can hardly be considered pleasant; the days went by, however, although there was but little incident to vary their monotony.

Passing through the Straits of Malacca, we steamed into Singapore on the morning of the 26th of August, and I was rather disappointed with its scenery, of which I had heard so much. The entrance to the harbour is certainly exceedingly pretty; there is a wonderful richness in the verdure, and the trees at the water's edge contrast beautifully with the deep red of the soil. Perhaps it is that after some days afloat people are always in a frame of mind to exaggerate the charms of the first land they see; or perhaps it is that the ships being able to come within twenty or thirty yards of the shore, the beauties are more apparent than in other places.

Government House is a fine building, on the top of a little hill, looking over rich green trees and green grass to the blue sea, the town of Singapore stretching out on one side along the edge of the harbour, where there is a great deal of shipping, and many boats. In the town there is an enormous Chinese population, and here for the first time I understood the mystery of using chopsticks. Up till now I had cherished the fond delusion that it was customary to take the rice up grain by grain; I had sorely exercised my mind on the consideration of the length of time that a Chinaman would occupy in consuming a hearty meal. I was therefore much interested in watching the process. The bowl, something like a large tea-cup without a handle, is held in the left hand close underneath the chin, the chopsticks being used as a shovel, by which the rice is pushed into the mouth, an extraordinary gobbling noise accompanying the proceeding. The grains of rice, moreover, even when cooked by a Chinaman, are not invariably all separate, and it is easy for a skilful performer to take a good deal of rice between his two chopsticks. The method of holding the chopsticks is almost impossible of explanation, but the art is acquired with a very little practice, and, once learnt, it is not difficult to pick up the smallest grain.

On the 29th of August we touched at Saigon, the capital of the French colony of Cochin China. The mouth of the river is rather pretty. As the steamer runs up, on the starboard hand are hills, about one hundred or two hundred feet high, covered with forest, in which there are here and there open patches of beautiful green grass ; the trees come down to the water's edge, the coast is broken into innumerable little creeks and bays, native villages are scattered about, and on the other side the low coast is seen two miles away. In a very short distance the hills disappear ; the river, about half a mile wide, is very tortuous, and winds through a flat, swampy, uninteresting country, covered with low jungle, where I was told there were a great many tigers; but as Frenchmen seldom hunt savage beasts for sport, they probably exaggerate the number of them.

The town of Saigon lies fifty miles up the river, and is close to a very large and important native town, the seat of ancient trade, which is inhabited in great part by a colony of immigrants from China. It was for commercial purposes necessary to establish the capital here rather than at the mouth of the river, where there would have been a more picturesque, more convenient, and far more healthy site. The French have certainly made more of the little that nature has provided them with, than we have at Singapore of a much better site. The principal street of the town is a fine broad boulevard, with trees on both sides, where there are a few French shops amongst those which are kept by Asiatics of various races. The public buildings are plain, and do not deserve much notice ; there are of course cafés and restaurants, in as close imitation as circumstances permit of the gay French capital. There is no gas at Saigon as there is at Singapore, but the streets and houses are well lighted with petroleum. This is said to be a very unhealthy place, residents being liable to a form of dysentery that nothing appears to cure; the governors, whose salary is 8,000*l.*, are rarely able to remain more than two years. We found that, with an admirable idea of how most to inconvenience the public, the post office was closed till 4.30 P.M., the officials being busy preparing their mails; so we took another drive, and when we returned we found that the *poste restante* business, the selling of stamps, and the receipt of valuable articles, were all conducted by one official at one little pigeon-hole.

People had been dropping in one by one during the past hour, and the street now presented something the appearance of one of our West End thoroughfares on the night of an entertainment, with a long string of carriages on each side of the road. When at length the pigeon-hole was opened, a crowd of Annamites, Chinamen, French soldiers, sailors, officials, and people of all sorts, fought for the services of the man inside; we also engaged in the conflict, and at length succeeded in posting our letters. Before returning to the ship we had to listen to the most doleful jeremiads of a sleepless night in store for us, from the size and virulence of the mosquitoes, with which the river was said to swarm; visions of large dragon-flies, with the stings of scorpions, presented themselves to me as I turned in; but happily the reports were exaggerations, and we none of us suffered much.

Leaving Saigon we steamed on again to the East, passing the Ladrone Islands, famous in the days of yore. When the old Portuguese navigators first entered these waters, and found themselves the unfortunate victims of the numerous pirates and murderers that cruised about among these narrow channels, they called this beautiful archipelago the Ladrone or Robber Islands.

The times have changed, but the nature of the people is not much altered; and though at a distance the fleet of junks, with their red sails bellying in the freshening breeze, might be mistaken for mackerel boats on our own English shores, and though by profession the people follow the peaceful avocation of fishing, they are still on occasions robbers, pirates, or buccaneers.

It was a delightful change at Hong Kong to pass a couple of days amongst kind friends; it was refreshing, too, once more to see English soldiers, looking as smart as only English soldiers do; and after so many weeks of walking up and down the deck of a ship, a real hill was a treat. But our time was soon up, Hong Kong gradually disappeared, and we sailed away again over the blue waters, where the extraordinary number of fishing junks formed a marvellous sight. All day and all night the steamer passed through a swarm of these vessels that seemed to fringe the whole coast; at one time I counted 150 in sight in one quarter of the compass, and we were obliged to stop our engines two or three times to avoid the nets.

My journey in the 'Ava' was drawing to a close, and on the morning of the 8th of September we entered the Yang-tzŭ-Chiang, or Ocean River, and soon dropped anchor off Shanghai. After greatly enjoying a dinner on shore, I took a 'jinnyrickshaw,' and went off in search of the steamer which was to carry me to Chi-Fu. The jinnyrickshaw, an importation from Japan, is the usual public conveyance of Shanghai, and is admirably adapted for the flat country, where the roads are good and coolie hire cheap. In shape it is like a buggy, but very much smaller, with room inside for one person only. One coolie gets into the shafts, and runs along at the rate of about six miles an hour; if the distance is long, he is usually accompanied by a companion who runs behind, and they take turn about to draw the vehicle.

The jinnyrickshaw is, however, only for the rich; for poor people there is another description of conveyance, the wheelbarrow, so well known in all the plains of China, with a seat at each side of one high wheel, on which the people sit sideways, as on an Irish car.

Except in Shanghai, the Chinese contrive that the wheels of these shall creak, for a Chinese coolie always seems to require some noise to assist him in his work: when carrying a load in the usual way, by means of a split bamboo over his shoulder, he gives a peculiar grunt at each step, and chair-coolies almost always do the same thing. I was told that in the early days of Shanghai, the noises made by coolies and creaking wheels became so great as to be at last utterly unendurable to European nerves, and a regulation was made, which was at first enforced with much difficulty, forbidding coolies to groan, or wheels to creak, within the boundaries of the Concession, and imposing fines for a breach of the rule. Inside the settlement both jinnyrickshaws and wheelbarrows abound. These are licensed, just as hackney carriages are in London; the tariff is fixed by law, and licences suspended for misconduct or breach of regulations. On my way to the steamer, in the cool of a glorious starlight night, the reverie into which I had been gently soothed by a fragrant Manilla such as is rarely to be met with in England, was suddenly broken by a violent bump, and I awoke to the fact that one of the wheels had suddenly come off the jinnyrickshaw. The driver, if such an appellation is permissible, did not seem at all disconcerted; he picked up his wheel, put it on, took a new linch-pin from some mysterious fold in his garment, whilst with a smart shake of his head he whipped the end of his pigtail into his hand. It was the work of a moment to unplait a little of it, break off a lock of his hair, and, by the light of the paper lantern always carried, put the tie thus improvised through the hole in the linch-pin. In five minutes we were off again as if nothing had happened, and I learnt that a Chinaman can find a use for anything, even for his plait.

The plait was first imposed upon the Chinese as a badge of servitude by the Manchus when they took the country; but the origin of the appendage has been long forgotten—it is now valued almost as dearly as life, and to be without one is considered the sign of a rebel.

I was told that once a Chinese gentleman was riding in the settlement of Shanghai in a jinnyrickshaw, when he allowed his plait to fall over the side; it was a long one, and the end was soon caught in the axle, which gradually wound it up. The poor fellow shouted to the man drawing him to stop, but the coolie, imagining that he was being urged to greater efforts, only went the faster, until the unfortunate occupant, with his plait nearly wound up to the end, and himself nearly dragged out of his carriage, was in a pitiable plight. A British sailor at this moment happened to pass that way, and observing the desperate predicament, with the readiness of resource for which nautical people are famed, he drew his knife and in an instant severed the plait from the Chinaman's head. He thought he had done a kindly act, but instead of thanks he received curses, and his life was not considered safe until his ship was well beyond the limits of the Shanghai river.

After steaming sixty-five hours against a heavy head sea we dropped our anchor in the quiet harbour of Chi-Fu, the watering-place of Shanghai, charmingly situated on a deep bay, sheltered on the north by a long low spit of land ending in some low hills; it is open to the N.E., and when the wind is from that quarter a heavy sea comes rolling in and prevents communication with the shore. To the E.N.E. are some rocky islands, which protect the harbour from that quarter; at the head of the bay is about a mile of flat country closely cultivated and very green; and at the back, a range of hills, which run down to the coast on either side, end in picturesque bluffs. To the west is the large and important Chinese town, where a fleet of quaint-looking junks were lying at anchor. The European quarter is small, containing not much more than the consulates, three hotels, and a few stores where European goods are sold at rather startling prices. Here, when the heat of Shanghai is at its worst, the wearied merchants find a pleasant and invigorating change in the fresh air and sea bathing.

The now celebrated Chi-Fu Convention was at this time being arranged, and Sir Thomas Wade, H.B.M.'s Minister, Li-Hung-Chang, the celebrated Chinese Minister, and some members of the other foreign legations were here, with three English, two French, and one German man-of-war in the harbour, besides Admiral Ryder's despatch boat the 'Vigilant,' and numerous Chinese war-vessels. I found two very fair rooms in an hotel close to the European town; my quarters faced the sea, and I could look out upon the British flag floating proudly from the mast of the 'Audacious.'

I was furnished with letters of introduction to Sir Thomas Wade, whose reputation for hospitality has become a proverb in Peking. Though pressed with business, he found time to talk over my plans, and I can never be sufficiently grateful to him for all his kindness and cordiality. Here also I made the acquaintance of Mr. Carles, a consular officer, who subsequently became my companion in my first trip in the province of Pe-Chi-Li, a trip that turned out to be but an introduction to Chinese travel, and the precursor of a much longer and more serious enterprise.

Taking a boat from the beach in front of the hotel, I went on board the 'Chih-Li,' an American vessel of about 1,200 tons, with the saloon and first-class sleeping accommodation forward, and had an excellent view of all the ceremonies and displays attendant on the departure of the great Li-Hung-Chang, one of the most powerful men in China. Li rode in a covered sedan-chair, preceded by a man carrying an immense red umbrella; his escort appeared to number about forty men, picturesque fellows in blue coats and red trousers, armed with rifles, and besides these there were some wonderful-looking men with cutlasses. The commander of the escort was a most unsoldierlike and ragged-looking person, perched on a Chinese saddle high above the back of an exceedingly small and abject pony. A battalion of infantry was drawn up near the landing-jetty, and about forty war-junks were anchored in a triple line close by. These most picturesque and old-fashioned vessels were armed with one gun each, and gaily decorated with an immense red flag, some of them having a second banner striped red and white.

The Chinese steam-gunboats in the harbour were all 'dressed,' as was the Chinese merchant steamer by which Li travelled. When he arrived at the quay, the battalion fired a salute, the Chinese steam-gunboats saluted, and the war-junks all let off their pieces somewhat promiscuously. The magnate then stepped into a cutter, which was towed by a very small steam-launch in command of Europeans, and was soon alongside his vessel. The soldiers on board fired a salute, the whistle gave a few screeches, the anchor was up, and away went Li, escorted by the steam-gun-boats.

The 'Vigilant' followed almost immediately, the soldiers marched home, the booming of the cannon ceased, the smoke cleared off, and as the sun descended in the western horizon, Chi-Fu, so lately the scene of such busy and hot arguments, so nearly the site of diplomatic rupture between England and China, seemed to throw off the garb of war, and, smiling pleasantly after the departing grandees, to wrap itself in the mantle of that peace that it had just given to the world.

At half-past six on the 15th of September our anchor was weighed, and, as the stars came out, we steamed across the Gulf of Pe-Chi-Li to the mouth of the Pei-Ho, or River of the North, which, with its wide expanse of mud flats, would certainly come up to any preconceived expectations of dreariness; but as Tien-Tsin is approached, although the country is still perfectly flat, the life, activity, and close cultivation around render the scenery, to say the least, cheerful.

Of any possible combination of annoying circumstances, the navigation of the Pei-Ho must be the most trying to the temper of a ship-captain. The river bends and winds about in the most exasperating manner with the sharpest turns; after a straight run of perhaps a little less than a quarter of a mile, it becomes necessary to round a sharp bend of at least a semicircle; if the bend is to the left, the bow of the ship is aimed straight at the bank on the starboard hand. All may seem to be going well, when the current probably catches the vessel, and, with the helm hard a-starboard, she runs hard and fast aground on the bank, in such a way that a pebble could be dropped ashore from the deck. The ship then sticks, and will not move; a warp is laid out to the bank on the other side of the river, and the donkey-engine set to work. Perhaps the strain is too great, and the warp parts; this has to be replaced; the engines then are backed, the helm put amidships, the donkey-engine set to work again, the helm put hard a-starboard, and at last her head is got round ; she moves again and reaches the next bend, when just at the critical moment a junk steers between the steamer and the shore. The engines must be backed to prevent the junk being jammed between the ship and the bank, and in three minutes as much ground is lost as has been gained in the last half-hour Now the steamer touches a bank in the middle of the river ; the current, running like a mill-race, slews her round right across the stream, and stops all navigation. Under these circumstances the captain seemed to me to exhaust the whole of his nautical vocabulary. Once we pulled the warping-post out of the bank ; once, in passing a great junk, whose anchor was laid out in a millet field, our wash was so strong that, taking her broadside on, she tore her anchor adrift and went afloat on her own account. Under similar circumstances the swearing of English sailors would have been terrible, but the worthy Chinese seemed to take it in the day's work, and, laughing all the time, quietly laid their anchor out afresh ; although I must admit that I subsequently found the swearing powers of the Chinese sailors to be in no way inferior to the capabilities of our troops in Flanders. From two P.M. until seven o'clock in the evening our captain struggled manfully with the twists and turns, when at last we ran so hard aground that with a falling tide no more could be done that night.

The captain must have been possessed of an angelic temper. He never said a single word except to give his orders in a quiet voice, but at the most aggravating moments, when most people would have used bad language, he would violently chew the end of his cigar, and by this means relieve his feelings. We all retired early, and it was well for us that we did so ; for at about four o'clock next morning the donkey-engine began to work. There was no more sleep for any one, and as we lay awake we could hear the captain's continued commands—starboard, port a little, &c. &c., and the same heart-breaking process was continued as we worked slowly up.

The morning broke, giving hopes of a lovely day that were by no means belied, and at eight o'clock we thought that we should breakfast at Tien-Tsin. There was only one more bend in the river, but that a very difficult one, and it seemed as if the vessel's head never would come round. No sooner had she come up half a point than she would viciously shoot forward a few yards, an eddy would suddenly take hold of her bow, and she would fly right off; at last, a tug coming down the river gave us a friendly pull, and we were safely round the last point. The command was given, full speed ahead—Tien-Tsin was but two miles off. The captain threw away the end of his cigar, and for the first time did not light another. We all began to prepare for going ashore, as the ship sped gaily on up the straight reach, when suddenly she ran on to a bank in the middle of the river, and, as the tide had now fallen too low, all the captain's efforts to get her off were unavailing. We descended to breakfast at nine o'clock, and afterwards, as the distance was so short, most of us went off in a boat to the bank, where landing in the mud was a matter of some difficulty. It was accomplished, however, with nothing worse than muddy shoes, and we walked to the British Consulate.

The journey from Tien-Tsin to Peking of a minister who is taking as his guests two admirals with their suites is a very serious matter; and I thought to myself that the British Legation must be a very elastic building to accommodate so many; but where a Minister is of such a royally hospitable nature as Sir Thomas Wade, difficulties soon disappear.

Sir Thomas and some of his guests were going by boat to Tung-Chou, whence a short ride would land them in the Legation. These river boats are long, flat-bottomed affairs, with houses on the stern, which a good travelling servant knows how to make fairly comfortable in a very short time. In cold weather the chinks must be covered with paper, but at this season it was unnecessary. One boat is usually kept as kitchen and dining-room, and at stated hours the different boats come together for meals. The vessels are mostly tracked against the stream by ropes made fast to the head of the mast, which is right in the bows; but if there is a fresh fair wind, they sail. In this manner the journey to Tung-Chou occupies from three to four days.

Another method of travelling is with carts, which perform the journey from Tien-Tsin to Peking in two days, unless the traveller prefers making three shorter stages; but the jolting and bumping of these springless carts over the rough tracks cannot be imagined by those who have never travelled but in carriages with springs over the made roads in England, and is really so unpleasant that this system would hardly commend itself to any one who was a good walker, and, by using his legs, could save his bones from being sorely bruised. The Chinese travel a great deal in this manner, and the Chinese ladies sit cramped and cooped up all day long with wonderful patience and endurance. European ladies, too, sometimes make long journeys in these carts; and though, perhaps, accustomed to all the luxuries of Western civilisation, put up with the discomfort attendant on a journey of this kind with a pluck that is delightful to witness.

One mule is generally put into the shafts and another as leader; the traces of the latter are both attached to the off-side of the body of the cart, passing through a steel ring six inches in diameter fastened near the end of the off-shaft. This ring is always polished up in a way that would refresh the heart of a captain of field artillery, and the carters keep their equipment altogether in first-rate order. The reins are generally of rope, very light—indeed, in China the lightness of the harness, in which strength and durability are quite sufficiently considered, is a remarkable contrast to the heavy and useless leather-work with which we in England load our horses.

One hundred *li*, or thirty-three miles, is considered an average day's journey, and when sufficient inducement is held out to the carters, the way in which their carts will day after day complete these long stages over the most trying roads—sometimes deep in mud, at others through heavy sand, or in the mountains, up and down severe and rocky gradients, where the ground is often strewn with huge stones and boulders—is very startling to any one who has been accustomed to the slow and short marches of carts in India.[1]

It was a long business, getting everything ready for the large party of the minister, admirals, and suites. All the luggage was in the 'Chih-Li,' hard and fast on a mud bank two miles down the river. Somebody had to find a steam-launch and go down after it; boats were to be hired, provisions bought, and all sorts of arrangements to be made; but nevertheless, some of my newly made friends found time to come and help me in my affairs. I had now to discover a servant and to buy ponies.

The word 'boy,' as applied to a servant, has been transplanted with curry and rice, punkahs, compounds, godowns, and tiffins into China, and the word 'servant' is scarcely ever used amongst Europeans at the Treaty Ports. In this capacity I engaged a native of Peking, Chin-Tai, whose name will often recur in these pages; and two ponies were eventually bought for forty dollars each, after the amount of mysterious bargaining usual in all countries.

There are numbers of ponies to be hired on the wharf, and on these the British sailors gallop wildly up and down the streets in the English settlement. Furious riding is as strictly prohibited here as it is in Rotten Row, but the prohibition is not quite so severely enforced. A couple of tars, just in harbour after a long sea voyage, will step ashore, and hiring each a pony, without stopping to critically examine the animals or their saddlery, will jump up and go off at full gallop, the proprietor sometimes running behind. Jack has probably no socks, and only a pair of shoes, so that the stirrup-iron catches his bare instep; but of this he takes little notice, nor of his trousers, which ruck up a long way above his knees. All goes well until the pony comes to a familiar corner, where, notwithstanding that Jack puts his

[1] Richthofen states that the journey from Si-Ngan-Fu to Ili (Kuldja), 2,673 miles, is performed as a matter of course by two mule-carts, carrying three and a half tons, in eighty stages, though practically more than eighty days are required for the journey.

helm hard a-port, the pony turns sharp round to the left, Jack falls overboard, the pony gives one kick of its heels, and gallops off to its home. Not in the least disconcerted, Jack jumps up behind his mate, who, on seeing the accident, has brought up all standing, and away they go again until the second pony manages to relieve itself of its double burden.

At last, at about 6.30 in the evening, the 'Chih-Li' succeeded in getting off the mud bank and reaching the wharf; so taking Chin-Tai on board, I pointed out my innumerable packages to him, and let him bring them to my rooms. This being finished, I went out to get some money. I found that the letter of credit I had provided myself with was more useful than circular notes would have been. It is not only in China that I have found this to be the case, and I mention it for the benefit of any who may be contemplating an expedition into out-of-the-way places. The money current here, as at Shanghai, is the American dollar. It is somewhat surprising that the use of a coin of fixed value has as yet penetrated so short a distance beyond the Treaty Ports, more especially as bank-notes are an ancient institution in China. A very few miles from the main road between Peking and Tien-Tsin, the dollar is of no use whatever, and recourse must be had to the cumbersome method of weighing out lumps of silver. For small change, the brass cash are universal: these are round coins with a square hole in the middle; there are some Chinese characters on them, and they vary in value from about one-tenth to one-fifteenth of an English penny, according to the exchange.

The next thing I had to do was to discover, and secure if possible, my guns and cartridges. Before leaving England I had been led to believe that almost wherever I went in China I should find birds and beasts of every description only waiting to be shot at, and I had provided myself with cartridges and firearms in proportion. These had been despatched by an agent in London direct to Tien-Tsin, but where they were I had as yet no conception; so I made the tour of all the foreign 'Hongs,' as the Europeans call their business establishments in China, and eventually found that my artillery was in the custom house, where it had caused much speculation.

At all the Treaty Ports the higher custom house officials are foreigners (mostly Englishmen) in the pay of the Chinese Government, and thus, as a rule, a European traveller has no difficulty about clearing his goods. In this instance, however, a number of cases, contents unknown, and consigned to nobody in particular, had suddenly arrived for an unknown person. They naturally drifted to the custom house, where, as naturally, they were opened by inquisitive Chinese, who suddenly discovered a very remarkable amount of gunpowder. This at once conjured up in the minds of the Chinese officials all sorts of fearful plots against the Imperial Government; an embargo was laid on the goods; and when at last I appeared to claim my property, I was introduced to a very polite French gentleman, who lectured me severely on the wickedness of which I had been guilty in sending out guns and cartridges without consigning them to some proper person; but who, at the same time, comforted me with the assurance that they would in all probability be handed over to me in the course of a few months. Thanks, however, to the English Consul, I at last rescued my artillery from the customs without much difficulty, and, after a final dinner at the Consulate, turned into bed ready for my first experiment in Chinese travelling.

CHAPTER II.

THE CITY OF CAMBALUC.[1]

Departure from Tien-Tsin—Rural Characteristics—Pictures by the Way—Chinese Hostelry—The 'Kang': Fittings and Furniture—Approach to Peking—Foreigners as seen by Chinese eyes—The British Legation—Visit to the Temple of Heaven—A Chinese Fair—Crambe Repetita—Chinese Dinners—Visit to the Summer Palace—Needless Havoc—Great Bell—Modern Cambaluc.

AFTER an early cup of tea we started at 6 A.M. on the 20th of September. A Ma-Fu (or horse-boy) rode in front on a very good iron-grey pony, in shape and size something like my own. The Ma-Fu had nothing on his head but his plait; he wore a loose blue coat padded with cotton-wool, and loose blue cotton trousers, and he rode on a Chinese-made English saddle. I rode next on a saddle that I had brought with me from England, with large flax-cloth saddle-bags and leather wallets. These saddle-bags proved excellent, and, if my experience is worth anything, good flax-cloth saddle-bags will last quite as long as any traveller can need; they are much more convenient and far lighter than leather ones, which latter become very awkward in rainy weather, but the seams should be lined inside with a strip of leather half an inch wide. At this season of the year in Northern China the sun has lost its power, and a helmet is not necessary. A white English felt hat, Norfolk jacket, breeches and gaiters, completed my costume.

My three baggage-carts came next, in one of which Chin-Tai reposed as comfortably as circumstances would permit.

At length we were clear of the town, and breathed the

[1] The name by which Marco Polo designates Peking.

fresh country air. The Ma-Fu, who knew nearly twenty words of English, took me under his care, and, leaving the carts to find their slow way behind us, we rode on ahead. The country here is quite flat, without an elevation of the smallest description except the houses and river embankment. Behind the latter, masts and sails of hundreds of junks can be seen. Every inch of the ground is cultivated with millet or Indian corn, and in the fields there is frequently an undercrop of sweet potato or a small bean. Cotton and castor-oil plants often border the edges of the fields; but the great feature is always the millet, standing about eight feet high, with reddish-brown or yellow stalks. The immediate neighbourhood of Tien-Tsin is not well wooded, but a little further into the country the villages have more trees about them, almost entirely willows and Chinese dates. These latter (in reality the *Rhamnus Theezans*, a kind of buckthorn or jujube, in no way whatever allied to the date-palm) bear a fruit in appearance and taste very like a small date; the tree itself is more like an olive than anything else, and is very common in Northern Persia about the neighbourhood of Sharood.

A few miles on, the road skirts large plantations of willows, and the landscape is very like the scenes in some of the pictures of Karl du Jardin. In the Dresden Gallery there is rather a stiff picture by this artist of a grove of trees, with a herd of swine underneath. Now, not far from Tien-Tsin, this landscape is reproduced almost exactly; there is the identical row of willow-trees in a perfectly straight line, and all of precisely the same height; and, as I passed, the very same herd of swine was feeding underneath—the only thing wanting to make it complete was the gay cavalier out hunting.

After a ride of about twenty miles, I arrived with the Ma-Fu at Yang-Tsun, the first halting-place, and here for the first time I made acquaintance with the luxuries of a Chinese inn. Riding through an archway, with a room on each side used as a sort of restaurant, there is an open courtyard. On one side of it there is what in England would be called a long low hut, divided into several rooms: these are the sleeping apartments of the guests at the hotel ; on the other side a large open shed is the stable or feeding-place for the horses and mules. At the farther end of the yard is the best room of the establishment, which is only awarded to guests of distinction—or, in other words, to those who can afford to pay.

Knowing nothing of the arrangements, I went, where I was shown, into one of the little rooms at the side, about ten or eleven feet square, and the same in height, the floor of brick and the walls of mud. Dirty paper, with many holes in it, pasted over the rafters formed the ceiling, and some wooden lattice-work, covered with dirty paper full of holes, did duty for a window.

The great feature in every room in every inn in Northern China is the 'kang.' This is a hollow raised dais, about eighteen inches high, covering half the floor, over which there is usually laid a bit of thin straw matting, the home of innumerable fleas. In the winter a fire is lighted under this, and through the bricks or mud of which it is built a pleasing warmth is imparted to the traveller, who, rolled up in his blanket, lies on it to sleep. During the day-time a little table about nine inches high stands on the kang ; a person sitting on the latter can just make use of this by twisting himself round into an impossible attitude, which after any length of time eventuates in aches all over the back. There may be in addition a broken-down and exceedingly filthy table and arm-chair, about the height of ordinary European articles : the chair very clumsy, heavy, stiff, straight-backed, and uncomfortable, with legs which, thrust out in a sprawling fashion, seem to have the most unhappy knack of being always in the way ; and the table with a ledge underneath just where an ordinary person wants to put his knees, and a bar below to interfere with the free movements of his feet. In some of the larger inns of the important towns things are better done, doors and window-frames being to a certain extent fitted ; but even in the best there is generally a big hole under the door, where the mud and bricks have been gradually kicked away. A window that will open is very rare in Chinese houses, and the doors are invariably fastened with a sliding latch. I do not recollect ever to have seen a door fastened on any other system, or hung in any other way, than with a couple of pivots, one above and one below, each fitted into a socket ; sometimes a hole in the floor is substituted for the lower socket.

Such is the accommodation and such the furniture a traveller invariably meets with in the inns of China. In the course of an hour my carts appeared. Chin-Tai was sorely indignant with the innkeeper for not having put me into the place of honour, and his contempt for a Ma-Fu who could care so little for his master's dignity was delightful to witness.

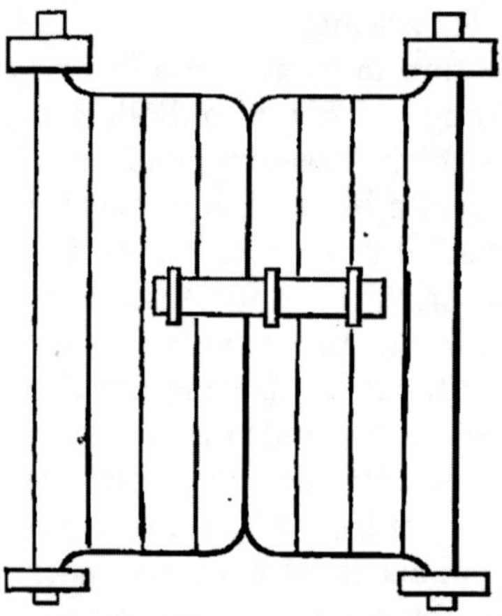

FIG. 1.—System of hanging doors.

Another ride of twenty miles brought us, late in the evening, to the inn at Ho-Se-Wu, the half-way stage to Peking. With my saddle-bags for a pillow I was soon sound asleep, and did not wake till Chin-Tai appeared with the carts and said that it was time for dinner.

Chin-Tai early discovered a weakness for cookery that subsequently proved very troublesome ; he never could be brought to understand that something to eat as soon as possible after arrival was better than an elaborate meal in the middle of the night. Once produced, however, my dinner was soon despatched, the mattress was laid on the kang, and at about midnight I was fairly in bed.

The carts were hired only for the journey to Peking, and it was therefore the interest of the driver to get there as soon as possible. The gates of the city are always closed at sundown, and as no power on earth can then get them open till the next morning, there was no fear of the carters starting late. The people of Northern China are all, however, very early, and when after a cup of tea a start was effected at 3.45 A.M. the town was all astir, many of the shops were open, and the furnace of a blacksmith cast a bright glare across the street as the sound of his hammer resounded in the clear morning air. Leaving the carts to follow, we started as soon as the ponies were fed. Riding still over the flat plains, the distant blue mountains presently came in sight, and soon afterwards the unmistakable walls of Peking,[2] with the great high three-storied building over the gate.

To-day there was some sort of fair going on in the city, and the spectacle was very remarkable—quite unlike anything to be seen elsewhere. The street was very wide, and on each side were the same wretched houses that so soon become familiar to the traveller in China. Between them the space was closely covered by the wares that the sellers of goods had spread out on the ground : old clothes, old rags, brushes, baskets, string, rope, eatables, drinks, fruit, crockery, and almost every conceivable article of household equipment, were exhibited for sale ; each seller was surrounded by a mob of buyers, their friends, and lookers on. The streets were absolutely thronged with people walking, riding, or in carts ; the hubbub and confusion were appalling, and progress at times seemed almost impossible. Pigs and dogs took their usual share in the proceedings, and evil smells were not absent. The inhabitants of Peking, and of all the towns and villages along the road from Tien-Tsin, have seen so many foreigners that a European causes little remark ; here they were mostly too busy with their buying and selling to pay much attention to anything else, and, with the exception of a few people who must have come in from the country, and who could not help laughing at the comical

[2] In Chinese, Pei-Ching, *i.e.* the northern capital. So also Nan-Ching (commonly called Nanking), the southern capital.

sight, no one took much heed of the Englishman moving slowly in the motley crowd. To a Chinaman's eyes a Western is as hideous and strange as a Chinaman at first is to ours; to his mind our clothes are not only uncouth and uncomfortable, but indecent; and to his ideas a light-haired being is diabolic—indeed the very animals seem to share this belief. A story is told of a red-haired, red-bearded Englishman who one day was walking in a country place; meeting a cart, the animals were so frightened by the extraordinary apparition, that they started, and upset the vehicle into a ditch. The Anglo-Saxon good-naturedly went to assist in setting matters straight, when the carter entreated him to get out of sight as soon as he could, as his awful appearance only terrified the animals the more.

We threaded our intricate way through the mazes of the fair for very nearly a mile, when, turning out of it into a by-street, a smart canter brought us at 4.45 P.M. to the gate of the British Legation, which stands in grounds sufficiently extensive to contain the minister's private residence and state reception rooms, chancery, houses for three secretaries, a doctor, and an accountant, quarters for ten students, a church, fives-court, bowling-alley, reading-room, and billiard-room.

Two large stone lions guard the entrance to the minister's house, and, passing between these, the first building is reached. This is nothing more than an empty antechamber, with a garden beyond, where there are a few trees; at the other side of this there is a second antechamber, with a suite of two or three rooms on each side; and, finally, traversing another garden, the door of the minister's residence is gained.

This was built by a former emperor for his son. There is no upper story, but the rooms are lofty, and beautifully decorated in the Chinese style, very different from anything European; the harmony with which, in the deep dark shadows, a brilliant lapis-lazuli blue will mingle with an emerald green is at first rather startling to an eye educated in the principles of modern high art.

An excursion to the Great Wall, and to the sea-coast,

through the interminable plains, among filthy though picturesque villages inhabited by a good-humoured population, need not be here recounted. The pleasant society of Mr. Carles, and his familiar acquaintance with the native manners and language, were advantages which cannot be overestimated, and the five weeks' journey 'athwart the flats and rounding gray' was a useful prelude and preparation for the more serious work to follow.

The days slipped by very pleasantly in Peking. During my stay a large party paid a visit to the Temple of Heaven, one of the sights of this metropolis. After riding through the foul streets, in which the smells and the dust impressed one most, we reached the Temple. The grounds are square, and enclosed by walls about half a mile long, where the fresh-mown grass is shaded by long straight rows of yews and laburnums. It is one of those places almost impossible to describe, and leaves upon the mind confused ideas of grandeur and utter ruin—recollections of wonderful blue encaustic tiles, and marble stairs, with rank weeds growing between the slabs—visions of elegant bridges, and rich but broken carvings—vivid impressions of a general covering of dirt and filth, and the surprise of a patch of kitchen garden in an unexpected corner.

The emperor comes here at certain times to pray, and on these occasions, after a bullock has been made a burnt-offering, he should pass the night sitting upright in a stiff and straight-backed chair; but the attendants naïvely exhibited the luxurious bed for which his Imperial Majesty vacates the uncomfortable arm-chair, and they had no hesitation in admitting that economy was now strictly carried out—that the flesh of the animal was sold, and nothing burnt but the skin and bones. Familiarity with Celestial affairs seems to have bred contempt in the minds of the servants about the place, for they were liberal in their offers of bricks, tiles, or bits of glass, of which tourists are generally so fond. I did not load myself very heavily, and trusted to my memory rather than my pockets to carry away souvenirs of the Temple of Heaven.

Men from the bazaars used to bring to the Legation

great piles of embroidery to tempt the unwary; costly furs of every description used to cover the floor of my room; old curios, and modern shams, bits of bronze worth almost their weight in gold, and marvels of ancient porcelain, were displayed in lavish profusion. But better than all were the newspapers and letters. I had not received a letter since leaving Europe, as I had travelled from Marseilles to Peking with one mail, and had left the northern capital before the arrival of the next.

A morning was spent in those quaint dark shops in the by-streets of Peking, and an afternoon in one of the regular fairs.

This was an amusing sight, and very like a European fair. There are stalls where every description of cheap trifles is sold, and nothing expensive is to be found. Children's toys, dolls, clay models of spiders, grasshoppers, and all sorts of insects; groups of men, women, and children, cleverly modelled in clay, and highly characteristic; ribbons and bits of finery for the women, pipes and chopsticks for the men. Then there are the eating-stalls, where divers savoury dishes are prepared, and the hot-potato men and the sweetmeat-sellers offer their attractive goods. Pigeons too are sold in great numbers, for the Chinese are great pigeon-fanciers. And in every corner there is a surging crowd of people, laughing, pushing, buying, or selling; the sellers calling out the virtue of their wares, and begging people to come and buy; the purchasers bargaining, and chaffering—and all enjoying themselves thoroughly.

One evening we had a Chinese dinner in the most famous of the Peking restaurants, the 'Restaurant of Virtue and Prosperity.'

I shall not attempt to describe a Chinese dinner, for although the subject may be of a nature to present some amusing details for a European, yet, as the humorous Abbé observes: 'These details are so well known that we should fear to abuse the patience of the reader. We have besides remarked in the 'Mélanges Posthumes' of Abel-Rémusat, the following passage, which would quite suffice to dissipate the idea, if ever it possessed us, of giving a nomenclature of the dishes which were served to us:

'"Some years ago, on the return of a European embassy from China, where the officers composing it had not found much to boast of in the success of their mission, it came into their heads to offer to the readers of the Gazette an account of a dinner that had been given them, they said, by the officials of some frontier town. According to their account never had guests been more sumptuously regaled; the quality of the dishes, the number of courses, the play-acting during the intervals, all had been carefully arranged, and furnished a magnificent example. To those who were in the habit of reading old books there seemed something familiar in the account of that dinner. More than one hundred years before the time of these officers, certain Jesuit missionaries had partaken of precisely the same repast, composed of exactly the same dishes, and served in the same style. But there are many people for whom everything is new, and although it is certain, '*qu'un dîner réchauffé ne valut jamais rien*,' this *réchauffé* at all events was found excellent, and the public, always greedy for peculiarities of customs, and even for the details of cookery, did not trouble itself as to who had been the real diners. It was pleased with the singularities of the Chinese service, as well as with the gravity with which the guests, in eating rice, executed manœuvres and evolutions which would have done honour to the best-drilled regiment of infantry."'[3]

If now I should present our bill of fare I should be suspected of having dined with, or of plagiarising, Mrs. Brassey!

Gelatine is the foundation of every delicacy that forms part of a high-class Chinese dinner. Swallow's-nest soup, shark's fins, sea-slugs, and sea-weed are nearly pure gelatine. For flavour, the Chinese seem to know but duck and pork; and the succession of gelatinous foods, flavoured the first with duck and the next with pork, is tedious in the extreme. European wines are utterly out of place with a Chinese dinner, and even the most conservative Englishman will find that hot rice-wine, with a bouquet of rose-water, sipped from cups not much larger than thimbles, is preferable to the

[3] Huc, *L'Empire Chinois*, vol. i. chap. v.

driest vintage of Heidsick, or the rarest *cuvée* of Lafitte. A European generally finds the first Chinese dinner he eats very good, the second indifferent, and the third nasty. The restaurant-keepers at Peking, Shanghai, and Macao doubtless invent fantastic dishes utterly unknown to an ordinary Chinaman, in order to satisfy the well-known English love of the marvellous. At all events, it would be as fair to judge of an English household dinner from a Greenwich feast, as it would be to consider one of these made-up and elaborate entertainments a type of a Chinese gentleman's usual meal.

But even of that, as well as of the diversified and lengthy repasts served up in these restaurants visited at intervals by curious Europeans, it may be said with tenfold the force with which the remarks may be applied to a Greenwich banquet, that 'the appetite is distracted by the variety of objects, and tantalised by the restlessness of perpetual solicitation, not a moment of repose, no pause for enjoyment; eventually a feeling of satiety without satisfaction, and of repletion without sustenance; till at night gradually recovering from the whirl of the anomalous repast, famished yet incapable of flavour, the tortured memory can only recall with an effort that it has dined off'[4] gelatine and grease!

I have heard it said that the Chinese use paper pocket-handkerchiefs. This, however, is not the case; but the idea may have originated in the little squares of paper that are laid beside each diner, and are used for wiping the chopsticks after partaking of any dish—for one pair of chopsticks must serve for the whole dinner.

The ruins of the Summer Palace, about ten miles from Peking, are very beautiful in the sadness of their desolation. One seems to be brought here face to face with the wreck of an empire. The builders of this palace seem to have been imbued with something of the spirit of those who in the middle ages raised in Europe such noble monuments of their devotion and piety. The whole soul of a man must have been in the work; no part was neglected, no money, time, or labour spared; infinite care was bestowed on every

[4] Coningsby.

detail—and, notwithstanding the desolations and ruin, there still seems to breathe over all the spirit of a master mind. Roaming about the palaces now overgrown with weeds, or looking out on that still lake whose mirror-like surface must have reflected so many and such curious sights, one cannot help feeling that the architect must have had a faith in something, even if it were only in the possibility of complete human happiness.

In the Wang-Tua-Shan enclosure there are now only two buildings left standing—one a beautiful little pagoda of red, yellow, green, and blue tiles; the other a temple in the same style at the top of the hill. Both were originally covered with porcelain figures of Buddha; but now the heads have been chipped off from all within reach, and in some places there are great cavities where people have been trying to extract whole tiles. It is very humiliating to see the greedy way in which Europeans chip off the figures that in their mutilated state can be of no possible utility, and are not by themselves in any way ornamental.

Surely the Chinaman cracking his water-melon seeds is at least as dignified as the wandering European desecrating shrines with his vulgar name, or destroying beautiful monuments, for the sake of glorifying himself in the eyes of his gaping country cousins, by the exhibition of a tile or the head of a Buddha!

Here, too, it would seem to be unnecessary to carry any further the cruel work of demolition, for, by groping in the heaps of rubbish that litter the place, amongst dust and stones and broken tiles, our party found plenty of relics, some of which, terra-cotta tiles with raised figures of Buddha on one side and an inscription in three languages on the other, were at least as valuable curios as bits knocked off a building.

The parks in which the palaces stand enclose many acres, interspersed with hills, some real and some artificial, looking over lovely lakes, where there are inlets spanned by elegant arched bridges. Standing on the crest of the highest of these hills, the barrier of the mountains that buttress the Mongolian plateau is seen to the north; whilst to the south the eye roams over the wide and rich alluvial plain, dotted with villages and trees, the walls of Peking in the distance showing sharp and clear through that crisp, dry, frosty air.

Here there were no noisy tourists to disturb reflection; no gabbling cicerone with his automatic tongue; and mournful though it must be to think of what has been and what now is, it is with difficulty that at length one tears oneself away from the scene, at once so fair and sad.

The last emperor ordered the palaces to be rebuilt. The ministers scraped together a small sum of money, and began to mend the roads and repair the walls; but the emperor dying soon afterwards the works were stopped.

On our way home we visited the 'Bell Temple,' where there is a bronze bell, eleven feet in diameter, fourteen and a half feet high, and about four inches thick. It is said to be the largest bell in the world that is hung. From rough measurements I calculated the amount of bronze in it at 300 cubic feet; this would make its weight about 160,000 lbs.

The bell is covered, inside and out, with Chinese characters, all of which are close together, and none more than half an inch long. It is said that the characters were cast on the bell, but this seems almost impossible. The whole inscription is a prayer for rain; and during a drought the princes and chief ministers come to this temple and pray for rain, remaining on their knees until the prayers are answered—a duty which they perform much as the emperor does his at the Temple of Heaven.

It is said that the tones of the bell are supernatural, and have the power of bringing rain. This superstition in all probability rests on a substratum of fact, for the vibrations of this mass of metal may cause the precipitation of rain from an overcharged cloud, just as the report of a cannon will sometimes bring on a threatening shower.

The largest bell in the world is that of Moscow, but this still rests on the ground, and has never been hung. It is nineteen feet high, with a circumference of sixty-three feet eleven inches at the rim, and its weight is computed at 443,772 lbs. Bells are usually cast with approximately the same proportions; a bell of the same shape and proportions as the Moscow bell, with the height of the Peking bell, would weigh 177,534 lbs. My rough calculation, as just stated, makes it 160,000 lbs., and it is not likely to be less.

'What is Peking like?' was a question that I knew I should often be asked on my return to England, and I determined that I would, if possible, be able to answer it; but the more I saw, the more hopeless seemed the task. I took a note-book out one day to try and write down what there was to be seen, but, as I began the task, I was nearly knocked down by a camel lumbering along with a load of brick tea.

I remarked to a friend, an old resident, that nothing but a series of coloured pictures or photographs could ever give an idea of Peking as it is: 'No,' he replied; 'and even then you would not get the stinks.'

As in old Marco's time, the streets are straight and wide, and the plots of ground on which the houses are built are still four square. There are many open spaces inside the walls, large gardens, and trees. But its grandeur seems to be gone; and if the old Venetian were now to return, the only part of his description that he would still adhere to would be that 'it is impossible to give a description that should do it justice.' There are still extensive remains of drains, but their place has long been taken by open sewers in some of the streets. The smells that pervade the city at all seasons of the year are abominable, and the black dust that sweeps in clouds about the streets is probably the most filthy in the world, not excepting even that of London. In dry weather, this dust lies deep in all the streets, and in wet it is turned to a horrible black mire.

CHAPTER III.

A CYCLE OF CATHAY.

Cradle of the Chinese Nation—Their Settlement in Shan-Si—Characteristics of Chinese History—Manifold Invasions of China, but Chinese Individuality always predominates—Imagination essential to Advancement, but the Chinese have it not—Inventions ascribed to Them—Stoppage of Development—China for the Chinese—Foreign Help Inevitable—The Woo-Sung Railway—Defects of Chinese Character—Pigeon-English—Perverse Employment of it—Preparations again for Travel—Detail of Packages—Additions to our Following.

THE birthplace of the Chinese nation is veiled in mystery. Mr. Douglas, in an exceedingly interesting article in the 'Encyclopædia Britannica,' observes: 'Some believe that their point of departure was in the region to the south-east of the Caspian Sea, and that, having crossed the head waters of the Oxus, they made their way eastward along the southern slopes of the Teen Shan. But, however this may be, it is plain that as they journeyed they struck on the northern course of the Yellow River, and that they followed its stream on the eastern bank, as it trended south, as far as Tung-Kwan, and that then, turning with it due eastward, they established small colonies on the fertile plains of the modern province of Shan-Se.'

Mr. Douglas also states that the nucleus of the nation 'was a little horde of wanderers roving amongst the forests of Shan-Se without homes, without clothing, without fire to dress their victuals, and subsisting on the spoils of the chase eked out with roots and insects.'

There were aborigines already here; but of them little is known; their remnants are said to exist at the present day amongst the Miau-Tzŭ of Kwei-Chou.

But the Chinese were the better race; they were also apparently already agriculturists, and as such in a higher state of civilisation. One result could but follow; the inexorable law of nature had its way—the inferior and less civilised race were pushed out by degrees, just as all the barbarous tribes still remaining are surely disappearing before the steady advance of the Chinese: as the New Zealand Maories and American Red Indians are dying away before the Anglo-Saxon race.[1] There is no record that the Chinese were ever a pastoral people, excepting that which lingers in some of the ancient characters of the language, and, as some say, in the wavy outlines of their roofs. However that may have been, they appear to have settled down as agriculturists in Lower Shan-Si.

Northern China had not yet been denuded of her forests; but though the climate may have been more favourable for agricultural pursuits than in the present day, the province of Shan-Si can never have been one that yielded a profusion of wealth without the steady application of labour.

Baron Richthofen remarks that 'the altitude of its arable ground renders nearly the whole of it unfit for raising two crops a year.'

Neither is the climate so severe that labour in the fields cannot be carried on at all seasons.

The Chinese race, therefore, in its infancy found itself in a country where steady labour and thrift were necessary for life; and here were perhaps the germs of the industry and exceeding carefulness so remarkable in the character of the Chinese of the present day.

Further, this was the order of things most suited for the production of a sentiment of equality amongst the people, for food was not too easily procured, and a sharp division between rich and poor would not immediately ensue. It is, therefore, not surprising that a strong demo-

[1] It will not do to argue from this analogy that so will the barbarians of Central Asia disappear before the European. The Anglo-Saxon cannot colonise there; if the Russians can, they have indeed a grand future before them.

cratic feeling should be another feature of the Chinese as they are.[2]

'The dim history of those days throws but a feeble ray of light, but it shows us that civilisation advanced, and the existence of trade is proved by the establishment of fairs.[3]

'The people now spread eastward, and in 2300 B.C. we find their capital in the neighbouring province of Shan-Tung, and their kingdom extending to the north and east of the present Peking, and as far south as latitude 23° N.[3]

'But the southern climate seemed to soften the hardy northmen, and the varied conditions of life to destroy their cohesiveness. . . . We read of a ruler in 1818 B.C. in whom were combined the worst vices of kings;[3] but the vitality of the people was still sufficient to make them rise against him and sweep away all traces of him and his dynasty.'[3]

During the next eight hundred years we hear of little but internecine wars, and consequent weakening of the kingdom.

Nigh two thousand years had elapsed since first the black-haired race had come from the north-west; three sovereign dynasties had reigned, of which the last was sinking amid the rivalry of feudal states, and China seemed rapidly disintegrating, when the Princes of Thsin, a state founded five centuries before with their capital at Chang-Gan in Shen-Si, conquering in succession the six or seven other states, restored (B.C. 251) a strong central power.

With the accession of new blood, China was reinvigorated, and this was one of the most flourishing epochs in the varied history of this marvellous empire: roads were made, canals were dug; and before long the powerful desert horde of the Hiung-Nu, who had long harassed the

[2] In China all judicial affairs are conducted more or less in public. Even in the presence of the highest officials any one can turn in from the street to see what is going on, no one trying to hinder him. A beggar will sit down and smoke his pipe in the presence of a magistrate, and sometimes join in the conversation unasked. The literary examinations are open to all—no matter how lowly a man may be, if he can pass his examination he may become the highest magistrate in the land.

[3] *Encyclopædia Britannica.*

Chinese, were completely routed and driven into Mongolia; and in the year 214 B.C. the Great Wall was commenced as a protection against the inroads of these barbarians. The veneration of antiquity preached by Confucius now seems first to take root, for at this time 'schoolmen and pedants were for ever holding up to the admiration of the people the heroes of the feudal times.'[4]

This reverence for antiquity throughout the ages that follow, amidst scenes of strife and disorder, as well as during the intervals of prosperity, sank deeper and deeper into the nature of the Chinese, and in it is to be found one of the causes of the present decadence of the nation.

History now repeats itself again and again with almost wearisome monotony; tumults and disorders, and the consequent weakness of the people, invite assaults from the north; but time after time the vanquished Chinese seem only reinvigorated by their invaders, and we find that each fresh incursion is followed by a period of glory.

In 121 B.C. the Hiung-Nu were driven to the north-east of the Caspian. Then succeeded the troublous time of the 'Three Kingdoms'; and in the fourth and fifth centuries of our era, the Wei, a race of Siberian nomads, conquered and ruled in Northern China. But in the seventh century arose the Thang, the most glorious of all the native dynasties. Under them Chinese rule extended to Turfan, Khoten, Kashgar, and even to the Jaxartes, whilst Chinese fame was so great that ambassadors came from the Caliphate, and even from Imperial Byzantium.

Thus the marvellous vitality of the Chinese disposed of successive races of invaders—either driving them far from their borders, or absorbing them and assimilating them when they could not be expelled.

But yet another army of barbarians appeared in the Khitans. These, however, never extended their rule very far south, although in 997 A.D. tribute was paid to them Later, the Chinese invited a fourth horde, the Kin or Niu-Chih, to expel the Khitans. The Kin succeeded in this

[4] *Encyclopædia Britannica.*

only too well, and in 1150 A.D. established themselves in the whole country north of the Yang-Tzŭ.

A new race, the Mongols, now came on the scene; they wrested province after province from the Kin, and the place of these knew them no more. This was in the thirteenth century, and in the brilliant light that radiated from these the most successful, the most glorious of all the conquerors of China, the feeble glimmer of Kin and Khitan was extinguished alike. This was the most celebrated era in the whole history of the Chinese Empire; but it was the Mongols, and not the Chinese, who made it so.

The latter were known to Marco Polo as the people of Manzi, who, if they 'had but the spirit of soldiers, would conquer the world; but they are (quoth he) no soldiers at all, only accomplished traders and skilful craftsmen;'[5] whilst Friar Odoric says: 'All the people of this country are traders and artificers.'[6]

True, both Polo and Odoric speak in glowing terms of the rich and noble cities of Manzi, of their wealth, magnificence, and luxury; but these were as nothing before the glories of the Great Kaan, whose subjects they were, and who was a Mongol. But the Mongol power waned, and by a turn in the wheel of fate the son of a Chinese labourer drove out the successor of Kublai. In more recent days, to quell rebellions in the south, the Chinese invited the aid of the Manchu Tartars, who now are seated on the Imperial throne.

Thus, through long ages of varied fortunes, the Chinese character has been formed; and it would be surprising indeed, if a nation that had survived so many and such great vicissitudes, had been conquered many times, and had each time risen superior to defeat, had absorbed one race of victors and driven out another, did not possess some characteristic that would mark it as a peculiar people—and this characteristic is the individuality of the race. It is, indeed, a matter for wonder that a people so numerous and covering so vast an area should everywhere appear the

[5] Marco Polo, book ii. vol. ii. p. 166.
[6] *Cathay*, vol. i. p. 105.

same ; who, whether they are found in the north, the south, the east, or the west of their own huge empire, who, whether they are observed as coolies in America or Australia, or met as ambassadors in London or St. Petersburg, should universally possess the same thoughts and the same feelings, wear the same clothes, and eat the same food, should be imbued with the same habits of intense industry and thrift, and should act precisely in the same manner as they did many hundreds of years ago.

Where else in the history of the world can we read of three hundred millions of people thus amazingly unchangeable? and who can doubt that they must yet remain for many centuries an important factor in the Asian problem?

Of all qualities that conduce to the advancement of a people, imagination is perhaps the most important ; without it a nation must remain stagnant, with it the limits of its forward march can never be reached.

No matter what branch of industry or science is examined, imagination lies at the root of its advance.

Surely it was in one of the most mighty flights of imagination that the keen gaze of Newton, sweeping across the wild chaotic waves of theory that each in turn must have leapt up towards his searching intellect, singled out the exquisitely beautiful and simple one of gravitation to account for the most complex motions of the vast masses that roll through space.

What but the richest imagination could have enabled Darwin to conceive the descent of man? or how could Professor Owen without imagination have built up from some paltry fragment the form of a gigantic mammal?

Who without imagination could from mere scratches on a rock have enunciated the theory of a glacial epoch? or how, without imagination, could the present marvels of electricity have been evolved from the twitching of the muscles of a frog?

Of art it is hardly necessary to speak ; no one can ever have attributed a want of imagination to either painters or poets worthy of the name.

Imagination and originality are more or less inseparable; an individual devoid of one will certainly be deficient of the other, and what is true of an individual will equally hold good of a nation.

In the Chinese character originality and imagination are conspicuous by their absence. The Chinaman is eminently a matter-of-fact person; sights that would be disgusting to a European have nothing unpleasant in his eyes, for everything is looked at from a utilitarian point of view. The beauties of nature have no charms for him, and in the most lovely scenery the houses are so placed that no enjoyment can be derived from it. If the unhewn log of a tree will serve as a beam in the wall, he does not think it worth while to spend money or labour in squaring it. A Chinaman may express the highest admiration for a pair of European candles, but if they cost a trifle more than his filthy oil lamp, he will rarely exchange the glimmer of his time-honoured institution for the brilliant light of a composite. A Chinaman will feel the texture of a European coat, and admit its superiority; but his first question will be, how much did it cost? In their pictures there is no imagination; they draw birds and insects as they see them, and really well. Animals also they attempt, but their ignorance of anatomy renders their efforts in this direction ridiculous; but abstract ideas, such as have made the memory of old European painters glorious, any attempt to portray Faith, Hope, or Charity, any effort to rise above the level of every-day life, are things unknown in Chinese art. So in their sculpture, they represent men, women, and children as they see them, but that is all; they can imitate admirably, but they can imagine nothing.

But the Chinese are credited with having invented almost everything: how can this be reconciled with a want of originality?

In the first place there are a good many things that the Chinese have never invented or discovered. The principle of the pump, the circulation of the blood, and the science of grafting are still unknown to the Chinese. It has frequently been asserted that they invented firearms; but the late Mr. Mayers, Chinese Secretary of Legation at Peking, has effectually demolished their claim to this discovery.[7]

The mariner's compass, however, appears to have been known to the Chinese at a very early date; and it must be admitted that the early use of bank-notes, and the knowledge of printing, give them some claim to originality in ancient days.

It would be a deeply interesting study, and one well worthy of the labour, for any one with sufficient acquaintance with the written language of China to investigate the ancient books, and from their internal evidence, and not from the prejudiced and superficial views of foreigners, to ascertain the history of the formation of Chinese character. It would appear, however, that originality, if they ever possessed it, has been stamped out, partly by the insane teachings of Confucius that everything ancient is sacred, and the still more insane idea that anything new, no matter what, is dangerous. Another cause for the disappearance of originality may be found in the preposterous system of examinations. Magisterial and official posts are awarded only to those who can pass the literary examinations: the 'literati,' or those who have passed high examinations, are the class most highly esteemed in China, and the desire to be numbered amongst them is almost universal. And what are these examinations? Examination only in the ancient classics, the obscure passages in which must only be explained in the orthodox manner.

It is not difficult thus to realise that the Chinese character may have changed during the last few centuries, and that the originality and power of conception they may have possessed may have been crushed out by the worship of antiquity and the system of examination.

If this be so, the extraordinary stoppage of the early development of the people may be accounted for; for without originality, and devoid of imagination, they must

[7] Morrison gives 1275 as the time of the invention of powder and guns, and was aware that what they called 'P'ao' were machines for throwing stones.

necessarily have stagnated, and have been arrested in the onward march towards a more perfect civilisation.[8]

Another feature in the Chinese character that may have assisted in some degree to retard their development is the intense desire of every man to do everything for himself. It is undoubtedly prompted by a sturdy feeling of independence, but carried to the excess in which it is seen in the Chinese it must be hurtful.

A Chinaman, if he can, will grow his own grain, grind it, or husk it, and cook it on his own premises. If possible, he will cultivate his little bit of cotton, and weave the cloth without assistance from beyond his household; all his clothes are perhaps made by his wife or family; and thus he is almost independent of any extraneous aid. We in Europe know that this is not an economical way of doing things; but the Chinese have done so for generations—and what was good enough for their fathers is good enough for them. Of course under these circumstances it is almost hopeless to expect any improvement in agriculture or agricultural tools, or any advance towards a use of machinery.

Thus with the nation, at the present moment, it is the extraordinary idea and wish amongst some of the most advanced thinkers to begin their mining operations, smelt their

[8] Another reason for the stagnation of the Chinese people may be possibly found in the fact that all the talent of the country is absorbed in the service of the State. This is partly because of the contempt in which the non-official class is held, and partly because there is no entrance to official life of any kind except by competitive examination. Now, even in progressive countries, a system which would divert from private enterprise all those who help to make the country great, would have lamentable results. How much more must this be the case in one where enterprise of any kind is almost unknown, and which has, as it were, been asleep for centuries. In Western States, honour, fame, and dignities attend those who succeed, no matter in what walk of life; but in China none but the officials can hope for any of these.

If we look back at the history of our civilisation we find that all the great strides in science, and nearly all the greatest works of literature and art, have been due to private individuals. The discovery of America, the establishment of the Overland Route to India by Waghorn, the extraordinary development of newspaper correspondence, are but a few of the instances that will occur to any one but slightly acquainted with history; and in our own country does not Government always look with distrustful eyes on any measure laid before it which would appear likely to interfere with, or to retard, individual effort?

iron with their own coal, and make their own rails for their railways, before they do anything else. They want to have China for the Chinese; they desire to do everything for themselves, and if possible to exclude foreigners. But how far they are from this, they little know.

True, the palmy days of the British merchants are over; the Chinese have at last learnt how to buy and sell without their aid, and they are fast ousting the foreigner from mercantile pursuits. We cannot of course but be sorry that the fine race of men, open-handed and generous, full of courage and enterprise, a type of all that is manly and thoroughly English, should die out and disappear, and mournful tales are told of the destruction in consequence of English trade. This is, however, but a superficial way of regarding the irresistible march of events. If the British merchant is ousted, it is because the Chinese can do things cheaper than the English; the result must be that we in England will get our tea and silk cheaper than heretofore, and that the people of China (if they buy it at all) will buy our cotton cheaper, and in consequence buy more. How then is trade injured: is it not rather on a better footing?

But although commercial pursuits may not be so profitable as they were, there must yet be a future for Europeans in China. Great as the opposition is at present, railways and telegraphs must certainly be laid down, and will for many years to come give employment to large numbers of Europeans, for, owing to the want of originality in the Chinese, they cannot hope to undertake the sole management of railways and telegraphs.

The Chinese may be taught almost anything—they are wonderfully quick at learning and imitating—and they would doubtless soon acquire the power of managing engines and telegraphs, as long as all went smoothly. But in the moment of difficulty, if any fresh combination of circumstances should necessitate some original action, or even the smallest amount of reasoning, a Chinaman would be found unequal to the emergency. The Chinese Government have for a long time owned steamers, but the engineers are still European, and it will be the same with the railways and telegraphs. There are at present no railways in China. Some of the merchants of Shanghai instituted a short line between Shanghai and Woo-Sung, but it came to an untimely end, not so much on account of the absolute dislike of the Chinese to railways, as from some unfortunate circumstances connected with its origin. Rightly, or wrongly, the measure adopted irritated the Chinese Government, who declined to have the Woo-Sung railway forced upon them, and when it came into their hands, contemptuously tore it up. During its construction, and in the early days of its existence, there was considerable opposition amongst the people of the adjacent villages, excited probably by the literati of Shanghai. There were even some attempts at suicide, the perpetrators being probably bribed to commit these acts. There was considerable method shown in the way that the attacks on the railway were carried out, and it may not be uninteresting to notice one in detail as an illustration.

There was a Chinaman living at Woo-Sung of a character so bad that, amongst the inhabitants of the place, he was known as 'The Pirate,' and of a reputation so evil that he dared not show his face in Shanghai. This man had a nephew who was a 'ganger' on the railway. Possibly bribed by the officials, or for some motives that never came to light, this man and his nephew incited the people of Woo-Sung and of another village to evil deeds. They proceeded to dig the ballast from between the rails, and pile it up on the line, in the hope of upsetting the train ; but as great crowds of people collected on and around the line at this point, when the train arrived at the obstacles the engine-driver saw that something was wrong, and stopped.

The train was then attacked, but the engine-driver and guard repulsed the mob, captured the nephew of 'The Pirate,' locked him up in a carriage with another prisoner they had caught, and went back towards Shanghai. On the way thither more mobs collected, and one man attempted to commit suicide by throwing himself down in front of the engine ; but the engine-driver was again able to pull up in time, and the would-be suicide was made prisoner, and, with the other two, conveyed safely to Shanghai.

One curious result of European intercourse with the Chinese has been the evolution of 'Pigeon-English,'[9] a jargon used in the Treaty Ports in the conduct of business matters. At the first appearance of the English in the country, the Chinese, who are naturally an imitative people, began to pick up a few English words, and soon constructed a language which was an unnatural combination of deformed English words with Chinese ideas and forms. The result was a jargon as hideous as it was illogical; but the English traders of the early days, finding they understood somewhat of this comic medley, instead of inducing the Chinese to make use of correct words rather than the misshapen syllables they had adopted, encouraged them, by approbation and example, to establish Pigeon-English—a grotesque gibberish which would be laughable if it were not almost melancholy. The English of the present day cannot do much to help themselves, but they might do more; for although it is to a certain extent true that Pigeon-English is understood, while the grammatical language is not, yet it is not possible to believe that when a glass of beer is poured out, even a Chinaman can more readily understand the idiotic expression 'can do' than the good English of 'that will do'; or that a Chinese boy would not in two days learn that 'upstairs' was the same thing as 'top side.'

But far from thinking it any shame to deface our beautiful language, the English seem to glory in its distortion, and will often ask one another to come to 'chow-chow' instead of dinner; and send their 'chin-chins,' even in letters, rather than their compliments; most of them ignorant of the fact that 'chow-chow' is no more Chinese than it is Hebrew; and that 'chin-chin,' though an expression used by the Chinese, does not in its true meaning come near to the 'good-bye, old fellow,' for which it is often used, or the 'compliments' for which it is frequently substituted.

Returning to Shanghai on the 21st of November, I began to make preparations for a long journey into the interior of

[9] 'Pigeon,' or, as it is often written, 'pidgin,' is a Chinese corruption of the English word 'business.'

China, and found plenty of occupation in getting stores of all kinds ready.

Mr. Baber, of the consular service, who was a member of the Grosvenor expedition to Yun-Nan, had invited me to accompany him to Ch'ung-Ch'ing. I eagerly availed myself of his invitation, but as yet formed no definite plans as to my future movements, only making up my mind that I would be ready for anything that might turn up.

I therefore prepared stores of all kinds, and arranged my provision boxes in pairs, each pair to contain a complete supply for two months. Chin-Tai used to carry out my orders with amazement. I had some large tin boxes, for soldering down, made to order, with strong wooden dove-tailed coverings, and inside these I had smaller tin boxes fitted.[1]

[1] I had 6 boxes packed each with 30 candles (English candles, six to the lb.)

1 tin box for tea, $5'' \times 5\frac{1}{2}'' \times 8\frac{1}{2}''$.
4 boxes of matches.
6 2-oz. pots of Liebig's Extract.
2 packets of Marseilles compressed vegetables.
1 bottle Worcester sauce.
1 tin box for cigars, $10'' \times 8\frac{1}{2}'' \times 2\frac{1}{2}''$.
1 box of toothpicks.
1 tin box of tooth powder, $3\frac{1}{2}'' \times 2\frac{1}{2}'' \times 1\frac{1}{2}''$.
1 small bottle cayenne pepper.

Six other of the large boxes were packed each with :—

30 candles.
1 tin of salt, $5'' \times 4'' \times 3\frac{1}{2}''$.
1 tin of mustard, $2\frac{1}{2}'' \times 4'' \times 3\frac{1}{2}''$.
6 2-oz. pots of Liebig's Extract.
1 tin for cigars, $8\frac{1}{2}'' \times 6'' \times 2\frac{1}{2}''$.
1 packet Marseilles preserved vegetables
4 boxes of matches.
4 cakes of toilet soap.
1 cake of yellow soap.
1 cake of carbolic acid soap.
2 little boxes of Brand's meat lozenges.

Each of these boxes, when finally packed and soldered down, weighed a little over 30 lbs.; quite enough for the mountainous countries.

The quantity of tea that I took was unnecessary, but I only had my northern experience to guide me; and in the province of Chi-Li, and beyond the Great Wall, tea can never be bought. In Southern, Central, and Western China, tea is always to be procured. The lids of the boxes were all screwed down, so that they could be opened and shut

The ordinary Chinese fashion of making tea (except in the West, where the tea of Pu-erh is taken) is to put about a teaspoonful of tea into the cup and pour boiling water on it. The Chinese drink it nearly scalding, and the cups are continually refilled with boiling water, fresh tea rarely being put into the cups. The object of putting a cover over the cup, instead of a saucer underneath, is to prevent the tea-leaves getting into the mouth. A Chinaman, before putting the cup to his mouth, always sweeps the surface of the tea with the cover, to push the floating leaves away from the side. He is very skilful in drinking, always holding cup and cover with one hand, and leaving just sufficient aperture for the infusion to pass without letting the leaves through.

The Chinese have a theory that if the water is properly boiling the leaves will not float on the tea, but if the tea has been made with water that does not boil, the leaves will at first come to the surface.

Before leaving Shanghai, Chin-Tai was instructed in the art of bread-making, so that during the two months on the river we were never reduced to chupatties. I also obtained possession of a dog, whose numerous good qualities, as appraised by his owner, would have made him cheap at any price. Baber and I laid in a considerable stock of provisions and delicacies for the voyage, amongst which two barrels of flour took a prominent position; and I engaged another servant, a friend of Chin-Tai. His name was Chung-Erh, and, according to his own statements, he threw up a marvellously lucrative engagement out of pure love and friendship for Chin-Tai.

as often as necessary; and as I could not manage to get sufficient candles into the boxes without unduly increasing the weight, I took besides an extra supply.

CHAPTER IV.

THE OCEAN RIVER.

Start up the Yang-Tzŭ—Names of the Great River—The Dog Tib, and his ethnological perspicacity—The Grand Canal—Arrival at Hankow—Manufacture of Brick-Tea—Tea in Chinese Inns—H.M.S. Kestrel—Boat engaged for Upper Yang-Tzŭ—The Lady Skipper and her Craft—Our Departure—Chinese Fuel—Our Eccentricities in Chinese Eyes—The New Year Festival—Chinese View of the Wind-points—Aspects of the River—Vicissitudes of Tracking—Great Bend—Wild Geese—Rice as Food—The Hills Entered—Walks Ashore—Population dense only on the River—Passage in a Cotton Boat—The Telescope Puzzles—Arrival at I-Chang.

At length the time came for our departure, and the cordial good wishes that I received from so many, whose acquaintance I had hardly formed, made me feel that I was leaving many good friends behind; it was not therefore without some regrets that, finally turning my back on Shanghai, I stepped on board the steamer 'Hankow,' on the night of the 23rd of January, 1877, and began my journey across China.

The great river up which we were now to work a devious way is known near its sources under various names. The Mongol name of *Murui-Ussu* is given by both Huc and Prejevalsky; the latter gives *Di-Chu* as a name in use by the Tangutans (as he calls the tribes of north-east Tibet); Burei-Chu, or Bri-Chu, corrupted by the Chinese to *Polei-Chu*, is another Tibetan name. The Tibetans again at Bat'ang, and a little lower, call it the N'jeh-Chŭ ('chŭ' is the Tibetan for 'river').

From Bat'ang to Fu-Chou it has the appellation of Chin-Sha-Chiang, or Golden Sand River, from the quantity of gold dust amongst the sand in its bed. No other name is applied to so long a stretch as this; and the Chin-Sha is the name best known of all.

Near its mouth, where it opens out to a width of some miles, the Chinese call it the Yang-Tzŭ-Chiang, or Ocean River. Friar Odoric, writing about A.D. 1320–1330 of the Great River, calls it the River Talay (Dalai), which is just a Mongol version of the Chinese name, and would seem, therefore, to have been applied to it by the Mongols then ruling in China.* The use of the word 'Dalai' in this way is therefore quite parallel to that of 'Bahr,' as applied by the Arabs to the Nile. So also the Tibetans apply the term 'Samandrang' ('Samudra,' the ocean) to the Indus and Sutlej.

I have seen it stated that the name Ta-Ho is applied also.

This is to a certain extent true; for there is scarcely a river in China that at some place is not called Ta-Ho, or Great River. Where an affluent enters a river, it is of most frequent occurrence to find the main river called Ta-Ho, and the affluent Hsiao-Ho, or Little River.

The French have invented a name expressly for themselves, and call it 'Le Fleuve Bleu'; and Prejevalsky has unfortunately adopted it.

The steamers that ply on the Yang-Tzŭ-Chiang, between Shanghai and Hankow, are built in the style of the American river-boats; they draw scarcely any water, are very light, and are perhaps the most luxurious steamers in the world.

Baber and I were the only passengers, and so there was plenty of room for us and our luggage, of which there was by no means an inconsiderable quantity.

Before turning into the luxurious cabin I went to see the dog, whose name was 'Tib,' but he barked at me as an intruder, and the endearing epithets and biscuits that I lavished upon him producing not the slightest acknowledgment of good-will on his part, I left him, to renew his acquaintance at a later date.

This dog had been almost entirely amongst Chinese, and either the appearance or the smell of a European was distasteful to him. The Chinese, who to a European nose always emit a peculiar odour, declare that they can perfectly well distinguish the smell of a European. There can be no doubt that 'Tib' could detect, even at a distance, a European by his smell, for he invariably barked at the French missionaries directly they entered the courtyard of my house at Ch'êng-Tu, although they were always dressed in Chinese clothes.

Any one who has been long in India will recognise the smell of a Hindoo; and although it is not flattering to our vanity to admit it, it certainly seems as if we, as well as all other people, had an odour peculiar to ourselves.

Near Ching-Kiang we passed the mouth of the Grand Canal of China, a work that has attracted much attention amongst Europeans, who have generally formed a vague idea of a magnificent highway, where great fleets of fine ships come and go, and where there is yet room for an unlimited increase of traffic. As a matter of fact, it is in many parts little more than a stinking ditch; it is already overcrowded to a degree almost incredible; and the water in it is often so low that a junk of very moderate dimensions may stick and entirely stop the traffic.

We reached Hankow on the morning of the 30th of January in a dismal downpour of rain, which soon afterwards turned to snow. In spite of the heavy northerly gale which had been blowing throughout the voyage, a damp mist generally hid the banks. Some idea of the magnificence of the Yang-Tzŭ may be formed from the fact that at Hankow, 680 miles from the sea, the river is still about 1,100 yards broad. It is embanked with a magnificent bund, which is the principal feature of this town. At the time of my visit the water was unusually low, being about thirty-five feet below the top of the bund. In the summer it rises sometimes even over this work, flooding the country and the town. Under these circumstances, supposing the average velocity of the current to be six miles an hour (and it certainly is not less), upwards of a million cubic feet of water per second must pass Hankow.

Hiring boats for the journey to Ch'ung-Ch'ing was not altogether a simple matter. It was necessary to let our servants make all the arrangements before disclosing ourselves, for boatmen sometimes object to taking foreigners, and always try to overcharge them. It was easier to settle our money matters. A firm at Hankow gave us a letter of credit on their Chinese agents at Ch'ung-Ch'ing, so we were not obliged to carry more silver than was necessary for the voyage.

During our stay in Hankow we visited the Russian factory, where brick-tea is prepared for the Mongolian market. Bricks are made here of both green and black tea, but always from the commonest and cheapest; in fact, for the black tea the dust and sweepings of the establishment are used. The tea dust is first collected, and if it is not in a sufficiently fine powder, it is beaten with wooden sticks on a hot iron plate. It is then sifted through several sieves to separate the fine, medium, and coarse grains. The tea is next steamed over boiling water, after which it is immediately put into the moulds, the fine dust in the centre, and the coarse grains round the edges.

These moulds are like those used for making ordinary clay bricks, but very much stronger, and of less depth, so that the cakes of tea when they come out are more like large tiles than bricks. The people who drink this tea like it black; wherefore about a teaspoonful of soot is put into each mould, to give it the depth of colouring and gloss that attracts the Mongolian purchasers!

The moulds are now put under a powerful press, and the covers wedged tightly down, so that when removed from the press the pressure on the cake is still maintained. After two or three days the wedges are driven out, the bricks are removed from the moulds, and each brick is wrapped up separately in a piece of common white paper. Baskets, which when full weigh 130 lbs., are carefully packed with the bricks, and are sent to Tien-Tsin, whence they find their way all over Mongolia and up to the borders of Russia. I was told that this tea could be sold retail in St. Petersburg, with a fair profit, at the rate of twenty copecks the pound. The green tea is not made of such fine stuff, but of stalks and leaves. The Mongolians make their infusion by boiling.

In this manner they extract all the strength, and as there is no delicate flavour to lose, they do not injure the taste.

The manufacturer here had set up a small steam-engine for the press, but found coolie labour cheaper. He told me that the tea the Russians usually drink in their own country is taken direct to Odessa from Hankow by the Suez Canal; and in answer to an inquiry that I made, he assured me that even before the Canal was opened it never passed through London. A better price is given by the Russians in Hankow than the English care to pay. This is the real reason why the tea in Russia is superior to any found in London; for caravan tea is a delicacy even amongst the nobles of St. Petersburg.

Anything but very ordinary tea is rare in Chinese inns or houses; occasionally, however, a cup of tea has been given me with a delicacy of flavour and a bouquet that I have never met with elsewhere.

A very delicate variety is grown in Pu-Erh in Yun-Nan; it is pressed into annular cakes, and can almost always be purchased in the large towns of Western China; even in Ssŭ-Ch'uan, cakes of the Pu-Erh tea were often given to me as a present. But these are exceptions to the general rule, as the tea in inns and private houses is indifferent. The brick-tea made for the Tibetan market is prepared entirely by Chinese at Ya-Chou. It also is made from dust and rubbish, and the manufacture is very similar to the process at Hankow.

H.M.S. 'Kestrel' was at Hankow, and a day or two before our departure she left for I-Ch'ang, now a treaty port under one of the clauses of the Chi-Fu Convention, carrying thither Mr. King, the newly-appointed consul to that place. The European officers of the Chinese customs service were also going up, so that Baber and I anticipated a merry meeting on our arrival.

When the mysterious process of hiring the boats had been accomplished by our servants, we went on board to be introduced to the owner and skipper, who was a lady. She declared herself capable of navigating the ship, taking the helm, working the *ulo*, and keeping the trackers up to the mark. Our subsequent experience showed that the last of these accomplishments was her strong point, for she had a tongue that nothing could withstand. The 'ulo' is a kind of gigantic scull that is worked by two or more people, sometimes from the stern, and sometimes at the side of the vessel. The old lady had suddenly discovered that a sail would not be altogether a useless article, and had sent to buy one. In the mean time I looked round the boat to see what manner of craft was to be our home for so many weeks. She was about eighty feet long and eleven feet broad, and the main deck, if such a term is applicable, was about two feet out of the water. The bows, for a space of twenty feet, were uncovered; aft of this a house about twenty feet long was built right across the deck, leaving no room to pass round the sides. There was a small open space aft of the house; and right over the stern another building, where our skipper lived, was piled up to a great height. The house was about seven feet high, and was divided into four compartments, giving us a sitting-room and two bedrooms for ourselves, and a room for the servants. Our heavy baggage was stowed away in a hold about three feet deep. In our sitting-room we set up a little American stove, which had the evil habit of becoming suddenly red-hot; at times the chimney would get twisted, and the wind blowing down would send great tongues of flame darting across the room; of course it smoked occasionally; but these little vagaries made us appreciate it all the more when it burnt properly.

Our party now consisted of Baber and myself, a photographer whom Baber took up with him, Baber's chief servant, Hwu-Fu, who had travelled some time with Baron von Richthofen; Baber's second servant, Wang-Erh, a giant of six feet two inches, who had been a soldier drilled by European officers, but who had never before been in the service of a European; my two servants, Chin-Tai and Chung-Erh, both over six feet high, and 'Tib,' a brown retriever. There was, in addition, an official sent by the Tao-Tai of Hankow to accompany Baber. On the 8th of February all the above ship's company was on board; but our skipper now said that the sail did not fit well, and must be altered before she could start. So we tried to shake ourselves down; we made bookshelves of the doors of our sleeping cabins, and pasted paper over the cracks in the wall, through which an icy wind was blowing. The sacrificial cock was expended during the day, and his blood sprinkled on the bow of the boat; for without this ceremony, and the subsequent more serious one of eating the flesh of the bird, it would have been nothing less than sheer madness to make a start—at least, so thought our skipper and his crew.

Towards the afternoon a fresh easterly breeze sprang up; the old lady suddenly declared that the sail was ready, and we started at 2.15 P.M., but only made seven miles before anchoring for the night.

Next morning the snow-storm was so heavy that the sailors would not leave their moorings, and we passed the time looking out of the window to see if there was a change of the weather, and in trying to stop up the cracks about the door through which the snow was driving. Our fireplace had not as yet proved by any means a success, and on thinking that the fuel was in fault we experimented on the Chinese mixture of coal and clay. The Chinese are too economical to burn coal alone, and mix coal-dust with a certain proportion of clay, making up round balls about as large as eggs. This burns well enough, and gives out a fair amount of heat; but it is, even in a house, a very unpleasant fuel on account of the dirt; and in our cabin, a gust of wind coming down the chimney, or a draught in an unexpected corner, used to blow this fine dust all over the room in clouds, and we came to the conclusion that we had not yet discovered a perfect fuel.

We were always moored at night in a crowd of vessels; and of a morning, when all was quiet, the whole place seemed to wake up suddenly. At six o'clock there was not a sound; but a few minutes later the crews of all the junks in the neighbourhood would arouse themselves with one accord. Then commenced the shouting and jabbering of all the people getting under way. Presently another junk would come against us with a violent bump, and threaten to carry away the chimney of our stove. This rouses the ire of our skipper and his crew, who all at once vociferate in the choicest terms that they can cull from their flowery language, the crew of the other junk returning the abuse; and amid the babel the shrill voice of the old lady is easily distinguished. Then it is our turn to run into something else; and so on, scraping and bumping, with all the timbers of the deck-house groaning and creaking, until we are clear of the crowd.

The Chinese used to think us very odd people; we never could sit in a room without a fire, although they never used a fire at all except for cooking, and were quite content to remain with windows and doors open, almost in the open air, trusting to their wadded garments and thick-soled shoes to keep them warm. They saw no harm in a gale of wind blowing in their faces; but we were always draught-hunting—stuffing in some cotton-wool here, pasting paper there, hanging curtains up, and taking an immense amount of trouble to keep out a little snow or a current of cold air; and as for our fire, we were perpetually fussing about it—if we found one kind of fuel did not burn, we were always worrying the servants to try something else, instead of doing without, like sensible people. Then they never cleaned their places—why should we?—but if we found an inch or two of harmless dust anywhere, or a pile of dirt in a quiet corner, nothing would satisfy us but having it removed. And notwithstanding all this, we, who felt the cold so much, were always taking off our clothes, and would in the morning sit, for no conceivable object, in a tub of cold water, instead of following their plan of keeping on the winter garments night and day, until the weather should begin to get warm. Then our clothes were preposterous—stupid, thin, tight-fitting affairs—as useless as they were hideous; no wonder we felt cold. We certainly did feel cold; but, notwithstanding the severity of the weather, we adhered to our national customs; and at length, by dint of perseverance, we made our room tolerably tight, and managed to keep up a moderate degree of warmth.

At the best of times, the scenery can scarcely be said to make this part of the river inviting; and we did not find much to regret in the necessity for keeping the windows covered. There was nothing to see but sloping mud banks, and a dead level beyond all white with snow; whilst a collection of miserable huts here and there, with a stunted and leafless willow, a few reeds, or bits of long grass, just appearing out of the white covering, only served to lend additional dreariness to the scene.

The 12th of February was the time of the Chinese New Year festival, which lasts about ten days. There was much feasting, popping of crackers, and beating of drums all the morning, and the people were so well amused they did not want to leave. We sent out at seven o'clock to know when they were going; they replied, 'Immediately.' At eight o'clock we wanted to know how long it would be before they started; they answered, 'No time at all.' At nine o'clock we said they really must get under way; they declared they were going to. At ten o'clock we threatened that they should have no New Year's present unless they moved at once; they sent back to say that we were just off. At eleven o'clock Baber ordered Hwu-Fu to go to our accompanying official; but they said he would be left behind if we let him leave the boat. At twelve o'clock we began to make a real disturbance, when they let go the mooring rope, and we went on to a place called Hua-K'ou. Here I asked our captain which way the wind was. She replied that the north wind was strong, but the east wind not so strong; by which she meant that it was about NNE., and made us almost think she had learnt mathematics, and understood the resolution of forces!

After passing the entrance to the Tung-Ting lake, on the 17th of February, we noticed that beyond this point the junk-traffic was very much less than lower down.

During the summer, the river overflows its banks and floods the surrounding country. There are extensive lines of embankment from one to two miles inshore, and all the villages are behind the inner line. This gives a dreary appearance to the landscape; and the traveller, walking for hours without seeing a village or meeting a human being, might easily be misled into the belief that he was in an uninhabited country. Nevertheless, there are a great many villages in the neighbourhood, which seemed in a very flourishing and well-to-do condition. The country was closely cultivated, the fields were protected by splendid embankments, and, as the snow had now all melted, the young crops coming up looked fresh and green.

It is a busy scene when a large number of junks are tracking together. Now an ambitious captain thinks he can shoot his vessel in front of another in-shore, and tries to pass his tracking rope over the mast-head of his rival. This excites the jealousy of the crew, and if the tracking ropes foul, or the junks bump together, it rouses their anger. The two captains then mount to the highest parts of the deckhouses, swear at one another, stamp their feet and shake their fists, both crews in the mean time shouting directions to the coolies on shore; but as they all talk at once, down to the smallest children, they are not generally very successful in making themselves understood. Then the confusion is tremendous; a track rope is unexpectedly tightened, and one or other of the vessels heels over so much that she is in danger of foundering. At last the junks shake themselves clear, but by pure good fortune, management having played a most insignificant part in the manœuvres. After they have been out of hearing of one another for some time the captains leave off swearing; but should accident again bring them together, the skippers at once mount to their elevated positions, and the commination service begins afresh. Although the trackers are often a quarter of a mile away from the boat, and at that distance the people on board naturally find it very difficult to make themselves heard, and though there is often such a crowd of junks whose crews are all shouting together that it would seem impossible for any coolie to distinguish the orders meant for himself, yet they never attempt to introduce a code of signals. It is customary, however, in the rapids, higher up the river, to use a drum, the coolies pulling as long as the drum beats, and stopping when it ceases.

There is a great bend between Last Bottle Reach and No Beer Channel,[1] where two points on the river are separated by a neck of land not more than three-quarters of a mile broad, the distance between them by the river being about fifteen miles. This neck must become more narrow each year, for the river sweeps down on to it at both sides. Blakiston represents it as one and a half mile across in his time. There can be little doubt that in a few years it will be cut through, and become the channel. Near this neck I could watch the movements of thousands of wild geese on a wide sandbank across the river. There were no people or boats on that side, but the birds appeared very uneasy. In their movements they put me very much in mind of swallows flocking at the approach of winter, and I wondered if they were preparing to leave the country before the hot weather. Every now and then they would get up with a great clamour, fly across the river, wheel round and round, and then return to the sandbank. They generally began calling just as they rose from the ground, but on one occasion they did not commence their hoarse croak until they were well in the air; and at the distance of about half a mile the simultaneous flapping of some thousands of big wings sounded like the report of a heavy gun very far away.

When we were favoured with a fair wind our crew would sit on the forecastle, eating, drinking, and talking incessantly, and 'whistling for the wind' just as European sailors do. On an occasion like this, when the breeze relieved them of their work, they used thoroughly to enjoy the unaccustomed treat of eating their meals in a leisurely manner. They would generally get up at a quarter past five, and roll up their blankets, and take down the framework and matting with which the front deck was always covered in at night. The start was usually effected immediately after this, and by seven o'clock the cook and cook's mate had prepared a gigantic bucket of rice and a few vegetables. The ship was then anchored for ten minutes, during which time the coolies would manage to eat each two or three basins of rice. In

[1] Names given by Captain Blakiston to these reaches.

the middle of the day, a quarter of an hour was allowed for a similar meal; but at night, when work was over, they could spend as long a time as they liked over their supper. Nine-tenths of the food of these coolies was rice boiled perfectly plain; they would eat some chopped vegetables with it, cooked in a great deal of grease; and when by chance we shot a gull, a crane, or other strange bird, it afforded them the rare luxury of meat; but the proportion of rice to all their other food was so large that the amount of grease they ate was not very considerable, though all their little luxuries, such as a bit of ancient fish, or a lump of fat pork, were cooked in large quantities of grease.

Rice is a food that is not well adapted for men doing hard physical work, except where it is so cheap that large quantities can be eaten at a less cost than a smaller proportion of more nourishing food; and, in travelling, it is very striking to note that the very day on which the rice-growing country is quitted, some other grain at once becomes the food of the people; rice is so bulky that even one day's carriage makes it too costly for any but the well-to-do. The grease eaten by the coolies, far from being an unaccountable taste, is an absolute necessity; no man can live without grease in some form or another, least of all those doing hard physical work on rice for their staple food.

About half our coolies were opium-smokers; but whether it was owing to the active life in the fresh air, or to the weakness of the drug they used, it did not seem to do them any harm.

Passing Sha-Shih we soon left the vast and monotonous alluvial plain of the lower Yang-Tzŭ, and were fairly in the hills. The ground was well cultivated, and the crops, which seemed to be growing by magic, were very green. Temples and pagodas here are perched on the highest points. Comfortable-looking farmhouses nestle in the hollows, surrounded by small bamboo copses. Children in the dirt, with pigs and dogs, play about the doors, where the women sit sewing and talking. On the hill-sides there are little clumps of cedars and firs, or patches of long grass; dog-violets are in blossom at the sides of the path, and the flowers of great fields of rape shine as brilliant streaks of yellow in the distance. The grand river, still half a mile wide, now clear and almost green, rolls below the cliffs of red sandstone, and numerous junks going up and down lend life and animation to the scene.

As we were sitting after dinner, with open windows, a man in a junk alongside said something I did not understand, when, to my astonishment, Baber took a header out of the window, and 'went for that heathen Chinee.' The man, however, escaped, and when Baber returned through the door, he explained that the object of his wrath had called us devils. Another man presently came, and resting his arms on the window stood calmly gazing at us. At last Baber politely asked him what he was looking at. Not in the least abashed, he quietly replied, 'I am looking at you sitting down'—an eminently matter-of-fact reply, very characteristic of the Chinese character.

On the 5th of March, as we were nearing I-Ch'ang, I took a walk inshore over the hills, about six hundred feet high. Directly the river is left, even by half a mile, the thinness of the population becomes apparent. Here the cultivation was only in the valleys, all the slopes and the tops of the hills being covered with beautiful long grass and low scrub. During a walk of more than two hours I scarcely saw a house, and did not meet half a dozen people.

After a time I returned to the river, and through a telescope saw the junk sailing away before a fresh breeze. I did not particularly wish to walk to I-Ch'ang, because I had heard that there had been some sort of disturbances there, and I had no wish to get into an unpleasant hooting crowd, if I could help it. So I told Chung-Erh to try and engage a boat. There was some difficulty about this, as all the boats belonged to fishermen, who did not care to do anything out of their accustomed ways; but I presently fell in with a small junkful of traders carrying cotton up to I-Ch'ang; they were very civil people, and took me on board. They looked at my gun and cartridges, for which they did not care much; but my telescope was a source of great merriment. They knew well enough what it was, though one and all completely failed to manipulate it. First one man took it, and the others eagerly asked him what he saw. After having pointed the glass steadily at the sky for some time, he answered in a doubtful sort of way that he could not see much; at which his friends jeered him, and made him give up the glass to the next man, who took it with a most superior air, as much as to say, 'Ah, just let me show you how to do it!' But after putting it out of focus, and looking straight into the bottom of the boat, he tried to see the inside of the telescope, and passed it on, with a shrug of his shoulders, distinctly under the impression that it was stuffed up. The third man, after I had again focussed it, chiefly poked it into the eyes of everybody else and knocked their hats off, at which he was voted a nuisance.

Then the evening closed in, and under the shelter of the straw covering we had tea, and smoked until we arrived at I-Ch'ang.

When I entered the cabin of our junk I was warmly congratulated on my safe arrival by a voice from a vast collection of opened newspapers. Careful search revealed Baber hidden in the product of three mails, and in answer to my question, he explained that his hearty reception was caused by my escape from the mob of I-Ch'ang, who at this time were very turbulent, so much so that the newly appointed consul had deemed it prudent to send out a strong escort to look for me.

I then learnt all the news. There was now a considerable European community at I-Ch'ang—the English consul and his Vice; the chief of the Chinese customs, with two assistants; the captain of a river steamer, who was up here to prospect, and three missionaries. The chief commissioner of customs had been the first to arrive, and after him the consul had come in the 'Kestrel,' to choose a site for the English settlement. At first they found the people civil and obliging; they were never annoyed in any way, and used to walk about anywhere and everywhere. The consul selected a piece of ground, made the necessary agreements, ordered the boundary-stones, thought that everything was comfortably settled, and was going to mark out the concession, when the aspect of affairs changed completely.

There was amongst the richer classes, and especially amongst the literati, a strong anti-European feeling. A report was spread that land was to be taken without payment, and other slanderous tales were invented by which the minds of the easily excited Chinese population were inflamed. One day, without previous warning, the consul was unexpectedly mobbed and insulted, and after that no European was able to walk on shore without an escort.

Such was Baber's news, and I heartily congratulated myself on the fortunate rencontre with the traders' junk.

Travellers' boat on Yang-Tzŭ, above I-Ch'ang.

CHAPTER V.

THE GORGES OF THE GREAT RIVER.

The I-Ch'ang Mob—Chinese Unreason—Departure from I-Ch'ang, and Adieu to English Faces—The Gorges Entered—Vicissitudes of Ascent—Scenery of the Gorges—Preparation for the Rapids—Ascent of Rapids—Yang-Tzŭ Life-boats—Dangers of the Rapids—View at Ch'ing-Tan—Ch'ing-Tan Rapid—Waiting our Turn—Pilots of the Rapid—Successful Ascent—Mode of Tracking—Long Gorge of Wu-Shan—Weird and Gloomy Aspect—Kuei-Chou-Fu—Method of Salt Manufacture—Extraordinary Richness of Soil—Chinese Skill in Agriculture Overrated—Their True Excellence is in Industry—St. George's Island—Cataplasm for a Stove-in Junk—The River of Golden Sand at Last—The Use of the Great Sculls.

WE were obliged to stop at I-Ch'ang for a couple of days. The vessels wanted recaulking, some fresh rigging was required, and, above all, a new crew; for the navigation of the Yang-Tzŭ above I-Ch'ang is very different from the simple tracking below, and the shoals, rocks, and rapids, some ot which are very dangerous, require a very skilful and practised crew.

The governor-general of the province had come up to arrange matters with our consul; but he went away two days after our arrival, either because he would not take the trouble to arrange matters, or because he was afraid of the responsibility of failure. No doubt he thought that things were going wrong, and in plain English his departure would have been called running away. When he left, of course all the people in the neighbourhood who had spare gunpowder let off guns.

At about ten o'clock the consul went ashore again with the Tao-Tai, attended by the other chief Chinese officials, and escorted by a regiment of braves. They were at once surrounded by a yelling mob: and as the officials and braves were quite unable to quell the disturbance, they retired to a temple, near which they succeeded in making prisoners of two men who appeared to be ringleaders, and these they carried off. When they were inside the walls of the buildings, one of the officials walked up and down, stamping and calling the people of I-Ch'ang by all the vile epithets he could think of.

The clamour outside now induced the officials to give up their prisoners, a concession which had much the same effect as a pot of Liebig amongst a pack of wolves. After a while a retreat was determined on; and the whole party returned to the landing-place, amidst a shower of dirt, stones, brickbats, and tiles. On the way the Tao-Tai lost his temper, and, stamping with rage, said to the mob, 'Here I am; why don't you kill me at once, and be done with it?' But the mob either had no reason in particular, or did not care to give one, and the party advanced without a reply to the question. The Tao-Tai still showed a bold front, until he was suddenly met by a hideous old woman with a ladle of filth; this was too much, for the awful nature of a ladle of filth in China can hardly be conceived.

When they again reached the shore, we could see the performance from our boat. About a hundred little boys led the procession hooting and shouting 'Foreign devil!'

Next came a dozen braves in red clothes armed with gingalls. The vice-consul followed under the protection of a gigantic brave from the north of China, with whose enormous strides he vainly attempted to keep step. After them the consul was walking with the Tao-Tai, who seemed rather glad to discard his red official canopy. Behind all was the howling mob; and the remainder of the braves were scattered about amongst the crowd.

The party regained the boats without a very serious butcher's bill: the vice-consul lost a button from his coat; and one of the braves was cut by a stone. He smeared the blood all over his face, and with this ghastly aspect rushed to the Tao-Tai and demanded an indemnity of ten taels.

There are no people more easily led than the Chinese, by those who have fairly established an influence over them; ordinarily, too, they are exceedingly respectful and obedient to authority. If instances were wanting, the way in which Gordon could do what he liked with his Chinese army shows how powerful in the minds of a Chinaman is the instinct to follow those who can lay claims to his fidelity. But it sometimes happens that in large towns some rich family may get more influence than the officials, especially if the latter are very corrupt or extortionate. This was the case at I-Ch'ang, where a family named Fu were believed to be the chief leaders of the people, and the instigators of the disturbance.

The Chinese are, moreover, eminently an unreasoning people; the movements of a mob everywhere are dictated rather by caprice than reason. It is very easy too to raise the devil of popular wrath, but it is generally a more difficult matter to allay it; and later, although it was supposed that the Fu family were desirous of doing so, they were quite unable to quiet the populace.

The extraordinary ideas that penetrate a Chinese mob of course help to make their conduct inexplicable. Here they had a notion that our consul was the brother-in-law of our queen, and agreed that, for that reason, it would not be proper to injure him. Although it is difficult to trace the logic in this reasoning, it shows the respect of the Chinese generally for high authority, even under circumstances where it would be least anticipated.

By the 8th of March the officials at length managed to effect some sort of compromise between the rioters and the Europeans, and the boundary-stones were successfully put up; after which the consul left for Hankow.

We saw the blood of the cock duly sprinkled on the bows of the boat, and our skipper and her crew were very busy making preparations: taking on board great quantities of ropes of all sorts and sizes, some of bamboo and some of hemp. Strong stanchions had been put up on the gunwale on both sides, to act as thole-pins for large strong oars. Then the forward rudder was arranged. This is a very strong oar, some forty feet long, which projects thirty feet beyond the bow. At the inboard end ropes are fastened, so that some half-dozen men can assist in the steering; and thus a very powerful steering apparatus is formed.

I-Ch'ang seemed to be a cheap place for cabbages, for the crew brought on board an enormous cargo. There is a peculiarity in the market of I-Ch'ang that I never heard of elsewhere; for the price of things never varies, but when they are dear or cheap, there are more or fewer ounces to the pound!

Before leaving we found a carpenter who was able to fix glass into the windows of our cabin, and as we succeeded in buying a couple of panes we very much increased our comfort.

On the 9th of March all English faces were left behind, and from this time until my arrival at Bhamo in November I saw no European save my travelling companions and the French missionaries. With many a hearty shake of the hand we said good-bye to the customs officers. At 7.30 the mooring lines were let go, and as the entrance to the gorges loomed before us, we seemed to have cast loose the last rope that bound us to civilisation.

After having been so long slowly winding up the tortuous reaches of the river, gliding through the alluvial plain, where there is scarcely anything to relieve the monotony of the landscape, the sudden change in the scenery that appears beyond I-Ch'ang is very striking.

The river soon narrows to a width of from four to five hundred yards. Steep spurs from mountains three thousand feet high run right down to the water's edge; their sides, wherever they are not absolutely perpendicular, covered with long orange-brown grass, that seems to grow almost without any soil. On the more gentle slopes terrace cultivation is carried on—little patches of the most brilliant green, sometimes a thousand feet above the river, and looking almost overhead, showing the presence of some industrious farmer, who will not leave a square yard uncultivated if he can help it. Sometimes the hills are broken into precipices, rising three hundred feet sheer up from the water, beneath which the river runs with a glassy surface; at others there are loose piles of *débris* or gigantic masses of rock strewn about the bed, where the water dashes in wild confusion. Now and then a cleft in the hill-side discloses a tiny stream leaping from rock to rock amongst ferns, long overhanging shrubs and brambles. Once the steep slopes running up a thousand feet were crowned at the top by a grim wall of white cliffs three hundred feet high and about a couple of miles long; and, looking up a valley, pine forests could be seen on the northern slopes of the snow-capped mountains.

Nor is it the change in scenery alone that causes a feeling of strangeness, but the mode of travelling itself combines to give a sense almost of bewilderment. Now there is no foothold for a goat at either side; the trackers come on board, and we have to row, five oars on each side pulled by ten lusty coolies, shouting to encourage themselves and mark the time. With each stroke of the sweeps the boat creaks and shakes, and from cliff to cliff, before and behind us, are echoed the regular cries of many boatmen, all urging their vessels against the rapid stream. Suddenly the cadence ceases, a confused babel of tongues swells in loud disorder, and, looking out, we find the trackers are being put ashore, the crew of every boat struggling to get before that of another. Every man with a different idea about the way something ought to be done, and proclaiming it as loud as he can, tries to shout down all the rest. The noise increases, and seems to peal from one end of the long reach to the other—when suddenly all on board is still ; we glide smoothly along, not a plank or a beam giving out a note of straining—but away ashore, quite softened down by distance, we still can hear the regular cry of the coolies, as, keeping step, they draw us quietly along. Now the towpath comes to an end, and the coolies must again come on board, but this time in a sampan, as here the vessel cannot run ashore. Now we cross the river to a path that runs up till the trackers look right over the mast-head. But one thing is never wanting at a critical moment, nor when the wild chorus of shouts is at its loudest ; for above the din, whatever it may be, the shrill tones of the old woman at the stern rise in hideous discord.

In the afternoon we made fast to one of the big rocks lying about, near some level ground in the bed of the river, where people living in a few small temporary huts were doing a little trade by selling odds and ends to the boatmen who stop here to rest. Stepping ashore we find little choice in the walks. There is but one path, and that soon leads to a zigzag track up the mountain-side. We follow up, but every now and then lose it, and have to clamber about with hands and feet from one rock to another, till we unexpectedly come upon a hut, perched on a tiny artificial plateau, surrounded by a few bamboos, orange trees, and a fir or two. Our sudden appearance startles a couple of fowls, who rush off cackling to a safe refuge by the fire inside. The never-absent dog comes out to see what is the matter, and does not cease barking until our retreating forms disappear behind some gigantic rock. Up we clamber, our protecting minions from the gunboat puffing and panting as they wonder why the mad foreigners want to be always going uphill. At length we reach a projecting point, where a bit of flat rock gives us a comfortable seat, and almost underneath us, a thousand feet below, the river, dwarfed by the distance, looks no more than fifty yards wide. To the south and west, the hills rise in masses one behind another—

mountains backed up by mountains, higher and yet higher, one giant leaning lovingly on the shoulder of the next, till, as we gaze towards the setting sun, with the eye of fancy, we can see them, range beyond range, stretching far over the borders of the Chinese empire, and at length culminating in the mighty peaks of the Himalayas.

In the afternoon of the 11th we reached the lower end of the Ta-Tung rapid, where we anchored and awaited our turn to ascend.

In the mean time the usual bamboo tracking line was cast off, and a strong hempen one substituted, and our old skipper, after much talking, concluded a bargain with the extra coolies required to help us up the rapid.

At the foot of all the serious rapids there are a number of temporary shanties erected—temporary, for the ground on which they stand is under water during the floods of summer. Coolies who come up here for the winter and spring live in these, and make a livelihood by assisting the ascending junks to pass the rapids, for a large junk may require an extra hundred of coolies to haul her up. Amongst these hired coolies there is always one who, owing to his skill, is a person of such importance that he is often saluted with an explosion of crackers when he first comes on board.

At length our turn arrives. We have now only five men left on the forward deck; four of these, picked for their nerve and experience, stand to the forward steering apparatus, and the fifth squats down with the drum between his knees. All give one anxious glance round to see that everything is right; the signal is given, the drum is beaten with a regular cadence, the coolies ashore shout as the rope tightens to their pull, and in a moment we are in the rapid. The water boils and foams about us, and leaps now and then up at the bow as if it would engulf us; but we steadily ascend; inch by inch we make our way; the coolies ashore attending carefully to the signals given by changing the cadence of the drum.

Now it is interesting to watch the movements of the agile

coolie who was received with so much respect. He seems to combine the activities of a goat and a fish. The bed of the river is strewn with granite boulders, some as large as a small house ; the tracking line catches in an uncompromising corner of one of them, in an instant the naked coolie—for he has disembarrassed himself of every shred of clothing—is at the top, and the line is clear. Now, behind a ledge of rocks, there is a backwater, and he has to swim across it to disentangle the rope from the mast of a fishing-boat anchored in the rushing torrent ; and again, active as he is, he is on shore only just in time to save the rope from another rock.

Little by little, though it seems slow work, the end is approached. At last, after three quarters of an hour, we pass the two hundred yards, and glide round a rock into a pool of still, calm water, where our coolies receive the congratulations of their friend, and we anchor for the night.

As we were looking straight up the Niu-Kan gorge a glorious mountain towered above us in the distance, seeming double its real height from the clouds that hung around its sides and left only its summit clear against the sky. Cliffs two hundred to three hundred feet high bounded the river on either hand, the hill-sides glowed in the rich colouring of browns and deep orange reds, and the huge boulders lying about gave a savage grandeur to the scene. The people here call the river the Ta-Cha-Ho, which means the river of lees or dregs—a most appropriate name, for the whole bed is strewn with *débris* brought down from the far-distant mountains.

On arriving at the foot of the next rapid, a very ominous sight presented itself to us. Stranded on a rock, with the water boiling and foaming around it, was half of a junk, which, coming down the river four days before, had driven her stern on to the pitiless ledge. In a very short time the furious stream had broken off the fore part of the vessel, and left the remainder an object of terror to the superstitious sailors. No lives were lost, and the greater part of the cargo was saved ; but the grim and shattered relic, with a coil of rope and a bundle of cabbages still lying on the after-house, formed a warning to rash navigators in the dangerous rapid.

To make the scene more thrilling there were a couple of life-boats paddling about close in amongst the rocks. These are not life-boats in our sense of the word, as to floatation,

Mouth of Niu-Kan Gorge.

but they are as to saving life. Strongly built, they are manned by a picked crew of six soldiers,[1] and stationed at the dangerous places, to rescue any unfortunates from a wrecked junk that may be struggling in the water. The boats are painted red, and have some characters written on

[1] The Chinese make little distinction between sailors and soldiers.

them. The men wear the usual blue trousers, blue tunic, and the blue Ssŭ-Ch'uan turban. Over the blue tunic there is a yellowish drab coat without sleeves; and on the front and back of this is a white circle inscribed with characters in red, indicating the company or camp to which the men belong.

They seemed to manage their boat in a quiet sailor-like fashion, and paddled steadily beside us as we went up. When once the junk was absolutely in a rapid our crew also worked very quietly; there was then always one guiding spirit, and, until we had safely passed, everything was left to his judgment. But the moment the danger was over, the shouting and noise began again, every one trying to make up by louder vociferation than usual for the few minutes of enforced silence.

Ascending a rapid in a big boat is in fact an operation that requires the very nicest skill and judgment and the most prompt and ready obedience to the smallest signal given by the commander. The very slightest error, or the smallest delay in executing an order, would often be fatal, and bring about a serious accident. The old lady never attempted to take charge under these circumstances, but generally the chief of the coolies she had hired at I-Ch'ang was in command, though on some occasions a pilot came on board with the extra coolies at the rapids.

Often the vessel will be driven violently ashore, or on to a rock, by an eddy, and to deaden the shock a simple kind of buffer is used. This is a very powerful spar on the starboard side, loosely lashed to a stanchion on the bulwark. When in use the forward end is pushed a long way in front of and below the bow, and the united strength of three or four coolies, at the inboard end of the spar, takes the first shock and lessens the concussion of the boat, though often, notwithstanding this, the blow is very violent.

When we looked out on the morning of the 13th, the steep slope of the Ch'ing-Tan rapid, the worst of all the rapids on the Yang-Tzŭ, was swelling and foaming almost under our bows. All night long we had heard its roar and rush, and now it seemed as if it were impossible for any boat to ascend it. Rocks cropped up in most unpleasant places, a broad sheet of white foam extended right across, and the very fish were jumping and leaping in their efforts to ascend.

Our accompanying official, Sun, sent to say that he had no intention of risking his valuable life in any boat up that awful torrent; and that we had better follow his example, and not only walk up ourselves, but send our valuables also by land. We, however, came to the conclusion that all our goods were equally valuable, and that unless we regularly unloaded the ship we could do little good; and as for ourselves, we determined that the excitement of going up was worth any risk there might be. We thought, too, that if we remained on board the people might be more careful than if we went ashore.

There was a long time to wait before our turn came, and we watched a small junk make several attempts to ascend before finally succeeding; whilst a crowd of people gradually collected who had come to see the unwonted sight of two foreigners going up the rapid.

The shore was strewn with gigantic boulders, amongst which knots of Chinamen in their blue cotton clothes sat and stood in every conceivable attitude; some were perched on the tops of the rocks, others at the edge of the water were catching fish about the size of sprats, and little ragged and dirty boys had arranged themselves in artistic groups that Murillo alone could have painted. A steep bank rose up thirty feet, on which the town was built; but the level ground was so scarce that the houses were obliged to seek extraneous aid, and support themselves on crooked and rickety-looking piles. Beyond towered the giant mountains above an almost perpendicular wall of rock that rose many hundreds of feet straight up from the river.

The ship was now lightened as much as possible by the removal of some of the heavy cargo, and all the morning was occupied in laying out warps. One, four hundred yards long, led straight up the rapid; and two other safety-ropes were made fast ashore, so that if the first and most important should have parted, we should have merely glided back whence we came, always provided that we did not strike one of the vicious-looking rocks whose wicked heads rose above the foam.

Just at this time a little sampan with two rowers and a helmsman came down, and it was really a fine sight. As they entered the broken water the boat disappeared altogether from view, and the fearless yet anxious look of the steerer was quite a study. A couple of seconds, and they were through, and floating in the smooth water below.

Presently a most important functionary came on board, a serious-looking man, with a yellow flag, on which was written, 'Powers of the water !! a happy star for the whole journey.'

This individual must stand in the bows and wave his flag in regular time; and if he is not careful to perform this duty properly, the powers of the water are sure to be avenged somehow. Another method of softening the stony hearts of these ferocious deities is to sprinkle rice on the stream all through the rapid; this is a rite that should never be omitted.

At this rapid it is necessary to take a pilot, and at three o'clock the chief pilot and his mate came on board. They were gentlemanly-looking men, dressed in light grey coats, and they gave their orders in a very quiet but decided manner. The pilot's mate was certainly the most quiet and phlegmatic Chinaman I ever met; but these men have to keep their heads uncommonly cool. Directly they came on board our crew became very silent, with the exception of one hungry-looking coolie, with a pair of breeches so baggy that he looked as if he could carry about all his worldly goods in them; but the severe looks thrown at him by the rest soon silenced him, and he seemed to subside into his capacious nether garments.

Just as all was ready a most ill-mannered junk put its head into my bedroom window, smashed it in, and threatened to do the same to the whole side of the deck-house. She was, however, staved clear, and eventually all damage was rectified with some paper and the never-failing pot of paste.

At half-past four our bows entered the foam. Everything creaked, groaned, and strained; the water boiled around us as we passed within a couple of feet of a black and pointed rock. The old ship took one dive into a wave, and water came on board at a rate that very soon would have swamped her; the drum was beaten and the flag waved; ashore the coolies (nearly one hundred of them) strained the rope, and their shouts could be heard above the roar of the foaming torrent; one line parted, and gave the vessel a jerk that made her shiver from stem to stern; but in ten minutes we were through, and anchored safely in smooth water.

Our small junk followed without much difficulty; the boat of our protector Sun received no more damage than the loss of her rudder; and our gun-boat, a handy affair, making very light of it, we all at last found ourselves together above the dreaded spot.

Ropes were then to be coiled down, and our junk made shipshape, before starting afresh and sailing through the Mi-Tsang gorge.

This is one of the most striking of all the gorges in the Yang-Tzŭ. Huge walls of rock rise up perpendicularly many hundreds of feet on either hand; the banks are strewn with *débris*; and where a gully or ravine opens up, nothing is seen but savage cliffs, where not a tree, and scarcely a blade of grass, can grow, and where the stream, which is rather heard than seen, seems to be fretting in vain efforts to escape from its dark and gloomy prison. A fair breeze took us through the gorge, and we anchored for the night at the upper end.

The coolies fasten themselves to the tracking line in a very ingenious manner. They wear a sort of cross-belt of cotton over one shoulder; the two ends are brought together behind the back, and joined to a line about two yards long. At the end of this line there is a sort of button or toggle, with which one half-hitch is taken round the tracking rope. As long as the strain is kept up, it holds; but if the coolie attempts to shirk his work, and slackens his line, the toggle comes unhitched, and his laziness becomes apparent to his comrades and to the overseer or ganger who superintends the work.

The ganger is armed with a stick, and it is his duty, by shouting or gesticulating, to excite and encourage the men. He rushes about from one to another ; sometimes he raises his stick high in the air over one of them, as if he were going to give him a sound thrashing, but bringing it down he gently taps his shoulders as a sign rather of approbation than of wrath. When all the coolies are harnessed, they walk forward swaying their bodies and arms from side to side, and shouting a monotonous cry to keep the time. Sometimes the path where they can track is only twenty or thirty yards long ; then as soon as a coolie arrives at the end he casts himself off, runs back to the other end, fastens himself on again, and begins pulling afresh.

The Wu-Shan gorge, which we entered on the 16th and did not escape from until the 21st, is twenty miles in length, being the longest on the river. In one part of this wild chasm in the limestone rocks I noticed that on the left bank the strata stand in an almost vertical position, and on the right are inclined at an angle of 45° below, turning over to a horizontal position up above.

On looking at these gigantic masses, which by some unknown force have been thus torn apart, it is easy to see that it is by some wonderful convulsion of nature, and not by the steady disintegration of a running stream, that these deep rents in the mountains have been formed.

The gloomy aspect of the gorge, shut in as it is by high limestone mountains and precipices, where vegetation was scarce, and where a narrow streak of dull leaden sky was all that could be seen above, was enhanced by the solitude in which we now found ourselves, for we scarcely saw another vessel. There was something weird and mysterious in that long silent reach, where there seemed to be no room for life, and it was not difficult to understand how the superstitious fancies had arisen that had attached some mystical fable to almost every point. In many places there are in the face of the rock innumerable long vertical grooves ; the surface of these is highly polished by the action of the wind and weather, and they look exactly as if they had been scooped out with a gigantic cheese-scoop. In other places the rocks are split up vertically into long needles and stalagmite-shaped masses.

The city of Kuei-Chou-Fu, which lies at the western mouth of the gorge, is surrounded by a very good wall, in much better condition than that of most towns. It is well situated on the slope of a high hill, and there are a good many suburbs, some permanent, and built on the high ground. But a very large population live in temporary huts of matting set up on the shingly beach. These are removed in the summer, as the river rises and covers all the ground on which they are built. Kuei-Chou-Fu is the seat of considerable trade, and at the time of our visit there were a great number of junks at anchor off the town. We found provisions here more plentiful than at any place we have visited since leaving I-Ch'ang, and were able to buy excellent vegetables and very indifferent beef and mutton.

A very large revenue is derived from the salt manufacture which is carried on at brine pits situated about half a mile below the city, on both sides of the river, where on low, sandy, shingly banks, close to the water's edge, holes are dug. The water finds its way into these through the soil, becoming in its passage impregnated with salt, but not strongly, for the taste of salt in it is scarcely perceptible.

Bricks are made from the salt earth in the neighbourhood, and with these dome-shaped ovens are built, having a door in front, and a hole in the top, in which a shallow iron pan, K, is placed. On the top of the oven, and concentric with the iron pan, a hollow in the brickwork makes a narrow trough, A C D B. Above the back of the oven, at E F, the wall is covered with, and made up of, cinders, slag, and earth. The brine is first poured into the narrow trough at A, and, running slowly round the top of the oven, discharges itself at E amongst the cinders, slag, and earth at the back. It permeates easily through these into the back wall of the oven itself, G H, and amongst the bricks of which it is built. Here the heat drives off the water, and leaves the salt deposited on and in the bricks.

After ten days or so the, fire is let out, the back of the oven pulled down, the bricks from it carefully removed, and the oven built with fresh bricks.

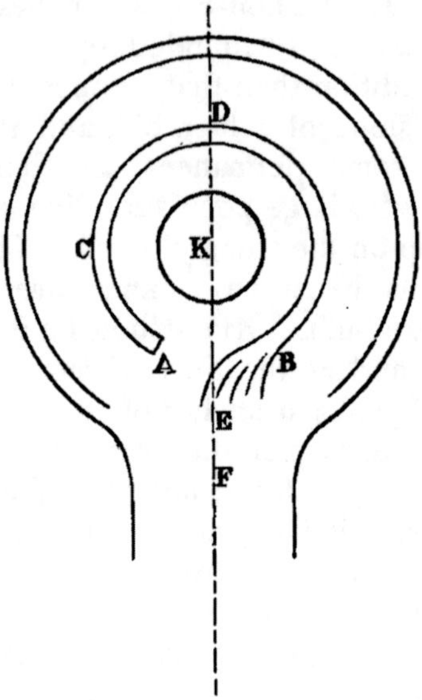

The stuff that has now been taken out is broken with hammers and stones, and put into a large wooden bucket; more brine is thrown into this mass, which seems to be dis-

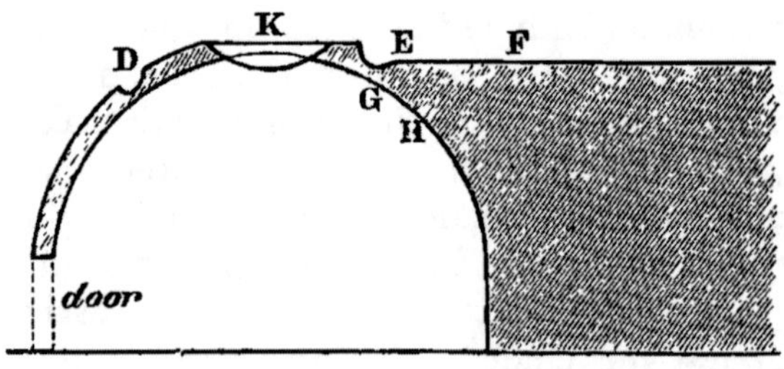

integrated by it, and now breaks up, forming with the water and the brine a black substance of about the consistency of freshly-made mortar. The water is poured from the bucket into the iron pan at the top of the oven, where it is evaporated, and very good salt produced.

We found the people at these pits extremely civil, very few troubled themselves about us, and our numerous and minute questions were patiently and politely answered. It is said that there are forty pits here, and that each pit produces one hundred catties (130 lbs.) of salt a day; this would make 890 tons of salt per annum.

The Government buys all the salt at a rate fixed by itself, and then sends it over the country for sale, making an enormous profit. I subsequently learnt from a banker at Ch'ung-Ch'ing that the salt in the province of Ssŭ-Ch'uan brought to the Government a revenue of six millions of taels annually—roughly, two millions sterling. The profit comes to about eighteen cash a pound, and, at the rate of 1,600 cash to a tael, this would make the annual produce of salt in this province 237,946 tons, an amount that seems almost incredible.

It may be well to record here the process of manufacture which I had previously seen in operation in the desolate salt-marshes near the coast in the north-east of China.

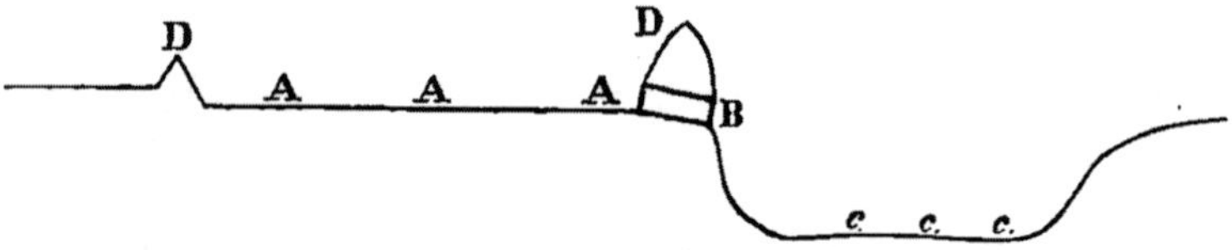

A A A. Tank where the earth is placed; B. Small drain; *c c c*. The receiver or hollow scooped out to receive the liquor draining from A; D. Earthen ridge.

A ridge of mud, six inches high, encloses a space twelve feet by four feet. At one end a little drain is formed by piercing the ridge, and a hollow is scooped out in the ground below the drain. The earth in the neighbourhood is all strongly impregnated with salt, and lumps of it are put into the tank formed by the mud enclosure. Fresh water is poured in, which drains slowly into the hollow, and in its passage becomes a strong solution of salts. The water is then boiled three times in flat circular dishes, and, by this successive evaporation, the different salts are thrown down at different temperatures, or by the varying strength of the solution. Common salt, or chloride of sodium, being the most easily held in solution, is not deposited until the final operation, and thus salt of more or less purity is obtained.

The process of evaporation is carried on in little circular enclosures of straw, to prevent the wind disturbing the surface of the liquor; and in the neighbourhood the whole plain is dotted with these queer-looking erections. Further on I shall have to explain a third system of Chinese salt manufacture.

We had now left the gorges, and the gentle slopes and open valleys of Ssŭ-Ch'uan, which province we had now fairly entered, were a pleasant change after having been so long shut up in the deep recesses where we could seldom see more than a narrow strip of sky.

The richness and verdure of this part of the country is almost inconceivable; the soil is bright red, and, where fallow, presents a delightful contrast to the fresh green of the young crops. The rape was now in flower, and field upon field of brilliant yellow rose one above the other. The terrace cultivation of rice occupied the bottoms of all the valleys, with patches here and there of wheat or beans. The houses looked comfortable and substantial, each enclosed in a clump of bamboo; handsome temples stood by themselves in groves of trees. Every here and there a species of banyan (without pendants) standing by itself, with perhaps a little niche underneath for burning incense in, was a graceful ornament to the landscape. All these combined to present a scene of richness and fertility that I have seldom seen equalled, and which fully justified the praise that has been lavished by travellers on this beautiful province. And more striking than all is the fine open countenance of the people, who, though very independent, are undoubtedly the most pleasant and gentle of all the people of China.

Notwithstanding the industry of the Chinese and their admirable system of irrigation and terrace cultivation, there can be very little doubt that the exceedingly high estimate in which their agriculture is held is very far from being deserved. This appears to have been derived from the French missionaries, for, as early as 1804, Barrow speaks of the way in which it had been overrated; nearly all moderns who have been in China make the same observation, and yet there remains amongst Europeans out of China the conviction that the Chinese possess secrets unknown to, or unguessed at, by Europeans.

The real point in which the Chinese excel is in industry. It is industry that leads them to take such care never to waste the smallest trifle; and it is industry that makes it worth their while to gather up the last fragments. Industry again enables them to dispense with any other manure than the sewage of the towns; for a peasant will walk into the town, fetch his manure, and take it to his field himself. It is by industry that in the large plains the Chinese are enabled to keep their rice fields properly watered; for it is not possible to conduct the water by canals to every part and every level of a wide plain; it must therefore be lifted artificially, and all day long coolies are to be seen in the extensive plains raising water by the means of little tread-mills.

But beyond their industry the Chinese can hardly lay claim to any superiority over other nations. They plough about as well as the natives of India, doing little more than scratch the ground. It is true that they can raise two crops on the same field—as, for instance, when they plant opium under rape, or yams beneath millet. But this is a system not altogether unknown to European farmers, and in the West Indies it is customary to grow yams underneath the sugar-canes. Some of Barrow's remarks appear to be worth quoting:—

'They have no knowledge of the modes of improvement practised in the various breeds of cattle; no instruments for breaking up and preparing waste lands; no system for draining and reclaiming swamps and morasses.

. . . .

'Levelling the sides of mountains into a succession of terraces is a mode of cultivation frequently taken notice of by the missionaries as unexampled in Europe and peculiar to the Chinese, whereas it is common in many parts of Europe. . . . Of the modes practised in Europe of improving the quality of fruit they seem to have no just notion. . . . Apples, pears, plums, peaches, and apricots are of indifferent quality. . . . They have no method of forcing vegetables by artificial heat, or by excluding the cold air and admitting at the same time the rays of the sun through glass. Their chief merit consists in preparing the soil, working it incessantly, and keeping it free from weeds.'

Thus wrote Barrow three quarters of a century ago. The Chinese are no further advanced than they were in his time; and it is hardly necessary to add anything to his remarks, except to observe that not only have the Chinese 'no just notion' of improving the quality of fruit, but that to this day they remain in complete ignorance of the science of grafting. To those accustomed to the appearance of European countries, the absence of hedges is at first sight strange; but in this country, as in many others, people recognise their own property by the divisions in the fields; and even where there are no marks, one man will rarely attempt to plough beyond his own land: boundary-stones to properties are, however, usual. It is not to be supposed that disputes never arise, but when they do they are generally, or almost always, settled by the people of the place.

In navigating this portion of the river, it is continually necessary to cross and recross from one bank to the other, partly to save distance by cutting off the angles of the numerous sharp bends, partly to get into the back eddies and avoid the current, and partly because it is often impossible to track on one side, while there is a fair path on the other. It is this that constitutes one of the chief difficulties of the navigation, and leads to most of the accidents. The junks are always rowed across towards some place where a landing is practicable. As a rule there is scarcely any room to spare, and unless the exact point is gained, the swirls and eddies that often run violently amongst the reefs will drive the vessel against a rock. Amongst these tides it requires the greatest skill and nicety to shoot the junk exactly to the desired spot, and it is under these circumstances that vessels are often wrecked or damaged. During the day we met with two accidents in this way; on the second occasion a big hole was knocked in our ship, which as usual was repaired with cotton-wool and paper.

Although in our walks we had frequently noticed little patches of opium, we had not seen it hitherto in any considerable quantity; but near the city of Fu-Chou we saw it growing in large fields.

The river was so low that when we arrived at the north end of St. George's Island (so named by Captain Blakiston), not only was there no passage inside it, but a reef, rarely visible, was now plainly to be seen beyond. Our small boat, and that of our official, made no attempt to pass inside this reef; but our people, seized apparently with a fit of temporary insanity, thought that, though our junk was much bigger and drew more water than the others, they would try the inner passage. So, as we were sitting in our room discussing the probability of our arrival that night at the city of Fu-Chou, there was a sudden bump that nearly shook us out of our chairs, followed by a babel of tongues, in which as usual the shrill and jarring voice of the old woman was painfully audible. Rushing to the window we found the tracking line adrift, and the vessel spinning round like a top; then the scrunching and grating sound of the junk dragging herself over some sharp rocks was immediately followed by the sudden irruption of three or four coolies into our room, who, without any preliminary remarks, moved the furniture, lifted the floor boards, jumped into the hold, and taking all our boxes out, hastily passed them up to other coolies outside.

Looking down we now saw a large stream of water running in through a hole in the side of the boat, and we comprehended what had occurred. We had not, however, much time to alarm ourselves, for we were fortunately able to run on to a bank of mud before the vessel filled and sank, which she inevitably would have done in a very few minutes.

After having cleared the hold, the men set to work baling with buckets, and gradually succeeded in reducing the water, after which they repaired damages. They first put on a kind of cataplasm of whitey-brown paper, mud, and grains of rice,[2] over which they nailed a piece of wood, and stuffed the interstices with cotton-wool and bamboo shavings. As, of course, when the hole was made the planks were driven inwards, this patch was put on inside. The operation was a long one, and, extraordinary as the method may appear, it eventually proved tolerably effectual, although, from the amount of baling that was always subsequently necessary, Baber suggested that our vessel should be called the Old Bailey.

We spent the afternoon walking round the island, and found some of the gold-washers, who above this are always seen in the sand and shingle beds washing for particles of gold. The quantity these men obtain is so small that it can repay none but a frugal Chinaman for the labour. Here the river is known as the Chin-Sha-Chiang, or River of Golden Sand, and this name is applied to it at least as high up as Bat'ang.

In these upper reaches it is often impossible to track, and the method of propulsion is by oars, or in some big junks by a very large scull, one on each side of the vessel. All the time that the coolies are at this work one of them chants a long story in time with the strokes, and at each stroke all the others join in a chorus of 'Hey-yea.' This will go on for ten minutes, when the story will end, and all will sing together, 'Yoi hai ay-a.' The tone is continually varying, but the chanting either of the story or the chorus never ceases. The method of employing the gigantic scull is quite unique. Every country uses it on a small scale, but I never heard of huge vessels being propelled in this way elsewhere. In any harbour in England dirty little boys may be seen sculling out of the stern of a boat. The Venetian gondolier also puts into practice much the same principle; but here huge junks, of some hundred tons burden, may be seen with an enormous scull on each side, worked by as many as twelve or fifteen men. These sculls are sup-

[2] The Chinese use a great deal of rice in this way. I have seen a kind of concrete for building purposes made of mud and rice grains.

ported at the fore part of the ship on a short outrigger, at the end of which there is a very short pin. This pin fits into a cup-shaped hollow in the scull, and, acting like a ball-and-socket joint, just keeps the scull in its place. The men stand in a row, fore and aft, facing the water. At the end of the scull there is a strong leathern thong, which, fastened down to the side of the junk, keeps the end of the scull moving in a circle. This method, which is in fact an application of the principle of the screw, is no doubt the most economical way of applying the strength of the coolies; it is more frequently seen in use on junks coming down than on those going up the river, for in ascending there are such frequent changes to be made—sometimes tacking, sometimes laying out ropes, and only occasionally rowing—that these large sculls are not so convenient as oars; but in descending, when the middle of the stream is always kept, when rowing or sculling is the only method in use for driving the vessel, and when the whole crew is always on board, then the large scull is found the most suitable method of working the ship.

Road-side Joss-house.

CHAPTER VI.

CH'UNG-CH'ING TO CH'ÊNG-TU-FU.

Arrival at Ch'ung-Ch'ing—M. Provôt, Monsgr. Desflêches, and the French Missionaries: Their Cordiality—The Last of our Lady-Skipper—We are satirised in verse, and enabled to see ourselves as others see us—News of Tibet—Unfavourable Change of Feeling in Tibet as to Admission of Europeans—Difficulties of Mr. Baber's Photographer—Preparations to start for Ch'êng-Tu—Elaborate Coolie Contract—Chinese Commercial Probity—Baggage Arrangements—Adieu to Baber—Good Manners of Ssŭ-Ch'uan Folk—Jung-Ch'ang-Hsien—Characteristics of a Restaurant—Coolies at their Meal—Realistic Art—Want of Ideality in Chinese Character—

The Brine Town of Tzŭ-Liu-Ch'ing—The Christian Landlord—The Brine-wells and Fire-wells—Mode of Boring and of Drawing the Brine—Further Details and Out-turn of Salt—Politeness of the People—Red Basin of Ssŭ-Ch'uan.

EARLY in the morning of the 8th of April we reached the outskirts of the great city of Ch'ung-Ch'ing; and, passing through a crowd of junks of all sizes, we hauled up to a position under the walls, where we very soon received a welcome batch of letters and papers. The Chinese merchants have an excellent postal system of their own: they arrange amongst themselves to send couriers or runners on foot at regular intervals, who travel very fast, and generally very securely. In this case the letters had been only fourteen days from Hankow, about six hundred miles by road. During the whole time I was in China I received every letter and newspaper sent me, except one letter, and that had been forwarded *viâ* Russia!

Soon afterwards Monsieur Provôt, one of the French missionaries, came to pay us a visit—a tall pleasant man, dressed in Chinese clothes, and with an artificial plait, for the missionaries in China invariably discard foreign clothes. He said that all sorts of conjectures had been rife about us amongst the Chinese. He asked Baber when he was going on to Yün-Nan; and, turning to me, said he hoped that I should like living here. When he saw that we did not exactly understand the remark, he explained that it was the general opinion that Baber had been appointed a consul in Yün-Nan, and that I was to be consul at Ch'ung-Ch'ing. We hastened to undeceive him; but even the missionaries could hardly believe in a gentleman travelling for his own amusement without any commission from the Government; the Chinese certainly did not.

In the afternoon we received intimation that Monseigneur Desflêches, the Bishop, was coming to pay us a visit. He was a small vivacious man, and a true Frenchman; he was most genial, and his expressions of delight and compliments to Baber knew no bounds. 'Ah, Monsieur Baber, it is you at last. How you are welcome!! Here is a grand thing that you have done—ah! it is indeed a victory. Yes!

yes ! a victory indeed. See how at last we have this great river opened to foreigners, thanks to you and your Government.'

Nothing could have exceeded the sincere cordiality of his welcome.

Probably besides missionaries there were not more than twenty or thirty foreigners who had ever been here, and the arrival of a real consul, accredited by the English Government, was naturally a glad event to the missionaries. But, for all that, we could not but feel it a pleasure to be so warmly welcomed, and received with such true and hearty friendship. The Bishop talked for a long time; first he told us about his flock, his converts, and his trials, of which he made very light, dreadful though they had been; he praised the English and the English Government, and declared that our country was the only one in which there was any real religious liberty. He naturally expressed great pleasure that war had not broken out between China and England—'for,' he said, 'if it had, we should all have been massacred here.'

The old lady who commanded our vessel came in afterwards with her child, and, kneeling on the ground, burst into a flood of tears, declaring that she was the most miserable and unfortunate woman in the world; that she was a lone widow, with no one to take care of her; that every one conspired against her; that she was no match for the wicked people by whom she was surrounded; and although she felt she had gained a high distinction by being allowed to bring our honourable selves up here, still her misfortunes had been many, and she was out of pocket by the transaction; and in pathetic tones, she expressed her hopes that our noble and honourable excellencies would not allow her and her orphan child to die of starvation. As a histrionic performance it was certainly creditable, the old woman having extracted from us half as much again as any Chinaman would have paid her. With a tongue so fierce and foul that it inspired awe if not respect, I could imagine no one better able to look after Number One.

Baber having found a house ashore, we said good-bye to

our ship, in which we had lived nine weeks. Our goods were first of all moved, and after everything had gone we followed in chairs. The coolies carrying the chairs bustled along at a great pace up the steep and dirty steps; three soldiers were in front to clear the way; nevertheless a good number of little boys followed, trying to lift the blinds and peep in; but there was no hostile demonstration of any kind. Besides the officials, the people of this province are mostly either merchants or agriculturists, the literati—that generally highly-favoured class in China—being held in light esteem by the men of Ssŭ-Ch'uan; and to this is probably owing the fact that foreigners are always treated with great politeness, as wherever opposition to foreigners is carried to any great extent, it will generally be found to be owing to the influence of the literati class. There were of course some literati here, and so good an opportunity of showing their talents was not to be lost. So they wrote a poem in very bad rhyme, which Baber translated and headed, 'As others see us':—

AS OTHERS SEE US.'

The Sea-folk, once a tributary band,
In growing numbers tramp across the land:—
English and French, with titulary sounds
As of a nation, are the merest hounds!
Nothing they wot of gods, in earth or sky;
Nothing of famous dynasties gone by!
One of their virgins, clasped in my embrace,
Told me last year the secrets of their race,
Taught me the foulness of the Western beast,
And, fouler still, the foulness of the Priest.
I know their features, Goblins of the West!
I know the elf-locks on their devil's crest!
Cunning artificers, no doubt, but far
Beneath our potency in peace, or war!
But now our opportunity is near;
Learning and valour are assembled here;
Let all to the cathedral doors repair,
Grapple the dogs, and never think to spare!
I rede ye right! shall savages presume
To harry China and escape the doom?
No! Let us all with emulous might combine
To crush the priests, and save the Imperial line.
First slay the Bishop, tear away his hide,
Hack out his bones, and let his fat be fried;

And for the rest who have confessed the faith,
Drag them along, and roast them all to death!
For when these weeds are rooted from the plain,
No magic art can give them life again.

The author begins by inquiring why foreigners should come to China; and though he shows an unusual amount of knowledge by stating that the French and English are different people, yet he denies nationality to either one or the other, who, he adds, are all mere dogs, and ignorant of the true religion. In the sixth line he refers to the features of foreigners, which all Chinamen consider worse than hideous. Foreigners are usually also credited with red hair, which, in their eyes, is an abomination; hence the reference to elf-locks. The author exhibits unexpected discrimination in crediting foreigners with being cunning artificers; Chinese generally think, or pretend to think, that we are ignorant of everything. In the eighth line, reference is made to the approaching examinations, when thousands of literati and students for degrees would be assembled at Ch'ung-Ch'ing. The last line refers to the popular belief that foreigners can after death return to life; and, once more showing more knowledge than might have been expected, combats this belief.

Monsieur Provôt had received a letter from Monseigneur Chauveau, Bishop of Ta-Chien-Lu, who said that a report had spread all over Western China and Tibet of the expected arrival of British and Russian missions at Lassa; that this report had caused a most profound sensation; that the Lamas were urging the people to refuse admittance to foreigners, and that forces were assembling on the frontier.

There can be no doubt that a great change has come over the feelings of the Tibetans since the days when Bogle visited their country and was so well received. There are two causes that may have combined to make the Tibetans afraid of Europeans. First, our power in India has so enormously extended that the Tibetans say, with much justice, 'Wherever an Englishman comes he soon possesses the country; once we let an Englishman enter ours, we shall lose it.' The second adverse cause is the presence of the missionaries. In the time of Bogle there had been few attempts on the part of these to approach Tibet, and in those days the Lamas had no fear of foreigners upsetting their power and their religion. But since then there have been many missionaries on the borders; and these being the only foreigners the Tibetans know, they naturally fear for the supremacy of their faith.

In the days of Bogle and Manning, and even as late as the time of Huc, it appeared that among the Tibetans themselves neither Lamas nor people offered any objections to the approach of Europeans; but that all the opposition, great as it was, came entirely from the Chinese officials. Since that time, however, it would appear that the Lamas, who absolutely rule the people, have conceived a violent hatred of foreigners, and have arrived at a determination to exclude them by every means in their power.

The town of Ch'ung-Ch'ing is built so crookedly, and with such tortuous streets, that the people are compelled to use the terms 'to the right,' 'to the left,' in giving directions about the way to any place. Ordinarily, in China, the towns are built with a certain amount of regularity, and the people say 'go north,' or 'go south,' &c. They become so habituated to this that, even out in the open country, they use the same expression, having, as a rule, not the most remote conception as to where the north point really is. This custom has had the effect of impressing on foreigners generally a most exaggerated belief in a Chinaman's knowledge of the points of the compass.

We went for a walk one morning on the other side of the river, and took the photographer with us and left him to his own devices. When we returned home he told us that the people had thrown stones and bricks at the camera. He said that his attempts had not been very successful. The Chinese people believe that foreigners make a juice out of children's eyes for photographic purposes; they say, 'A man, or a dog, or a horse cannot see without eyes; how then can that machine? If it has not got eyes of its own, it must have the eyes of somebody else.' Their logic is unanswerable, especially the brickbats and stones. The next time that Baber's photographer essayed his art, he went out under the guidance of a fat Christian, Mê by name, who could talk to the people in their own dialect—the photographer, who was a Shanghai man, finding the language of Ssŭ-Ch'uan quite unintelligible. Mê returned triumphant from the joint expedition; his part of the business had been satisfactorily accomplished; but the photographer's efforts can hardly be said to have been crowned with success. He could not show us much except some clouded glasses, and I never heard that any pictures were subsequently achieved.

I now began to make preparation for a journey to Ch'êng-Tu, the capital of Ssŭ-Ch'uan.

There are no mules in this part of the province, and it was therefore necessary to look for coolies; but, as I was able to send most of my goods by water, I did not require a great number of carriers. I had to buy a chair also for myself to ride in, because, in this province, a chair is the usual means of locomotion; and to have travelled otherwise would not only have been against the inexorable law of custom, but would have entailed a loss of dignity that might have been inconvenient. After I had once started, however, I rarely rode in the chair, except when entering or leaving a large town; in the country I invariably walked, or rode on a pony. The chair was, nevertheless, invaluable for carrying a few things in, for with four coolies, and no one riding in it, it could always travel very fast, and in the plains could even keep up with me when I was walking, so that when I arrived at my destination, the chair was seldom far behind, and I had not to wait an interminable time for all the odds and ends, writing and drawing materials, &c., &c., that I wanted immediately.

In a large city like Ch'ung-Ch'ing there was no difficulty in finding any number of coolies, and Chin-Tai soon found a coolie-master willing to provide for all my wants. An elaborate agreement that would have refreshed the heart of a lawyer in Chancery Lane was now drawn up between this coolie-master and myself: detailing specifically what I might and what I might not do; the places at which we were to halt, and how long we were to stop at them; and the extra amount to be paid, in case I wilfully delayed on the journey. The coolie-master on his side pledged himself to use all reasonable care and forethought for the safety of my goods, and to arrive at places specified within a certain time. But, unlike English documents, this charter, once drawn up and verbally agreed to by the coolie-master and myself, required neither witness nor signature; but, being confided to the depths of my pocket, was as valid, according to Chinese usage, as the most formal document that ever issued from Lincoln's Inn.

This confidence that people in China have in one another is a feature in the character of the people that has been strangely unnoticed by foreign writers. Merchants in China rely implicitly on one another; indeed, if they did not, all business would come to an end at once. In my position I was over and over again compelled to trust the Chinese with large sums of money without receiving any receipt, and in other ways to rely on their probity to a far greater extent than I should have trusted Europeans, or Chinese if I could have avoided it. But I was never deceived in the smallest degree, nor did I lose anything during all the time I was travelling. Of course if I had set my wits against those of the Chinese I should have been taken in continually; and if I had tried to drive bargains, I should certainly never have succeeded. A Chinaman, if he is selling anything, will always ask as much as he thinks he can get, even if he knows it to be ten times the value of the article. But amongst the respectable Chinese there is a strong feeling of commercial morality. It probably arises, not from any natural inborn virtues, but from the necessities of the case; for there is no reason to suppose that the Chinese race forms an exception to the general rule of humanity, the heart of which is declared to be by the highest Authority 'deceitful above all things, and desperately wicked.' If a Chinese weaver adulterated his silk, it would be known at once, he would be a marked man, and his trade would cease. If the English manufacturer never sold his goods at a greater distance than one hundred miles from his doors, it is probable that he also would find the advantages of honesty in his policy. Necessity is not only the mother of invention, but the origin of all custom ; and custom in time becomes, not law, but something even more binding.

When I called to say good-bye to the missionaries, I found that they were firmly persuaded that political missions from every quarter were being poured into Tibet, and that Baber and I were connected in some mysterious manner with the inscrutable purposes of these expeditions. When I assured them that I had nothing whatever to do with Government or Government missions, and that I was a private individual travelling for my own objects, they smiled incredulously, as if unwilling to be thought simple-minded enough to believe so foolish a story ; and, even with the proverbial politeness of Frenchmen, they could hardly help showing that they thought Albion was as *perfide* as ever ; and if reasonable Europeans could not believe it, how could it be expected that the Chinese would ? In fact, they never did ; from first to last I passed for an important official on some secret service, and was invariably treated as such.

On the 26th of April everything was at length ready for a start, and I found coolies sitting about, waiting for their loads to be adjusted. A chair that I had bought was now fresh from the painter and decorator ; there were, besides, small chairs that were hired for the servants, and a pony about eleven hands high was ready to be saddled. Twenty coolies sufficed for my luggage ; besides these there were four coolies for my chair, four for the chairs of the servants, and one man, who glorified himself with the title of Ma-Fu, with the pony.

With a hearty shake of the hand I said good-bye to Baber, whom I hoped to see, in the course of a few weeks. Without this expectation I should not have parted with a light heart from one who had been a cheery companion for so many weeks. But 'Dieu dispose,' and I still have to look forward to the pleasure I hoped for so long ago.

I started in my chair, and as, with the exception of a short ride in the city, this was the first time I had tried this method of progression, I found that dignity and discomfort were in about equal proportions, for, to one unaccustomed, the motion, especially in hilly countries, is very disagreeable. When I was well clear of the town I descended, and found walking preferable. The road ran for some distance by the side of the river, winding about amongst hills five hundred to a thousand feet high, sometimes shaded by hedges of pomegranates from the sun, which was now becoming powerful. The hill-sides were dotted with the white-walled Ssŭ-Ch'uan farmhouses in their clumps of bamboos, looking the very emblems of peace. Yew trees often sheltered fine large graves, and here and there we passed one of the small

Grave near Chung-Ching.

religious shrines which Europeans call joss-houses.[1] Everything was very green, fresh, and, as nearly all the rice-fields were under water, there was very little dust. The coolies in the fields were busy at work raising water from the lower to the upper terraces, sitting under the shelter of big umbrellas; and from the top of a hill these looked like a number of gigantic mushrooms dotted about over the plain below.

Every day I was more impressed with the gentleness of

[1] See illustration, p. 82.

the people. After having been accustomed to find myself universally regarded as a fair and legitimate object of ridicule and wonder, it seemed quite strange to be able to come in of an afternoon and sit down to write for a couple of hours quietly before dinner. In many places in this part of the country I was left as much alone as I should have been in England—certainly much more so than a Chinaman, in his long coat, long plait, queer shoes, and huge spectacles, would be in any English market town.

At Jung-Ch'ang-Hsien, a town which we passed through on the 29th, I had the misfortune to rest at a hotel where the number of travellers was so great that the place appeared to be a small city.

The travelling Chinaman, when he has arrived at his destination, usually divides his time between eating, drinking, smoking, and sleeping; he seldom enjoys any excitement, not from lack of power so much as from want of opportunity. The afternoons and evenings of these people must be appalling in their monotony, and melancholy illustrations of the truth of Talleyrand's prophetic warning to the young man who did not play cards.

It would have been unreasonable to expect the three or four dozen inhabitants of this inn to miss so rare an occasion of amusing themselves, and such an expectation would have been completely falsified. My door, therefore, was soon blocked up with stolid gazers, and the somewhat unsavoury air that had previously entered entirely excluded.

A little further on I turned into a tea-shop for breakfast, and sat down at a table, on which there were about half a dozen cups with a pinch of tea at the bottom of each. The boiling water was poured into one of them immediately, and the refreshing draught was ready as soon as it was cool enough for my pampered throat. One of the waiters went round the room every five minutes or so and filled up the cups with boiling water from a huge kettle. While my breakfast was being cooked I looked round. The tea-house, open along the whole length of its front, faced the road, but a wooden wall, coming down from the roof to within seven feet of the ground, kept out the heat and glare; and a thick straw matting, projecting from the top of the open part, cast a grateful shade across the road, tempting the voyagers to stop and have a dish of tea. As I sat facing the front, a short, benevolent-looking old man, with a grey beard and mustachio, stood behind a counter at my left. At his back there were a number of small square drawers, and above these some porcelain jars and bottles contained the various ingredients for preparing his savoury dishes. Some big wooden tubs for rice or grain were at his side, and a little child holding his hand joined in the gaze of wonder that some coolies, leaning against the front of the counter, bestowed on me, as over their trivial pipes they discussed my remarkable appearance. The cooking-place was on my right, with a smoke stack passing out through a hole in the roof. The centre of the room was occupied by small square tables, and there all my coolies were having their breakfast, and enjoying the unwonted treat of plenty of time to eat it in. That they found this a luxury I could guess from the way in which some of them dallied with their beans before commencing serious operations on the rice, instead of shovelling the latter down in the fashion of the boat coolies on our old junk. The people here seemed very fond of broad beans roasted. I watched several of the coolies commence their meal with a dish of these; one man in particular took them up one by one with his chopsticks, and chose them carefully from his little dish with the air of a *gourmet* who feels that, having plenty of leisure, it will never do to throw away the opportunity of playing the epicure. Directly on my right, and near one corner of the room, a huge tub, kept warm by steam, contained the rice (boiled in some other place); and while I was looking on, a coolie came in with a fresh tub, taking away the other, which had just been finished. An attendant dips a large wooden ladle into the steaming tub, and takes out the rice; with an artistic turn of the wrist he puts it into a bowl about as large as a small slop-basin, and, giving it a dexterous pat, the clean white grains are piled up in a smooth and regular dome above the edge of the cup. This tub of rice gives plenty of work to the attendant. Another coolie demands a second portion. In an instant the waiter fills a bowl, walks quickly to the customer, and transfers the contents to the other cup without dropping a grain. The scene is full of life: the busy attendants with their bowls of rice, or pots of boiling water; others cooking, and more taking away the bowls and dishes that have been used. All the time coolies on their journey pass in front to and fro at the quick, half-walk, half-run, sort of gait they adopt. Now a big chair, with red outside, and an official hat fastened behind, followed by a man with a red umbrella, proclaims an official of some importance; but the drawn blinds prevent my seeing what he is like. Now a very small and shabby two-coolie chair comes along, with a fat Chinaman half asleep and stupid with several hours of this unpleasant motion. Perhaps the coolies stop here for their food; but the sallow Chinaman sits stolidly without moving until they have finished. Most of the people at this time of day pass the tea-house, but some turn in for a little refreshment; and others, walking straight to where a tub of cold water is standing, rince out their mouths, and proceed on their journey. As a counterfoil to all this busy activity, across a field, I can see, about a quarter of a mile away, a clump of bamboos lazily waving their tops to the gentle breeze, and sheltering a house the roof of which just appears above a hedge of pomegranates and brambles. This is backed up by a fine clump of firs and willows, standing in bold relief against the liquid blue of a range of hills in the extreme distance.

The P'ai-Lou, or triumphal arches that are so frequent in Ssŭ-Ch'uan, are generally of stone, and on the superstructure at the top are elaborate carvings in relief; these are most artistic in their execution, and represent officials administering justice, and various other scenes of domestic and public life, in which the expr ssions of the faces are caught with a wonderfully sympathetic spirit, and delineated with a masterly hand.

Yet in everything there is the Chinaman's want of ideality; his carvings represent nothing but what he has absolutely seen over and over again with his own eyes; he is quite incapable of forming an idea of anything beyond.

His pictures are the same : insects of life size, magpies on willow trees, bridges, ponds, and hills, all realised, but with not enough imagination in the whole to produce even perspective. Even in the representation of Hell we saw the other day there was no imagination. The demons were people such as themselves, with painted faces ; and the tortures such as might be inflicted by their own officials. Of Heaven they have no idea, and that they never try to conceive. Everything they do is material and realistic, and imagination does not exist in their nature. From imagination springs the power of inception, or, in other words, originality ; and, as might be expected, or rather as must follow by a natural sequence, the Chinese are remarkable for their want of originality. In the course of ages, as the necessity arises, as population increases, and life becomes more difficult, the law of the survival of the fittest may come into play, and the reign of intellect begin. But at present, with the want in the national character of the power of inception, they must be for a long time to come dependent on the aid of foreigners.

I came from Marseilles to Hong-Kong with two Chinese who had been to Europe to learn European naval tactics, European ship-building, and European navigation. They were returning to their country no doubt highly instructed and much benefited ; but one of them, by the permission of the captain, who wondered greatly, copied the log of the ship carefully every day. He was under the impression that if he should ever take a ship from Marseilles to Hong-Kong he would be able to do it by carefully sailing the same course.

On the 2nd of May, after a journey of seven days, we came in sight of Tzŭ-Liu-Ching, famous for its immense production of salt. Approaching this town the number of tall scaffoldings around it at once attracts the notice of a traveller : some right on top of the hills, others on the sides, and a few close down to the river. At a distance they look just like the tall chimneys of some manufacturing town in England. The town is prettily situated on the river, which is about one hundred yards wide, and is here bunded back ; its banks are steep, and run straight up to little hills about two hundred or three hundred feet high, where, as the cultivation is not very close, there is a great deal of fresh green grass.

The inhabitants of this neighbourhood have the reputation of being very rude, but I nowhere in China found more civil people. The town is a wretched place, and its people bear all the indications of their miserable poverty. I had what seemed an interminable ride through narrow and more than usually dirty streets, all of them staircases of the steepest and worst description. The shops were very inferior, and the only novelty I remarked was a Chinaman sitting in an easy-chair. As a rule, a Chinaman sits in the usual high, stiff, straightbacked chair, so painfully familiar to any European who has penetrated into these regions. I never before saw anything like a lounge, but here there were low chairs with sloping backs, and a semi-circular projection to fit into the neck, very like the cane chairs so much in use by Europeans in Singapore or Ceylon. Amongst the Chinese, none but very old men use them, and a youth would be guilty of the most gross disrespect who should seat himself on an easy-chair, or even loll about on an uneasy one.

My sedan-chair was put down for some minutes in the middle of the main street; a few woe-begone-looking people and children with pinched faces came to look, but seemed to take but little interest; and when we moved off and turned into a bye-lane, not a dozen people thought it worth while to follow me to the inn.

This was really a fine building, with three courts separated from one another by strong gates. I had a capital room, opening on to a yard where there were a few flowers. The surrounding rooms were occupied by respectable well-to-do people; and the quiet of the place was most delightful after the noise and hubbub that there is usually in the courtyard of an inn, even when a crowd of men and boys are not fighting for a look at the foreigner. In most inns in this part of China the front court is more or less of a restaurant; people are continually coming and going, coolies shouting, customers quarrelling with the landlord about a cash, itinerant vendors of patties and cakes shouting out their wares, all at the top of their voices; while here there was nothing but the croak of the bull-frog, and the distant bark of some unquiet dog, varied by the low hum of conversation in an adjoining room.

I found the dogs about here more savage than the ordinary Chinese cur, who usually beats a speedy retreat at the motion of picking up a stone. But there was a sense of independence and a democratic spirit about the dogs of this neighbourhood. They had no respect for anything, not even for good blood; and the life of poor Tib, whose valour was not equal to his breeding, was made very burdensome to him.

The landlord of this inn was a Christian, or, as Chin-Tai put it, 'he liked the French Joss.' He expressed great pleasure at seeing me, and, after my dinner, came to pay me a visit. Our conversation soon descended into the trivialities usual under similar circumstances. I asked him if he knew what was the annual produce of salt. 'Oh, yes,' he said, 'a great deal.' 'But how many catties?' I continued. He thought that there would be a vast number. But did he not know what number? Yes, for there were a great many people always at work. 'But how many pits are there?' I said, trying another tack. He thought that there might be a thousand, but of these a large proportion were not working.

He then looked at all my things, asked what everything was for, and, above all, he wanted to know the cost of each. Amongst my dressing apparatus there was a relic of European travel that could hardly be considered a *sine quâ non* in China, a railway key. He asked Chin-Tai what it was. Chin-Tai was quite equal to the occasion, and I was much interested at the readiness with which he evolved out of his own inner consciousness a long and elaborate dissertation on the uses of an article of which by no possibility could he have known anything.

Eventually, when his curiosity was satisfied, I extracted from him, after much cross-examination, that salt went from here to I-Ch'ang, Ch'ung-Ch'ing, and Kwei-Yang-Fu, but not to Ch'êng-Tu-Fu. He told me that the people were wretchedly poor, and said that no foreigner had been here before except the French missionaries, who always dress, talk, and travel as Chinese. Before going away he informed me that he liked my cigars and my claret, and hinted that a small quantity of either one or the other would be a welcome gift.

Next morning he came again to take me to see his salt wells, for he was part proprietor of a very extensive establishment. We crossed the river by a good bridge, and after partaking of the inevitable cups of tea we proceeded to the works. Here some of his people were engaged in boring one of the holes; this was already 2,170 feet deep, the average rate of boring being, if all went well, about two feet a day; but they said that they often broke their things, that accidents happened, and that it was thirteen years since this well had been commenced.

The jumper for boring is fastened to a bamboo-rope attached to one arm of a lever; the weight of three men who step on to the other arm raises the instrument, the men then leap nimbly off the lever on to some wooden bars fixed for the purpose, and the jumper falls. Another workman stands at the mouth of the bore, and each time the jumper is lifted he gives a slight twist to the rope; the rope untwisting gives a rotatory motion to the jumper. This operation is continued all day, the coolies employed showing the most extraordinary and untiring activity.

A few yards off was a finished fire-well, somewhat deeper than the one in progress; a bamboo-tube about three feet long had been put into the mouth of this boring, and some clay was plastered over the upper end to prevent the bamboo from burning. Up this well, and through the bamboo, the gas ascends from the bowels of the earth, and is lighted at the top; when the light was extinguished the odour of the gas was very powerful of sulphur, and very slight of naphtha; the latter smell was imperceptible when the gas was burning.

At no great distance was a brine-pit, which, I was informed, was two thousand and some hundreds of feet in depth, and about three inches, or perhaps a little more, in diameter at the top; immediately over the mouth was erected a scaffolding a little over a hundred feet high. To draw the brine from this well, a bamboo-tube, a hundred feet long, open at the top and closed at the bottom by a valve, serves as a bucket. A rope, fastened to the upper end of this, passes over a pulley at the top of the scaffolding and round an enormous drum; this drum, turning on a vertical axis, was eight or nine feet high, and about twenty feet in diameter. Four buffaloes are yoked to this, and thus the rope is wound up. Near the end the rope is marked with bits of straw, like a lead-line on board ship, so that a man watching knows when it is near the end, and warns the drivers. The process of raising this bamboo once, occupied ten minutes. There is a driver to each buffalo. The bamboo being raised from the well, a coolie pushes the end over a receptacle, opens the valve with his fingers, and allows the brine to escape. When the water has been let out, the buffaloes are unyoked, and the bamboo and rope descend of themselves. This sends the drum round with a frightful velocity, which, in rotating, of course produces a violent wind. The 'break' for this is simplicity itself—a few strips of bamboo pass horizontally half round the drum, and both ends are made fast to the wall. These strips hang quite loose, until a coolie, leaning against them, tautens them up, checks the pace of the drum, and stops it in a very few seconds. The brine thus raised is conducted to the evaporating-pans over the fire-wells I had already seen.

In this establishment, by no means the largest in the place, there are employed forty coolies and fifteen buffaloes, the latter in a stable kept beautifully clean (a most remarkable thing in China). They produce here 8,000 to 10,000 catties (10,000 to 13,000 lbs. avoirdupois) of salt per month; the proprietor pays no duty, but sells it for eighteen to twenty cash a catty (½*d.* to ¾*d.* per lb. avoirdupois); the purchaser then sends it away by coolies, paying duty at the barriers, 300 cash (13½*d.*) per coolie-load, whatever that happens to be—it generally runs from about 160 to 200 catties (210 to 260 lbs. avoirdupois).

In some places they have the fire without the brine, and

at a place about five miles up the river there is brine but no fire; the brine is therefore brought down from here in boats, of which I counted about one hundred lying by the bund constructed to keep a sufficiency of water in the river for these vessels.

At the top of the hill, close to the town, there is a fire-well without any brine. The principle of the pump being unknown, the method of raising the water is the clumsy and laborious one of a row of small buckets passing round two wheels, one at the bottom and the other at the top of a tower, of which there are a good many about in different directions. A blindfold mule going round and round at the top is the motive power. The water is thus raised twenty to thirty feet at a time, a trough leading from the top of one to the bottom of the next tower. In this case the brine was lifted seven stages before it finally reached the fire.

Some years ago some Chinese connected with a European firm attempted to introduce pumps. They only had their heads broken for their pains by the coolies, who declared that their labour was being taken away from them; since this no further innovations have been attempted. Baron Von Richthofen states that these wells are lined with tubes of cedarwood. I did not see any lying about, nor was I told of them; but my interpreter was nothing but a servant, and it was difficult to obtain technical information. Baron von Richthofen also states that when a portion of the rock is mashed, clear water is poured into the hole, and the turbid water raised by a bamboo-tube.

The number of pits in this place must be greater than the thousand hazarded by the innkeeper. The produce of a thousand would be from fifty thousand to seventy thousand tons per annum; but as Tzŭ-Liu-Ch'ing must supply from a third to a half of the salt manufactured in the province, and as, according to the statistics of the Ch'ung-Ch'ing banker, that amounts to 238,000 tons, the out-turn at these wells must be from 79,000 to 119,000 tons—from 1,200 to 2,300 pits would be necessary to furnish that quantity.

I found that the people of Tzŭ-Liu-Ching entirely belied

their bad reputation. I stood about the fire-wells for a couple of hours without being pressed upon in the least; and I never saw people anywhere with a more respectful demeanour.

The incidents of the remaining part of the route to Ch'êng-Tu scarcely call for narration. We travelled pleasantly along through what Baron von Richthofen calls the Red Basin of Ssŭ-Ch'uan—and a most appropriate title it is. The formation here is a layer of dark red clayey sandstone; and wherever the soil is bare the ground is of a rich dark red-brown colour. The tops of the hills are nearly all on the same level, some three hundred or four hundred feet above the river. On their upper slopes there is a good deal of wood and coarse grass; and the bright green of a kind of low thorn contrasts pleasantly with the deep red of the clay. In the bottoms of the valleys, which are tolerably flat, all the ground is cultivated; but the formation does not seem well adapted for rice. The villages and towns were scarce, the country-houses less numerous, and the traffic on the road was not nearly so great as during the first few days after leaving Ch'ung-Ch'ing.

Man-Tzŭ village, near Wên-Ch'uan-Hsien.

CHAPTER VII.

A LOOP-CAST TOWARDS THE NORTHERN ALPS.

Ch'êng-Tu to Sung-P'an-T'ing.

Arrival at Ch'êng-Tu—Public Examinations—Arrangements with Mr. Mesny—Pleasures of French Society—Proposed Excursion to the North—The Man-Tzŭ, or Barbarian Tribes—Leave Ch'êng-Tu-Fu—The Escort—Irrigated and Wooded Country—Halt at Kuan-Hsien—Frantic Curiosity of People, but no Incivility—Irrigation Works—Coal-beds—Hsin-Wên-P'ing—Wên-Ch'uan-Hsien—First Man-Tzŭ Village—Pan-Ch'iao—Traces of War—Relentless Advance of Chinese—Miraculous Sand Ridge—Hsin-Pu-Kuan—Rapid Spread of the Potato—Excursion to Li-Fan-Fu in the Man-Tzŭ Hills—Scenes that recall the Elburz—Carefully-made Hill Road—The 'Sanga' of the Himalayas—Village of Ku-Ch'êng—Peat Streams—Musk Deer—Arrival at Li-Fan-Fu—The Search for a Man-Tzŭ Village—Man-Tzŭ here a Term of Reproach—The I-Ran Tribes and their Language—Return to Hsin-Pu-Kuan—Resume Valley of Hsi-Ho (or 'Min River')—Wên-Ch'êng—The Himalayan Haul-Bridge in Use—Polite Curiosity at Ma-Chou—Grandeur of the 'Nine Nails' Mountain—The Su-Mu, or White Barbarians—Alpine Scenery—Tieh-Chi-Ying—The Yak seen at last—Glorious Mountain View (Mount Shih-Pan-Fang)—Ngan Hua-Kuan—

Delicious Tea—Smoking in Ssŭ-Ch'uan—Country of the Si-Fan—Sung-P'an-T'ing—Reports of Game—Crops—Butter, Fish, Yak-Beef—Bitter Alpine Winds—Foreign Remedies Appreciated—The Traveller quits the Valley ('Min River') and turns Eastward—Si-Fan Lamassery—Herds of Cattle and Yaks—Desolate Hospice at Fêng-Tung-Kuan—Tibetan Dogs—Reported Terrors of the Snow-Passes—Summit of the Plateau of Hsüeh-Shan—Descent begins—Forest Destruction—Verdure of Eastern Slopes—Splendid Azaleas—Slaughter by the Si-Fan—Luxuriant Gorges—Miracle-Cave—Hsiao-Ho-Ying—Iron Suspension Bridges—Mauvais Pas—Lung-An-Fu—P'ing-I-Pu—Boat Descent of River (Ta-Ho)—End of Excursion.

WE entered Ch'êng-Tu on the 9th, at a somewhat unfortunate moment, for the examinations were now being held. These always bring thousands into the capital from every part of the province; and, in addition to this, the provincial governor-general was just leaving, and a new one being installed. Consequently, the city was full of Fu-T'ais, Chen-T'ais, Hsieh-T'ais, and T'ais of every description, not to mention the lesser lights of Fus, Chous, and Hsiens. Every hotel was crowded, and after hunting up and down the town Chin-Tai had only been able to get a place in an exceedingly dirty inn outside the east gate. The walls were hung with cobwebs of the blackest description. There was a bedstead with some carving at the top, the interstices in which were nearly filled with dust and dirt; bits of string hanging from the beams had nearly lost their original character from the coating of filth that had accumulated on them, and every gust of wind brought down a shower of dirt from the roof on to my head. Under the bed I dared not look. This unwieldy piece of furniture had probably stood there for years, and, according to Chinese custom, whenever the room had been swept during that time, the sweepings had been left underneath it. To clean the room would have taken at least a couple of days, and to have half cleaned it would, by stirring up the accumulated abominations, only have made matters worse.

When at Shanghai, I had been in communication with Mr. Mesny, an officer in the service of the Chinese. He ultimately arranged to join me at Ch'êng-Tu, and subsequently travelled with me to Bhamo; and to his intimate knowledge of the language and ways of the people, I am mainly indebted for the friendly relations we always maintained with the Chinese officials. At present, he was still buried in the depths of the province of Kwei-Chou, although I was under the impression that he was well on his way to Ch'êng-Tu, and expected him every day. Hearing nothing of him, however, I determined, instead of waiting idly for him in Ch'êng-Tu, to make an expedition to Sung-P'an-T'ing. The trip was sure to be an interesting one; no European, not even the missionaries, had ever been to Sung-P'an-T'ing, and it was almost on the borders of the Koko-Nor district.

Paying a visit to Monseigneur Pinchon, the Bishop of Ch'êng-Tu, I found it a delightful change from my own company to that of some half-dozen lively Frenchmen. The mode of the meal, as they put it, was *moitié Chinoise, moitié Européenne*; one missionary was eating rice with chopsticks, and cracking jokes with a Chinese minister who also sat at table; another was washing down a Chinese dish with a glass of Tinto, which, contrary to usual custom, was taken in my honour. Excellent bread was on the table, for wherever a Frenchman is found there is sure to be good bread; and Chinese dishes succeeded others that might rather have come from the Boulevards than from a kitchen in Ch'êng-Tu. The meal passed very pleasantly, and afterwards I spent the greater part of the afternoon in the delights of hearing a familiar tongue. The Bishop informed me that Li-Fan-Fu, a place which I proposed to visit on my way to Sung-P'an-T'ing, was inhabited by the Man-Tzŭ—or Barbarians, as the Chinese call them; a people who, amongst other pleasing theories, were possessed of the belief that if they poisoned a rich man, his wealth would accrue to the poisoner; that, therefore, the hospitable custom prevailed amongst them of administering poison to rich or noble guests; that this poison took no effect for some time, but that in the course of two or three months it produced a disease akin to dysentery, ending in certain death.

Monseigneur Pinchon advised me to take my food from Ch'êng-Tu, and to avoid the temptations of feasting as a guest of this singular people. This superstition is almost an exact parallel to one related by Polo as in vogue amongst a tribe in Western Yün-Nan (*vide* Yule's 'Marco Polo,' 2nd ed. vol. ii. p. 64). It may be doubted, however, whether much more of the custom remains than the tradition.

There are altogether eighteen of the Barbarian tribes spreading over the west of Ssŭ-Ch'uan. Each tribe has its king—one of them a queen—and they live almost entirely by agriculture and cattle-keeping. The king usually derives a considerable revenue from his lands, and every family in his kingdom has to send one man for six months to work on his estate. In other cases he receives an annual amount of eggs, flour, or wheat from each household. He has absolute power over all his land, assigns certain portions of it to certain families, and, if they displease him, or he has any other reason for doing so, he displaces them at once, and puts others in their stead, all the houses and farm-buildings passing to the new comer.

One of these royalties, that of Mou-Pin, was at this time distracted by disturbances—a civil war, bandits, robbers, soldiers, and evils of every kind. The king had died not long previously, leaving a wife with three daughters, and a sister-in-law, who set herself up as the protector of an illegitimate infant son. There was at once a disputed succession, for, by the law, a female could not sit on the throne. The sister-in-law and the wife both wanted the ruling power. The sister-in-law succeeded in stealing the seal of State. She obtained some boy, who was permitted to go and pay his respects to the widow as sovereign, and who, while making his obeisance, managed to snatch the seal and escape to the sister-in-law.

A war then broke out, some people taking part with the queen widow, and others with the sister-in-law. As usual in such cases, all the bad characters flocked to the place to feed on the booty; both the queen widow and the sister-in-law were obliged to take refuge in Ch'êng-Tu, and now the whole kingdom was given over to pillage and the villanies always accompanying a civil war.

After spending a day or two in completing arrangements, I sallied out of the north-west gate of the city on the 18th, with eight baggage coolies, besides the usual chair coolies, and four Ting-Chais, or official messengers, furnished for my protection and guidance by the magistrate. I proceeded in great state with my four satellites, who shouted to every one they met to get out of the way. Perhaps a poor man would come staggering along with an enormous load on a wheelbarrow, just where the track for these machines was very narrow, but where there was plenty of room for me at the side. Nothing, however, would satisfy my gentlemen, unless he cleared right out of the course; and once, when one of these unfortunates was not quick enough, they upset the wheelbarrow into the brook at the side of the road. I remonstrated with them, but it had no effect whatever, as they had made up their minds to maintain their own dignity, however little I might care about mine.

Whenever I got on and off my pony, as much fuss was made about me as about a jockey mounting for the Derby: one man to each stirrup, another to the pony's head, a fourth to his tail, and the Ma-Fu to give me a lift, as if the animal was about eighteen instead of eleven hands high.

We halted for the night at Pi-Hsien, the magistrate of which town insisted on sending me an escort of twenty soldiers. After some remonstrance I succeeded in reducing to ten the number of these useless but exceedingly picturesque braves.

Over the ordinary dress they wore a loose red tunic without sleeves; four of them were armed with spears terminating in an arrangement like Neptune's trident; and four others with weapons ending in short square swords. The heads of all the poles were adorned with large rosettes of blue and red, with ends hanging down. The other two men bore flags, one in front and one behind.

The Hsien also sent his steward, a functionary of much importance. This man rode a pony, and gave me a good deal of assistance—praise that I can hardly lavish on the remainder of the procession, who were about as useful as the men in armour in a lord mayor's show.

Leaving Pi-Hsien, we marched over the beautiful fertile plain; and after about an hour the mountains appeared through the haze. The whole country is a perfect network of canals and watercourses; and, as the plain here begins rising rapidly (at least ten feet per mile), the streams are all very swift. The number of trees everywhere is enormous; the sides of the road are bordered with a small kind of beech, and also willows; there are often rows of trees between the fields, and clusters round the houses. Here is a line of fruit trees, oranges or apricots; there a temple enclosed by a wall with a number of fine yews; and in every direction the view is bounded by trees. The beeches are used only for firewood, and for the manufacture of charcoal, which, as well as coke, is made in great quantities at Kuan-Hsien; and vast numbers of coolies are seen on the road carrying these in the usual way, or wheeling them in barrows.

There was no lack of tea-houses by the roadside, and I breakfasted in one close to the river, which, here sixty yards wide, and running swiftly over a pebbly bottom, looked a glorious place for throwing a fly. A little higher up it was crossed by a neat trestle-bridge in nine spans. The frame-work for the usual roof had just been put up over the road-way, and people were at work completing it.

As fresh coolies had to be hired before entering the mountains, we halted for a day at Kuan-Hsien. The people of the place do not enjoy a high reputation, and I found no reason to make my opinion of them an exception to the general rule. I was followed about by a gaping crowd, who exhibited more than the usual amount of the frantic curiosity of the Chinese people, who, notwithstanding their outrageous inquisitiveness, seem yet utterly devoid of the power of observation. I have looked at the faces of some thousands, and in scarcely one have I seen the smallest appearance of observing power. Where the eyelid ends, the forehead begins, leaving no room for the organs of this faculty. After I had returned from my excursion, my people managed to keep the courtyard clear; but in the door of it there was a little open latticework, and hour after hour it was blocked by heads, whose owners all that time can have seen nothing foreign save a bath-towel hung out in the sun to dry.

No one who has not gone through this process of being continually stared at, can thoroughly realise what it is. Sometimes after arrival at an inn, when the fearful hubbub, which usually lasts about an hour, has somewhat subsided, and when at last the courtyard has been cleared, and the traveller fondly hopes the reign of peace is about to commence, he suddenly becomes aware of a whispering carried on somewhere near him—a conversation carried on in a whisper is always disagreeable, but under these circumstances it is peculiarly irritating—he lays down his pen, and listens, and the sound of a scraping noise outside the wall is heard. Presently a finger is cautiously thrust through the paper that covers a little bit of window which he fancied far beyond the reach of escalade, and that well-known eye appears. He suddenly looks up, the eye disappears, a thud is heard on the ground outside, followed by the rumbling sound of some thirty or forty feet, as their owners scamper off, ashamed of having been found out.

Writing is recommenced, and the traveller is soon again absorbed in his work, when presently a scratching and scraping, accompanied by the same horrid whispering, discovers some one picking away the plaster of a lath-and-plaster partition. If one hole is covered up, another is made somewhere else, until at length even if people should appear underneath the floor it would not cause the least surprise.

Besides their reputation for turbulence, the people of Kuan-Hsien are said to be miserably poor ; the latter they certainly are, for Chin-Tai was unable to change his silver. I did not find their turbulence exhibit itself in any other way than excessive curiosity, which was so great that not only were the foreigner, the foreign dog, and foreign clothes objects of intense interest, but the wonder with which these were regarded was extended even to the servants, and a crowd of people, who apparently thought that a Chinaman who could perform the astounding feat of entering the service of a foreigner must bear in his body some outward and visible sign of the fact, followed Chin-Tai when he walked about the streets. Notwithstanding this insatiable inquisitiveness, I found them quiet enough, and no one said an uncivil word.

Leaving the west gate of the city, the road ascended the left bank of the river, here about two hundred and fifty yards broad, a rushing torrent of beautiful clear water. This river debouches from the hills at Kuan-Hsien, where the valley is a mile wide; and, immediately below this, the ingenious contrivances commence for dividing the river, and directing the numerous branches into the desired channels. The works are most simple. Large boulders, about the size of a man's head, are collected and put into long cylindrical baskets of very open bamboo network. These baskets are laid nearly horizontally, and thus the bund is formed. The streams into which the river is in this manner split up, irrigate the Ch'êng-Tu plain; and lower down again unite, to form the 'Min River' of geographers.

The road, following the river, at once plunged into the mountains, which rose about twelve or fifteen hundred feet. The first were of sandstone, and in this a couple of seams of coal, though only a few feet thick, gave plenty of occupation to a considerable population. The beds were here inclined 45°, and the strata ran up in a north-east direction, at right angles to the valley. These formations soon gave way to the inevitable limestone, here exceedingly rich; and large numbers of lime-kilns, and many coolies laden with lime, attested its value. Eight miles further on we turned to the right up a stream, where the vertical strata were well exhibited in some small cliffs, the strike being nearly north and south. The sides of the hills were almost too steep for cultivation, of which there was very little; but grass, flowers, shrubs, and trees were growing luxuriantly, and the richness of the verdure was charming.

The road was much traversed. We met great numbers of coolies carrying timber on their backs; the logs were generally about eight feet long by ten inches square. Some were even larger, though these would weigh at least 200 lbs. There was evidently a great trade in timber, for at all the villages on the river there were large stacks.

On the 22nd we followed up the river all day by a very fair path, in which there was a good deal of up and down. The mountains here rise about three thousand feet; their sides are very steep, in places almost precipitous, and here and there there are cliffs, sometimes four hundred or five hundred feet high; but where they are not absolutely vertical, a luxuriant vegetation of grass, brambles, beautiful flowering creepers, jasmines, and ferns gets a hold in the crevices of the rocks. Small ashes, beeches, and other trees grow in profusion; and the mountains are clothed in green to their very summits. Down at the bottom, if the valley opens out and leaves a little level ground, there is sometimes a patch of cultivation, and, growing amongst the big rocks which lie tumbled about, there are quantities of a kind of barberry, just now in blossom, with a scent like wild thyme. Round every little village are fine clumps of trees, walnuts, peaches, apricots, and large numbers of Pi-Pa (*Eriobotrya Japonica* or *loquot*), the last now bearing fruit, which, although the people here seemed very fond of it, appeared to me to have no taste whatever.

At every two or three miles ropes are stretched across the river; the people make a sort of raft of two logs of wood, a line from this runs on the rope, and they cross on the raft—rather an unpleasant operation in this foaming torrent, which falls one thousand feet before it reaches Kuan-Hsien, a distance that, taking all the windings into account, cannot be more than fifty miles.

I breakfasted at the little hamlet of Hsin-Wên-P'ing, built on exactly the same model as all the other mountain villages, with one inn, at which no one appeared to stop. It had only just been built, and the fresh clean wood panels of the wall and boards of the ceiling were quite a pleasure. The people treated me with the greatest civility, even taking the trouble as we passed the houses to keep their dogs from barking at mine. Some of them would come in and have a quiet talk now and then, or show me their curiosities in return for a similar exhibition on my part. Here they told me there were deer and wild boars in the mountains; that some of the latter were found weighing three hundred catties (four hundred pounds); and, as a proof, brought me a young one about a foot long which was striped longitudinally.

On the morrow the tops of the mountains were hidden in rain clouds, wreaths of mist hung about the lower slopes, and a steady rain did not tend to enliven the scene, or render the taking of notes more easy or more agreeable. The road ran close to the edge of the water, the path being cut out of the rock, in many places propped up from underneath, or cut into steep and irregular steps which the rain made very slippery. The place was very desolate, and there was not a great deal of traffic, although every now and then we passed a good many coolies carrying loads of wood and roots; and at long intervals a small string of mules.

As Wên-Ch'uan-Hsien is approached the valley opens out, the sides of the hills are less steep, and there is some cultivation below. This town is a miserable place, and has a poverty-stricken air. The missionaries warned me to be very careful here; they advised me to shut myself up in my chair and draw down all the blinds, for, as they put it, the inhabitants were very 'mauvais;' but it seemed to me that, however vicious their inclinations might be, there were not enough people to put them into practice. I saw scarcely any one about, and the streets would have been absolutely deserted but for a few old women, who seemed ashamed of themselves for being there. The town is only about three hundred yards across, and we found a filthy inn in a wretched suburb on the northern side.

I had been told that I could get yak-beef here, as the mountaineers were said to keep yaks in a domestic state, and kill them for beef. This, however, was a pure fable, invented to put me in good humour.

Soon after starting we saw the first Man-Tzŭ village on the top of the mountains. I was walking ahead with two of the Ting-Chais, and, pointing to the village, asked if it was not one of the Man-Tzŭ. 'No,' replied the man, 'it's a village.' After which brilliant effort on his part the conversation dropped. The Man-Tzŭ build their villages in quite a different style to the Chinese. The houses are of stone, and the lower part is like a fort, with a few narrow windows like loopholes; there is a flat roof, and on part of this a kind of shed is erected, also flat-roofed, and open to the front. There is a high tower in each village. These are usually square; but I once saw an octagonal one. I never succeeded in getting a very satisfactory explanation of these towers; some people told me that the possession of one was a privilege enjoyed by the head-man; but as I almost immediately afterwards saw three or four in the same village, this did not seem as if it were altogether to be relied on.[1]

The inn at Pan-Ch'iao, though small and dirty, was quiet; but the righteous soul of Chin-Tai was sorely vexed at the robbery of a coat by one of the lodgers. But it was not so much the loss of his coat that grieved him, as the injustice that permitted an inn to be kept by two women so wretched that he could not extract from them the value of the stolen article.

With much difficulty I tore him away from the scene of this disaster, and, leaving Pan-Ch'iao on the 24th, we continued our journey. The river still wound about in a narrow gorge, and soon after starting the clouds lifted for a minute from the head of a fine snowy mountain. About two and a half miles from Pan-Ch'iao, the valley on our side opened out, and there was a little grassy plain, where a stream running down from the east joined the river. Here, hidden amongst the thick foliage of walnut-trees, there was a little village, whose inhabitants cultivated the patch of level ground. It was a pretty place. There were a few apricot and peach trees by the roadside, and a couple of brilliant yellow birds were flying about amongst the branches.

Perched like an eagle's eyrie on the tops of the almost inaccessible hills, or like wild birds' nests on the faces of perpendicular cliffs, there were many villages of the Man-Tzŭ; and down below, on the banks of the smiling river, there were the blackened ruins of many another once peaceful hamlet. In one place, close to the ruins of some Man-Tzŭ buildings, that I could plainly see had been burnt not very long ago, there was a new and flourishing Chinese village, where the Chinese, having ousted the aborigines, had established themselves. A little further on there was a

[1] See illustration, p. 102.

cluster of inhabited houses, built, in the Man-Tzŭ style, close down to the river, that had formerly been occupied by Man-Tzŭ, but had now been taken possession of by Chinese. I noticed that the Chinese, in one or two very new villages, were adopting in part the Man-Tzŭ style; but in these the high tower was always wanting, and the difference in the appearance of the new semi Man-Tzŭ villages and of the regular Man-Tzŭ buildings was most apparent.

The relentless advance of the Chinese was thus presented to the eye in a very striking manner; every village had its tale of battle, murder, or sudden attack by the barbarians on the peaceable Chinese. In imagination it was easy to fill the picture with living figures. I could in fancy hear the clash of arms, or see the flight of the Man-Tzŭ from their ruthless enemy, who left nothing but the smoking ruins of some once quiet hamlet to bear witness to the cruel tragedy. The story as told me was always the same. How the Chinese came peaceably up the valleys, and were received by the inhabitants with every show of welcome; how unprovoked and unexpected attack was made on the new comers, who, at first fighting only for existence, ultimately secured the victory, and established themselves in the place of their treacherous foes. The Chinese, as at each successive village they narrated with never-varying details the events of every battle, dwelt with delight on the valour of their race and the cowardly conduct of the barbarians, and never thought it possible that I should wonder what account these same barbarians would render, should they have the opportunity of telling their tale.

But the irrevocable law of nature must have its way; the better race must gradually supplant the inferior one; the Chinese will continue their advance, stopped only where the climate aids the soil in its refusal to produce even to these industrious agriculturists the fruits of the earth in due season.

These mountains, whose heads are crowned with dazzling snow, into whose inmost recesses man has never penetrated, and whose rugged sides and mighty precipices must inspire awe in the most unpoetic soul, have not been without their influence on the minds of the inhabitants.

Not only the shout of battle, but the miracle wrought by some Buddhist saint, the mystery attendant on some freak of nature, and even the gentle song of love, finds its place in the legends that cling to the sides of these romantic valleys.

Leaving behind us the melancholy records of a fast dying race, we cross a little ridge, and my attention was called to a spot surrounded with all the halo of the miraculous. On our left was a long ridge of loose sand, that fancy might conjure into the semblance of a gigantic snake ; and hidden in its mysterious depths some marvellous creature even now resides. And with awe the tale was told me, how no effort of man has ever succeeded in clearing away that ridge of sand ; for even if by dint of desperate labour during the day a portion is removed by nightfall, when the labourer returns to his work on the morrow, lo ! all is as it was, and everything must be commenced afresh.

The fable has its origin in truth. No doubt there is a backbone of rock to this ridge of sand, and the wind coming out of the valley causes the drift, that even if cleared away would of course soon again collect.

There was yet something more wonderful about this place, and Chin-Tai told me an interminable story about a Fu, five dragons, and five swords ; but it was very long, and he became so interested in it as to give it me more in Chinese than English, by which the moral, if there was one, is lost to posterity for ever. He, however, impressed upon me very strongly the fact that it was a miracle, and that, as it was told him by some one who lived here, it must be true.

Hsin-P'u-Kuan boasts a wall and gate, and is presided over by an official called a 'T'ing.' He asked me to stop here all day, and placed his house at my disposal, an offer that he did not expect me to accept. He sent me the usual unromantic fowl, some potatoes, which were very acceptable, and a piece of pork, which my servants gladly disposed of for me ; for nothing short of absolute starvation would have induced me to touch the flesh of a Chinese pig, a peculiarity that afterwards obtained for me the title of a foreign Mahometan.

The potato is despised by the Chinese as food only fit for pigs and foreigners, but, introduced into the mountainous regions by the missionaries not much more than fifty years ago, the valuable properties of this useful root have already made themselves appreciated, and steadily, but surely, gaining ground, notwithstanding the contempt of the Chinese, it is destined at no distant day to take its place amongst the agricultural products of China. In all the mountain regions in Western China and Tibet potatoes are found, and as far as Ta-Li-Fu I was never without them during the whole of my journey.

Marching out of Hsin-P'u-Kuan the river was immediately crossed by one of the rope suspension bridges that had by this time become familiar. Six ropes, one above the other, are stretched very tightly, and connected by vertical battens of wood laced in and out. Another similar set of ropes is at the other side of the roadway, which is laid across them, and, since it follows their curve, is rather steep at the two ends. The bridges themselves sway about a good deal, especially if there happens to be any wind, and walking on them is something like walking on the deck of a rolling ship.

The volume of the river is here swelled by the tributary from Li-Fan-Fu ; this is passed by a similar bridge, and, leaving the main road to Sung-P'an-T'ing, the road to Li-Fan-Fu ascends the right bank of the tributary stream.

The scenery now changed entirely. At the bottom of the valley there was here and there a little flat ground, where fields of barley were divided by loose stone walls, the mountains rising up behind almost precipitously. With the exception of a few scanty blades of grass, these were perfectly bare, and, standing like a long wall, almost unbroken even by a gully, presented a remarkable contrast to the magnificent verdure we had left behind.

In one or two places the Man-Tzŭ villages were now inhabited by Chinese ; and up on the tops of the mountains, when the clouds lifted, the present dwelling-places of these aborigines could be seen. Some of them put me much in mind of many a Persian hamlet lying hidden in the valleys of the great Elburz; one in particular, close down by the stream, half hidden amongst trees, with a little patch of cultivation round it, and with the bare and rugged mountain rising like a wall behind, needed only a few tall straight poplars to complete the likeness, and almost made me think I was nearer to the Atrek than to the Yang-Tzŭ. In places the valley narrowed, and the hills running sheer down to the water, the road was supported from below, or rested upon horizontal stakes driven into the face of the rock. The road was everywhere in an excellent state of repair; great care was evidently bestowed upon it, and it must have cost much money and labour to keep it up. The Chinese are not as a rule in the habit of repairing roads; but in a case of this kind a road left to itself would very soon cease to exist. In one place it had been found impossible to avoid a short tunnel, and when it had been necessary to cut steps in the rock, these were very regular, and carefully made.

A little less than nine miles from Hsin-P'u-Kuan there is a bridge precisely similar in construction to the Sanga bridges of India, and to many others that subsequently became familiar to me in the mountainous regions between Tibet and Western China.[1]

On the 25th we continued our march up the desolate valley, where the cultivation on the little level patches of ground close to the water's edge only served as a foil to set off the bare and precipitous mountain-sides. The streams that came down from these ran through deep and gloomy gorges, tumbling in little cascades between almost vertical walls of rock; many of them were of a brown colour, so like the peat streams of Scotland that I almost think there must be fields of peat in the unknown mass of mountains to the south. There was scarcely any traffic on the road, the villages were few and very small, and half hidden in walnut and willow trees, with a few apricots and firs.

Li-Fan-Fu is situated on a little triangle of flat ground, at the mouth of a narrow gully. The river runs swiftly in front, and separates it from a wild and bare mountain,

[1] See illustration, p. 273.

crowned with huge precipices that rise up some three thousand feet at the opposite side. It is enclosed by a wall, in many places broken down. This wall runs between the houses and the river, and then climbs a long way up the crests of two spurs which enclose the deep ravine running up at the back of the town; but, as the houses are only built on the flat ground close to the river, the walls enclose a considerable vacant space. I counted the houses as well as I could,

Gorge of Li-Fan-Fu.

and at a rough calculation put them at about one hundred and twenty. The houses here, unlike those in other parts of China, are two-storied, generally built of stone below, with a wooden upper story and a balcony. Nearly all the roofs are flat, but a few of them are made of sloping battens of wood. There is a small suburb on the eastern side, but none elsewhere.

A rushing torrent comes down the ravine, flows through the town, and serves to turn numerous water-mills, for, as this is a corn and not a rice-growing country, there is a great deal of grinding to be done. The wheels are nearly always horizontal, and are enclosed in little low, round, flat-roofed houses, which look like small forts; they have one little door, and are hardly high enough for a man to stand in.

There is another Chinese town, called Cha-Chou-T'ing, twenty miles up the river, which is the last Chinese station.

Crossing the river by a rope suspension-bridge, the roadway of which was merely a few hurdles laid down, and walking about half a mile up the river, we turned into a deep ravine and came upon a couple of houses, where, as an illustration of intermarriage, about which I had been making inquiries, I was shown a Chinaman who had a Man-Tzŭ wife.

The people who were with me evidently thought that now we should go back.

'But where is the Man-Tzŭ village?' I said.

'Oh!' they replied, 'that is too far; ten miles away up there.'

I looked, and saw a village on the side of the mountain, about four miles off, and two thousand feet above me. Fortunately the people had not time to make up a story, as they had simply trusted that the mere sight of the village perched up above me would be quite enough to damp my ardour; but, to their astonishment, I insisted on going there. Chin-Tai was the most disgusted of all, for the sun was shining, it was somewhat warm, and he appeared to be wrapped up in an infinite number of wadded coats. He very soon became a piteous object. The road was desperately steep, and very stony; every step he took was a labour to him. He was compelled to sit down and rest every few yards; sometimes he threw himself flat on his back with a groan. He several times declared that he was going to die, and I found it far greater trouble to look after him and make him come on, than to walk the distance myself a dozen times. My satellites kept their countenances fairly, but were evidently desperately amused, and I could easily see that amongst themselves they thought the whole proceeding eminently ludicrous. By dint of perseverance and much waiting, we at length succeeded in getting him to the top, and when there it was with true religious fervour that he 'knocked his head.' I found that the Man-Tzŭ people cultivated far more ground than I had thought. The upper slopes of the hills were all laid out in terraces, where barley and wheat were grown.

In this part of the country the term Man-Tzŭ is, amongst the aborigines, considered a term of reproach, they themselves preferring to be called I-Ran, or I-Jen. This is very unusual. The aborigines in the province of Kwei-Chou would rather consider I-Ran an insulting epithet; but here the term Man-Tzŭ is considered so bad that Chin-Tai would not let me go on, until he was perfectly sure I should make no use of the word 'Man-Tzŭ;' and in the conversations that afterwards passed in this village the term I-Ran was repeatedly used, and the word Man-Tzŭ not once.

This village was about two thousand two hundred feet above Li-Fan-Fu, but was not on the top of the mountain, which rose another thousand feet behind it. The houses were all of loose stones, with little windows like loopholes; the streets were not more than three feet wide, and everything was more filthy than usual. As we sat outside the entrance to the village, waiting for Chin-Tai to drag himself up the last few yards, the clouds lifted from the head of a grand mountain to the south of Li-Fan-Fu, disclosing vast fields of snow. This is called Hsüeh-Lung-Shan, or Snow Dragon Mountain, and the people said there were fields of ice where it was too cold for any one to live.

In the village we all had tolerably good appetites, and did justice to a huge loaf of Indian corn bread that one of the Ting-Chais brought straight from the ashes in which it was baked. I then asked to be taken to a house where I could sit down, and the village school was selected. Here I soon gathered a few people around me, who gave me what little information they themselves possessed. There are two kinds of I-Ran people, those living at Cha-Chuo and beyond having a language different from those who live here. The I-Ran of this place are very like the Chinese in appearance; they wear the same dress, as well as the plait, but they have good teeth. The Chinese, as a rule, have vile teeth, ill-formed, irregular, very yellow, and covered with tartar. The I-Ran here all talk Chinese, as well as their own language. Their writing is Chinese, and the school children were learning to write that language. The I-Ran of the West have quite a different writing, which appears to be alphabetic; but I completely failed in my attempts to get the alphabet; all they could say was that they had a great many characters. I, however, made one of them write me a couple of lines, and on comparing their writing, which is from left to right, with pure Tibetan, there is really no difference, and their statement that the number of characters was very great was probably some confusion. They gave me the numerals and a few words, in which the connection between the two languages is quite apparent, although they are very different.

We turned our backs on Li-Fan-Fu on the 27th, and, as we marched down towards Hsin-P'u-Kuan, the clouds lifted from a magnificent snowy mountain in the east. It is called the White Cloud Mountain, and it must be fourteen or fifteen thousand feet high; for I subsequently found the snow-line at this season at an altitude of thirteen thousand feet; and the summit as I looked on it was at least one thousand or two thousand feet above the line of snow. Moreover, the snow lies on this peak all the year round, and the limit of perpetual snow must here be at least fourteen or fifteen thousand feet above the sea.

From Hsin-P'u-Kuan we marched up the banks of the main river; and now the beautifully wooded slopes and magnificent verdure had disappeared, and the rocks were very bare. The I-Ran villages were seen on the tops of the hills all the way to Wên-Ch'êng, which we reached just before a good downpour of rain commenced.

Next morning the sun dispelled the mists; and every now and then there was a glimpse of the grand snow-capped mountains on which snow lies all the year round.

In many places along the river ropes were stretched from bank to bank; the inhabitants manage to cross by these, and even carry goods. An opportunity was soon afforded to us of watching a man cross with a heavy sack; a sight that was all the more thoroughly enjoyed when he stuck in the middle immovable until another man came to his assistance. There are always two ropes, one for going, the other for returning, so arranged that each has a considerable slope downwards. A small runner is first placed on the rope. This is a hollow half cylinder of wood, about eight inches in diameter and ten inches long. The runner is placed on the rope (a very large twisted bamboo rope). The man takes a strong line, ties it round his body, and then, by

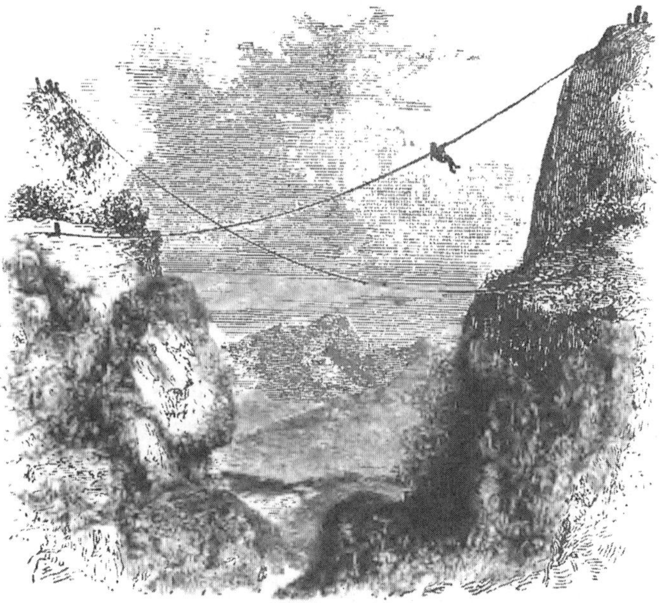

Haul-bridge near Mao-Chou.

passing it two or three times over the runner, makes a kind of seat for himself; it is then again passed round his body, and firmly secured. He is thus suspended close below the big rope; then, with both hands on the runner, he raises his feet from the ground, and shoots down the incline at a tremendous pace. Of course, with a width of about one hundred yards, it is quite impossible to have one end so high that there shall be a regular slope all the way; so, notwithstanding the impetus he gets in descending, which shoots him some way up, the passenger always has to pull himself up the last few yards, which is done in the natural hand-over-hand fashion. This is a method of crossing a river that must require a considerable amount of nerve, when the torrent is roaring some two hundred feet below, dashing over most ugly and cruel-looking jagged rocks.[2]

Two miles beyond Mao-Chou, on the 30th, I had a magnificent view of the Nine Nails Mountain, so called on account of its summit being broken into sharp peaks or points; but as for the number Nine, it might just as well have been anything else. I had not before been able to appreciate the grandeur of this mountain, in which I could now see great fields of snow descending quite two thousand feet below its highest point. I stood and admired it for a long time, the people all wondering what I was looking at.

Near this point the mountains again close in on the river, which now runs through a series of narrow and precipitous gorges, great bare slopes and precipices running down to the water, and leaving scarcely a yard of level ground—except here and there, at the end of a projecting point, or up the bottom of a little valley, where a few flat acres are found and cultivated. The great mountain-sides are ragged and torn about in a marvellous manner, and huge masses broken from them lie strewn about. The road is cut out of the sides of the rock, and is often supported from below, or propped up for a few yards by horizontal stakes driven into the rock. When a valley opening disclosed a view of the interior, the tops of the higher mountains to the west were seen to be well wooded; but there was no opportunity of seeing what lay to the east, as none of the valleys were sufficiently open.

About six miles from Ch'a-Erh-^{Ng}ai the river receives a considerable affluent from the west, called the Lu-Hua-Ho. A six days' journey up this river is the home of another of the Man-Tzŭ tribes, the Su-Mu, or White Man-Tzŭ—as the people here call them—a tribe numbering some three and a half millions; and the Ju-Kan, or Black Man-Tzŭ, live in

[2] This is the *Chiká* of the Kashmir Himálya (see Drew's *Jummoo*, &c., p. 123).—*Y.*

the interior, an indefinite number of days beyond. The sovereign of the Su-Mu is always a queen. When the Tartars were conquering the land, this tribe happened at that time to have a queen for a sovereign, who gave the Tartars great assistance, and as an honorary distinction it was decreed by the conquerors that in the future the Su-Mu should always be governed by a queen.

The Su-Mu have been pillaged by the Ju-Kan, their houses burnt, and their villages destroyed. The Ju-Kan now wanted peace, and had offered an indemnity sufficient to rebuild the houses; but the Su-Mu were eaten up with the desire of revenge, and their queen was now at Ch'êng-Tu praying that soldiers might be sent to punish the Ju-Kan. If she ever succeeded in her mission she probably will find herself in the position of the horse in Æsop's fable, who desired the help of man.

On the 30th we marched all day through the same wild gorge, hemmed in with bare cliffs and ragged rocks, broken at the top into pinnacles and crags of fantastic shape. Now and then some of the valleys opening out to the right or left were less precipitous, and were well wooded on their slopes. Once or twice I caught a glimpse of a snowy peak, but nearly all day we were shut in by the steep hill-sides, and could see little besides them and a narrow streak of heaven above. When the road descended to the river, there might be a few yards of level ground, where the barberry and other shrubs seemed to grow luxuriantly amongst the rocks; but the general aspect of the scene was barren and somewhat dreary.

From Ta-Ting the road at once climbed up the precipitous side of the valley by a tolerably gentle slope; and we soon began to breathe the pure and invigorating mountain air.

As we ascended, instead of being shut in by steep hills and cliffs, the slopes became more gentle; though often high above us, at the very summits, there were again great precipices. Amongst the slopes and crags were many tiny plateaux, cultivated by a few people, who seemed to gather but scanty crops from the unfruitful soil. The sides of the valleys were either well wooded with pines, or covered with close and thick brambles, barberries, thorns, and all sorts of shrubs which were deliciously fresh and green. Many varieties of wild flowers grew luxuriantly, numbers of the purple iris in blossom, and acres of a kind of purple crocus; many sweet-smelling herbs shot up amongst the grass, and the whole scene is very fair to look upon. As we ascended, we saw a great many cock-pheasants strutting about, crowing loudly, quite innocent of fear, and unsuspicious of any harm from the hand of man. On this occasion their confidence was misplaced; and thenceforth my table was daily supplied with game, which varied the monotony of diminutive kids, shrivelled ducks, and emaciated fowls.

A steady pull of eleven hundred feet in four miles brought us to an inn close to the village of Shui-Kou-Tzŭ, where I found a room looking over the valley of the river. Here the air felt crisp and pure, and, though the sun was shining brightly, the thermometer at 9 A.M. was only 58° in the shade. Across the valley, a grand mountain ran down in precipices and steep and bare slopes, about three thousand feet, to the river; up a gorge, to the left, a deep green forest of firs crowned the summit; to the right, on a small plateau, a Man-Tzŭ village hung over the stream, with a little terrace cultivation at its side; in the background here and there a patch of snow was lying on the higher mountain-tops, and below in the bottom we could just hear the murmur of the invisible river as it tumbled over its rocky bed. The tinkling of the goat-bells sounded pleasantly in the morning air, and, after having been shut in for so many days in the close gorges, the place and all around it was very delightful.

After breakfast another steady pull of one thousand feet brought us to our highest point, and from here we had a fine view of the town of Tieh-Chi-Ying. This place is on a flat plateau, bounded on three sides by precipices, or exceedingly steep slopes, which fall down to the river fifteen hundred feet below. On the fourth side, apparently inaccessible mountain crags rise abruptly behind it, the roads to and from it being cut out of the face of the mountain, making it a very strong military position.

We descended to the river by a steep zigzag, where loose stones lay scattered about the narrow path, and then followed the river bank to Sha-Wan (the Sandy Hollow).

There was a freshness in the early morning air that now made us feel we were thoroughly in the mountains, and far above the oppressive heat of the steaming plains below. The road from Sha-Wan was very good, and the scenery most picturesque. On the right, crags and precipices rose into pinnacles generally crowned with clumps of pines; the northern faces of the hills were almost always well wooded with fresh green or yellow trees; and in the valley all sorts of shrubs grew luxuriantly. On the opposite bank of the river the hills sloped gently, and their sides were beautifully green with grass and shrubs. Presently on the road a string of yaks was encountered, and a number of coolies laden with red deers' horns, some of them very fine twelve-tyne antlers. The deer are only hunted when in velvet, and from the horns in this state a medicine is made that is one of the most highly prized in the Chinese pharmacopœia; the antlers that are shed are collected and brought down to the plains for sale, where they are converted into knife handles, and used for various other purposes. These are sold at Kuan-Hsien at the rate of fourteen taels for one hundred catties (about sixty-five shillings for one hundred pounds).

About eight miles from Sha-Wan, on turning a corner, a glorious view suddenly burst upon me. Right in front was a perfect pyramid of virgin snow; the sun was shining brightly, and the brilliant white of the peak was all the more dazzling from the contrast presented by the deep shadow on the wooded flanks of the nearer mountains. This was Mount Shih-Pan-Fang (the Stone Slab House), and I stood almost spell-bound, lost in admiration. Long I gazed at this majestic peak, whilst my unsympathetic companion seized the opportunity to sit down and smoke a pipe, wondering the while what I could find to look at or admire.

The morning air of the 3rd of June quite made my

fingers tingle; and I thought with pity of Baber sweltering at Ch'ung-Ch'ing, with the thermometer at 100° in the shade. The road was now good and level, and kept close down to the water-side. The scenery was very beautiful; the tops of the mountains were crowned with dark forests of firs, and the valleys, opening east and west, disclosed a vast extent of pine-clad heights. The bed of the river was much wider, and bounded by slopes clothed with shrubs of many descriptions, amongst which wild flowers grew in profusion; in one spot there was a field of wild roses, one mass of blossom, and the air was literally laden with the delicious perfume. On the northern slopes were charming little woods of the freshest green; and the yellow flowers of the barberry, everywhere abundant, helped to give that warmth to the colouring that always seems to characterise a Chinese landscape. Five miles from Ch'êng-P'ing-Kuan a valley opening to the east gave a near view of the snow pyramid Shih-Pan-Fang, whose summit, as I now could plainly see, must be at least two thousand feet above the snow line.

The landlord of the inn at Ngan-Hua-Kuan had heard of my approach, and had cleaned up his house three days before in expectation of my arrival. Directly I came in he brought me a cup of the most delicious tea I ever tasted in China. It was of pale straw colour, like all tea taken by the Chinese, and the steam that rose from it diffused a delicate bouquet through the room. I was very glad to buy a packet of this from the friendly landlord; for as I had left Ch'êng-Tu with the intention of being absent for a few days only, I had brought with me a very small supply, which, like my candles and cigars, had now come to an end. I had been for a long time endeavouring, unsuccessfully, to make myself believe that I enjoyed the aristocratic water-pipe; but at last the conclusion was forced upon me that my tastes were vulgar, and, venturing one day to borrow a pipe from a coolie, I never again resorted to elegant but trivial hubble-bubbles.

The coolie's pipe is the same all over China; but in Ssŭ-Ch'uan the method of smoking seems in accordance with the character of the people, who, being more independent in spirit, and less narrow-minded, are not so addicted to trivialities as the Chinese of other provinces. They, therefore, do not content themselves with the homœopathic doses of tobacco usually taken, but roughly roll a leaf of tobacco into a kind of cigar, and use the pipe as a mouth-piece.

We now entered rather a different country, the scenery everywhere indicating the proximity of the plateaux. The river valley opened out to nearly half a mile, and the bed itself became wide and shallow, the stream being broken up into several small channels. The mountains were now rounded, and separated by open level valleys, instead of the close narrow gorges which had hitherto been almost universal; the main valley was all cultivated, whilst the hill-sides were cut into terraces, and crops grown all over them.

The Man-Tzŭ people had now been left behind, and we were approaching the country of the Si-Fan. These are a very wild-looking people. Some of them wear hats of felt, in shape like those of the Welsh-women, and high felt riding-boots, and in their dress are much the same as the regular Tibetans. Now and then we met three or four, riding all together; and my truculent Ting-Chais always made them dismount as I approached, in no way attempting to conceal their contempt for the conquered barbarians.

Sung-P'an-T'ing is on the right bank of the river, with an extensive walled suburb on the left; a hill runs down from the right bank, ending in a small cliff; and the wall of the town runs right up the side of the hill, taking in a great deal of open ground where barley and wheat are grown. The place seemed to have an enormous population for its size.

I was informed that, at a place two days' journey to the west, there were great numbers of red deer; and I was promised excellent sport if I felt inclined to make an expedition. Wild sheep and goats were said to live amongst the crags and rocks in the neighbourhood of Hsüeh-Shan; and the people told me that on the road to Lung-An-Fu I should see plenty of hares, musk-deer, and pheasants—a prophecy that was belied; for although there were a great many pheasants for the first few days, I never saw a hare, a musk-deer, or any other game. There must, however, be a considerable number of musk-deer amongst the mountains; for the price of musk at Sung-P'an-T'ing was only three times its weight in silver. The musk-deer are not shot, but trapped; for there is a belief that if one of them is wounded he tears out the musk-bag, and so disappoints the hunter. It is possible that terror or pain, or both combined, may cause the animal to eject the musk, as the sepia, under similar circumstances, squirts out its ink, and as, on the authority of Æsop, the beaver is said to tear out a certain gland and cast it to the hunter.

The crops here are nearly all wheat, oats, and barley, as it is too cold for Indian corn. There are also potatoes in the neighbourhood, and the market produced a vegetable like spinach. The principal food of the people is barley-bread, and barley-porridge, for which the barley is roasted before grinding it into meal. There is also some buckwheat, from which a heavy unleavened bread is made. The market produces the leaven and steam-baked bread, in the shape of dumplings, which seems to be universal wherever Chinamen are found.

Butter is made in the mountains by the Mongols; but it is not brought down here in any quantity, as this place is entirely populated by Chinese, who never make use of butter or milk in any form whatever. The landlord of the inn, however, had some, and made me a present of a circular cake about an inch thick and six or eight inches in diameter, similar in shape, taste, and appearance to the cakes of butter found all over Eastern Tibet. The river produces a few little fish, very much like sprats in taste and appearance. Yak-beef is plentiful, and costs forty cash a catty, and eggs cost seven cash each.

In the month of July there is an annual fair, when the Si-Fan, the Mongols of the Ko-Ko-Nor, and the Man-Tzŭ bring in their produce to sell. Skins of all kinds, musk, deer-horns, rhubarb, and medicines are the chief articles brought down, for which they take up in exchange crockery, cotton goods, and little trifles.

My landlord was a Mahometan, and his respect for me was much increased by my reputation for never eating pork or ham. He told me that he had been to the Ko-Ko-Nor, and that the journey occupied three months in going, and the same time in returning; the road, he said, passed over dreadful mountains, the very recollection of which made him shiver. In winter-time the cold is intense, and the wild winds that sweep across the frozen plateaux cut great gashes in the face or any part of the body exposed. He asked me to give him some medicine against the wind; and as Chin-Tai declared that the possession of a bit of diachylon plaster would render him exceedingly happy, I felt I could not deprive him of the pleasure, although I rather spoilt the effect by telling him I was afraid he would not find it a certain remedy.

The ignorant superstition of the Chinese attributes to the foreigner all kinds of supernatural powers, which are even extended in their minds to European goods. Amongst many Chinese the application of grease from a foreign candle is considered a specific for small-pox; and European sugar is almost a pharmacopœia in itself.

On the 6th we left the valley of the river which had been our constant companion for so many days, and, climbing up a gorge, we soon obtained a good view of the town. Ascending a little more, we crossed a ridge, here only eight hundred feet above the river, to the valley of another stream, running nearly parallel to the main river. We now ascended this valley by a good and easy road, and kept up above the stream as far as the Lamassery, a low wooden building, very irregular in shape. About some of the chief rooms there was some coarse embroidery; round the largest of the chapels hung a number of rough pictures of saints, painted on a sort of cotton stuff; in one there was an image of Buddha, who here is known by the name of Khătye-Tăbā;[3]

[3] Buddha is usually called in Tibet *Shakya Thubpa*, 'Mighty Sakya.'—*Y.*

in front of him there were a number of lotus-flowers, and ten little brass bowls of water. They introduced me into the cell of the chief Lama, who acknowledged my presence by a slight inclination of the head; he was squatting before an immense pan of ashes, counting beads and muttering prayers.

I did not stop here long. The Lamas, though exceedingly polite, were excessively dirty, and smelt horribly. This elevated plateau-land being ill-adapted for agriculture, but few Chinese are found, and we were now almost entirely amongst the Si-Fan. Their architecture is very much the same as that of the Chinese, but they do not turn up the ends of their ridges and gables; indeed, at a distance, the houses look very Swiss. On the hill-sides the roofs are made of planks, laid anyhow, with big stones on them to prevent their being blown off, just as in Switzerland.

The march was up the valley, bounded on both sides by rounded hills and low mountains, all covered with grass and brushwood full of pheasants; but not a single tree or wild flower was to be seen. Here the Si-Fan keep immense herds of cattle and yaks that feed on the splendid pasture. We passed no village all day, a single house, surrounded by a little patch of cultivation, at about every mile and a half, being the only sign of a population.

For the last two miles and a half of the journey we did not pass a single habitation. We were obliged to stop at a solitary wayside hut, as there was not another roof for many miles; and as a heavy chilly rain came on, and wild gusts of wind swept down from the snowy heights, none of us were loth to take shelter in the hovel at Fêng-Tung-Kuan, or Wind Cave Pass, as it is most appropriately called. This place is not visited by any but a few of the poorest coolies, and the accommodation was suited to the requirements. It was a long low house of uncut, flat stones, between which the daylight was more apparent than the mortar. The single room, that constituted the public accommodation of this luxurious hotel, was sheltered by a gabled wooden roof, the ridge of which was left open in its whole length as an exit for the smoke of the fire, a most unlooked-for piece of thoughtfulness on the part of the architect. One end of the room, above which there was a loft under the gable, was divided off by a wooden partition; this portion formed the private residence of the hostess, and was on this occasion given up to me.

The people here keep very large savage dogs; in shape they are more like a colley than any other English breed, but much heavier about the head, neck and fore part of the body. They have a very deep voice, and one of them would hardly let us enter the inn—if inn it could be called, for there was absolutely nothing to be purchased but a little buckwheat or barley-bread.

Chin-Tai brought me awful tales of the terrors of the road that we were to traverse the following morning. He warned me that going up we must all be very quiet; any one calling out or making a noise would be certain to bring on a terrific wind, a violent snowstorm, hailstones of gigantic dimensions, thunder, lightning, and every evil the elements could inflict. If a man on this mountain should express feelings of hunger, thirst, fatigue, heat, or cold, immediately the symptoms would be intensified to a very great degree. He told me that once a military official with an army of soldiers came to cross this mountain. He had with him his sedan-chair, to which about twenty men were yoked, before and behind, who could not get on without shouting. The troops also marching always made a great noise. This high functionary was warned that he should not attempt to cross the mountain, for if he did some fearful accident would befal him. He laughed, however, at the warnings, saying that he had the emperor's order, and must go on. So he went. A fearful storm of wind and snow came on; half his army perished; and he himself very nearly lost his life. Such were the tales about Hsüeh-Shan with which I went to bed; and if I did not shiver it was thanks to the quantity of clothing with which I covered myself.

The floor of the loft made a sort of ceiling to my apartment; but there was a large square hole in it, and through this, as I lay in bed, I could see the long opening in the roof, and the stars beyond, when not obscured by clouds; and at intervals the rain came in for variety. Fêng-Tung-Kuan is 11,884 feet above the sea. It fully justified its name, for it blew a violent gale all night; but I put on a considerable number of garments, rolled myself up in three blankets, and neither the wind, nor the rain, nor Chin-Tai's weird stories disturbed my peaceful slumbers. The story of the general who cried 'Excelsior' was familiar to me; but whether it was told me before, *à propos* of this mountain, or whether I have read it somewhere, I am not sure. I have no doubt that it is a tale tacked on to many mountain passes.

When the morning broke on the 7th of June low clouds were scudding across the sky, driven by the wind, that howled amongst the crevices in the walls of the hut. A chilly rain that turned to sleet did not enliven the scene, and soon we plunged into the dank mists that swept over the summit of Hsüeh-Shan. One single partridge, startled from its bed, was the only living thing we saw as we made the dreaded ascent. The plateau, as the summit is approached, is bare and dreary; a climb of about one thousand feet brought us to the first sprinkling of snow, at an altitude of 12,800 feet above the sea; there was no snow on the path, but it was lying in little patches amongst the rocks, here all quite bare. A short distance more, and at an altitude of 13,148 feet above the sea we stood at length upon the summit of Hsüeh-Shan (Snow Mountain). At the very top there was a little hut without any inmates, but no one seemed anxious to remain here in the cold sleety rain; and, quickly descending the steep path that leads to the west, we left the chill mists behind us, and soon reached a warmer climate.

Riding down another valley, that ran nearly east and west, on our northern side there was but little wood, all the slopes being covered with a rich green grass; but on the south, a serried ridge, whose summit was torn into wild crags and ragged pinnacles, bounded the valley, throwing out long spurs, where pine forests clothed the northern faces of the lower slopes, and masses of a shrub with white blossoms and a scent like our lilac grew amongst the trees in lavish profusion.

These forests are being cut down in a ruthless manner, and as of course no attempt is made to plant young trees, of the ultimate fate of these beautiful valleys there can be but little doubt. The trees gone, the rains will cease; and then these ranges will become dreary, bare, and useless masses, like the mountains of Northern Persia.

A march of ten and three quarter miles, during which we passed only three small huts, brought us to the village of Hung-[Ng]ai-Kuan (Red Rock Pass), where the community lived in three houses. Here we halted for breakfast, and immediately afterwards heavy rain commenced, evidently no unusual occurrence, for the rich green of the dense woods that now surrounded us, and the wonderful verdure of the open slopes and valleys, were unmistakable signs that the climate of the eastern is much more moist than that of the western face of the great spur from the Himalayan plateau, which stretches to the south between the valleys of Sung-P'an-T'ing and Lung-An-Fu.

The ridges from each side every now and then threw out great masses of rock, ending in huge precipices over the valley; and, between these, green grassy slopes, with clumps of trees scattered about as in a park, ran up to the heights above. The bottom of the valley was wooded with low trees, and we marched all the afternoon through a thick copse, where there were not so many wild flowers as on the other side of the mountain. Here and there there was a house quite new, showing how recently the Chinese had reached this point.

The Si-Fan live only on the tops of the hills, and, as before, every opening had its tale of horrors. At one of them my attendants stopped, and said that here the Si-Fan had suddenly descended from their fastnesses, butchered five hundred soldiers in cold blood, and burnt all the houses without any provocation on the part of the Chinese.

'But what were five hundred soldiers doing here in the country of the Si-Fan?' I asked.

The question remained unanswered, and we marched in silence to the village of Chêng-Yuan, three thousand feet below the summit of Hsüen-Shan.

The river now ran for six miles through a narrow gorge, not more than one hundred yards wide, bounded everywhere by almost vertical cliffs, and clothed with the most dense foliage. In the valley there were azaleas fifteen and twenty feet high, covered with a mass of blossom as if prepared for a show at Kew. Wild peonies proudly flaunted their gorgeous flowers, and the delicate foliage of a small wild bamboo almost hid itself amongst the broad fronds of many a magnificent fern.

We passed three wretched huts, but, except the little patch of garden round them, there was absolutely no cultivation all the morning.

The affluent streams ran through exceedingly narrow precipitous gorges; but the foliage was so dense that it was impossible to see more than a few yards in any direction, except where the road rose a little above the river. Once I heard the roar of a waterfall; but, though I was not above a few yards distant, I was quite unable to get a view. The road was strewn with sharp stones, and, although it never rose more than thirty or forty feet above the river, frequent ascents and descents of no more than this were sufficiently troublesome over the slippery and broken rocks.

We halted at Yueh-Erh-Ngai, a little hut by the wayside. It was but a mere shelter, the back wall being made of a few loose stones, on which the roof-beams rested. Here I breakfasted, and two of the Ting-Chais seized the opportunity to lie down in a corner, where there was enough shelter from the draughts for the lamps of their cherished opium-pipes.

Beyond this place the gorge became more narrow, and the sides of the hills more steep, until the river ran between two vertical walls of rock, running up a clear five hundred feet, separated from one another by but a few yards, where with marvellous pertinacity the trees and shrubs, which still grew in rich luxuriance, continued to get a hold for their roots in every crevice in the cliffs. The road was dreadful, the descents were desperately steep, and the slippery rocky path was often blocked by great masses of pointed stone ; where this occurred, as it often did, in places almost like an exceedingly steep staircase, not more than two feet wide, with a rough wall of rock at one side and a precipice at the other, the travelling was not exactly pleasant for us who were going down ; and it seemed as if the ascent must be an impossible task for either coolies or mules.

The river (for it had become one now) dashed in a succession of waterfalls over its uneven bed, now blocked by some gigantic rock, or almost stopped by the perpendicular cliffs, that hem it in on either side so closely that it sometimes seems an easy jump across the top. It is quite impossible to give any idea of this extraordinary gorge ; I could hardly have believed in the existence of a rift so narrow and so deep, and yet so wonderfully clothed with trees, ferns, and shrubs. On emerging from it and looking back, there was nothing to be seen but a giant wall of rock ; the chasm through which the torrent finds its way was nowhere visible, and it seemed almost impossible that there could be a road through that apparently impenetrable barrier.

In one of the gloomiest recesses of this remarkable chasm, it is said that a long time ago a hermit took up his residence in a cave ; but finding that, even for Chinese eyes, it was exceedingly dark, so dark that he could not even see to boil his rice, he fixed a mirror on the opposite side, which not only reflected the rays of the sun into the sombre dwelling, but (such was the holiness of the man) it had the additional useful property of reflecting the moon also, whether that luminary happened to be above the horizon or not. The hermit has long since been transported to a better sphere ; but they say his looking-glass still remains, and the traveller who should have the misfortune to be benighted in this desolate gorge may still see the weird glimmer of the mirror on the darkest and thickest night.

The valley opens out near Hsiao-Ho-Ying, and about nine miles further on the river is crossed by one of the iron chain suspension-bridges, so familiar to travellers in Western China, but of which up till now I had never seen a specimen. Seven iron chains extend from bank to bank; these are tightly stretched by powerful windlasses, bedded in a solid mass of masonry. The roadway is laid on these chains. There are piers at each end; and from the top of these (about eight or nine feet above the roadway) two other chains are stretched, one on each side. These two chains droop in the middle to the roadway, which is suspended from them at this point; but as these extra chains are intended only to prevent the structure from swaying about, and not as an additional support for the weight, the roadway is attached to them at this central point, and at no others. This method of applying the two side chains is rather unusual; for generally they are parallel to the roadway, about three feet above it, and are chiefly of use as hand-rails.

The valley from Yeh-T'ang to Shui-Ching-Chan is very open, and the road generally fair, though bad in places. Every now and then it would rise a couple of hundred feet above the river; at other times it was scooped out of the side of the rock, or propped up from below in the usual way. The hill-sides generally were not too steep for the cultivation of Indian corn; and close down to the river the quantity of rice was rapidly increasing. This was now planted out in beds from which a crop of opium had already been gathered. Round the villages there was a little wheat and tobacco. We had the same wild flowers by the roadside, but by no means in the rich profusion of the upper part of the valley. There were a few shrubs of barberry, some magnificent white lilies in blossom, and flowering pomegranates clustered round the houses.

Below T'i-Tzŭ-Yi the sides of the hills again became more steep; but still, wherever amongst precipices or steep slopes a few roods of ground not steeper than 30° could be found, there was sure to be a patch of Indian corn. This is about the steepest slope up which a man can walk unaided by his hands. From the opposite side of the river the face of a slope of this kind has all the appearance of being nearly vertical, and the people hoeing on it look like flies on a wall. There are generally ten or twelve together, dressed in a line that would please the eye of a British drill-sergeant; and as they advance from the bottom upwards, seen from this point of view, it seems that they must slip down and be precipitated into the river below.

The road as yet did not improve—rising up one side of a spur, and zigzagging down the other by a desperately steep and slippery ladder of rock. Wherever there had been land-slips, the track was strewn with gigantic rocks and sharp stones. All the projecting rocky points were exceedingly precipitous, and generally almost vertical on their western sides, the eastern faces of the spurs sloping more gradually, and clearly indicating the direction of the geological up-heaval. The river twisted and turned in a most incomprehensible manner, and wherever it washed the foot of one of these cliffs, the road was scooped out of the face, or propped up in the usual fashion. In one place, instead of using poles, long stones were put horizontally into holes bored in the face of the rock; across these other stones were laid—and thus the road was formed. Here and there, there was only just room for the ponies' feet; and in one place, when I was looking at the scenery rather than at the pony, he stepped so close to the edge of a rotten bank as to elicit a shout of dismay from the usually phlegmatic Ma-Fu. This individual would walk behind, and where the descent was a very steep one, over big stones or down a slippery staircase, he would hold the animal's tail, to prevent the glissade into space that would inevitably have ensued on a false step.

Lung-An-Fu is situated at the foot of a spur thrown out by the mountains towards the river, the valley of which opens out considerably just before reaching the city. It is enclosed by a very long wall, running nearly a mile up both sides of the spur and across the top. It seemed a very small place; and, as Chin-Tai remarked, there was a good deal of wall, but not much house.

An adventurous raft was here seen on the river; but, considering the nature of the torrent, I was not surprised to find it alone in its ambition for the perils of shipwreck. The iron chain suspension-bridges now became so frequent as to make it a matter for sincere congratulation that the Chinese had not discovered the irritating Western system of the toll.

On the 15th we had entered the country of stone bridges, and a little below Hsiang-Ngai-Pa there was an exceedingly elegant one-arched stone bridge. Ssŭ-Ch'uan is justly celebrated for its stone bridges, and we all began to realise the proximity of the plains. Nearly all the water was off the rice fields; the Indian corn was high; there were melons in the gardens; the climate was hotter; the grass by the wayside was rather burnt; and for the first time in this trip there was dust upon the road. The river had at length escaped the trammels of the mountains, and, though still a rushing stream, much encumbered by rapids, boats now navigate it, and can descend all the way to the Ocean Sea. The coolies had counted on an idle day, but Chin-Tai brought back the mournful news that the craft at this place were not large enough for us; so, with sorrowful countenances, they shouldered their loads and tramped to P'ing-I-P'u.

The 16th of June was a joyous day for the coolies. We walked about a quarter of a mile to where a boat sufficiently large to accommodate us all was waiting for us. We were soon all packed and under way, and began the descent. There were rapids at about every half-mile, and the current was everywhere very strong. Many boats were tracking up, and the old familiar songs of the trackers resounded amongst the rocks. We seemed to fly past the shore, and several times in the shallows there was a scraping and bumping and a taking in of water over the bow that would have been alarming to weak nerves.

The first part of the journey was through narrow gorges,

with precipices at each side; but at last the valley opened out for good, and we bade a final farewell to the mountains. Two days' boating carried us to Mien-Chou, a distance of forty-five miles, where we disembarked, and a march of three days brought us back to Ch'êng-Tu.

Mill at Li-Fan-Fu.

Tibetan Bridge over Torrent.

CHAPTER VIII.

CH'ÊNG-TU, AND THE ROAD TO TIBET.

Account of Ch'êng-Tu, as given by Marco Polo—And by Padre Martin Martini—Description of the Modern City—The Rivers, and Probable Changes—Destruction of Documents—Arrival of Mr. Mesny—Political Aspects compel Change in Traveller's intended Route—Decision to Travel Homeward viâ Bat'ang and Bhamo—Visit to the Great Monastery of Wen-Shu-Yüan—Its Buildings and Curiosities—Chapel of Meditation—Antiquities of Ch'êng-Tu—Invitation to a Picnic—Notable Guests—The Dinner and its Peculiarities—Table Manners and Customs—Threatenings of Drought—'Organisation of Departure'—To Shuang-Liu—Superstition as to Fires in Towns—Vast Fertility of Country—Personal Criticisms on Travellers—Chinese Idea of Foreigners in general—First Sight of the

Mountains—Fine Bridge on the Nan-Ho—Great Coolie-loads—Tibetan Embassy—Pai-Chang-Yi—Paved Road in Decay—Ya-Chou-Fu—Its Commercial Importance—Cake-Tea—Coolies employed on the Traffic—Traffic from Yün-Nan—Mountains begin to close round—The Little Pass—Alleged Terrors of the Hills—The Great Pass, and the T'ai-Hsiang Pass—'Straw-Sandal Flat'—Ching-Chi-Hsien—Huă-Ling-P'ing—River of Ta-Chien-Lu—Bridge swept away—Lu-Ting-Chiao and its Iron Suspension bridge—Dominoes—Character of People of Ssŭ-Ch'uan—Hsiao-P'eng-Pa—Scantier Vegetation—Arrival at Ta-Chien-Lu.

MARCO POLO thus describes the plain and city of Ch'êng-Tu-Fu :—

'When you have travelled those twenty days westward through the mountains, as I have told you, then you arrive at a plain belonging to a province called Sindafu, which still is on the confines of Manzi, and the capital city of which is also called Sindafu. This city was in former days a rich and noble one, and the kings who reigned there were very great and wealthy. It is a good twenty miles in compass ; but it is divided in the way that I shall tell you. You see, the king of this province, in the days of old, when he found himself drawing near to death, leaving three sons behind him, commanded that the city should be divided into three parts, and that each of his sons should have one ; so each of these parts is separately walled about, though all three are surrounded by the common wall of the city. Each of the three sons was king, having his own part of the city and his own share of the kingdom, and each of them in fact was a great and wealthy king. But the Great Kaan conquered the kingdom of these three kings, and stripped them of their inheritance.

'Through the midst of this city runs a large river, in which they catch a great quantity of fish. It is a good half-mile wide, and very deep withal, and so long that it reaches all the way to the Ocean Sea—a very long way, equal to eighty or one hundred days' journey; and the name of the river is Kian-Suy. The multitude of vessels that navigate this river is so vast that no one who should read or hear the tale would believe it. The quantities of merchandise also which merchants carry up and down this river are past all belief. In fact it is so big that it seems to be a sea rather than a river. Let us now speak of a great bridge which crosses this river within the city. This bridge is of stone; it is seven paces in width, and half a mile in length (the river being that much in width, as I told you), and along its length, on either side, there are columns of marble to bear the roof—for the bridge is roofed over from end to end with timber, and that all richly painted; and on this bridge there are houses, in which a great deal of trade and industry is carried on. But these houses are all of wood merely, and they are put up in the morning and taken down in the evening. Also there stands upon the bridge the Great Kaan's Comerque—that is to say, his custom-house, where his toll and tax are levied; and I can tell you that the dues taken on this bridge bring to the lord a thousand pieces of fine gold every day, and more. The people are all idolaters.'

The city of Ch'êng-Tu is still a *rich and noble* one, somewhat irregular in shape, and surrounded by a strong wall in a perfect state of repair, in which there are eight bastions, four being pierced by gates. It is now three and a half miles long by about two and a half miles broad, the longest side lying about east-south-east and west-north-west, so that its compass in the present day is about twelve miles. A stream, about thirty feet wide, runs through the city from west to east; parts of this are embanked with perpendicular revetments on either side.

At one point it is spanned by three bridges close together, each of stone, with a single arch. The one in the centre has at one time evidently been larger and of more importance, for on the other side of the road that lies between the water and the houses, almost buried in the buildings, there is a stone lion with his back to the brook. This has clearly been the former end of the bridge, so that the houses must have advanced some yards since this was built.

The city is well laid out, the streets, straight and at right angles to one another, well and carefully paved. One of them is very pretty, and runs by the side of the stream that flows through the city. Looking in at the doors of the fine shops on the right, respectable old gentlemen can be dimly discerned in the semi-obscurity smoking their long pipes. Overhead, a bamboo matting, or a bit of trellis-work covered with creepers, shelters the street from the glare of the sun; while on the left hand is a strip of garden, a yard wide, enclosed on either side by trellis-work covered with scarlet-runners, whose small red flowers form a pleasing contrast to the fresh green foliage, and through the leaves the brook is seen sparkling in the sun. The shops in Ch'êng-Tu are very good, with handsome fronts; every description of goods is sold in them; there is especially a very large trade in silk, and Ritter quotes Martini as saying:

'In the river Kin, which flows on the southern side of the city, they wash the silk, which thereby attains an extraordinary brilliancy.'

The main river still runs at the south side. It is about a hundred yards wide, and crossed by many bridges; one of them, ninety yards long, has a roof, and, as is the case on nearly all covered bridges, hucksters sit down under the shelter on both sides, as in the days of the old Venetian traveller, and sell whatever they can to passers by. There are still large numbers of junks on this river, which come up from Ch'ung-Ch'ing, and possibly some from the 'Ocean Sea.'

It is difficult to account for the great difference between the state of the city as it was in the time of the early writers and the present condition of Ch'êng-Tu. The hills, however, that enclose the plain of Ch'êng-Tu are of sandstone, and are of course easily worn away by water. The drainage of the basin is by a river of considerable size, which must in the course of five centuries have deepened its bed at its point of exit from the plain, where it is closed in on both sides by the sandstone hills. At the same time it would seem probable that the *débris* brought down by numerous streams from the surrounding mountains would rather have tended to raise than to lower the general level of the plain itself. Anyhow, when we consider how very flat the plain now is, we should, without the aid of the historian, be almost driven to the conclusion that it was in former ages the bottom of a lake.

Martini tells us that some of the ponds, lakes, rivers, or canals were artificial; and the river full half a mile in width spoken of by Polo may, in reality, have been a shallow fleet crossed by a causeway, or even by a long bridge such as he describes.

In the course of the last five centuries, as the bed of the river at its exit has been deepened, the plain has gradually been drained: and thus will nature have performed her part of the change.[1]

It is an historical fact well-known at Ch'êng-Tu that the city formerly covered a very much larger area; for in olden days, the temple of Wu-Hou-Tz'ŭ, now a mile or two outside the city to the south-west, was within the walls.

Since the days when Marco Polo travelled this way, the times have been turbulent indeed: the city has been pillaged, lawless bands have roamed with fire and sword across the fertile plain. In the early part of the Ming dynasty (commenced A.D. 1368), the whole province was overrun by a brigand named Chang-Shien-Chung; he went about ravaging and destroying everything, and is pictured as a devil incarnate; amongst other things he destroyed all the books, so that the ancient written history of the place is lost. There is therefore nothing improbable in the total disappearance of the fine works spoken of by Polo. Thus may the hand of man have combined with nature to change completely the appearance of the city of Ch'êng-Tu.

On the day after my return to the provincial capital, I called upon the French missionaries in the afternoon, and when I went home (for I had succeeded in engaging a private house, into which I gladly moved from the uncleanly inn) I found that Mesny had at length arrived from Kwei-Yang-Fu, where he had been living for many years.

Now the very serious question presented itself, whether

[1] The fact that an actual bifurcation of waters seems to take place near Ch'êng-Tu (see Richthofen's *China*, p. 327)—one branch flowing south, as the Ta-Kiang, Min-Kiang, or what not, to Siu-Chou-Fu, and the other south-east, as the To-Kiang, or Chung-Kiang of maps, to Lu-Chou—renders change in the distribution of the streams about the city highly probable.—*Y.*

I could carry out my intention of travelling through Kansu to Kashgar. My whole difficulty lay in European politics. Supposing that I had found myself unable to proceed any further towards Kashgar than Urumchi, I could have passed through Russia, if there had been no danger of England being entangled in a war with that country. But with England and Russia at war, this of course would have been impossible; and if unable to enter Kashgar, I should have had no choice but the dreary journey in mid-winter back to Peking; and even should the road to Kashgar have been clear, the mountain passes would not have been open, and I must have waited north of the Himalayas until the spring. This would not have deterred me for one moment but for the critical state of affairs between our country and Russia; in the event of war it was equally my duty and desire to be somewhere within hail, and I could not feel myself justified in running the risk of being buried for so many months in Central Asia.

This was the more disappointing, as I had everything prepared for the journey—provisions, clothes, and about three thousand taels in silver. I was very loth to give it up; but after anxiously reading every word in the scanty items of European news that were available, and after thinking over the matter night and day, sorely against my will, and with a heavy sigh, I at last determined to come home with as much speed as possible, but at the same time to travel by some new road.

The only route left was that by Bat'ang and A-Tun-Tzŭ; for the objections that applied to the Kashgar route applied equally to the only alternative, a journey *viâ* Lassa, which might or might not have been practicable. The die was cast at length. I made up my mind that I would travel with the utmost speed *viâ* Bat'ang. My desire to get on was ably seconded by Mesny; and, considering the nature of the country, and the difficulties always to be encountered, the journey actually was a very fast one, and we had the satisfaction of thinking that during the whole sixteen weeks we never lost a single hour.

Before leaving, however, I thought it well to take the

opportunity of seeing something of Ch'êng-Tu and the manners of its inhabitants. The city still bears on its face all the evidences of wealth and prosperity; the people are well dressed, and some of the temples in the city are richly endowed.

We paid a visit one day to the Wên-Shu-Yüan (Literary Book Hall), a very fine monastery near the north gate, built some time during the Sung dynasty (from A.D. 960 to 1279). It was then called the Chin-King-Sze; it fell into decay during the Mongol occupation, and was rebuilt by the second emperor of the present dynasty, the famous Kang-Shi (better known in the form of Khang-Hi), who reigned 1662–1722. This emperor richly endowed it with lands; but, notwithstanding its wealth, it seems to have been predestined to misfortune, for it was again neglected, until the time of Kia-Ching (Kia-King), the fifth emperor of the present dynasty (1795–1820) when it was rebuilt by public subscription with stone instead of wooden pillars. Since that time it has gone on increasing in wealth and magnificence, and is now one of the richest in the country. To have the right of living at this monastery it is necessary to be a priest of a particular sect; but, besides the priests, there are resident here a number of students qualifying themselves for holy orders; altogether there are about one hundred and fifty inmates.

A remarkable air of refinement and cleanliness pervaded the place. The courtyard was laid with smooth-cut flagstones, not one out of its place, and not a weed or blade of grass permitted to grow in the interstices. All the buildings were in perfect repair, and a man was walking about the court with a cross-bow. His employment was to shoot stones at the sparrows that nfested the roofs, and which, if left to their own devices, would do serious damage. Immediately on the right of the entrance was a very clean reception-room; and whilst preparations were being made to escort us over the establishment, we were refreshed with the usual cups of tea. We were not kept waiting above a couple of minutes, and then we were invited to proceed. The refectory, a long wooden building on the right-hand side, opened into the court; here were twenty-five tables, each prepared for six people. For each person was laid one pair of red wooden chopsticks and three porcelain bowls, one for rice, one for vegetables, and one for tea, no meat of any description ever being permitted here; everything, the tables, bowls, and chopsticks were beautifully clean—a most surprising thing in this country, where usually dirt reigns supreme. Passing this, we entered a chapel, where, at the end, the repulsive countenances of a number of huge and hideous images were partially obscured by a kind of throne for the prior, whence he discourses on the religious classics to the students.

On either side of the chapel was a reception-room. The general arrangement of these rooms is almost always the same, and whether a private house, a ya-mên, or a temple, the description of one stands as a representation of all the others: no furniture in the middle of the room; along two sides are arranged, in symmetrical though inartistic order, the usual heavy, stiff, uncompromising, and utterly uncomfortable arm-chairs of China; between each two is a little high and square table, all corners and angularities, like the Chinese character. At the end of the room is the kang, or raised dais, ten feet long, four feet broad, and two feet high, where in the centre is placed a small table, six or eight inches high, between two cushions of the most brilliant scarlet—these are the seats of honour; and footstools of wood for those seated thereon complete the furniture.

For ornament, a few bronzes, or the roots of trees carved into representations of impossible dragons, are arranged behind the kang; while from the ceiling hang paper lamps, some of them really artistically painted, and arranged just low enough to knock off the hat of a foreigner. In China, etiquette rules that in polite society the hat is kept on the head, and at a dinner party it is amusing, when all the guests are intimate and of the same social standing, to see the alacrity with which permission is always asked and given to exchange the official hat for the little skull-cap, which each person's servant has somewhere secreted about the capacious folds of his garment.

A collation of tea and cakes, sweet but nasty, was looked at rather than partaken of, while the monks gave us what history of the building I have been able to relate, sitting, as etiquette ordains, with their backs quite stiff, on the extreme edges of their chairs, and with their bodies slightly turned round to their guests.

From this we ascended to the upper story, where the principal room was a magnificent chapel filled with gifts and curiosities, a very fine and richly-decorated altar, rubbings from ancient tablets, a great deal of blue and white china, pictures painted on glass from Canton, and, amongst other things, a present from a young lady of a piece of embroidery entirely worked with her own hair. This represented the goddess of mercy sitting under a bamboo, the leaves of which were really most admirably represented.

In this chapel also the contributors to the building, maintenance, or decoration of the temple are immortalised, their names being written in gold on black tablets and put under a glass case. Here also is the library, where huge cupboards are filled with books of the religious classics, which form the unique and dreary study of the inhabitants.

We passed on to another chapel set apart for meditations. Here the priests and students, in yellow robes and with shaven heads, come at least once a day, and, lighting an incense-stick before one of the images, sit down at the side of the room and meditate, trying to work themselves into a state of religious ecstasy, in which they shall be entirely withdrawn from impressions from the outside.

A few of them appeared to be really in this state of semi-unconsciousness ; but the majority, though trying to look as if they did not see us, could not resist a sidelong glance every now and then. They remain in this state about half an hour at a time. The impression formed upon my mind by the appearance of those who had succeeded in their extraordinary task was rather a painful one.

Passing through another chapel, where a number of beautiful red and yellow lotus-plants were growing in pots, where a tailor was at work in a corner, and in which were the portraits of all the deceased priors, we again came to the gate, where a number of huge and hideous figures—the guardians of the place—were grinning horribly, and where the monks with exquisite politeness bade adieu to their unwonted guests.

We went from this, along a road between walls that enclosed magnificent vegetable gardens, to the grave of a concubine of Shu-Wang.

Shu-Wang ('King of Shu') was the aboriginal king of this country before its conquest by the Chinese, and he lived in the time of the Chinese emperor T'sin-Shih-Hwang-Ti, the builder of the Great Wall of China, in the third century B.C.

The grave is an artificial mound of yellow clay, about one hundred yards long, running north-west and south-east, and about twenty yards broad; its two ends being raised about ten feet above the other parts. At the south-east extremity, half buried in the clay that has fallen on it, is a huge limestone disc. Neither its diameter nor its full thickness are exposed, but, judging from the segment, its diameter must be about sixteen feet, and there is a thickness of three feet visible; how much more there may be I cannot say. Near the circumference of the stone, there is a circular hollow about six inches across, but it is very irregular, and I should say was accidental. The stone has evidently fallen from its place, so that any examination as to its position was useless. But it must have been a great labour to bring this enormous slab from beyond Kuan-Hsien, the nearest place where the limestone is found.

We were invited to a picnic at a temple not far from the Wu-Hou-Tz'ŭ, at which place it was agreed that our party should meet.

Though the sun was powerful there was a little air moving outside the city, and the heat was by no means oppressive. We were about an hour reaching the Wu-Hou-Tz'ŭ. Here our friends were waiting for us, and we all went on together to a temple, built, during the seventh century, by the great poet Tu-Fu, as a country residence. The buildings include a number of rooms, covered passages, corridors, and pavilions, furnished with little tables and chairs, where the people of

Ch'êng-Tu come to picnic. The grounds are large, containing fine trees and great numbers of large bamboos, that everywhere cast a pleasant and grateful shade. There are ponds with tortoises and fish in great numbers, and a couple of dwarfs with enormous heads earn a livelihood by selling bread and cakes for the people to feed the fish with.

We first went into a nice large cool room, where all the woodwork was painted black; but, as the upper half of both the long sides was entirely window, there was no sombre impression. All the windows were open, and the eyes rested on the fresh green foliage, which almost completely excluded the mid-day glare, whilst the breeze gently rustling the bamboo leaves, and the occasional caw of a rook or a magpie, produced a pleasant feeling of repose.

We found the company assembled. There was a very fat, heavy-looking man, a civilian, with the rank of Fan-Tai, by name Wei, whose manners were polished to the highest degree, and who would have been profoundly shocked at the smallest breach of the intricate etiquette of the Chinese. In remarkable contrast to him, a tall thin man, with the rank of Chen-Tai, was walking about. His face differed much from the usual Chinese type: he looked as if he was more of a man than the Chinese generally appear; and, although his face and manners betokened a love of ease, there was none of the listless, apathetic appearance about him so often seen in this people.

After our hot ride (in chairs) we sat down, and the grateful beverage was soon introduced. Mesny and I were pressed to take seats on the kang; but among so many we left it unoccupied and sat down on the chairs at the side of the room.

A basin of hot water and a piece of rag were brought in. An attendant, whose hands must have been made of cast-iron, dipped the rag into the almost boiling water, and wrung it out several times. He brought it to me, and I wiped my face and hands in correct Chinese style. The rag, or, as Huc calls it, a linen table napkin,[2] was dipped afresh and wrung out for each person present.

[2] Huc, *L'Empire Chinois*, vol. i. p. 184.

Mesny then opened the conversation by asking every one he did not know, 'What is your honourable name?' 'What is your honourable age?' 'Where do you come from?' and in return answered similar questions with true celestial politeness, and although I did not know a dozen words of Chinese I could see what was going on.

The secretary then proposed to take me round the temple, and we walked about looking at the tortoises, the ponds, the dwarfs, and the idols.

He showed me an isolated building in one place, with four very large images of Buddha in the centre, and upwards of a thousand pictures of the head of Buddha on the walls. We then came back, and after a time signs of dinner appeared in the form of a *zakouska*, for, before seating ourselves at the round table, a bowl of soup and four little puddings, with minced meat and onions inside, were handed to each person.

I did not know how to manage these things; but I watched the others take up a pudding, put it into the soup, partially break it, and so eat it. I did the same; but there was too much garlic for my taste. This appeared to me quite a meal in itself; but my Chinese friends finished their four puddings, and looked upon this exactly as the Russians do upon the little bit of salt fish or caviare they take to whet their appetites. The pudding to put into the soup also is quite a Russian custom.

Soon afterwards, at about half-past four, we sat down to a very extensive dinner. To every man was assigned a pair of chopsticks, one little piece of paper, one little saucer of soy, one china spoon, one saucer of water-melon seeds and kernels of peach-stones, and one cup about as big as the bottom of an egg cup (without a handle).

At a given signal every one at once dipped their chopsticks into the centre dish and commenced operations. The silk merchant was very polite to me, and always assisted me if he saw I was not sufficiently skilful with my chopsticks. The guests thus went through about twelve dishes that were on the table, some sweet, some sour, some raw, and some cooked. They were much the same dishes that I had seen at Shanghai or Peking—shrimps raw, duck or ham cut into little bits, sugar-candy, lotus-root, walnuts cooked in soy, giblets, with preserved eggs, shrimps, and other things, all equally flavourless. A servant then came in, and removing two or three of the nearly empty bowls, brought in others; and so on, dish succeeded dish in somewhat weary monotony; duck appeared in two other forms, fowl came on twice, tripe was dressed in two ways, and a dish of peaches stewed in arrowroot was given in the middle of dinner. There was one dish of really excellent mutton, and of course at least half a dozen of pork in different forms. The greatest delicacy was minced pork, dressed with something sweet, and wrapped up in a huge lotus-leaf. To our Western ideas the mess the table and floor get into on an occasion of this kind is horrid. There are no plates; when the dishes are brought in, if they are solids they are piled up as high as possible, and if they are soups the bowls are filled to running over. In helping himself with a chopstick the most skilful will now and then drop something, and to eat the gravy the spoon is dipped into the central bowl, and then put down wet and greasy on the table.

The *débris* also collects on the table more or less, though a person accustomed to these things does not leave much, for he spits or throws it on to the floor. Bread is not offered until the end of the meal, and when I asked for some, earlier during the entertainment, a whole baker's shop of loaves was brought in for me. The drink was a very palatable fermented liquor made from rice, and was taken hot.

Directly two guests have taken wine with one another the cups are filled by the attendants. The silk merchant was very anxious on my account, and asked me to drink with him after each course, and seeing that the mutton was the thing I really liked, he had it specially left for my edification.

The waiters were all naked to the waist, and the guests would have been the same if Mesny and I had not been present; but out of deference to us they kept on a thin garment over their bodies.

The last dish of all was a bowl of what Europeans call 'conjee'—rice boiled almost to a pulp, and served up with the thick rice-water. In ordinary society a bowl of plain rice takes the place of this; but at these grand entertainments it is customary to have conjee instead.

After this the guests laid their chopsticks across the empty bowl, rose up and saluted one another, and then, again putting the chopsticks on to the table, the dinner was over.

I gave each of the gentlemen a Manilla cigar, produced a penknife, showed them how to cut off the ends, and offered them a light from a box of wax vestas, at which they were much delighted. The general and my French-speaking friend lighted their cigars; but the Fan-Tai and the silk merchant put away theirs for some other opportunity.

While the servants were clearing up the mess we strolled about the grounds. The general, pacing up and down smoking the cigar, had far more the air of an Englishman than a Chinaman; but the secretary, although he seemed to like the smoke, did not quite manage it *à l'Européenne.* We loitered about some time, and many amusing stories were told.

The 9th of July, our last day in Ch'êng-Tu, was, as may be imagined, a busy one. We paid a final visit to our kind friends the missionaries, and then all our acquaintances came to say good-bye to us. We were informed that the drought was becoming very serious, even in this province; at the time of my visit there was as yet no scarcity of food, but in the neighbouring provinces the famine eventuated in the awful calamities that have filled the readers of our daily papers with horror; and even in Ssŭ-Ch'uan the drought, though not so disastrous as elsewhere, was in 1878 very dreadful.

In the fertile plain of Ch'êng-Tu itself, the rice crop never fails, even in the driest season; for the brimming brooks that course by the roadside and sparkle in the sun derive their supplies from the streams which, descending from the snow-clad heights, are never-failing, and unite to form the considerable river of Kuan-Hsien. There the impetuosity of the turbulent torrent, which dashes and foams over its rocky bed, is curbed by the irrigation works that divide the river into numerous streams, and those, meandering through the beautiful plain, and subdivided into canals and yet smaller ducts, and finally pumped up by the simple treadmills, leave not an acre of land without its perennial supply of water. Thus, even at a time when all the horrors of famine and pestilence were desolating the lands that lay just beyond the surrounding hills, this favoured spot was still enabled to present a scene of comfort and tranquillity.

When at last our preparations were complete, our baggage was weighed and divided into forty portions, for forty coolies were required to carry it; and a bargain was eventually struck with the coolie-master to supply us with sixty coolies, to take us, our chairs, our baggage, and our servants to Ta-Chien-Lu, at the rate of 3·2 taels per coolie.

The mosquitoes had already sounded their warning notes, and although they had not yet given me any trouble, Mesny had been so devoured that I thought it advisable to see about mosquito curtains. The Chinese have a capital

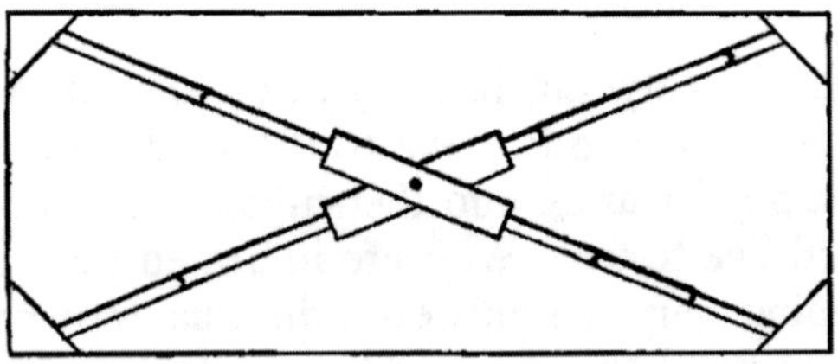

arrangement for travelling-curtains. The top is made with a little triangular pocket at each corner. The ends of four light bamboos are joined together by two brass tubes, and the other ends of the bamboos inserted in the small pockets stretch the top of the curtain. One nail in the wall or the ceiling is all that is required, and the curtain can be put up or taken down in a few minutes. The bamboos, being of no great length, are easily carried. I bought one of these, and found some regular Indian mosquito-gauze in a shop in the city, with which some curtains were made that served me in good stead. I used them almost every night throughout my journey, and they effectually kept out, not only mosquitoes, but insects of many other kinds.

It is not customary in China for a servant to ride in a chair with more than two coolies, and an official is forbidden to permit his servant to do so; but I did not feel myself bound by Chinese customs, for my boys, both over six feet, would always have been miles behind me if I had not allowed them three coolies each.

The organisation of departure, as Huc is pleased to term the disorder of a start in China, was now complete; the baggage was all packed, the coolies' bickerings gradually were settled as they moved off one by one, and at length, on the morning of the 10th of July, we left the provincial capital, and started joyously on the high road to the Tibetan borders.

The march to Shuang-Liu was over the busy, fertile plain, entirely given up to rice cultivation. In the gardens there were melons, cucumbers, all sorts of vegetables, and patches of Indian corn. The country was beautifully watered; little rills brimming with water coursing by the roadside, or among the fields; and, as elsewhere on this plain, there were numerous detached farmhouses embowered in trees and bamboos. West of Shuang-Liu the road still led us over the level plain, where the amazing fertility of the soil was apparent in the magnificent crops of rice that now, from two to three feet high, presented to the eye a vast expanse of the richest green.

Riding through a town, where, as it was market-day, all the streets were crowded, I was much edified by the remarks passed by the crowd upon my person. I wore a helmet, and one man said, 'Does not he think himself a swell with a hat like a ram's horn?' 'Yes,' replied another; 'but look at his nose; he might be an official with that nose.'

The Chinese are great physiognomists, and always admire a good-sized nose; generally, their own noses are perfectly flat, without any bridge, and by saying I might be an official, the man meant that my nose was good, and that therefore I ought to possess some talent that would fit me for an official position.

Another man said that I had tremendously long legs. The Chinese always wear such loose baggy raiment, that in appearance the length of their legs is very much diminished.

The observations that are made are not as a rule very flattering, and forcibly illustrate the old proverb about listeners. I once heard of an English gentleman of whom an educated Chinaman remarked with the intention of being highly complimentary : '*Why, he is not so dirty as a Mongol.*' A Mongol never takes his clothes off all the winter, eats fat and grease by the pound, wipes his fingers on and drops messes all over his leather coat, and is about as greasy and dirty a personage as can well be imagined. On another occasion, an Englishman was told that he did not smell so bad as a Man-Tzŭ. However little it may flatter our Western vanity to admit it, there can be no doubt that every nation has its peculiar odour ; but on this point I have already remarked.

It may seem impossible for us to understand how such remarks can be made seriously, and without the smallest offensive intention ; but this is only another proof of the difficulty of understanding the Chinese. To judge of a Chinaman's character, we must look with the eyes of a Chinaman, and put ourselves outside every conviction that we have formed, even about ourselves.

A Chinaman from his earliest infancy is brought up to believe that besides the Chinese nation there are in the world only some few insignificant barbarians. The chief knowledge of foreigners was originally derived from intercourse, peaceful or warlike, with the Man-Tzŭ, Tibetans, or Mongols ; and even now the number of Chinese who have been in contact with Europeans is very small. When, therefore, a Chinaman had to form his idea of foreigners, there was nothing very wonderful in his comparing them with the Man-Tzŭ, the only type of foreigners known to him ; nor was this idea, after all, very much more erroneous than that prevalent not so very long ago amongst many English people, that frogs formed the principal part of a Frenchman's diet, or the opinion that is even now indulged in by many of our home-staying countrymen, that all foreign cookery is greasy.

It was with intense pleasure that, at half-past two in the afternoon of the 12th, when the sun was darting its most fiery rays upon us, we caught the first sight of the mountains on the horizon; and our minds dwelt with pleasure on the snow-fields, and awful glaciers, so vividly depicted by former travellers in the regions we were now approaching. Soon afterwards, as if to cheer us, an easterly breeze sprung up, and the thermometer falling to 93°, the weather felt quite pleasant.

On the 13th we came to the river called Nan-Ho, the bed of which, where we struck it, was about one hundred yards wide; but, following down stream about two hundred yards, we crossed by a remarkably fine fifteen-arched bridge of red stone, two hundred and forty yards long and nine and a half yards wide, with a somewhat boastful inscription on a tablet proclaiming it the finest in Ssŭ-Ch'uan.

After passing the river, we entered an undulating country, the hills of a reddish-yellow clay, and well wooded, principally with pines in small clumps. The road, running in many places between hedges, would have put me much in mind of some of the Hampshire scenery, if it had not been for the rice in terraces. The cultivation was only on the flat ground, the slopes being everywhere given up to trees. The road was exceedingly tortuous, winding about and twisting in a most perplexing manner, following the summit of a ridge from one hundred to two hundred feet above the valleys. We met coolies carrying logs of wood, sometimes as much as two hundred pounds in weight. These enormous loads are carried about ten miles a day, the wood being principally for coffins, which, when made from a particular and much-prized species of tree, cost sometimes as much as 300*l.* or 400*l.* Here nearly all the women had feet of the natural size, and many of those whose feet were cramped had not squeezed them in nearly to the usual extent; but those seen about were mostly of the poorer class, for the richer folk do not permit their women to walk about much in public.

At Pai-Chang-Yi, we found one of the embassies that were just now on the Tibetan road established in one of the inns. The ambassador, if he can be dignified with such a title, was an official of very inferior position. The Chinese always send petty officials as ambassadors, in order to show their immense superiority to foreigners; it is as much as saying 'Oh! anything is good enough for a foreigner;' and it must have gone sorely against the grain to despatch two men of high rank to England.

The people here are not such early risers as in the north of China; as we marched through Pai-Chang-Yi [3] in the morning none of the shops were open, and there were very few people about in the streets.

A Chinese town with its shops all shut up is even more dreary in appearance than Regent Street on Sunday. The shop fronts—when open there are no fronts—are made of dirty wood, from which the paint has long worn off; and everything looks shabby to the last degree.

The road was most unpleasant for walking on. It was paved, and the original intentions of the constructor had evidently been excellent, for most of the stones had been cut quite flat, and as the ground was tolerably level, if the execution had been as meritorious as the conception, the road would have left nothing to desire. But the contractor, in order to save money, had made use of the rough stuff he found lying about, and had put in at every foot or so an uncut boulder that thrust itself above the general level in a most obtrusive and unpleasant manner. No doubt, by bribing the road surveyor, he had obtained a good report of his performance.

Between Ming-Shan-Hsien and Ya-Chou, the country was more broken, the smaller ridges giving way to detached hills of red clayey sandstone, all still well cultivated and wooded.

We followed a little stream through a miniature gorge, and, ascending a branch, gained a saddle four hundred feet above the plain, whence we had a fine view of the Ya-Chou valley. This is about two miles wide, is quite flat, and bounded on each side by mountains from eight hundred to fifteen hundred feet high. The river bed is about two

[3] *Pai* means a hundred. *Chang* is a measure of ten Chinese feet.

hundred yards wide, though at this season the water is not more than forty or fifty yards across. The stream ran at the rate of about four miles an hour, and was now very shallow. A little lower down, the valley closes in on the left bank, and steep red hills, clothed with deep green foliage, hang over the water, forming little cliffs, and making a very pretty picture. We ascended the river about three miles, and crossed it in a ferry, just below the city of Ya-Chou-Fu, where we found a particularly nice inn with an open court in front.

In front of some of the houses, before reaching Ya-Chou, we saw a few vines, trailing over a trellis-work above the road. There was also some tea put out to dry, of which a little grows here. At Ming-Shan-Hsien some very celebrated tea is grown, but only in small quantities.

Ya-Chou is a place of great importance, as it is the starting-point of all the commerce to Tibet, to which place tea and cotton are the chief exports.

The most remarkable trade of this place is its commerce in tea, vast quantities of which are sent from here through Tibet, and up to the very gates of our own tea-gardens in India. The tea for the Tibetans is merely the sweepings that would elsewhere be thrown away, the poor Chinese in Ya-Chou paying seven or eight times the cost of this for what they drink themselves. It is pressed into cakes about 4 feet long × 1 foot × 4 inches, each of which is wrapped in straw, is called a *pau*, and weighs 24 lbs. The average load for a coolie is about ten or eleven of these packets. I have seen some carrying eighteen—that is 432 lbs. Little boys are constantly seen with five or six *pau*—120 lbs. These men wear a sort of framework on their backs, which, if the load is bulky, often comes right over the head, and forms in rainy weather a protection from the wet. Each of them carries a thing like the handle of a spud, with an iron shoe and point at the end, and when they rest themselves the handle is put under the load, the point into the ground, and thus they relieve their backs from the weight. A coolie gets 1·8 tael to carry six *pau* (144 lbs.) from Ya-Chou to Ta-Chien-Lu, 150 miles over an exceedingly mountainous country—a distance usually accomplished in twenty days. The pay would seem barely enough to keep life in them under their tremendous loads. They eat scarcely anything but Indian-corn bread, made up into round cakes nearly an inch thick, and from six to ten inches in diameter.

Beyond Ya-Chou we left the main river at once, and, crossing a little ridge, entered the valley of a tributary, ascending which we gained Yung-Ching-Hsien on the 16th. As we marched through the town early next morning, the shops were just opening, and I was not very favourably impressed with the place; but I had perhaps been spoiled by the very fine cities in the Ch'êng-Tu plain, for certainly even these towns of Western Ssŭ-Ch'uan would compare favourably with those in the north of China. The streets are wide and fairly paved, though there are a great many round stones used, which are equally disagreeable for man and beast. The unfavourable impressions are also partly owing to the abominably shabby state of the houses, which never seem to be painted, white-washed, or repaired. All the woodwork is black with dirt, the paint is rubbed off, and everything looks dreadfully dilapidated. This is most apparent before the shutters are removed, for the fronts are quite open, and in the day all the inhabitants of the town collect in the main street, and in a measure conceal the imperfections; but in the morning, when the greasy shutters close the fronts, and there are only a few sleepy coolies about, or an early pieman selling his hot cakes, all the dirt is seen in its full glory.

We met a long train of mules bringing opium from Yün-Nan, and others carrying brass. There was a man with a cargo of parrots, which, he said, came from the mountains in the interior; but he did not know much about it, as he did not get them himself. We afterwards found the home of these birds in the neighbourhood of the Chin-Sha-Chiang, south of Bat'ang.

About six miles from Yung-Ching we left the main river, and ascended a tributary up a very pretty valley bounded by sandstone hills. The red sandstone formation presented a remarkable contrast to the limestone of the valley of Sung-P'an-T'ing. The limestone is always broken into sharp crags and pinnacles, leaving tremendous precipices. The streams find their way through long and gloomy gorges, sometimes winding for miles between perpendicular walls of rock, scarcely broken by a chasm.

Gradually the mountains began to close around us, and the amount of cultivation seemed to decrease with every step in advance, until the limit of the Indian corn and bamboo was passed at 4,132 feet above the sea. Between that point and the summit of the T'ai-Hsiang-Ling-Kuan, or the Pass of the Great Minister's Range, there was, with the exception of one tiny patch, absolutely no cultivation, the hill-sides being clothed with a rich and brilliant green foliage of trees and undergrowth, which completely obscured the red colour of the granite, of which the whole of the mountains here are formed.

Quitting the river, we ascended a tributary for a short distance, and then, crossing a little spur, a descent of fifty feet brought us back to the main stream. The road over this spur is closed by a gate called Hsiao-Kuan (Little Pass), and the village at the foot of it bears the same name.

Whilst sitting at breakfast Chin-Tai came in with a sad look about his face, and after a cough that was the invariable prelude to a miraculous narrative he began :—

'The road goes over a very big Shan.' (He never succeeded in learning the English word 'mountain.')

'Yes,' I said ; 'so I understand.'

After a moment's pause he continued, 'We must not make much talk on the big Shan.'

'Indeed,' I said ; 'I suppose a great wind would come if we did.'

'Yes,' he answered ; 'there was once a big military official who——'

'Ah,' I interrupted, 'he was advised not to go up with his army?'

'Yes ; all the people tell him that——'

'That is enough,' I said, 'I have heard the story before ;[4] and as these mountains seem to have been so fatal to

[4] Page 131, at Fêng-Tung-Kuan.

military officials, you had better go and knock your head that you are but a humble civilian.'

Beyond the Little Pass, the road followed the valley, and was one of the worst I ever travelled on. Now zigzagging up the side of a mountain, the path was cut in steep steps over sharp pointed rocks; and now winding along the side of a gully, some stream was crossed by a ford or a bridge. Everywhere the wooded hills rose above us some one thousand or two thousand feet, very steep but never precipitous. Sometimes we were down at the level of the stream, at others far above it, but the steady ascent always continued. After a time, again leaving the main valley, we ascended a steep spur by a long zigzag, and reached its crest at Ta-Kuan (Great Pass), 5,754 feet above the sea. Near here we passed an unfortunate pony that had fallen down under its load, and was left to die by the roadside. I wanted to shoot it and put it out of its misery, but was told that its owner would be sure to come up and accuse me of having killed a fine and healthy animal. After this the road again rejoined the river without descending appreciably, and another long pull of four thousand feet brought us to the summit of the T'ai-Hsiang-Ling-Kuan, 9,366 feet above the sea.

Directly we crossed this, the landscape changed entirely, the mountain-sides being all green grassy slopes, very little cut up by valleys, and not so steep as those on the other side. There was no wood, no cultivation, and little undergrowth, but the ground was covered with beautiful rich grass and many wild flowers.

The rain had been falling on the eastern slope, which, from the luxuriance of the foliage, appears to possess a much damper climate than the western face; but as the ridge arrested the clouds, we were now in tolerably fine weather, and from the little tea-house close to the summit we could see the city of Ch'ing-Ch'i at the foot of a steep spur 3,888 feet below. This tea-house rejoiced in the name of Ts'ao-Hsieh-P'ing (Straw-Sandal Flat), and was doubtless so called on account of the numerous straw sandals expended in the passage of this terrible mountain.

Another wearisome zigzag led us down a very steep spur. On the way, the first cultivation was a patch of tobacco, and a little lower, the familiar fields of Indian corn and beans again covered the hill-sides.

Ch'ing-Ch'i seemed a wretchedly poor place; when we started there was no one in the streets, the shops were all shut, and the city generally bore a miserable aspect. I have a very vague idea of the day's march, for everything was shrouded in mist and fog. This is amply compensated for by the remarkably vivid impressions retained of the road. In many places there was no road at all—we had to cross ravines, where the torrents, swollen by the rain, had altogether carried away the goat-track that did duty for a path, and sometimes in these narrow gullies it was almost impossible to get the chairs round the sharp corners. The soil was a soft sticky clay; the chairs were continually bumped about by projecting rocks; the coolies stumbled, the rain fell, and altogether it was anything but a lively performance, as may be gathered from the fact that we were six hours covering the nine miles to Fu-Hsing-Ch'ang.

On leaving Ch'ing-Ch'i we descended to a stream, crossed it, and ascended the hills bounding it on the other side, until we gained the crest of a ridge that separated it from another valley. From this point the main road to the province of Yün-Nan leads to the south-west. We left it on our left, and, crossing the ridge, followed up the stream to Fu-Hsing-Ch'ang.

On this road we continually passed long trains of coolies, carrying tea on their backs, climbing mournfully and with measured tread the desperate and staircase-like tracks. There was something very sad in the aspect of these men—they seemed more like beasts of burden than human beings; they never smiled, and scarcely ever said a word; and as our lively Ssŭ-Ch'uan coolies, ever ready with some banter passed them, they would stand on one side, with rigid countenances that scarcely relaxed into an expression of wonder as the two strange foreigners came by. These coolies, who do the chief part of the mountain transport, are quite a different class to the comparatively well-paid coolies of the plains; they carry the tea as far as Ta-Chien-Lu, beyond which point that extraordinary and hardy animal the yak is almost solely employed.

The people had told us that there were no more regular mountain passes before reaching Ta-Chien-Lu; but mile after mile we ascended, in continual showers of heavy rain. The road was broken into rocky steps, sometimes so steep that it seemed as if neither ponies nor coolies could possibly mount, and sometimes so slippery that I was quite unable to walk in European boots, nothing but the straw sandals that the coolies wear giving any hold on these steep paths. At last, after a long clamber up many a weary zigzag, through a dank mist that shrouded everything from view, we gained the summit of the pass called sometimes Wu-Yai-Ling (which means the Range without a Fork) and sometimes Fei-Yueh-Ling (Fly beyond Range)[5] 9,022 feet above the sea. From here, as the clouds lifted for a few minutes, there was a fine view in both directions. The valley on the northern side was rather more open, and the hills less steep, and we descended about a couple of thousand feet to the town of Hua-Ling-P'ing, perched, among many walnut and other trees, on a little plateau about five hundred feet above the stream, where there was a small but very comfortable inn.

The last shower fell as we left the town on the 22nd of July, the day cleared up, and in the valleys the damp heat was again almost oppressive after the chilly air of the mountain-tops. We descended the stream until some people met us with the pleasing intelligence that the bridge by which we ought to cross had been washed away in the morning, and that we should probably have to wait until it should please the river to subside. We went to look for the remains of the bridge, but there were absolutely none to see, and the muddy torrent, roaring and foaming over huge rocks and stones, was evidently quite impassable. Our guides and the inhabitants of the place, with one consent, now tried to frighten us, and assured us that there was no road; but, not heeding them,

[5] Correctly, I believe, *Ling* is the pass, or *col*, not the *range*.—Y.

we found a track through a field of Indian corn, which, leading above a little cliff that bounded the stream, led us down to a village, whence the road was very fair to the junction of this stream with the river of Ta-Chien-Lu.

At Lu-Ting-Ch'iao, which we reach on the 23rd, the river is crossed by an iron chain suspension-bridge, of one hundred yards span. The roadway is laid on nine iron chains, and there are two other chains at each side for hand-rails; the links are of seven-eighth-inch-round iron, and are about ten inches long, but those underneath are much eaten away by rust. The roadway consists of planks laid across, which were originally lashed to the chains; but all the lashings were now adrift, and the planks quite loose, with wide gaps between them. There is a deep pit at each end of the bridge, into which the chains are brought, and where, if they get slack, they can be tautened up with powerful windlasses. I crossed with a good many people, and there was very little vibration; but Mesny, during the afternoon, walked over by himself, and found it swayed about a good deal.

On arrival at the bridge I was directed to cross it; I dismounted, and walked across to examine the structure, and pace its length, and I did not take much notice of what my people were doing with the ponies. These animals were rather frightened at the loose planks; but the men, instead of letting them go slowly and put their heads down to see what they were doing, dragged at the bridles, and attempted to pull them over by main force. The poor brutes, in consequence, could not see where to put their feet, one false step was made, both the animals started, and in a moment all their eight legs were in the openings between the planks. By the aid of a number of coolies, however, they were lifted up bodily from their perilous position, and reached the other side more frightened than hurt.

There was an archway at the end of the bridge which seemed to be the principal seat of trade as well as of amusement; for here there was a large party of coolies playing dominoes, with pieces not very different from those used in Europe.

After having crossed and waited about some time searching for the inn, we found that our men had taken up our quarters at the other side; so, leaving the ponies here, we recrossed to the left bank of the stream, where we found a delightful inn, large and comfortable, with two good bedrooms, besides the sitting-room; but of course with the invariable bad smells from piggeries and other foulness. There was an upper story also, and for the first time in China I heard people walking about overhead.

The people here took very little notice of us; as they are accustomed to the constant presence of Tibetans, and, as all foreigners (including these) are classed together, we did not attract much attention. But the dog was still an object of much curiosity, and a good many people came about on his account. Chin-Tai, finding access to our room incommoded by the people, told a man rather sharply to get out of the way, and not come staring at us; to which the man replied, not exactly 'a cat may look at a king,' but something very like it, for he said that he might look at the Emperor of China, and he supposed that an Englishman was not better than that. Whereupon high words ensued, and something like a fight, and Chung-Erh came in, breathless with rage and excitement, with no other purpose whatever than to tell me that he had made up his mind to kill one of the men of Ssŭ-Ch'uan before he left their country.

Both my boys had taken a violent dislike to the people of this province, chiefly because on one occasion when Chin-Tai had bargained for a fowl for a hundred and twenty cash, and had been obliged to go and fetch the money, he had been told on his return that the price was a hundred and thirty. This rankled in his bosom ever after, and now neither he nor Chung-Erh missed any opportunity of abusing these people.

Airing ourselves at the inn door, we entered into conversation with a man, who told us that the bridge was three hundred Chinese feet long, and had thirteen chains. On inquiring the reason of this gratuitous information, we were told that our reputation for asking questions had preceded us, and that the bridge had been measured for the first time within the memory of man expressly for our gratification.

The road from Lu-Ting-Ch'iao ran along the side of a mountain on the right bank of the river, keeping generally about five hundred feet above it, but descending once or twice to reach a village or cross a torrent. The river valley now closed in, the hill-sides became more steep, and the cultivation almost entirely disappeared; but in the bottoms of the valleys there were still some tiny plots of rice, the last we saw for many a long and weary day. The little agriculture carried on on the slopes produced as usual chiefly Indian corn and beans, with small quantities of pearl barley.

Beyond Hsiao-P'êng-Pa the river ran between precipitous mountains, with here and there wild bare slopes running down sharply to the stream; the road was not very good, in some places ascending long and steep inclines or steps, and at others rounding a bluff at an angle rather too sharp to be easy for a chair. Seven miles beyond Hsiao-P'êng-Pa the road crossed a torrent by a covered wooden bridge, and an icy breath that suddenly saluted me made me look up the narrow gorge, and between the clouds that rolled up the mountain-sides some snow was visible lying on a peak at no great distance.

Wa-Ssŭ-Kou, where we slept, is situated at the junction of the stream that comes from Ta-Chien-Lu with the main river. Both streams here flow through narrow gorges, and at their junction there hardly looks as if there was room to pitch a tent; but the Chinese do not mind being crowded, and have managed to find place for the few houses that make the village.

The valley, for the first ten miles beyond Wa-Ssŭ-Kou, is closed in by steep hills, whose rugged sides have been rent by the rigours of the climate, and torn into cliffs and precipices, that overhang the roaring stream. As Ta-Chien-Lu is approached the valley is more open, but the ground and river-bed are everywhere strewn with great boulders, and the water leaps down in a succession of falls over huge masses of rock. At this time the rains had filled it, and it thundered down a mass of foam, falling nearly three thousand feet in the twenty miles from Ta-Chien-Lu. The road is in harmony with its savage surroundings, but in three or four places there are remains of what appears to have been a fine ancient road, fifteen feet wide, evenly paved, and on which all the gradients were easy.

At Ta-Chien-Lu, the end of the first stage in our journey, Bishop Chauveau received us with every expression of cordiality and friendship, and we spent a delightful half-hour before seeking our lodging.

Ta-Chien-Lu.

CHAPTER IX.

TA-CHIEN-LU.

Ta-Chien-Lu—Native King—Indian Rupees Current—The Place and People—'Om Mani Pemi Hom!'—A House found for us—The Local Government—Transport Arrangements—The Lamas and the Dalai Lama—The Prayer-Cylinder and the Multiform Mani Inscriptions—The Lama Ambassadors—Menaces of our Fate if we entered Tibet—The Servants begin to Quail—Chin-Tai, his Greed and his Tempers—Heavy Provisioning for the Journey—Contrast of Tibetan and Chinese Habits—Of Tibetan Simplicity of Fare with Chinese Variety—Kindly Aid rendered by the late Bishop Chauveau—The New Ma-Fu—Visit to a Lamassery—Currency for the Journey—The Tibetan's Inseparable Wooden Cup—Tib left behind—Fresh Selection of Nags—Fatality of Small-pox in Tibet.

TA-CHIEN-LU may be considered as the boundary of China, for up to this point the people are directly governed by Chinese; but beyond this there are native chiefs who, subject to China, rule over the people.

There is a native king here whose territory extends to Ho-K'ou, a few days' journey to the west. Although he enjoys the rank of king, he is obliged to pay an official visit twice a month to the Chinese chief magistrate (a Kiun-Liang-Fu). The king always refused to see Europeans, because he was afraid that the formalities of an inferior to a superior that are exacted from him by the Chinese officials would be demanded also by foreign visitors.

It seemed very strange to us to find the Indian rupee in use here. The Tibetans and mountaineers of these countries find themselves so cheated by the Chinese in their money dealings that they have abandoned the cumbersome method of making payments by weight, which lends itself so easily to every kind of trickery, and have adopted the rupee, which has now become the current coin of the country. There is no coin less than a rupee, and for small payments it is cut up into little bits, which are of course weighed by the careful Chinese at Ta-Chien-Lu; but the Tibetans do not seem to use the scale, and roughly judge of the value of a piece of silver. Tea, moreover, and beads of turquoise are largely used as a means of payment instead of metal. These rupees come in thousands all through Tibet, Lassa, and on to the frontiers of China, where the merchants, who eagerly buy them up, are, by melting them down, able to gain a slight percentage. Only those who have gone through the weary process of cutting up and weighing out lumps of silver, disputing over the scale, and asserting the quality of the metal, can appreciate our feelings of satisfaction at again being able to make purchases in coin; and it was very pleasing, and somewhat flattering to our national vanity, to see the portrait of our Sovereign Lady Queen Victoria on the money we used. The rupee is the current coin as far as Lu-Ting-Ch'iao. Below that place the rupee may be met with, but does not pass current. The value of a coinage is thus practically demonstrated to the Chinese; but it is probably not so much their conservative instincts that prevent them establishing a coinage for themselves, as the knowledge that a Government mint would only open another door for the cheating, bribery, and corruption that infest the land.

At the time of our visit, we found it difficult to obtain a large number of rupees; for the embassy that had just arrived from Peking, and was on its way to Lassa, had bought them all up; but Monseigneur Chauveau contrived to find one thousand for us amongst his friends and acquaintances.

Ta-Chien-Lu is situated in a small open valley at the foot of mountains enclosing it on all sides except to the east, and is surrounded by a wall in a poor state of repair. The brawling stream which divides the city into two parts is crossed by a wooden bridge, and a good many trees grow about the banks. The streets of the place are narrow and dirty, the shops inferior, and in them are all sorts of strange wild figures—some dressed in a coarse kind of serge or cotton stuff, and wearing high leathern boots, with matted hair or long locks falling over their shoulders; others in greasy skin coats, and the Lamas in red, their heads closely shaved, twisting their prayer-cylinders, and muttering at the same time the universal prayer, 'Om Ma-ni Pe-mi Hom.'

Both the women and the men wear great quantities of gold and silver ornaments, heavy earrings and brooches, in which are great lumps of very rubbishy turquoise and coral. They wear round their necks charm-boxes—some of gold, others with very delicate filigree-work in silver. These are to contain prayers. Some of the women are good-looking, and all are utterly unlike the Chinese in every way.

For lodging we engaged, not without some difficulty, two fair rooms, and one very small one, all on the upper floor. The stairs were outside, and led to a verandah that ran along the front of the house; there was a small courtyard below enclosed by a high wall, in which there were several sheds and tumble-down buildings.

Ta-Chien-Lu is under the jurisdiction of a Chinese Prefect, who has the further title of Kiun-Liang-Fu (Commissary), because he is in charge of the provisioning of the soldiers in the district. The name of the official who held this position at the time of our visit was Pao.

The chief military officer had command of three hundred soldiers quartered in the city. A land-tax is imposed on the occupants of the soil, who are obliged to bring a certain quantity of grain to the Kiun-Liang-Fu, by whom it is distributed to the soldiers in his district. His income is derived principally from presents or bribes, according to the almost universal system in China ; and the position is a very remunerative one.

The Kiun-Liang-Fu collects his taxes and imposes his *corvées* through the native king ; the latter are chiefly the supply of food and transport for travelling officials.

The transport is often a very serious matter, and is usually called the Fu-Ma (men and horses). On this high road to Tibet, officials are continually passing, and embassies without number. All of them are provided with Fu-Ma ; and, as no payment is exacted, it becomes a very serious tax upon the people of this poverty-stricken land.

It was very difficult to make it understood that we intended to pay our Fu-Ma ; hence there was, at first, great unwillingness on the part of the mule and pony owners to let us have animals, and we were considerably delayed in consequence. We obtained them eventually through the steward of the native king, who collected them from the petty farmers or mule owners in the neighbourhood. Nearly all the trade of the place is done on yaks, hence there are no forwarding houses where, as in Peking, large numbers of mules are kept, or where, as in Lower Ssŭ-Ch'uan, coolies may be hired. Beyond Ta-Chien-Lu, instead of hiring our own animals without official assistance, we were obliged to apply to the magistrates for the regulation Fu-Ma. This was always an annoyance ; the people of course thought that, like others, we should not pay them, and naturally disliked lending their animals for long and arduous journeys to foreigners for whom they cared nothing.

Everybody here, from the Kiun-Liang-Fu to the lowest coolie in the streets, believed that we were on our way to Lassa; and it was simply impossible to convince them of the truth of our assertions that we were going to Ta-Li-Fu. The Chinese officials professed their willingness to assist us, but at the same time asserted their inability to protect us against the avowed hostility of the Lamas of Tibet. Properly speaking, the Lamas are the priests of the Buddhist religion; but the Chinese, always very loose in their nomenclature, apply the term somewhat indiscriminately to laymen who profess the strict tenets of the Buddhist faith. The Lamas throughout Tibet wield a power that is as tyrannical as it is absolute; huge communities live together in the Lamasseries or monasteries, and it is said that they form one-third of the whole population of Tibet.

The head of the Buddhist faith is the Dalai Lama, resident at Lassa; and he is supposed to be an incarnation of a divine being. When the Dalai Lama dies, the true believers in the Buddhist faith consider that his spirit has entered into the body of a young child. Search is then made over the whole empire for a child, who is recognised by certain mysterious marks, the secrets of which are known to the Lamas. There seems to be very little doubt that this search is honestly carried out, the Dalai Lama often being chosen from the house of a peasant. The Dalai Lama who was living when Huc was at Lassa was selected from a poor family resident at Ta-Chien-Lu. Those who have seen a Dalai Lama speak in raptures of the singular beauty of his countenance, and in all probability he is chosen in accordance with the laws of physiognomy, so that a mild and contemplative disposition is found in the head of the Buddhist faith. This is well for the Lamas, for if a man of energy, with ideas of reform, should ever succeed to this extraordinary position, their power would probably receive a blow from which it might never recover.

The Lamas shave their heads, are filthy in their person, and their dress is poor. They wear a garment of a coarse red serge or sackcloth. This has no shape, but is simply an oblong piece of cloth thrown over one shoulder, the other being generally bare; for the Lamas, not less hardy than their lay brethren, seem absolutely impermeable to cold. They wear another length of cloth wound two or three times round the waist, which forms a skirt reaching to the ankle. Many of them are barefooted, others wear high boots of red cloth, with the lower parts made of leather. A yellow scarf is sometimes worn round the waist, and, with a string of beads and a prayer-cylinder, completes their costume.

The prayer-cylinder, or prayer-wheel, as it is often most inappropriately called, is usually about three or four inches in diameter and in length; the mystical invocation, 'Om Ma-ni Pe-mi Hom,' is written on the outside, whilst a small weight at the end of a short string keeps the affair in rotation; and all day long, not only the Lamas, but the people may be seen muttering the universal prayer, and twisting their cylinders, invariably in the same direction with the hands of a clock. One or more great cylinders, inscribed with the sentence, stand at the entrance to every house in Tibet, and a member of the household, or a guest who passes, is always expected to give the cylinder a twist for the welfare of the establishment. At almost every rivulet the eye is arrested by a little building, that is at first mistaken for a water-mill, but which on close inspection is found to contain a cylinder, turning by the force of the stream, and ceaselessly sending up pious ejaculations to Heaven, for every turn of a cylinder on which the prayer is written is supposed to convey an invocation to the deity. Sometimes enormous barns are filled with these cylinders gorgeously painted, and with the prayer repeated on them many times; and at every turn and every step in Tibet this sentence is forced upon the traveller's notice in some form or another.

A string, called a Mani string, is often stretched between the two sides of a tiny valley, and hundreds of little bits of rag are tied to it with the prayer written on all. At the top of every mountain there is a cairn made of stones cast there by the pious, thankful to have escaped the dangers of the mountain roads, and on each stone the prayer appears.

Many sticks are planted in the cairn, with a piece of rag or cloth at the upper end, on which of course the prayer is written; and by the roadside are heaps of flat stones with the inscription roughly cut on them. These are especially frequent in the valleys; sometimes only a few hundred yards apart, they would appear to serve as a means for marking the road, when covered by deep snow-drifts, as well as for some pious purpose. Sometimes the road passes between walls of flat stones, on every one of which the sentence may be read by the passing traveller. A light pole, from which a piece of rag flutters, inscribed with the prayer,

Mani String.

is placed at the top of every Tibetan house; and wherever a traveller may go he is constantly reminded that he is in the home of the Buddhist religion.

There must be some deep meaning attaching to a torn piece of cloth. The same idea is seen in Persia, where, at the summit of the mountain from which the pilgrim's eye first lights on the sacred shrine of the Imam Reza, the bushes are covered with hundreds and thousands of little pieces of cloth, which each devout pilgrim leaves as a memento of the blissful moment.

The Lamas in Tibet wield a power unequalled by a similar class of people in any other country, and every position of importance outside Lassa seems to be filled by a member of this strange community. There is a Lama at the head of every embassy; and the Chinese always insist on a very high Lama from Lassa residing at Peking; this is partly as a hostage for the safety of the Chinese officials resident at Lassa.

Those of the Lama ambassadors whom we saw seemed woefully poor; they always had something to sell, and were ready to dispose of any article of clothing, equipment, or adornment, except the prayer-cylinders, which were very difficult to buy. It is said that in Peking the ambassadors part with nearly everything, and no doubt a rare collection of curios from Lassa might be made in that wonderful city.

The Chinese officials resident in Tibet are not permitted to take wives with them, the ambassador resident at Lassa being no exception to the rule. The officials and soldiers, therefore, when in Tibet take to themselves Tibetan wives. The children thus become entirely Tibetan; and when the Chinese officials return to China they usually leave their family behind them. The Tibetans in this are wise in their own generation, for if they permitted the Chinese to bring their wives with them, and raise Chinese families, the country would soon become altogether Chinese.

The Lamas made no secret of their intentions to oppose our entry into Tibet. They had already given orders that if we attempted it we were to be starved out; all the people were forbidden to supply us with food for ourselves or with forage for our horses, or to assist us in any way. We did not ourselves hear very much of this, but of course all sorts of idle tales were spread about the place, and our servants, always willing to gossip, lent a ready ear to every silly rumour. These were very rife; and, if absolute threats were not thrown out, hints were not wanting that neither our own lives nor those of our servants would be safe in Tibet. Menaces of this sort would under no circumstances have met with much attention from us, and, as we had no intention of crossing the Tibetan frontier they had no effect whatever on our peace of mind.

Mesny's boy was the first to quail before the prospects of fatigue, not by any means imaginary, and still more before the idea of terrible dangers, altogether visionary ; he wanted to go home, but being a poor feeble thing was terrified at the idea of returning by himself, and persuaded my man Huang-Fu that he would never get back alive if he ventured beyond Ta-Chien-Lu. Huang-Fu then made up his mind to desert, and Chin-Tai also became faint-hearted, or said so, which came to the same thing ; but, probably, although he was by no means a courageous person, his discontent was chiefly caused by the addition to our party of Peh-ma, a Tibetan whom I had engaged as my interpreter, and who would have the management of all money matters. This did not suit Chin-Tai, who every day became more greedy of gain, and his avaricious propensities were carried to such an extent that if I ever employed any one else in the smallest money transaction, the loss of the squeeze, which he now seemed to consider as his sole and absolute right, so stirred his bile that he was in an ill temper for the rest of the day. It was very soon evident that no love would be lost between Peh-ma and my servants ; they had already begun to quarrel, and one day Chung-Erh, in a violent passion, went out and abused Peh-ma in the language of Shimei the son of Gera. 'Who pays you to curse me?' said Peh-ma, who was a heavy powerful man. What the result would have been, if our attention had not been attracted, it is impossible to say, for the Tibetans are a very independent people, and will not brook insults from any one, high or low.

We were told that the journey to Bat'ang would occupy eighteen days ; that the intervening country was little better than a desert, the higher portions of which were covered with wide fields of snow ; and that until our arrival at Bat'ang it would be quite impossible to buy food of any description. In accordance with these gloomy prospects, Chin-Tai was soon in his glory laying in an amount of provisions that would have sufficed to stock a troopship. He at once bought one hundred pounds of beef, which he salted, and butter in quantities that would have puzzled a Laplander, or even a Tibetan—and the amount that a Tibetan will eat is startling! The chief food of a Tibetan, is *tsanba*, or oatmeal porridge, generally mixed with a large proportion of butter; and buttered tea—that is, tea with enormous lumps of butter in it. In their food, as in all their ways and customs, and even in their buildings, the Chinese are in striking contrast to the pastoral people found on their frontiers. In the habits of these there always remains a trace, and often something more than a trace, of the nomad life; whilst in China proper, and amongst the Chinese, everything betokens the ancient and high civilisation of a people that have taken root in the soil.

In every city and almost every village in China inns are found, an indication of a people accustomed to live in houses, and who, when obliged to travel, must have a roof to shelter them; the very coolies, poorly as they are paid, never sleeping in the open, but invariably expending some portion of their small earnings for night accommodation. Amongst the Tibetans, and the Man-Tzŭ, or barbarian population in the mountains, this is not the case; the people all originally leading a wandering life, the idea of inn accommodation has not penetrated into their habits. A Chinaman will under no circumstances sleep outside if he can help it; in Tibet the master of a good house will as often as not be found passing his night on the flat roof; whilst the hardy people in the winter-time can sleep with their clothes half off, and with their bare shoulders in the snow. In China no house is complete without its table, chairs, and bedsteads, rough and clumsy though they often are; in Tibet these accessories of life in a fixed habitation are always wanting. Amongst the Chinese, mutton can rarely be obtained at all —they themselves think it very poor food; the love of a Mongol for a fat-tailed sheep is proverbial, and the natives of Tibet are not behind them in this taste. Although not exactly forbidden by their religion, the idea of killing an ox is very repugnant to the agriculturists of China, because, they say, it is ungrateful to take the life of the useful animal that draws the plough, and in the large towns the butchers are nearly always Tartars. The Chinese, as they never were a pastoral people, never kept flocks and herds; milk and butter are therefore practically unknown to them; while Tibet may safely be called a land flowing with milk and butter. As a rule, the Tibetan does not drink much milk: partly because it is all made into butter, and partly because, owing to the filthy state of the vessels, milk always turns bad in a few hours; but the traveller who makes his tastes known can always obtain an unlimited supply. Tea is often brought to him made altogether of milk, without any water at all. The Tibetans also eat sour cream, curds, and cheese; and this brings a Tibetan bill of fare to an end, which, in its constituents and in its simplicity, bears the stamp of the nomad pastoral race.

I had already found it very inconvenient to carry about the enormous bulk of silver that I had with me, and as very pure gold comes from Lit'ang to Ta-Chien-Lu, Monseigneur Chauveau, who lost no opportunity of assisting me in all my troublesome transactions, found a trustworthy merchant, from whom I bought a considerable amount. It is cast into ingots about three inches long, and, instead of the uncouth lumps of silver, it was quite a pleasure to handle these dainty morsels of pure and glittering gold. I could not help reproaching myself for the trouble that Monseigneur Chauveau took to supply the wants of an utter stranger, for I felt that I should never have an opportunity of repaying any part of it; but I little thought that in less than a year this noble-hearted missionary would be no more.

A man came in to visit us one day, and, after many preliminary inanities, remarked that he had a son; as he seemed unable to get any further in his narrative, we warmly congratulated him upon his fortunate possession. Thus encouraged, he observed that the youth would be invaluable to us in any capacity in which we might employ him, and at once introduced a boy of remarkable, though unprepossessing, appearance, dressed in a costume in no way peculiar, except for a pair of enormous English sea-boots. We declined his services; but as I went out for a stroll a short time afterwards, Boots followed me, and arriving at a temple he insisted on acting as cicerone. On my return I told Chung-Erh to give him a few cash, and asked where he had found those boots. It appeared that they were relics of poor Cooper. The boy was very proud of them, believing that when he had them on the spirit of an Englishman had entered into him, and that he was treated with distinction in consequence.

The boy was not easily rebuffed; and Mesny being in possession of a pony that Pao had given him, Ting-Ko (for such was his name) constituted himself Ma-Fu.

Monseigneur Chauveau, never at a loss for some fresh method of obliging us, had been at infinite trouble to find two trustworthy Ma-Fus from amongst his flock; and in the course of the day two men came to be engaged. They presented a strong contrast to one another in appearance. One of them, named Shuang-Pao (Double Gem), a silent and grave man, scarcely ever said a word. The other, Chang-Shou-Pao (Long-lived Gem) was always laughing, whistling, or singing, and even in the most depressing circumstances of wind and rain would trip along beside me in the most cheery manner. Shuang-Pao was a musk-hunter, and Chang-Shou-Pao hunted the red deer for their horns in velvet.

Walking about the streets of Ta-Chien-Lu we attracted very little attention; even the Chinese boys did not follow us, and people scarcely turned their heads to look as we passed, though our costumes sometimes elicited a laugh. In this border-town there are so many strange wild figures of different kinds that one more makes little difference. By the Chinese we were all classed together as barbarians, and a man who turned up one day with a slight knowledge of the Bengali language thought we were Nepalese,[1] and said our countrymen were the richest people in Lassa. He wanted Mesny to go there and establish himself as a watch and clock maker. This was very generous on his part, for he told us he had a monopoly of the business; he acknowledged that he could do no more than oil the clocks that

[1] The Chinese name for Nepal is Pi-Pon-Tzŭ.

were entrusted to him, and owned, with admirable candour, that he had never succeeded in making one go for more than a fortnight.

There are three large Lamasseries in the neighbourhood of Ta-Chien-Lu and we went one day to visit one of them. For a mile or two we rode between stone walls almost entirely built of loose flat slabs, with the sacred inscription 'Om Ma-ni Pe-mi Hom' on each. On the way we met great droves of yaks, with enormous horns and heads like bisons, huge shaggy tails, and hair under their stomachs reaching to the ground. These were coming into the city in charge of some wild-looking, shaggy-haired fellows, with two or three of their large savage dogs. Yak is the Tibetan name for the bull, and the cow is called Jen-ma.[2] Europeans apply the word yak indiscriminately to both sexes, as do the Chinese their word Mao-Niu (Hairy Ox).

Ta-Chien-Lu being situated at the very edge of the great Himalayan plateau, one day's march to the west brings the traveller to the glorious pastures of this magnificent table-land, and here the yak is naturally the almost universal means of transport. Very slow in his movements, and accomplishing but a few miles a day, this hardy animal is nevertheless the cheapest that can be employed. Requiring no attendance, and no food that cannot be picked up on the mountain-side or in the rich grass-lands of the upland plateau, the cost of keeping a yak is absolutely nothing. A caravan of yaks on the road will, when they arrive at a fine pasture, halt for a few days and let their animals feed; after which they will perhaps travel for three or four days more in the wild stony mountains, with scarcely any food until they reach the next grazing-ground.

We stood aside in the narrow path to let these lumbering beasts go past with their loads, and then proceeded up the valley. Steep rugged hills running down on each side, and great rocks strewing the ground—it was a wild, desolate

[2] According to Jaeschke's dictionary the cow yak is *di-mo*, of which *jen-ma* is possibly a local variation. In Ladak it is pronounced also *bri-mo*. But Jaeschke gives also *zhon-ma* or *shön-ma* as 'a milch-cow,' which is more probably the word given to Captain Gill.—*Y.*

scene, closed at the back by snowy mountains, from which the clouds lifted now and then.

Crossing the arched bridge that spans the roaring torrent, we met a dozen Tibetan coolies carrying a huge log, keeping step to a kind of chaunt, by no means unmelodious, and in which a sort of first and second could be distinctly recognised.

The Lamassery is finely situated on the slope of a hill, and is surrounded with many trees. Outside, the walls are whitewashed and well kept. There is a slight batter to them, and, as they look very thick and massive, there would be something of the appearance of a fortification, if it were not that the windows are large, and outside many of them flowers were growing in pots. We entered a quadrangle, on the eastern side of which is the gate. This and two other sides are occupied by living-rooms in two stories, and the fourth—that opposite the entrance—is taken up with the principal chapel. This was not very gorgeous. There was a gigantic statue of Buddha at the end. The Lamas said it was all of brass, but it looked like clay coated with that metal. On each side of this was the tomb of a very sacred Lama, enclosed with iron-wire netting, on which a few scarves of felicity, called 'Khatas,' were hung. There were seven copper bowls of water before Buddha. We asked if any meaning attached to the number seven, and they replied that there were so many mysteries in it it was quite impossible of explanation. On each side of the chief chapel is a corridor leading into other rooms, into one of which they showed us. It was very dark, and, as far as we could gather, seemed to portray the horrors of hell. Outside it, hanging from the roof of the corridor, were skins of dogs, deer, bears, and other animals, roughly stuffed with straw. In many of these the sewing had burst and the straw protruded in a melancholy fashion, whilst the hair had fallen off in patches from all of them. Some of them were provided with glass eyes of awful dimensions, and they were fearful objects to look upon. To these also there was some mysterious meaning, but the Lamas would not tell us what it was. We were treated to a cup of tea each, and entertained by one of the chief Lamas, who, in his dress, did not differ from the others.

There were some fierce black dogs in the quadrangle, who, when we entered, gave tongue furiously, in a deep baying voice. These dogs had heads something like mastiffs, with an overhanging upper lip; they had shaggy tails, and some long hair about their head and neck. Here also a flock of enormous geese that were quite quiet before we arrived set up a loud cackling on our approach. In some parts of China geese are frequently kept as guards to a house, as they always cackle at the appearance of a stranger on their premises.

Early one morning, after a stroll outside the city, as we were sauntering homewards, we saw a flock of sheep. Mesny declared he had not eaten mutton for years; I had not tasted it for months, and our mouths watered at the sight of this unwonted food. From Ch'êng-Tu to this place we never had any other meat than chicken, and since our arrival at Ta-Chien-Lu our sole diet had been beef; for fowls were not to be bought, grain being so expensive that few people could afford to keep them. Wonderful for China even eggs were scarce; ordinarily, all over China, eggs can be bought in any quantity at a ridiculously low rate. Now, although by the aid of skilful cookery we had thrown as much variety as possible into our meals, yet the *toujours bœuf* had given us a decided desire once more to taste the flesh of a sheep; so, calling the coolie who was following us, we bade him address the gentle shepherd and demand the price of one of his flock, and in the mean time we sauntered home to breakfast. But the coolie, instead of doing as we told him, informed the Bishop that we wanted a sheep, and soon afterwards Monseigneur Chauveau sent us one of the fattest from his own flock.

We were told that most of our payments between Ta-Chien-Lu and Bat'ang would be made in tea and beads; so at Ta-Chien-Lu we bought a horse-load of the common inferior tea that we had seen carried by coolies all day long, and nearly every day, on the road from Ya-Chou; and we told Peh-ma to try and get some beads. We were somewhat astonished at the dirty-looking stones that he brought and said were turquoises. They were of all sizes, some as small as No. 2 shot, others as large as No. 12 bullets. To me they looked the veriest rubbish; but, as Peh-ma assured us that they would pass current as small coin, we bought three hundred and fifty for twenty-one taels.

The Tibetans, both men and women, are possessed of a taste almost amounting to frenzy for coral and turquoises; and the immense quantity of these that are used is surprising. The scabbards of their swords, the covers of their charm-boxes, their earrings or bracelets, all are ornamented with coral and turquoises. Quantity, however, is more regarded than quality, and in the whole of Tibet it would be difficult to find any pieces that would have any value whatever in the European market.

A sack of rice for our servants, another of wheaten flour, and a few dozen *khatas*, or scarves of felicity, completed the purchases that Peh-ma deemed it advisable to make.

The 'khata' is a great institution in Tibet. It is a little scarf, of some common material, that may be any colour except red, but is generally white gauze. Etiquette ordains that every present should be accompanied by a khata, and pious people visiting a Lamassery generally tie one to the rails in the front of the image of Buddha.[3]

We were invited to breakfast one day with Monseigneur Chauveau, who said that he had not entertained European guests since the late Mr. T. T. Cooper was at Ta-Chien-Lu, just nine years before. The feast terminated with buttered tea, made with the Bishop's own butter. The butter to be bought at the houses in the country and in the towns invariably has a somewhat rancid taste, owing to the filthy vessels in which the milk is kept and the butter manufactured; but that made in Bishop Chauveau's establishment would have rivalled the produce of Devonshire and Alderney, as indeed it should, considering the wonderful pastures on which, during the short summer, the animals can graze.

In a cold climate, buttered tea, made with good tea and fresh butter, is not such a repulsive drink as would be

[3] On the *Khata*, and the manifold occasions of its use, see Huc, *Souvenirs*, &c., 1850, i. 86.—*Y.*

supposed, and is admirably adapted for a people living at the great altitude of the Tibetan plateau. In the summer-time, when the climate is pleasant, much heat-giving food is not required, and the people can take their tsanba and tea with the least amount of butter; but when the howling winds of winter sweep across those dreary wastes of snow, they can only maintain their vital heat by large quantities of carbonaceous food, and butter is the most suitable of all that can be obtained. For animal food is most plentiful in the season when it is the least required; in the winter, the cattle and sheep can scarcely find anything to eat, and become miserably lean, out of condition, and totally unfit to provide the fatty food necessary for the people; while the butter, made in large quantities during the summer when the animals are at the height of their condition, is easily stored up for winter use.

This shows also why so little milk is drunk by the people. The winter is the season of trial, and it is for that time that all provisions are made; in the summer large quantities of milk or butter are unnecessary, and every available drop of milk is made into butter for the winter. In the long winter, again, milk must be exceedingly scarce, and thus drinking milk has never become one of the habits of the people.

The afternoon in the society of Monseigneur Chauveau was a most pleasant one, for though he had lived thirty-two years in China, time had not dimmed his interest in European affairs, nor his affection for his country. His courtly manners, those of a nobleman of the old French *régime*, were in striking contrast to the wildness of his surroundings, and would have made me forget that I was on the borders of an almost barbarous country, if his enthusiasm for the propagation of the faith had not kept it constantly in view.

He used to speak with great affection and admiration of the English, and of the religious toleration experienced under their rule; and he looked forward with the keen eye of faith to the day when, the English being established at Lassa, the missionaries would be able to follow, and, sweeping at last across those wild wastes of superstition, carry the

Christian faith to the very home of the Dalai Láma, shake the throne of that arch impostor, and strike with mighty strokes at the very root of the Upas-tree of Buddhism.

'Ah,' he said, 'my proper title is, Vicaire Apostolique of Lassa ; but I call myself by the less pretentious one of Vicaire of Tibet, for I feel that my eye can never look over the border into the promised land. But,' he added, with flashing eye, 'I feel sure that my successor will reach the goal denied to me.'

Listening to him, as the colour mantled to his cheeks, I could not help sharing his earnest enthusiasm, and wishing that it might be he who should be the first to enter the haven so long desired. But a few short months elapsed, and he went to his last rest, bitterly mourned by his faithful little flock in those far-away regions, and deeply regretted by all who knew the nobility and grandeur of his nature. To me he was almost more than a friend. I owed him a debt of gratitude that nothing could have repaid, and never shall I forget his venerable figure as, standing at the door of his palace, he bade me a final adieu, and, quoting the passage in which Goldsmith, who was his favourite historian, narrates the last speech of our unfortunate monarch Charles, said the one English word, '*Remember* !'

During our stay traders came pouring in with all sorts of ornaments, enormous finger-rings, barbaric ear-rings, brooches and buckles, some of silver and some of gold, and all set with huge lumps of coral and turquoise. The greatest curiosities, and the best worth buying, were the charm-boxes, made of gold or silver. On the top of these there is generally some filligree, quite equal to any of European manufacture, and it is surprising how the handicraftsmen of Lassa, where these things are made, can, with their rough clumsy tools, produce work of such extreme delicacy. These boxes, which are invariably adorned with a lump of coral, are to contain a slip of paper, on which is written the usual formula, 'Om Ma-ni Pe-mi Hom.' No Tibetan is ever without one of these, no matter how poor or dirty he may be. A miserable yak-driver, with perhaps no home, and no worldly possessions but a bit of serge for a coat, will invariably have a charm-box which may be worth some twenty or thirty taels. It is very curious to see the women, always dirty, often ragged, and sometimes almost too poor to afford themselves clothes, wearing massive ornaments of silver or gold, and immense plates of silver in their hair. I bought a very heavy bracelet of solid gold, embossed with some emblematical design, and a good many finger-rings, ear-rings, and charm-boxes.

There is another article that almost forms a part of every Tibetan. This is the wooden cup, or Pu-ku, in which he eats his tsanba or drinks his tea. It is always kept in the bosom of his capacious garment, a space that serves not as a pocket merely, but rather as a portmanteau, in which he can carry about the whole of his not very extensive possessions.

These cups are made of different woods, and polished; no Tibetan is ever without one; he seems to be born, not with a silver spoon in his mouth, but with a wooden cup in his bosom. The cup never leaves him, night or day, as long as he lives, and would no doubt go down to the grave with him, if burial were the custom of the country. Some are supposed to have the valuable property of annulling the effects of poison, and others are lined with silver; but none of these priceless articles were to be bought to add to our collection of Tibetan curiosities, and we contented ourselves with plain, simple, but useful cups, like those of our coolies.

A prayer-cylinder also was brought, which I began to twist the wrong way, much to the consternation of the people; they were really seriously alarmed, for they seized my hand and stopped me immediately.

In the afternoon I made an agreement with eight chair-coolies, for whom I was obliged to provide four ponies, partly to carry their food, and partly to enable them to take an occasional ride to relieve themselves amongst the mountain roads. I took my chair to Ta-Li-Fu, chiefly because it was so very useful for carrying the small odds and ends I always wanted on the march or immediately on arrival at the halting-place. It would also have been invaluable in case of sickness. The other chairs were taken no further than Ta-Chien-Lu.

Poor Tib was also left behind; he had supported the difficulties of the road very badly, and, much to the discontent of the coolies, had been carried more than half-way from Ch'êng-Tu in my chair. Had I taken him further he would probably have broken down altogether, if he had not been killed by the savage dogs of the Tibetans; and as Monseigneur Chauveau offered him a comfortable home, I accepted it for the poor beast, though in China the presence of a dog is a great safeguard against thieves.

Later in the day a number of ponies were waiting for me, and, after trying a few of them, I was just going to make a bid for one or two, when a man came in with a grey and a chestnut. The grey, though small, at once attracted my fancy, as he had more breeding about him than any of the others, and the shape of his head, and the way in which his tail was set on, were quite of the Arab type. I had him saddled, and taking him over the worst bit of road I could find in the neighbourhood, the way he came down hill on the stony path at once determined me to buy him. My Ma-Fu had followed on the chestnut barebacked; the saddle was changed, and I found that I liked the second almost as well as the first. On returning I asked the price of the two; the horse-dealer demanded forty taels, and I promptly offered twenty. After a time I went up to twenty-nine, and the dealer coming down to thirty a bargain was struck. The dealers here have a curious way of telling the price to one another by putting their hands together under their sleeves, and, by signs well understood, communicating the figure without the bystanders knowing anything about it.[4]

None of our coolies or Ma-Fus cared to engage themselves to come beyond Bat'ang; for the Tibetans have the greatest dread of entering China, on account of small-pox —a disease almost unknown in Tibet. A Tibetan once attacked by small-pox never recovers. The Chinese look

[4] The Burmese have a similar method of bargaining, which is not, I believe, used exclusively for horse-dealing. It is in occasional use almost all over Asia. See *Marco Polo*, 2nd ed. ii. 486.—*Y.*

upon this disease much as an Englishman does on a cold ; they are generally ill for a few days only, and get over it, though of course there are a large number of severe and fatal cases. But when a Tibetan is attacked, his family take him outside the village, out of the way, and put him under a tree, or in a cave, with some tsanba and cold water, and leave the poor wretch to die.[5]

[5] Colonel Prejevalski notices that the inhabitants of the Lob-Nor district have very similar customs.

Tibetan Chodten.

CHAPTER X.

THE GREAT PLATEAU.

1. *Ta-Chien-Lu to Lit'ang.*

The Departure from Ta-Chien-Lu—The Cavalcade described—A Supper of Tsanba—Village of Cheh-toh—A Wreck of the Crockery—Tibetan Salutation—Delicious Air—Half-bred Yaks—Splendid Alpine Pastures—Wild Fruits—The Sacred Cairn—Ti-zu—Delightful al fresco Breakfast—A Land of Milk and Butter—Hot Spring—The Buttered-Tea Churn—Tsanba—Tibetan Houses—An-niang—Wild Flowers—Roadside Groups from the Fair—A Galop over Turf—Pass of Ka-Ji-La—Magnificent Alpine Prospect—The 'King of Mountains'—Pine Forests—Huang-Fu—Descent towards the Ya-Lung River—Appearance of Green Parrots—Ho-K'ou or Nia-chuka, on the Ya-Lung River—Ferry over the Ya-Lung—Re-ascent towards the

Plateau—Mah-geh-chung—A 'Medicine Mountain'—Crest of the Ra-ma Pass—Female Decorations—Lit'ang-Ngoloh—Description of House and Appliances—Domestic Sketches—Deh-re Pass—The Rhubarb Plant—Rarefied Atmosphere—Pass of Wang-gi—Abundance of Supplies—Shie-gi Pass—The Surong Mountains—Lit'ang in View—Arrival there.

IT was just noon as we rode away on the 7th of August and turned our backs on Ta-Chien-Lu. We were a goodly company, though somewhat quaint to look on: Peh-ma riding first on a light-coloured chestnut with a white tail, enveloped in all sorts of blankets and wraps; Peh-ma himself in a garment gathered in at the waist, where in a gigantic fold he seemed to be carrying all his worldly goods, and whence, later on, when I began to be unpleasantly sensible of the fact that I had not breakfasted, half a loaf was produced. Mesny, dressed in a kind of patrol jacket, European trousers, Chinese high-boots, and a Kuei-Chou pancake hat, and mounted on a very gorgeous Chinese saddle, with short stirrups that drew his knees somewhere up towards the vicinity of his chin, would at least have attracted notice wherever he might have been. Huang-Fu had, by a quantity of bedding, clothing, and saddle-bags, raised the altitude of his small pony almost to that of an elephant; and he looked the picture of contentment, as he sat perched up with a long pipe and a red umbrella. Chung-Erh wore a large straw hat over a long black coat; and Chin-Tai, and Mesny's coolie (now raised to the rank of 'Boy,' *vice* Hsi-Sen resigned), with one of the pony-drivers, formed our mounted party. But Ting-Ko (or 'Boots,' as we called him), in the hopes of gathering up some fragments, came with us for one day's journey, as he said, and made himself generally useful. My laughing Ma-Fu, dressed all in red like a Lama, the other Ma-Fu, and our two spare ponies, completed our caravan; while behind us the chair, with its eight coolies and four ponies, and the twenty-nine baggage animals, followed in beautiful disorder.

Our course lay up a valley, nearly due south, past the Lamassery we had visited a day or two before. On each side hills covered with low green brushwood sloped down to the river; in the valley the fields of oats and barley, nearly ready for the sickle, were divided by stone walls, and a good many fine large trees lined the edge of the water. To the south, right in front, a fine snowfield on Mount Ru-ching glittered in the bright sun; and to the south-east another mountain every now and then showed in patches of snow, as the clouds came and went from its lofty summit.

At a little less than four miles from Ta-Chien-Lu, the road leaves the main river, and strikes to the west, up the valley of a smaller stream. There is but little cultivation, and scarcely any wood, the hill-sides being all covered with a dense green undergrowth. The road is good, ascending steadily without any of those desperately steep zigzags that we now looked upon as almost a necessary part of a day's march.

On the way we passed the house of one of the Ma-Fus. It was a poor shanty, standing by itself in the middle of a little cultivation, but it was his home; and his wife, children, and dogs, all ran out to welcome him. The Ma-Fu found four eggs, which he brought as a respectful present, and was very pleased when we told him to stay for the night with his family. We rode on to the little village of Cheh-toh, where we halted for the night, and, as there was no immediate prospect of the arrival of our baggage, we both had a bowl of tsanba, which we ate after the manner of the country. A large basin of oatmeal, two good-sized cups, a kettle of buttered tea, and two pairs of chopsticks were brought to us—these last, a Chinese innovation, never used by a Tibetan, who finds his fingers sufficient. A Tibetan first helps himself to what oatmeal he requires, the buttered tea is poured over it, he stirs it up with his fingers, adding oatmeal and tea to suit his taste, and then eats it. It is very like porridge, and, as in Scotland, the oats are grilled before grinding them into meal.

The mules did not arrive till six o'clock; and then Chin-Tai told me that all the plates, dishes, cups, glass, and crockery had been smashed. I consoled myself with the reflection that as the plates and dishes were of iron, there was a certain amount of exaggeration, and went out to see the wreck. The muleteers had stopped behind us at Ta-Chien-Lu, to have a final drink and glorification before starting; and in attempting to make up for lost time, had only succeeded in producing the alarming catastrophe reported. They were now in a state of wholesome fear that they would be made to pay for the damage done; and when introduced into the august presence, to explain matters, they went down on their knees, thrust out their tongues, and repeated at intervals the word 'La-so.' Protruding the tongue as far as possible is a respectful salutation in Tibet, and 'La-so' is a term of respect used by inferiors; it means also 'be merciful.'

Our dinner did not appear until very late. At first there were no candles to be found, and Chung-Erh said everything was 'east and west,' a Chinese expression for a general state of disorder.

The cooking things were again all 'east and west' in the morning, and the time consumed in getting ready was frightful. Chin-Tai had an extraordinary genius for putting two forks into three boxes, and dividing his cooking things amongst the greatest number of packages possible, so that every time he wanted to prepare a meal he had to pack and unpack boxes enough to load a good-sized caravan. But in the course of time, and by the exercise of patience, everything was at last ready, and we made a start. The morning was beautifully fine; there was a delicious feeling in the air, and, looking back down the valley, there was a glorious view of a snowy mountain, whose edges were just lit up by the rising sun, and whose glittering pinnacles of ice and snow shone like points of brilliant light.

The road was broad and good; there was not much traffic, but we met great droves of yaks, and half-bred oxen, a cross between the yak and the ox. We ascended steadily by an easy gradient to the head of the stream; here the valley opened out, and formed a little basin, enclosed by bare and rugged hills, with a strip of green grass beside the tiny rill that trickled at the bottom. A few yards more, and, reaching the summit of Cheh-toh-Shan, we at length looked upon the great Himalaya plateau. The pass of Cheh-toh-

Shan (the Jeddo of Cooper) is 14,515 feet above the sea; and from this point, with the exception of a dip into the valley of the Ya-Lung-Chiang, the road is always at an altitude of 12,000 feet above the sea, until the descent into the valley of the Chin-Sha-Chiang is commenced at Pun-jang-mu. There was no snow here, but a few small patches were lying two hundred or three hundred feet above.

I had outwalked everybody, and I sat down to wait for the rest of the party. My merry Ma-Fu alone was with me, and he whistled and sang as he let Manzi browse on the delicious herbage.

Stretched at our feet lay a beautiful valley, closed on both sides by gently sloping, round-topped hills; a carpet of luxuriant grass covered the whole surface of the hills and dales; the richness of the pasture was astonishing, and thousands of yaks and sheep were feeding on the magnificent vegetation. The ground was yellow with buttercups, and the air laden with the perfume of wild flowers of every description. Wild currants and gooseberries, barberries, a sort of yew, and many other shrubs grew in profusion, but there were no large trees. There were a few gooseberries on one or two of the bushes, but they were quite unfit to eat. The Tibetans said that the gooseberries never ripened, but that the currants were sometimes eaten.

At the summit of the pass there was a huge pile of stones; and bits of rag, inscribed with the sacred sentence, fluttered from the heads of long poles set up in the heap.

At this altitude there is great difficulty in breathing. The Tibetans ascribe this to subtle exhalations, which they say rise from the ground; they call all high mountains 'Medicine Mountains,' and so universal is this custom, that the comparative heights may be roughly guessed at by the amount of 'medicine' attributed to them by the people.

In the winter many travellers are said to die here; the passage is greatly dreaded, and those who arrive safely at the top add a stone and a rag to the trophy, as a thank-offering for dangers escaped.

When the rest of our caravan arrived, one of the horse-owners, a sort of petty chief, with a sword-scabbard set with great pieces of turquoise and coral, tied a rag to one of the poles, and cast a stone on to the pile.

To my surprise Ting-Ko turned up again; he said he had come another day's march for the fun of the thing, and begged to be allowed to come with us to Bat'ang; when at last I consented, he grinned with delight, and seemed to think more highly than ever of his remarkable boots.

A descent of about three and a half miles brought us to a solitary hut, glorying in the name of Hsin-Tien-Chan, or New Inn Stage; the Tibetan name is Ti-zu, which has the same meaning. Here we halted for breakfast, but it was such a miserable place that we at once passed a unanimous vote for a picnic.

A couple of boxes were placed beside a low table on the delicious fresh grass; a gentle breeze, and now and then a passing cloud, moderated the sun, which was almost strong enough to make itself felt, and helped me to give myself up for a while to day-dreams and the charms of scenery and climate.

This was one of those days, which come sometimes to a traveller, when he feels so thoroughly happy, that the pleasures of civilisation are forgotten, and he dreams of perpetually seeking fresh fields and pastures new, and of spending his life amongst the mountains. It must be confessed that these days are rare; but, sitting outside the little shanty, the scene was so peaceful, and there was such an exhilaration in the air, that I thought I could contentedly spend the rest of my life in this lovely valley.

Continuing our march we presently came upon a little tent pitched by the hill-side; here some Tibetans were lying about, their fierce dogs tied up to pegs in the ground, and innumerable herds of cattle and sheep grazing round them. Outside the tent a quaint and wild group of Tibetans was gathered round the buttered-tea churn, making their mid-day meal. A bag of oatmeal lay on the ground by the churn, and one of the men was filling the wooden cup with a brass ladle. Like the wooden cups, the churn is almost a part of every Tibetan community. On entering a house at any hour, some one is certain to be seen making buttered tea in the churn ; a mule, with a sack of oatmeal, and a churn for every three or four men, forms part of every caravan ; at a halt the churn is immediately produced ; and, in fact, wherever there are half a dozen Tibetans gathered together, there the churn will be found.

This churn is a cylinder of wood about two feet long and six inches in diameter. The butter is churned up in the boiling tea, and there is some art in doing this in such a manner as to make the ingredients mix properly.

The tsanba is prepared in various ways according to fancy ; the meal is sometimes kneaded with the fingers into a stiff paste, and eaten like a cake, and at others it is mixed with sufficient tea to be almost thin enough to drink.

Further down we came to the first Tibetan house, at a distance looking like a strong castle, and up a little valley behind it were two or three others, together forming a small community or village, and from here to An-niang, houses, separated from one another by about a quarter or half a mile, stand singly on the right bank of the stream. These houses are great piles of loose stone with scarcely any mortar, sometimes three or four stories high ; the roof is always flat, and a gable is never seen. With their little slits of windows, they are gloomy in the extreme, and, looking as if they were half in ruins, give an idea of great misery. They are, nevertheless, very picturesque, and the view down the valley as the sun was setting would have made a lovely picture.

All this valley is covered with wild flowers, from one of which a paper like parchment is made ; another has the valuable property of killing lice ; caraway grows wild, and is also cultivated. Barley and oats grow well in the valley, but the people do very little but keep cattle, sheep, and ponies—of which there are great numbers, some exceedingly good looking, with quite an Arab head.

Marching down the beautiful valley, on the 9th, by an excellent road, amongst the fresh green grass, buttercups, and wild flowers, we met large parties of Tibetans returning from a fair that had been held at a Lamassery a mile or two away. Women, as well as men, were riding ponies *à califourchon*, and as we approached they turned a few yards aside and dismounted. As they stood about, or sat on the grass, they formed most picturesque groups. The men were wild-looking fellows, with long shaggy hair, whose garments, always with a bit of red about them, seemed to have no shape in particular, and were gathered in with a cloth tied round the waist, leaving a fold in which they carried an immense amount of property, not only in front, but at the sides and behind their backs. The women, too, all wore something bright-coloured, and fastened up their hair with a circular disc of silver engraved with Tibetan characters, and set with coral beads. No matter how poor and dirty, they all wore this expensive ornament. Both men and women had necklaces of turquoise, coral, or coloured glass, from which they hung charm-boxes of gold or silver.

The turf was so tempting, and the air so delicious, that Chin-Tai and Chung-Erh could not resist the excitement of a gallop, and were soon racing over the level plain. Mesny's boy, ambitious to emulate their example, essayed to follow them; but, never before in his life having ridden a horse, he had a tremendous fall. He was carrying Mesny's somewhat crazy gun, and, though he did not hurt himself, he lost one of the locks; this was not noticed at the time, but by the aid of the almighty rupee, a search that was subsequently instituted proved successful, and this ill-used weapon was put again in order.

At Ngoloh, which we quitted on the 11th, the local official furnished us with an escort, and we were astonished to observe on one of their coats the buttons of the 47th regiment. After this we noticed that half the men we met buttoned their coats with British regimental buttons. These find their way from the old clothing in India, through Tibet, to the very frontiers of China.

The first crest we reached is called in Tibetan Ka-ji-La, or in Chinese Ko-Erh-Shi-Shan, 14,454 feet above the sea. The view when we reached the summit was superb. Looking back in the direction from which we had come, range after range of mountains lay at our feet, culminating at last in the most magnificent snowy heights, one of which raised its head about four thousand or five thousand feet above its neighbours. It was a magnificent peak, and at this distance looked almost perpendicular. Its name in Tibetan is Ja-ra (King of the Mountains), and I never saw one that better deserved the name. Never before had I seen such a magnificent range of snowy mountains as here lay stretched before me, and it was with difficulty I could tear myself away from the sight.

Our road now lay for a couple of miles over an undulating grassy plain; at the centre of this our escort left us, and marched back across the ridge of Ka-ji-La.

The official in charge of the ferry at Ho-K'ou passed us here. Pao had sent for him to give him instructions about us, and he was now on his return journey.

From the western side of the plateau, there was a still finer view, and, as the day was fortunately very clear, our guide could show us where Ta-Chien-Lu was lying, at the foot of a grand snowy range.

We now descended a narrow valley between steep hills, well wooded with firs, some of very large dimensions. Next day we observed numbers of green parrots flying about from tree to tree. The proper *habitat* of these birds is, doubtless, in the warm climate of Southern Yün-Nan; but during the summer, short though delicious, they fly up the two rivers, the Chin-Sha and Ya-Lung, and scatter about amongst the entrances to the valleys of the tributary streams. They may be seen during one or two marches on both sides of both rivers, but no further; and as soon as autumn tinges the leaves, in all probability their green plumage disappears.

Nia-chu-ka (Ho-K'ou, 'River Mouth' in Chinese) is situated at an altitude of 9,222 feet, at the junction of two streams with the Ya-Lung-Chiang, and is surrounded on all sides by bare and precipitous mountains, that run sheer down to the water, leaving no flat ground for grass or cultivation, and very little for building. Opposite the town, and dividing the river from the stream we had followed, a bare rock, seven hundred feet high, rises almost precipitously from the surging water; a pile of stones marks its summit, and the flutter of the pious rags that wave from the usual poles can just be discerned from the houses below.

Though at a greater elevation, the climate is warmer than that of Ta-Chien-Lu, which place is particularly cold, owing to the masses of snowy mountains that surround it on every side.

The ordinary way of crossing the Ya-Lung is in a coracle the shape of a walnut, made of raw hides stretched over wicker-work; and as the current is rapid, and the water broken, it does not look a very pleasant operation. Animals of all kinds have to swim; even the soldiers carrying the imperial despatches are obliged to leave their horses behind.

Our baggage animals swam across in the evening; we were ferried over the next morning with our servants and horses, and waited in one of the few houses on the right bank of the Ya-Lung, opposite Ho-K'ou, whilst our caravan was re-assembled. Our animals were at length all collected, and we started with two fresh soldiers; those that had come with us from Ta-Chien-Lu leaving us here, and returning to their own quarters.

The road from Ho-K'ou again ascends to the plateau from the warm valley of the Ya-Lung. Climbing up the bed of a tributary stream, the same order of vegetation and trees is seen as on the eastern side of the river. At first, there is neither cultivation nor pasture-land, but the road at once enters another dense forest of magnificent pines. Near Ma-geh-chung I measured the largest I saw, and its girth, at a height of four feet from the ground, was thirteen feet six inches. There were oaks also—poor scrubby things; indeed it was only here by the discovery of acorns on them that I was able to satisfy my mind as to their identity, for anything less like our oaks it is hard to imagine. The parrots were seen no more, but amongst the trees there was some large jungle-fowl, called pheasants by our people—pheasants, however, they certainly were not, they looked more like jays, though much larger, and made the same kind of chattering noise.

Gradually, as we ascended on the 14th, an open valley here and there showed us grassy hill-tops, where not even those hardy oaks and pines would grow. The forest became thinner, and the trees smaller, and at about four hundred or five hundred feet below the summit the last of the pines and oaks were left behind.

The summit of Ra-ma-La is 14,915 feet above the sea, but none of our party seemed to experience the evil effects of the great medicine mountain. Of course those who walked found breathing difficult; but neither Mesny nor myself noticed anything unpleasant, unless we stooped, when we felt giddy. This appeared to me the more remarkable, because in other countries, at much less altitudes, I have found difficulty in breathing even when sitting down.

The crest of Ra-ma-La may be said to divide the plateau from the valley of the Ya-Lung-Chiang, and once across it we again find the green pastures, the wild flowers, the great herds of yaks and sheep, and the profusion of milk and butter so characteristic of the upland country. The plateau extended for many miles, and the rich grass was covered with buttercups and other yellow flowers, that grew together in great masses; there were patches of red, purple, or blue, and the variety of colour was wonderful.

The droves of yaks, ponies, and sheep were tended by Tibetans armed with swords and guns; for the Tibetans, unlike the Chinese, always carry a long matchlock, and a sword studded with turquoise and coral.

From the next crest of Ra-ma-La, 15,110 feet above the sea, which we reached soon after breakfast, we should have had a very fine view, had it not been for the heavy clouds on all the mountain-tops. It was, however, tolerably clear the west. They showed us where Lit'ang lay, about seventy miles distant, and an occasional flash of sunlight struck some snowy pinnacle on the high mountains surrounding that place. The descent was not very long, and, once down, a level bit brought us to the village of Lit'ang-Ngoloh. The largest house in the place belonged to the father of one of our muleteers, a wealthy man in these parts, as he was supposed to possess property to the value of a thousand taels (about 300*l.*).

Our muleteers had ridden on ahead, and all the family, including the ladies, came out to welcome us. The damsels were dressed in their best, which included a considerable amount of dirt, and were covered with beads and jewelry. On each side of the head they wore a disc of chased silver about the size of a saucer; these, meeting above, formed, to a front view, an inverted v, thus ʌ. Another smaller disc was worn behind; and all were loaded with coral, and sham or real turquoise. A lock of hair, about an inch broad, was brought vertically down over the centre of the forehead, and cut off at a level with the lower part of the nose. They had necklaces of beads, and great silver ornaments, and charm-boxes were hung from chains of beads that seemed to be wound about all over their bodies.

We were led into the house with great pomp and ceremony, and, as soon as we had been installed in the best room, the women quickly brought us buttered tea, milk, and sour cream. The house was really a well-built solid structure, quite a palace after our recent accommodation, and betokened the comfortable position of its owner. The whole of the lower area formed a covered and extensive stable, divided by immense pillars of wood, that supported the ceiling and the house above. Instead of the usual notched log, a sumptuous ladder led through a spacious trap-door to the upper story. This consisted of a quadrangle, the floor of which was planked, the living and sleeping rooms being arranged round the four sides. The roof of these was flat, and projected far enough to shelter a large portion of the quadrangle and the inmates of the house from the rays of the sun in the summer and from the snow in the winter. The roof was gained by another ladder, and was surrounded by a parapet; and a covered shed was erected on part of it, where piles of hay were stacked. The room we occupied was lofty and commodious, the back wall of solid mud, the others of wood. The floor was planked, and the windows looked upon the quadrangle. We had some difficulty in manufacturing a table, as the simple people themselves having nothing that they can want to put upon a table are unaccustomed to the use of this article of furniture. There is, however, an object of household equipment of which we Westerns are still in ignorance.

Shaped like a table, eight feet long by two feet broad, and nine inches high, there is a large circular hole in the centre, in which a pan of charcoal or wood is put. This is the fireplace of the country, and two persons can sit on it, one at each end. Finding one of these in the room, we raised it on stools and packets of tea, and improvised for ourselves an excellent table. I was always astonished at the miserable appliances for warming rooms that are used in Tibet: a wretched fire lit on the floor, emitting far more smoke than warmth, or a pan of charcoal, such as we found in this room, would seem to be but a poor protection against the frightful severities of the climate during the winter in these elevated regions; yet nothing better is ever seen, and it must be chiefly by clothing and food that the Tibetans keep themselves from perishing of cold.

We halted here a day, and when I went out on the roof early in the morning to put out my thermometer, I found the old master of the house sleeping placidly under a shed, wrapped up in a heap of ragged skins. Presently one of the girls came up with a jug of hot buttered tea and a cup; she poured out a cupful, which the old man consumed, and then, leaving the jug beside him, she retreated below. There were two girls here, one the wife, and the other the sister of one of our muleteers. The wife was always gorgeously arrayed with strings of beads, from which great gold and silver ornaments were suspended; she seemed to sleep with her jewelry on, for, no matter how early or how late, if we ever caught a glimpse of her she was still covered with these uncomfortable-looking accoutrements. We wanted to buy the complete set; but she would not part with them, because she said it would be like dying before her time, and very unlucky. She did not show herself very much, and always hid if she thought either of us was looking at her. The other girl was dressed quite plainly, and seemed rather to like being looked at. There seemed to be a certain amount of polyandry, not to say promiscuousness about their arrangements, and I never thoroughly understood the degrees of relationship, which would have puzzled even so able a genealogist as Sir Bernard Burke.

Rain clouds were hanging about the hill-tops as we left the hospitable village of Lit'ang-Ngoloh and marched up the pretty little valley between the fields, divided by stone walls, or hedges of wild gooseberry bushes. We then ascended the hills at the other side, and entered an undulating country, where pines of the most beauteous form were disposed by nature in such lovely groupings that they would have brought feelings of despair and envy to the owner of the noblest European park.

I was riding ahead with the 'Long-lived Gem' through the silent woods, when we started a musk-deer from its lair; it bounded down the side of the hill, and disappeared in a thicket beyond. It was the only game I saw in all the journey.

From the summit of Deh-re-La (about 14,584 feet above the sea) we had a fine view over one of the valleys so characteristic of this part of Tibet. A small stream meanders through a little plain, enclosed on both sides by hills, rising sometimes as much as a thousand or fifteen hundred feet above the valley below. Nowhere is there any cultivation, nor is there a tree to be seen, nothing but gentle slopes and rounded tops all covered with grass, the richness of which is marvellous, and is only seen in places where snow lies for three-quarters of the year. In these valleys there are quantities of the rhubarb so valued as a medicine; it is a fine-looking plant, of which there is a very good picture in Prejevalsky's book. Another herb that grows in profusion is something like a gigantic dock; its leaves are sometimes as much as two and a half feet long, and it throws up a straight thick stem, at the top of which is a large bunch of small yellow flowers; it is not used for anything, nor in itself is it particularly ornamental, but the masses of big leaves by the side of a stream look fine and handsome amongst the delicate grass and wild flowers.

From the summit of Deh-re-La, we looked across this plain to the mountains on the other side, and to the pass Wang-gi-La, a mountain of which Peh-ma now observed that, though it was not very high, there was plenty of medicine in it.

The summit of this mountain is 15,558 feet above the sea, and the excessive rarefaction of the air renders breathing difficult; but as the ascent is commenced from only a thousand feet below the top, and the road leads up by an easy gradient, the Tibetans do not realise its great altitude, and being quite unable to comprehend the sensations they experience, attribute them to noxious vapours, or other causes, and call the mountain a medicine mountain.

The sun was shining brightly, and there was a gentle breeze; as we marched across the little plain, the road lay along turf, which was simply perfect for a horse's foot; all nature smiled upon us, and I began to think that the happy valley of Rasselas must have been in Tibet! But ominous clouds were gathering, rain soon began to fall, and a change came o'er the spirit of the scene. When we reached the summit a pitiless sleet was driving before a cutting wind, and there was a dreary view down a narrow valley, where the tops of the hills were shrouded in mists. It was very cold, and another degree or two would certainly have changed the sleet into snow. What a difference a couple of hours made in my estimate of things in general! Two hours before I had been living in a sort of heaven, and now the happy valleys had lost their charm, and a coal fire in an English house seemed infinitely more desirable.

There was nothing to vary the monotony of the march down the mountains. Seven miles in the driving wind and rain brought us to the Chinese village of Ho-chŭ-ka, consisting of two or three miserable tenements, of which the house we stopped in was the best, a wretched place with but one small room. One end of this was occupied by the dais usual in a Chinese house; there was a hollow for a fire in the mud floor, but there was no window, and no hole for the escape of smoke; the roof leaked horribly, and the drops coming through brought large quantities of mud with them. Some wet sticks were brought, with which a little fire was made, that filled the room with pungent smoke. But if our accommodation was not luxurious, we soon found that the tales with which we had been frightened of the impossibility of obtaining food were, as usual, utterly untrue. First, some people brought dried fish; and immediately afterwards we were offered, for a rupee, twenty good fresh fish just out of the water, averaging about half a pound each; another man brought us a dozen hen's eggs and fifteen pigeon's eggs. Some mutton and a fowl of a certain age arrived as presents; the village produced one turnip, and two cabbages; Chin-Tai discovered some flour, and eventually we had a sumptuous repast.

On the morrow the road up the valley was good, and nowhere steep. We ascended through the same undulating grassy country; great herds of cattle and sheep and good-looking ponies were browsing on the slopes, and the silence was occasionally broken by the whistle or cry of the herdsmen, or the deep bay of a dog belonging to one of the numerous encampments dotted over this magnificent plateau. As we proceeded, the rain clouds cleared off, and the sun now and then shone out in fitful gleams. The people say that here, as well as in the Lit'ang plain, it rains every afternoon in the summer, but that the mornings are generally fine. The pass Mount Shie-gi-La (14,425 feet above the sea) is only 1,170 feet above Ho-chŭ-ka, and the ascent to it is gradual and very easy. From here gentle slopes lead down about seven hundred feet to the plain. This is from eight to ten miles wide, and stretches out for many miles east and west. Opposite, a range of hills bounds the plains; behind it rises the magnificent range of the Surong Mountains, stretching as far as the eye can see to the east and west, snowy peak rising behind snowy peak, where even at that great distance vast fields of snow almost dazzle the eye as the sun shines on them.

After a march of seventeen miles Lit'ang came into view, a cheerless place, and one of the highest cities in the world, situated at an altitude of 13,280 feet above the sea.[1] No cereals of any kind, nor potatoes, can be raised. Just round the houses a few half-starved cabbages and miserable

[1] Potosi is 13,330 feet above the sea.

turnips appear to be the only things that can be produced.

Although there are only a thousand families in the city there is a Lamassery within the walls containing three thousand Lamas, and not five miles away, another of nearly equal size. Notwithstanding the miserable poverty of the people, the Lamassery in Lit'ang is adorned with a gilded roof that cost an immense sum of money. The roofs of all the Lamasseries that I have seen are gabled like the Chinese roofs, and those at Lit'ang are no exception.

Huc finds that Lit'ang means the 'Plain of Copper,' but I could hear of no such interpretation. There are three hundred Tibetan and ninety-eight Chinese soldiers in the neighbourhood, under the command of a Shou-Pei.

Nen-da.

CHAPTER XI.

THE GREAT PLATEAU.

2. *Lit'ang to Bat'ang.*

Departure—Quit the Lit'ang Plain—High Pass of Nga-ra-la-Ka—Cold Granite Region—Alarms of Robbers—Dzong-da—Pine-clad Valleys again—The Cairns and Mani Inscriptions—Stupendous Alpine Scene—The vast snowy Peak of Nen-da—The Guide's Head turned with Wonder—Sublime Aspect of the Mountains—Rhododendrons—Striking Picture—The J'ra-ka-La—Savage Desolation—Our Guide—Welcome on Arrival at Bat'ang—Chao the Magistrate, and Favourable Impressions—Abbé Desgodins—Discharge of our Suite—The Name of Bat'ang—The Plain—Possibilities of Navigation on the Rivers—Earthquakes—The Great Lamassery—Number of such—Causes that fill them—The Lamas a Curse to the Country—Eccentric Chinese System of Accounts—Slavery and Cattle-holding—Gradual Depopulation of Tibet—Hostility of the Lamas—Alleged Muster to bar our Advance.

THE road from Lit'ang was said to be infested with robbers, and we were furnished with an escort of twelve Tibetan soldiers—the men who had come with us from Ho-K'eu leaving us. In accordance with what the people said was the custom of the place, it rained all the morning, as we marched over the low ridges thrown out into the plain from the mountains on the northern side. This plain is a favourite summer resort of the Tibetans, and numerous encampments of the black tents were dotted about. Immense herds of cattle and sheep were browsing around them, and the quiet was broken by the deep bay of the watch-dogs.

On the 20th we crossed the dreadful summit of Nga-ra-la-Ka, 15,753 feet above the sea. The mules were a few hundred yards ahead of us, and we heard the muleteers set up a shout of joy as they gained the highest point. They say that in foggy weather people often swoon here. Ting-Ko, the boy we picked up at Ta-Chien-Lu, seemed to feel the rarefaction of the air very much, and could hardly drag himself along. Here and there, just at the top, there were a few patches of snow lying in the road, but they were very small. After passing the crests we descended over dreary wastes of huge granite blocks. All this mountain mass is of a very hard, whitish-grey granite, and is much colder than the sandstone ridge at the other side of the Lit'ang plain. A good many skulls of oxen were lying about here, and it can be no matter for surprise that great numbers perish in the winter months, when the whole place is deep in snow. There are no poles and no cairns to indicate the path. It must then be a matter of the greatest difficulty to find or keep the road; and a wretched animal, stumbling between two boulders, each as big as a small room, would have little chance of escape.

The native chief of Lit'ang had sent off parties of soldiers to scour the hills in all directions directly he had heard of our approach. This was owing to the attentions of Pao at Ta-Chien-Lu, who was an excellent magistrate, and had sent most stringent orders regarding us. He had been at one time Liang-Tai at Lit'ang, and when he first came he took such active measures, and made such severe examples of the first robbers he caught, that during the rest of his term no more brigandage was heard of in his district; and, though we were no longer within his jurisdiction, his name was still so highly respected that we were well taken care of.

We halted for breakfast at a place called Dzong-Dā, which means 'dry sea.' It is 857 feet below the summit, and is a sort of marsh in a valley 200 yards wide and one mile long, running up to the east between low granite ridges covered with loose stones. Here we were astonished by a swarm of mosquitoes, most unexpected assailants, for we had not seen a mosquito for weeks. Dzong-Dā consisted of no more than one hut, and we left it to march over the same granite waste for four miles, when, after crossing a stream, we suddenly struck the sandstone, and the scene changed as if by magic. We again entered the rounded grassy hills, and a little lower, descending a stream, the pine-clad valleys appeared, and the lovely landscape that had charmed our eyes in the sandstone at the other side of Lit'ang was again spread out before us. We descended rapidly, and every now and then caught a glimpse of a grand snowy range in the distance; the sun came out, the air was delicious, and the afternoon ride was most enjoyable.

Thirteen and a half miles from Dzong-Dā, the stream we were following was joined by another equal in size, the two together forming a fair-sized river; and here the welcome sight of barley met our eyes, the first cultivation we had seen for a long time; and another mile and a half brought us to La-ma-ya.

On the 21st we found the road was very fair, though a little stony in places, and the ascent to the summit, through sloping hills covered with beautiful grass, was neither long nor difficult. We were still in the sandstone, and the hills were smooth and rounded. The pass is called Yi-la-Ka, and is 14,246 feet above the sea. Looking over the valley to the mountains on the other side, we caught a glimpse every now and then of a magnificent snowfield, as the clouds came and went across it. Down below us the road was marked out by the familiar religious cairns, immense piles, with 'Om Ma-ni Pe-mi Hom' roughly engraved on every stone; and from a hill on which we were standing these heaps appeared like some gigantic serpent twisting through the valley.

We now descended 884 feet, and mounted 250 feet to a pass called Man-ga-La. Down again a little way, and once more up, we found ourselves on another of these magnificent grassy plateaux, with a splendid panorama of snowy mountains.

Our escort halted here a little while, and we spent the time in getting the names of the different peaks; but the natives are so ignorant of these, that a mountain seen from one point can hardly be identified from another. Nen-Dā and Gombo-kung-ka appeared to be the names of the two highest; of the former we were afterwards thoroughly satisfied, but the other remained doubtful. Here enormous fields of snow seemed close to us, huge icy pinnacles frowned above us, and we could not wonder at the superstitions engendered in the ignorant minds of those who live amongst these scenes. In the icy breaths wafted from that pure expanse of dazzling white, imagination could hardly fail to feel the presence of the spirit of the frost and snow, or in the fitful gusts that murmured through the gullies to hear the rustle of that spirit's wings. The ice-blue water of the stream below, as it dashed over its rocky bed, seemed to leap for joy at its escape from the frosty trammels that had bound it, and the spray that broke from the rocks in sparkling gems seemed, in the very wantonness of mirth, to cast defiance at the hoary giants above. It was a scene never to be forgotten, and we both gazed long, with mingled feelings of wonder and admiration. But time is inexorable—our journey was not yet finished, and, mounting our ponies, we continued our march.

Towards evening we had a glorious view of Mount Nen-Dā, and, as the setting sun cast its last ray on the summit, I could well appreciate the solemn beauty of the scene. No words can describe the majestic grandeur of that mighty peak, whose giant mass of eternal snow and ice raises its glorious head seven thousand feet above the wondering traveller, who yet stands within five miles of its summit. He can but gaze with admiration, and appreciate the feelings of the Tibetans that have led them to call it Nen-Dā, or The Sacred Mountain.

During our march on the 22nd, every valley which opened on our right disclosed the vast snowfields of Nen-Dā, and with my glasses I could discern the blue glint of the ice. On the western side, which we saw at the end of the day, the snowfields seemed unlimited. With its spurs it covered the length of our day's march, and its summit is 20,500 feet above the sea.

Ra-ti, the Tsanba of Cooper, is situated at the end of a charming little green plain about two miles long, with a width in the widest part of a little less. The village consists of eight families, living in two or three houses ; but in the plain there is a large nomad population in black tents, who feed their cattle in the level valley, and on the sides of the gently sloping ridges that enclose it. These wandering shepherds remain here during the short summer, but at the approach of winter move lower down to some less rigorous climate. It is believed that more than half the population of Tibet live in these black tents ; but, giving this due consideration, the population must be exceedingly sparse. In our marches we rarely passed a habitation of any kind between the villages. The generality of these contained no more than ten or a dozen families, and the largest eighty, or a hundred families at most. There were some Chinese at Ra-ti, and we stopped in a new Chinese house, built of wood, very roughly put together.

On the 23rd we gained the summit of Rung-Se-La or San-Pa-Shan, 15,769 feet above the sea. From here we had a magnificent view of fog in every direction ; and the distance we could see was nearly a hundred yards all round !

We had a guide with us who had never seen a foreigner before. He was a half-breed, and rode a pony that had been mauled in the flank by a wolf. He was so much interested in us that he rode the whole way with his head turned round, and left the pony to find the road, which it did admirably. I at last began to think the guide was riding backwards. I was wrong, however : he was sitting the proper way, and none of my anticipations as to his head falling off came true. They say there are great numbers of enormous wolves here; and in the forests, on the western side, there are (so they say) every kind of wild beast—tigers, panthers, bears, wolves, and monkeys. The descent of the mountain was much more difficult than the ascent; but after three miles we escaped from the mist, and our toils were forgotten in the wild scene that lay before us. Bare crags towered above a sea of pines, and a weird forest of naked and blackened trunks seemed like the relics of some huge strife of the elements—indeed, it was not difficult to fancy the fierce conflict still being waged, and it only wanted the crash of thunder to complete the illusion. To the left a vast forest of pines rolled up the mountain-side, as though to storm its summit; but far above the highest, and laughing to scorn their efforts, the grim and savage rocks rose high towards the heavens. Thousands of dead stems in the van of the attack looked like the victims of this furious combat, whilst down below myriads of mighty pines seemed marshalling their hosts for a renewed assault. On the other side green grassy slopes looked calmly on at the desperate battle, whilst right in front a gigantic wall of rock, towering up nearly perpendicular, as though ready to hurl itself into the fray, reared its stupendous head into the clouds that sometimes swept across its summit. Not ten yards from us, the blackened stems of two colossal pines twisted their withered branches into all sorts of fantastic shapes, standing like spectre sentinels over the struggle.

We gazed some time on the magnificent scene, and then, descending a steep and rocky path, plunged into the dense forest.

Here there were vast numbers of rhododendrons, called by the Tibetans 'Ta-ma.' After much inquiry I elicited a Chinese name; but as in all probability it was invented expressly for me, I did not put much faith in the title Yang-Ko-Chai. There were also great quantities of the holly-leaved oak.

This is the forest of which Huc speaks in such raptures as the most beautiful he had seen in the mountains of Tibet;[1]

[1] *Souvenirs d'un Voyage*, vol. ii. chap. viii.

but in enumerating the trees he miscalls the holly-leaved oak a holly—a mistake very easy to fall into when acorns are not to be found.

When we halted to use the hypsometer a little below the summit of the pass of Ta-So, the scene would have made a splendid picture—the wild surroundings of bare rocks, and the still more wild-looking fellows grouped about, with their tall felt hats, their sword scabbards set with coral and turquoise, and long matchlocks, with prongs at the end of the barrel; Mesny with a long scarlet cloak reaching almost to the ground, the ponies with their queer saddles covered with felts and sheepskins, and the transparent water of the little pond reflecting the proceedings. We were 16,129 feet above the sea, and the summit of the pass was 540 feet above us.

The rocks here were full of iron, and affected the compass, how much I could not tell. I took a bearing as an experiment close to a rock, and, moving only a few yards, found a difference of a degree and a half. The tops of the crags were all yellow with iron, which sometimes produced remarkable effects.

The Tibetan name for this mountain is J'Ra-ka-La; but, strange to say, this is almost forgotten, and it is usually spoken of as the Ta-So-Shan; even Peh-ma and the Ma-Fu, whom we had questioned on the subject, had forgotten the native name, and it was not until after some conversation with the muleteers that they recollected it.

We reached the summit without much difficulty; there was no snow anywhere visible, nor was there any view, as the mountains were all shrouded in heavy clouds. Here, on the razor-like edge of the ridge, there was a pile of stones; the pious of our party added to the heap, and knocked their heads in thankfulness to Buddha for the dangers happily passed.

Just over the crest of the pass there is a great basin two miles in diameter, and such a wild and savage scene I never before looked on—a very abomination of desolation. Great masses of bare rock rising all round; their tops perpendicular torn and rent into every conceivable shape by the rigour of the climate. Long slopes of *débris* that had fallen from these were at the bottom, and great blocks of rock, scattered over the flat of the basin, lay tumbled about in most awful confusion amongst the masses that cropped out from below the surface. Three or four small ponds formed in the hollows were the sources of the stream that, descending from the basin, plunged into another valley, and, falling rapidly, soon became a roaring torrent, dashing through mile after mile of dense pine forest. The stillness of this place was very remarkable. The air was so rarefied that I could hardly hear the horses' feet only a few yards off, and when quite out of hearing of these, as I walked on alone, the silence was most impressive.

The road began badly, over the rugged stones of this desolate spot; it went on worse, as, descending sharply, it plunged into the enormous pine forest of which we now only saw the commencement; and it ended worst of all in a sea of black mud spread over the same unpleasant masses of rock.

The guide, who rode ahead, was a very remarkable figure. He had no head-dress whatever, and his hair fell in tangled locks over his shoulders. He had a very long nose, like many of the people here—a great contrast to the small features of the Chinamen. He had no hair on his face, and he was dressed in one garment of coarse sacking. A long matchlock with prongs and a huge cooking cauldron were slung at his back; the end of a coral-mounted sword projected from his clothes. His little pony was covered with felts and sheepskins, and at each side of the saddle were two great sacks. All the way down the 'Long-lived Gem' walked beside him, and narrated some wonderful stories, probably about ourselves, and his exclamations of surprise were continued. 'Arī-ī-ī,' he would say, dwelling on the final ī, and drawing it out for nearly a minute. Then, as evidently the Ma-Fu made some more than usual astounding statement, the guide would turn his head, and look at us with wide open eyes, and exclaim 'Eh-h-h-h, ī-ī-ī-ī.'

We trudged into Bat'ang on the 25th, and were conducted straight to the house prepared for us, where we immediately received an exceedingly kind note from Monsieur Desgodins, accompanied by a loaf of excellent bread, a bottle of wine, and some peaches.

We had barely washed our hands when the Liang-Tai 'Chao' was announced, and the chief military officer with him. After complimenting me on my literary ability, he said we could hardly get away in two days, but that he would have everything ready if we remained three days. This announced rapidity of action was as unexpected as it was gratifying, and I could scarcely believe that the performance would equal the promise. Chao was a man with a very agreeable countenance, bearing on it the signs of his active mind; unlike most Chinamen, both he and the military official here cut their nails short. I remarked on this to Monsieur Desgodins, who answered, 'Ah! but they are real workers.' Chao always appeared to be at work, writing or reading despatches, and his physical was almost as great as his mental activity. He was a remarkably small eater; I scarcely ever saw a man who ate less, and I had many opportunities of forming an opinion. Monsieur Desgodins always spoke of him as a model magistrate, who endeavoured to deal fairly with all classes: altogether he was a remarkable man, and a bright contrast to the generality of Chinese officials.

After the usual complimentary questions regarding our honourable names and honourable ages, Chao asked if we had any rifled artillery in our portmanteaus. This question was not put as a joke, but meant in all seriousness. On our replying in the negative, he said, 'Ah! if you only could have given me one or two I soon would have made these Tibetans say "La-so"; now I often have to say "La-so" to them.' This unpremeditated question and remark did more to show the true nature of the relations between the Chinese and Tibetans than anything else I had seen or heard. After he had gone, we called on Monsieur Desgodins, who was living alone. He is a most interesting and intelligent man, and has made many valuable observations on the geography of a totally unknown country, which he has had rare opportunities of studying.

The first business to be undertaken in the morning was the payment of the muleteers, chair coolies, Ma-Fus, and interpreter, and the presentation of gifts to the many soldiers who had accompanied us.

We had bargained with the muleteers to do the journey in twenty days, and, as they had accomplished it in nineteen, they were well entitled to the extra payments that made their eyes glisten with delight, and they thrust out their tongues further than I could have deemed possible. They afterwards returned, bringing a present of a jar of spirit made from what is here called black-wheat. In the process of manufacture, sticks of juniper, a shrub that grows in profusion on the mountains, are thrown in, and the taste of the liquor is very much like that of weak gin. When the gift had been accepted, they begged that if any other of our countrymen should pass this way we would recommend them, and they would serve them as well as they had treated us.

The chair coolies were so pleased with their rewards that they determined at once to take me further; this was a great convenience, as they had now fallen into my ways. The Ma-Fus, however, wished to return to their families, for which I was sorry, as they had both been exceedingly good servants; Peh-ma also returned to his little bit of land—though they all three seemed doubtful of reaching their houses in safety, on account of robbers. I subsequently learned that they would have been willing to come with us to Ta-Li-Fu, had it not been for Chin-Tai, whose overbearing manner they were unable to endure.

Now, every person who could possibly frame an excuse brought presents; first they came singly, then collectively, till I began to suspect they were like an army on the stage, and refused to pay for any more of the so-called gifts.

The Abbé Huc declares that the name Bat'ang means the 'Plain of Cows,' though in what language he does not say.[2] The Tibetan name of the place is Ba, a word that has

[2] Without presuming to have an opinion, let it be said, in justice to Huc, that Jaeschke's Tibetan dictionary gives *Ba* or *Bha* = 'cow,' and *thang* = 'plain.'—*Y.*

no meaning; the Chinese have added their favourite termination T'ang, which may mean either a place or a post station. The name the 'Plain of Cows' would certainly be inappropriate, for the plain, such as it is, is nearly entirely given up to cultivation.

There is a fable connected with the origin of the name, which is probably without any foundation of truth, but the existence of which clearly shows that the word 'Ba' can have no meaning. The story goes that once upon a time an old man and his wife wandering over the mountains with one sheep, their sole possession, in search of a habitation, came upon this place, and, enchanted with its position, warmth, and fertility, decided to settle here, but could not think of a suitable name. Whilst they were discussing the question, the sheep began to bleat, and they agreed at once that the animal had decided the matter, and called it 'Ba.'.

Bat'ang is well situated on a stream; it is about half a mile from the left bank of the river, and in a somewhat commanding position overlooks the plain.

The plain of Bat'ang, described by Huc as 'La magnifique, la ravissante plaine de Bat'ang,' lies at an altitude of 8,540 feet above the sea; but, notwithstanding this, its sheltered position, and distance from the mountains of perpetual snow, render the climate temperate and agreeable. At the time of our visit it was very warm, and the number of house-flies that swarmed in the houses, the streets, and even in the fields, was very remarkable, and equally disagreeable. The plain is not more than two or three miles long and one to two miles wide, and is enclosed by almost bare and precipitous mountains. There is scarcely a tree to be seen in its length and breadth, and it is nearly altogether given up to the cultivation of wheat, black-wheat, buck-wheat, barley, and Indian corn. Before the earthquake in 1871 the vines of Bat'ang were celebrated, and the native chief used to make great quantities of wine; but since that year, the vines have either not been replanted, or they have not had time to grow, for now there are very few, and wine is made only in very small quantities. Mulberry-trees grow well in the vicinity, but silk is not manufactured, as killing the cocoon of the silkworm is a mortal sin.

The Bat'ang river, a rapid stream twenty-five yards wide, winds through the plain, and joins the Chin-Sha-Chiang five miles below the town. Neither river is navigated, though there are a few boats on the Chin-Sha, a little lower down, at a place called Niu-K'ou. These, however, are only used for local purposes, and do not venture more than a few miles. I subsequently had many opportunities of forming an opinion, and certainly the river Chin-Sha is, generally speaking, not navigable above Shi-Ku, though there are many long, broad, quiet reaches where boats could be used. The boats in use at Niu-K'ou are mostly made of about eight raw bullock hides stretched over a wooden framework; one man only sits in them, and he steers from the bow with a paddle. They descend the stream in this way, and are carried back by land, the boat being sufficiently light to be easily carried on a man's back. There are also a few wooden boats at Niu-K'ou, that can be tracked a short distance against the stream, but these only ascend a few miles.

In 1871 Bat'ang was visited by a frightful series of earthquakes, which, lasting over many weeks, devastated the whole neighbourhood. In the town itself not one house was left standing, and the loss of life was awful; there was not one family in which there was not one dead. The traces of this appalling calamity are still to be seen for many miles around this ill-fated town. The hill-sides are rent and torn, and huge slopes of *débris*, hurled from the mountains, have in many places buried and obliterated the ancient paths.

The town is now perfectly new, and every house is fresh; of these there are about two hundred, containing three hundred families, who are chiefly remarkable for their reputed immorality.

Close to the bank of the little river of Bat'ang, in the midst of the waving cornfields, like the monks of old, the Lamas of Bat'ang have built their Lamassery, and, sheltered by the golden roof that cost upwards of 1,000*l.*, thirteen hundred Lamas live in idleness. Lama is the Tibetan word for 'monk,' and means in their language 'superior person;

the French use the term 'Bonze;' and the Chinese in the west have another name which, translated into English, means neither more nor less than 'criminals whose lives have been spared,' although the word in its application has lost somewhat of its signification. The story is that when the religion of Buddha was first established here, it was impossible to find inhabitants for the Lamasseries that were built, until they sent to these institutions all the criminals condemned to death. The Chinese now use this phrase for their priests, and see nothing incongruous in the epithet.

The number of Lamasseries throughout the country is astounding. At the small town of Ta-Chien-Lu there are three. At Lit'ang—a town of a thousand families—there are three thousand Lamas in the principal Lamassery; and outside the town is another building containing nearly as many. At Bat'ang, where there are only three hundred families, the Lamassery contains thirteen hundred Lamas. The traveller may march for days, passing by only a few straggling villages, containing at most ten or a dozen houses, and yet every now and then he is sure to hear of some huge Lamassery not far from his road.

Whatever may have been the difficulty in filling these institutions in the early days of the Buddhist religion, it is only too easy now. Parents who have a son, or sons, with whom they can do nothing, or whom they cannot afford to maintain, send their useless offspring with a gift to the nearest Lamassery. If a man gets into debt and cannot pay, he enters a Lamassery, where he is safe from any assault on the part of his creditor. If any one owes money to a Lamassery, as soon as the Lamas can get no more interest from him, they seize his land, he soon follows his possessions, and becomes a Lama.

The idle member of a family will turn Lama; he can then rejoin his relations for short periods of amusement or distraction, during which time he lives at their expense. All those who, having committed crimes, wish to escape their deserved punishment, enter a Lamassery, and shelter themselves under the cloak of their assumed sanctity. The Lamasseries are further peopled by the country-born children of the Chinese soldiers of the garrisons in Tibet. When these return to China, the foreign wives and children are left behind, and the latter, in that case, generally enter a Lamassery.

Occasionally a Chinese soldier will take his wife back with him ; but to do this requires an amount of moral courage not often found. For, instead of being admired for his constancy, he will meet with nothing but the gibes and sneers of his companions for his folly and ill-taste in burdening himself with a barbarian woman and her children.

The Lamas and Lamasseries are enormously rich. They certainly possess the greater part of the cultivated land in the plain of Bat'ang, and now must own nearly half of the country. Their wealth is daily increased, partly by legacies—for a dying man generally leaves something to the neighbouring Lamassery—but still more by usury. Being the only people in the country who have any property, a man in want of money always applies to the Lamas, and then his fate is sealed as surely as when some spendthrift in London commences dealings with the Jews. The rate of interest they exact for loans, even when real property is mortgaged, is fatal to the borrower. Interest mounts up, and, left unpaid, interest on interest, till at last, utterly crushed by the extortion of his creditors—his land gone, and with nothing left—the unfortunate debtor mortgages himself and his services for some temporary loan, and ultimately becomes a Lama.

The Lamas do not spend all their time in the Lamasseries entirely given up to devotion. On the contrary, theirs is a life of freedom. Whenever so inclined, they leave their Lamassery, return a while to their families, or to almost any house they choose to enter, spend their days as they please, and take anything they fancy away with them. This priesthood assists in no way in the maintenance of the State ; their lands are free from taxation ; they never lend their horses or animals for the public service, and do not pay one iota towards the Government expenses. They scarcely work in their fields themselves, as every Lamassery possesses hundreds of slaves. Thus the Lamas, by profession celibates, but in practice profligates, live in idleness and immorality—a curse to the country and the people.

The chiefdom of Bat'ang is governed by its native chief, under the immediate supervision of a Chinese official, who is paramount in the place. The taxes are collected by the native chiefs, who pay the imperial taxes to the Chinese official, who in his turn remits them to Peking. Not very long ago, the system of accounts adopted by the Chinese Government being imperfect, it was customary to send the whole of the imperial taxes in bullion, at least as far as Ya-Chou; the pay of the Chinese officials and soldiers being also sent in bullion back to Bat'ang. In recent years, however, knowledge of book-keeping has advanced sufficiently far amongst the Chinese to enable them to abolish this clumsy process, although the novel experiment has not been quite so successful as might have been expected, for the predecessor of Chao, in the office of Liang-Tai of Bat'ang, was a careless, indolent person. He spent the money himself, or allowed the native chiefs who collect the taxes to spend it, and neglected for some years to render an account to the governor-general of Ssŭ-Ch'uan, to whom he was responsible.

This governor-general must have been a careless person also, and probably the Liang-Tai trusted to this weakness in his character; but he suddenly demanded not only the year's taxes but all the arrears. The Liang-Tai failed to produce them; he was deposed, and Chao appointed in his stead.

Chao was at first afraid that he would have been called upon to pay the arrears, and, knowing how ill the miserable people whom he was to rule could afford any extra taxation, he refused the appointment, until it was clearly and plainly agreed upon that he should not be expected to produce anything more than the taxes for the period of his service.

Besides the imperial tax that is sent to Peking, there is another tax for the native chief. The assessment is per village. The amount that each village has to pay was settled a hundred years ago, according to the number of families residing in it. Since the date of this assessment the lay population of the country has diminished fifty or sixty per cent., and, as it continues to diminish, the tax becomes yearly heavier, and is now almost unendurable : so much so, that from this part of Tibet the people emigrate in considerable numbers to avoid the pressure of taxation and the hated rule of the Lamas.

Slavery is a great institution in Tibet. There are rich families who own five or six hundred slaves. These are hereditary, and are often treated very cruelly. A family always counts its riches in slaves and cattle ; but in Tibet proper, more by the number of slaves than by the head of cattle.

In this part of the country a man with three or four hundred head of cattle is rich, while one who has only twenty or thirty is considered poor. Even the agriculturists reckon their fortunes in mules and ponies, and not in land ; for in a family there is rarely enough land to support the whole. One or another of their number then undertakes the trading, and has charge of the mules, yaks, or ponies, used as beasts of burden, which thus become the measure of the family fortune.

Tibet is being gradually depopulated ; partly by the oppression of the Lamas, who are detested by the people as much as they are feared, and partly by emigration to Yün-Nan. Empty and deserted villages are constantly seen, and Monsieur Desgodins informed me that, even during the short time of his stay in the country, the decrease of the population in those parts well known to him had been enormous.

As the lay population diminishes by emigration, the land that the emigrants leave behind does not go to increase the fortunes of the remainder ; but, on the contrary, these are the more impoverished, for nearly the whole of this land passes to the Lamasseries, and, being no longer available as a source of taxation, the burden on the remainder, who still have to pay the same amount, is increased.

There can be no doubt that the Lamas were very strongly opposed to our entry into Tibet. Rumour, with her thousand tongues, had already been abroad, and the Lamas were expecting an attempted entry on the part of both Russians and English, which they were determined to resist. Whether the Chinese power in Tibet is as feeble as it is represented, it is difficult to say, but in all probability the Chinese have but a slender hold on the Tibetans, who, if it were not for the convenience of trade, might cease the payment of tribute. It was perfectly clear from the manners of both Chao and the military official, that they were exceedingly uneasy at the idea of any attempt to enter Tibet proper. Chao said that if we wished to go, he was bound by the letters he had received to do his best, but that it would be quite impossible to enter peacefully, and if we insisted on making the attempt, we should, in all probability, be obliged to fight our way. That he was really concerned for our safety was sufficiently proved by the fact that, even after he was quite satisfied that we really were going to A-tun-tzŭ, and not to Lassa, he not only came with us himself an eight days' march, but brought the native chief and an immense escort with him. That this was mere espionage is quite impossible; he could have sent half a dozen spies, if he had been so minded, who would have reported our most minute actions as closely as he could have observed them himself; and certainly, without some grave reason, he would not have put himself to the trouble and discomfort of this journey.

We were also told that the Lamas had ordered out six thousand men to guard the frontier, and our informant said that he had met the messenger sent by the Lamas to report our arrival. Numbers are of course always enormously exaggerated, and the six thousand was not, in all probability, as many hundreds; but there can be little doubt that the Lamas, whose power is almost absolute, had made up their minds to resist any attempted advance on our part; and even if open hostility and violence had not been attempted, they would have simply starved us out. The whole country is in their hands, and if they had forbidden the inhabitants to give us food for ourselves and people, and forage for our animals, or to receive us into their houses, or supply us with transport, their orders would have been obeyed to the letter.

Father Desgodins.

CHAPTER XII.

REGION OF THE RIVER OF GOLDEN SAND.

1. *Bat'ang to Sha-Lu.*

Departure from Bat'ang—Adieux to MM. Desgodins and Biet—Broad Features of the Geography, and Relation between Road and Rivers—Valley of the Chin-Sha or Golden Sand—A False Alarm—Journey across the Chin-Sha—Fine Scenery of the Kong-tze-ka Pass—Quarters at Jang-ba—Growth of our Escort—Armed Opposition on the Lassa Road—The River of Kiang-ka—Hospitable People—Desolated Country—Chŭ-sung-dho (Cooper's 'Jessundee')—Tsaleh—'The Boy the Father of the Man'—Watershed between the Chin-Sha and the Lan-T'sang—Camping Ground of Lung-zung-nang—The Bamboo seen again—The Gorge of Dong—Parallel Fissures from North to South—The Town of A-tun-tzŭ—Evil Character of A-tun-tzŭ—Prevalence of Goître—Water Analysis—Farewell Visits from Chao and the Native Chief—Ceremonies of Adieu—Prevalence of Opium-smoking in Yün-Nan—Long and Moist March.

BEFORE leaving Bat'ang the native chief sent soldiers out over the mountains to look for robbers or others who might wish to molest us, and when we left he came with us himself at the order of Chao, and brought a considerable escort with him; so that, with mules and muleteers, Chao and the chief, besides soldiers Chinese and soldiers Tibetan, as well as coolies and servants, we were more like an army than a private party.

Soon after leaving, we met Messieurs Desgodins and Biet, who escorted us a little way; and then Peh-ma and the two Gems were by the roadside with a tray of wine, which we tasted.

Half a mile further we met the native chief, and all rode on together till Messieurs Desgodins and Biet bade us adieu, and turned their horses towards Bat'ang. During my short stay Monsieur Desgodins had been a delightful companion; full of intelligence, his conversation had been most interesting, and it was with great regret that I parted from him. Monsieur Biet has now taken the place of the late Monseigneur Chauveau, and is the Bishop at Ta-Chien-Lu.

The great plateau that extends over the whole of Central Asia throws down a huge arm between the Chin-Sha-Chiang (the River of Golden Sand) and the Lan-Ts'ang-Chiang, gradually diminishing in altitude as it extends to the south. The northern portion of this arm partakes more or less of the characteristics of the main table-land, but even in the latitude of Bat'ang the difference is apparent, and it becomes more striking as Ta-Li-Fu is approached. This arm is not more than thirty-five miles wide in the latitude of Bat'ang; and as the crest is generally about five or six thousand feet above the river, it is little more than a ridge of mountains running nearly due north and south between the two streams. A-tun-tzŭ lies on the western slope of this huge rib, the road from Bat'ang crossing the crest at the pass of Tsaleh-La-ka, 15,788 feet above the sea. This is the main road to Yün-Nan, and is so conducted, in all probability, partly for the sake of passing through the important town of A-tun-tzŭ.[1]

[1] The Atenze of T. T. Cooper.—*Y.*

It might be expected that, as the road to Yün-Nan again returns to the Ching-Sha valley, south of A-tun-tzŭ, there would be another and easier road, by following the valley of the great river instead of leaving and returning to it. But in all probability there is no road down the valley of the Chin-Sha; the river appears to run through a succession of deep gorges, much as it does between Ch'ung-Ch'ing and I-Ch'ang, and as the Lan-T-s'ang does near A-tun-tzŭ, as well as further south, where the same river is crossed by the road from Ta-Li-Fu to Burmah.

Moreover, the road from Deung-do-lin to Tz'ŭ-kua keeps to the eastern face of the ridge, or, in other words, to the Chin-Sha basin; but near Deung-do-lin one glimpse is all that is gained of the river, a few miles distant, evidently tearing through an exceedingly steep gorge. The road then leaves the river to the east, and, by two exceedingly difficult passes, crosses two very elevated spurs thrown out to the east from the main ridge, which still runs north and south. The crossing of each of these spurs is at least as difficult as the passage of the main ridge; for the valleys dividing them are four thousand feet deep, and their sides excessively steep. In crossing these spurs, the road passes no town whatever, and there is clearly no reason why it should not follow the river, if there was a practicable route. The probable conclusion is that the river, at all events between Deung-do-lin and La-pu, flows through narrow gorges, where there is neither a road nor a possibility of navigation; and it would seem reasonable to believe that the case is the same between Bat'ang and Deung-do-lin, and that all the rivers running nearly due north and south of this region maintain the same characteristics of rapid streams in deep and narrow rifts.

We descended the Bat'ang river, a little stream of clear water twenty-five yards wide, for five miles; then leaving it we crossed a low spur that divides it from the Chin-Sha, a muddy turbid river one hundred and seventy to two hundred yards in breadth.

The valley of the Chin-Sha is somewhat dreary. The steep and broken sandstone hills descend at a very steep angle sheer down to the water, leaving—except at the *embouchure* of some small stream—no place for cultivation. The path running along the edge of the river is strewn with stones; the hill-sides are nearly bare; and every now and then there are long, steep slopes of loose rocks and *débris*, or small precipices by the road or up above it, the result of the convulsions that destroyed Bat'ang and tore the mountain-sides in all directions.

We breakfasted at Niu-Ku, where there were a few leather boats, by which some of our coolies relieved themselves of their burdens. Here some despatches arrived for Chao from Lassa; he swallowed a mouthful of food in a hurry, and set to work to answer them before proceeding on the march.

Our cooking things were either in front of us or behind; and, much to our astonishment, the people of the house produced three little tin plates with an English alphabet round the edge, and a picture in the middle of Sir Henry Havelock, K.C.B., on a prancing horse. By what route they had come here we failed to find out.

In the afternoon, as I was riding in front, I suddenly heard a shot; and, looking up, I saw half a dozen wild-looking fellows, with guns, behind a rock. For a moment the idea of an attack came into my head, but it was soon dispelled by a Chinese soldier dashing forward, for I knew that no Chinese soldier would voluntarily expose himself to danger. It is customary for large parties of a wild tribe of barbarians, sometimes two hundred or three hundred strong, to descend to this spot from the opposite side of the river, and attack the caravans of passing officials or traders. If these are Tibetans, or half-breeds, they do no more than rob them; but if they are Chinese they take them prisoners, and keep them until ransomed. There is a little square fort here for some guardians of the place; and it was these who had fired a salute in our honour, for which act of homage they of course expected a few rupees.

Crossing the Chin-Sha near Chu-ba-lang, we reach Kong-tze-ka, 11,675 feet above the sea, on the 30th. The scenery round this village would make the fortune of a Swiss hotel proprietor, if only it could be moved a few thousand miles in a westerly direction. I ascended to the housetop in the early morning, and thence my gaze roamed over a valley of wondrous beauty, enclosed by grassy hills, where masses of primrose-coloured flowers brought to mind many a bank in England. On the hill-side the pines and holly-leaved oaks contrasted their deep green with the brilliant yellow of the flowers. Here and there lovely slopes of the freshest grass were dotted with trees of the most graceful forms and delicate hues. In the distance rolling mountains filled the background; and the stream was heard rushing four hundred feet below. Herds of sheep and cattle luxuriated in the pasture, and round the village there were fields of wheat, barley, buckwheat, and pease. The usual wild gooseberry formed natural fences, and a road led along the hills right through lovely woods of pines, yews, and juniper. The road followed up the side of a stream. As we ascended, the hills became less steep, and presently we entered a charming plain about half a mile to a mile wide. Here the French missionaries have built a house on some property they have bought, and for a summer residence it is hardly possible to imagine a more delightful spot. The house is situated at the foot of a gentle spur thrown out from rugged mountains behind. A waving field of barley surrounds it; a meadow of grass, yellow with a carpet of flowers, lies beyond, where a stream meanders by a few large trees, and where great herds of cattle, sheep, and ponies stand up to their knees in the luxuriant herbage. Opposite the house the valley is closed by spurs of bright red sandstone from a range of higher hills behind. Just above the little building a Lamassery stands on a grassy knoll; and two Lamas dressed in red, crouching under the hedge of the missionaries' enclosure, scowled at us as we passed. Some time back the missionaries' house was destroyed at the instigation of the Lamas, but Chao rebuilt it at his own expense.

In this valley the usual piles of stones are capped with flat slabs of white marble. These heaps are of a pyramidical form; at a distance the white tops have the appearance of a row of English bell tents; and, looking through my glasses, I almost expected to see a red-coat pacing up and down in front.

The morning of the 31st had been very fine, but before we had finished breakfast heavy clouds were gathering ominously, and promised us a wet afternoon. Chao and the chief started off before us, and, following them, we rode over an undulating plateau, about thirteen thousand feet above the sea, whence we could see a high range of snowy mountains to the south-east, their tops hidden amongst heavy clouds. We had not long left the shelter of the village when the thunder began to roll in the distance, and a heavy downpour of rain descended.

I noticed that our escort, which had been gradually increasing, had by this time reached formidable proportions, and that now there were some two hundred men and officers with us. The officers wear felt hats, of the shape of our tall hats, but rather lower, with a broader flat brim. The men and officers are generally armed with a long matchlock, with prongs to rest on the ground, and two swords, one for cutting and the other for thrusting. All are mounted on Tibetan ponies, and carry great rolls of blanket and felt on their saddles.

I was riding on ahead of Mesny, and, in the wind and driving sleety rain, took but little heed of a man muffled in a big cloak crouching down on the opposite hill. A few yards further I suddenly found Chao and the native chief behind a knoll surrounded by about a hundred horsemen; and a quarter of a mile distant, on the opposite hill, some three hundred Tibetans were encamped, who had come out to oppose us if we should attempt the road to Lassa. When first they saw us coming they had fired off warning guns, although Chao had sent to them to say that we were going to A-tun-tzŭ.

When we had safely passed the encamped Tibetans, but not till then, Chao followed us, and, with two hundred soldiers, we marched in the drenching rain along slopes cut up by deep ravines and valleys, where the red sandstone, breaking through the rich grass, contrasted with the dark hue of the pines and oaks on the hill-tops.

I was assured that the woods were full of monkeys; but my scepticism was apparent, and it was with an air of triumph that my people called my attention to what they said was a monkey. The truthful field-glass, however, discovered nothing more inhuman than a boy; but, still, the repeated assertions of the people that the woods are full of monkeys are probably not without foundation.

The river of Kiang-ka, or the Vermilion River of Cooper, takes its rise in about latitude 30° 20′, and, passing the town of Kiang-ka, waters the plain of Dzung-ngyu, where it is about fifteen yards wide. The basin of the upper portion of this river is composed nearly entirely of red sandstone and red clay, which gives the water the remarkable red-brown colour observed by Cooper.

We followed the twists and turns of this tortuous stream through a rather dreary valley, where the view was limited to about half a mile of steep, high, and almost bare hills, and after a few miles we found Chao and the Bat'ang chief waiting for us in the house of another petty chief, where a few carpets were spread on the floor, and where butter, cheese, and tsanba were laid out on a low stool. It is a strong instinct of hospitality that prompts the master of a house thus to put food and drink ready for his guests; nor is this done with any niggard hand—a huge circular pat of butter about an inch thick, a cake of cheese of the same size, and great jars of oatmeal with gaily painted wooden covers, invite the travellers to partake freely of the best the household can produce; the tea-churn is not far distant, and, taking his wooden bowl from the fold of his coat, a Tibetan soon makes an ample and luxuriant repast.

From here we marched over an execrable road; and although Chao had taken care that the worst places were repaired, the track was so narrow and fearfully stony that it was necessary to dismount once or twice where steep and slippery steps had been cut out on the face of the cliffs. Wherever the valley opened a little, there were a few houses close down by the river, all built, as at Bat'ang, of rammed earth, and embowered in clumps of walnuts, peaches, and weeping willows. The number of inhabitants was small;

and the frequent ruins were sad proof of the diminution of the population, and the oppressive rule of the Lamas. We had been making inquiries for Jessundee, with the intention of saying a few words if possible to the old man who had treated Cooper so well; but in Chŭ-sung-dho we failed at the time to recognise the name, and so we lost the opportunity. Chŭ-sung-dho means the 'meeting of three waters.' Here we left the muddy river, and, ascending the bed of a beautiful clear stream, we plunged into a desperate gorge shut in by walls of bare rock eight hundred and nine hundred feet high. Here the native chief pointed out some wild oxen at the top of an almost inaccessible cliff, and a little further on, half-way up the mountain-side, there was a cave that our people told us was inhabited, although it seemed impossible to believe that any human being could clamber to it. About three miles from Chŭ-sung-dho the perpendicular cliffs gave way to slopes, where, though the hill-sides were still very steep, the road was somewhat better, and we could see a little more than a few square yards of heaven.

The village of Tsaleh is 12,690 feet above the sea, and is said to be a very rainy place; but, although it had rained all night, it was fortunately a fine morning. The muleteers had told us that, if wet, it would have been useless to start, as the mountain Tsaleh-La-ka was very difficult at all times, and quite impossible to pass in rain.

The morning of the 4th of September felt very chilly, as, in order to prepare for an early start, we turned out into the keen air, and watched the people of the village wading about in the mud in their long leather coats, which, as I remarked to Mesny, probably lasted from the day of birth to the hour of death.

'How can that be?' said he; 'do people never grow in this country?'

In reply I pointed out a touching sight that was at that moment presented to our view. An old man was performing the morning toilet of his son, a boy of about nine years of age. A huge coat, big enough for the father, was thrust upon the child, the sleeves were turned back till they were not more than a foot or so too long, the skirts were then drawn up, and a girdle being tied round the child's waist it was tightened up till we expected to see the boy drop into two pieces. This process providing the usual substitute for pockets, the father drew a parcel about the shape and size of his head from his own capacious fold, and thrust it into the child's bosom, with several articles, amongst which there was of course a Pu-ku, or wooden bowl. Then the boy was ready for anything. As he grows bigger his pockets will become smaller, but otherwise his coat will fit him well for the rest of his life.

From Tsaleh we continued our ascent of the stream, as menacing clouds were gathering amongst the mountain-tops. The valley was entirely without population, and we passed only one ruin before halting for breakfast.

At first the road was fair, and through woods of pines, oaks, and poplars.

There were long stretches of dead pines on one or two of the slopes, and the usual gooseberries, currants, and briars grew in the valley. We ascended gradually into the rain; but it was curious weather, at one moment it was raining, the next the sun was shining, and soon after we would have both at the same time. Once there was a magnificent rainbow down at our feet in the valley below, and the effect was very beautiful. After marching four miles we found ourselves amongst ragged peaks and slopes, broken into spires and pinnacles, where the road became very rocky, and we again entered the region of rhododendrons, and soon after we commenced the final zigzag that took us to the summit of Tsaleh-La-ka. There were a few small patches of snow at no great distance from us, but none on the road. The crest of this mountain, 15,788 feet above the sea, is the water-parting between the Lan-T'sang and Chin-Sha rivers. It marks the boundary between Yün-Nan and Bat'ang, and here the jurisdiction of Chao and the native chief comes to an end. But Chao was afraid that the Lamas of A-tun-tzŭ, who are directly under the King of Tibet, and are very hostile to foreigners, might try to annoy us, and, being determined to see us safely through all difficulties, he came with us to A-tun-tzŭ.

There cannot be much disputing about boundaries here, and no one runs much danger of being cursed for removing his neighbour's landmark. There can hardly exist a sharper line of demarcation, for the top of the mountain is like the edge of a knife.

We descended by an exceedingly bad zigzag for about half an hour, and then followed the stream to a little grassy opening, where we found our retainers near the remains of a hut, with a fire of sticks and a churn of buttered tea. The people here have a name for every opening in the forest, and this, being particularly small, rejoices in the remarkably long title of Jieh-kang-sung-doh. The rain held off for a little just as we arrived, so, seating ourselves on waterproofs on the grass, we breakfasted as well as circumstances would permit. The Tibetans do not seem to share in the superstitious dread of the Chinese for mountain passes—they sing and shout as they go up without any fear of evil consequences, and they regularly whistle tunes. The Chinese are unable to whistle, or, at all events, have never acquired the art.

From here the road took us to our camping-ground, through a pine forest very like that on the western side of J'ra-la-ka. The spot was charming for a camp, or would have been but for the rain, which effectually deprives camp-life of its pleasures. A rivulet came down from the mountains through a dense forest of pines and oaks, and just at its junction with the main stream there were a few hundred yards of open space covered with grass and wild flowers, and, though there were not even the remains of a hut, it was called Lung-zung-nang. Tents had been brought by Chao, and we found the native chief in a good-sized marquee, in which he and twenty men were going to pass the night. The tent that had been brought for us was not ready, so we sat down for a while with the Bat'ang chief, until our modest residence was prepared. This was a *tente d'abri*, of one thickness of cotton, ten feet by eight, with many holes in the sides, and nothing to close the front; but as the rain did not come down very heavily, and there was no wind, we were fairly water-tight all night. The servants and followers slept as best they could under trees, or elsewhere, and the place had probably never before seen so many horses and people encamped at once ; for altogether, with Chao and the chief, and their retainers and baggage, we numbered fully one hundred animals. We turned in early, and were lulled to sleep by the pattering of rain on the top of the tent, the chattering of the brook close beside us, and the more cheerful sounds of the crackling of numerous fires outside, where many picturesque groups of men, smoking, drinking, or sleeping, could be seen as the pine logs blazed up in the dark night.

It was a long time before we could prevail upon any one to start in the morning, and our time was beguiled with fearful stories of the dangers of the road before us. At length, however, everything was ready, even Chin-Tai and his cooking things, and we continued our descent. My Ma-Fu was now a beautiful sight, as he marched ahead of me in the rain. He was six feet high, and always out of breath ; he wore a rough felt hat, with his plait twisted round it, a red serge coat, and trousers reaching to his knees. His legs and feet were bare, and he trudged along with his boots in his hand. A gun was slung at his back, and he was further armed with a pair of field-glasses and a couple of swords. He carried the remains of a Chinese umbrella over his head, but as there was little left beside the framework, it hardly seemed a useful article of equipment.

We presently found a bamboo, a poor miserable thing, but we had not seen one since leaving Ta-Chien-Lu, and we hailed it as the first sign of a return to a warmer climate.

Two and a quarter miles over a villainous road brought us to the entrance of the gorge of Dong, called by Cooper 'Duncanson Gorge.' The river here runs between walls of rock, rising up almost vertically from the stream, whose bed is but a few yards wide ; the cliffs, however, are not altogether continuous, but are broken in places by exceedingly steep slopes clothed with dense foliage of pines and oaks, which seem to find sufficient nourishment in the crevices of the almost perpendicular cliffs. The road led us amongst trees, many of which had just been cut down to render the path practicable for us; but the branches of those remaining threatened every minute to knock us over, and made us stoop low over our horses' heads. We crossed and recrossed the torrent several times, and now and then the track was actually in the water. A huge sentinel rock marks the entrance to the gorge of Dong, which is two and a half miles long, and ends most suddenly in a little grassy opening, covered with trees, where the stream, as if weary of its headlong descent thus far, now ripples pleasantly and gently in a wide bed. After leaving the gorge the road is very fair, and, rising above the river, crosses a spur which divides it from another stream, and from this point the two rivers run for two and a quarter miles, nearly parallel to one another, only half a mile apart, and separated by a very steep and rocky ridge. A mile and a half beyond their junction the road is but a narrow track, eighteen or twenty-four inches wide, about two hundred feet above the stream, and it runs along the side of the hill, which is here at a slope of about 60°.

All the ponies with one accord used to insist on walking at the extreme edge of the paths. At this point Chung-Erh's pony, putting his foot over the edge, lost his footing; Chung-Erh was fortunately able to jump off, but the pony rolled down, and was lost to view among the bushes. A number of people clambered down to help it, but the poor brute was beyond all help, quite dead.

Soon after this the stream was joined by another running also parallel to it, and separated by another steep and narrow ridge. It is interesting to notice that all the great rivers, the Chin-Sha, the Lan-Ts'ang, and the Lu-Chiang, run nearly north and south, separated at comparatively short distances from one another by steep and high ranges of mountains, and that here their tributaries partake of the same character. It is as if some violent convulsion of nature in ages gone by had cracked and split up the surface of the country with huge rents all parallel to one another.

No sooner had we started from Dong than the rain again

came down, and descended on us without intermission until we arrived at A-tun-tzŭ.

We again mounted one of those steep and dreadful roads, which were now becoming somewhat wearisome, and for three hours we toiled over the accustomed rocks and stones to the summit of mountain Jo-ka-La, 12,389 feet above the sea, 3,389 feet above Dong. From this the road improved, the valley opened, leaving a little grassy space, where there were plenty of sheep and cattle, and further on there was a patch of cultivation, and a hut. Five-and-thirty minutes of very steep descent down a slippery zigzag brought us at length to the end of our first stage on the journey homewards, at the Chinese town of A-tun-tzŭ (Cooper's Atenze), which nestled in a little valley between high hills. We had made the journey very fairly—170 miles in eight days, a performance that reflected great credit on Chao, who had made all the arrangements for us.

Just outside the town the chief Lama came to meet us in a costume that would have put a beef-eater to shame; he had a wonderful red garment, the mysteries of which I had not time to penetrate, as I was fully employed in observing and admiring his hat. It can only be described by a sketch, and when it is added that it looked as if made of wood, and was gilt all over, a faint idea of the magnificence of the costume may be obtained. We visited him a day or two afterwards, and he wrote out the sacred ejaculation for us on a slip of paper. He told us that he was appointed by the spiritual authorities at Lassa, but was subject to the temporal rule of the second chief of Bat'ang.

A-tun-tzŭ is a Chinese town, and nearly all the people in it are Chinese; but, through long residence amongst Tibetans, they speak Tibetan better than their own language. They are not altogether Chinese in appearance, and the women were certainly better looking than any we had seen since leaving Ta-Chien-Lu. The immorality of the place is said to be very great, even worse than that of Bat'ang, the reputation of which town is about on a par with that of the worst in Eastern Europe.

The prevalence of goître in these districts is frightful.

The Chinese attribute it to the salt; but, whatever the cause, at least one third of the population are afflicted with this hideous disease; the swellings in the throat of some of the people being of appalling dimensions. It is said that the Chinese are not so liable to this malady as the Tibetans, possibly because they have not lived here so long, possibly because they never drink cold water.[2]

The houses in A-tun-tzŭ are nearly all built in the form of a quadrangle, with the stables below the living-rooms, and with flat roofs; but the evidences of Chinese civilisation are not wanting; some of the walls are whitewashed, and tables and chairs can be obtained.

As we were now almost out of Tibet I was very anxious to buy a prayer-cylinder; but the people had a superstitious objection to parting with them, and it was difficult to prevail on any one to sell one. They had a curious superstition also about their wooden bowls; they said that if they sold the bowls from which they had eaten to a foreigner, their country would fall into the hands of the nation whose representative had bought them.

We paid our farewell visits of ceremony to Chao and the native chief, and I was very sorry to say good-bye to the

[2] At Deung-do-lin, where there was a beautiful stream of clear water, and where goître was as prevalent as at A-tun-tzŭ, I procured a bottle of water. I believed at the time that it was drawn from an unpolluted source, but I am afraid that I was deceived. This water reached London in safety, and was minutely analysed by Mr. Bernard Dyer, F.C.S., &c., &c., who showed it to contain:—

	Grains per gallon
Total solid matter in solution	8·68
Loss on ignition (chiefly organic matter)	3·92
Chlorine	0·42
(Equal to chloride of sodium)	0·69
Nitric acid	0·059
Free (actual or saline) ammonia	0·077
Organic (albuminoid) ammonia	0·119
Oxygen, absorbed by oxydisable organic matter	0·406

After an elaborate, but by no means complimentary, description ot the water, and the effects that it would be likely to produce, Mr. Dyer concludes:—'In short, as far as I can judge, any peculiar properties this water may possess are to be attributed solely to the presence of a large quantity of organic filth.' An awful warning to future travellers to be careful whence they procure the water they destine for analysis.

excellent Chinese magistrate, who had taken such good care of us. Our visits were returned with all the rites attendant on so solemn an occasion. At these visits, Chinese officials are always in full dress, with their official hats on. There are usually cakes and fruits on the table, but they are seldom offered, being more for show than anything else; water-melon seeds of course there are, and these delicacies can seldom be resisted by a Chinaman, even under the most serious circumstances. Tea is always produced, but the visitor does not drink it until he takes his leave; then he rises from his seat, and holding the cup in both hands, raises it to his forehead, lowering his head at the same time. He then sits down again, while the host, who has performed a similar ceremony, calls for the horses or chairs of his guests. After this, the guest sips a little tea, rises, and walks to the door. When there, he clasps his hands, and, stooping, brings them to his knees; he then straightens his legs, bows his head, and brings his clasped hands to his forehead, thus completing the complicated movements necessary for making a Chinese bow. The host follows his guest into the outer court, where similar salutations are exchanged, the horse is mounted, or the chair entered. But the ceremonies are not yet complete, for now again the clasped hands are brought to the bent head; after which, the rigours of Chinese etiquette having been complied with, the guest moves away.

On our return I made Chin-Tai turn out all the provision boxes, the number of which had been increasing during the last three weeks instead of diminishing. It nearly broke his heart to part with some ancient hams and joints of beef that had accumulated in quantities sufficient to stock Noah's ark, but I succeeded in reducing by six the number of useless boxes we had been carrying. Still the muleteers declared that I must have six more animals than I ever had employed before, and the talking that ensued attracted the attention of most of the people in the town, who dropped in casually, one by one, to see what was going on. The chaos that reigned it seemed impossible to regulate; but order, if not harmony, was at length attained, and the greater part of our baggage was sent off the day before we left ourselves, as there was said to be no halting-place between A-tun-tzŭ and Deung-do-lin. Of the distance no one could give us any more exact information than that when people went there they started very early and arrived very late, and that at this season of the year, as the days were short, it could only be done by riding very fast.

As we had such vague ideas of the distance before us we were anxious to make an early start; but we were now in Yün-Nan, the province of China in which more opium is smoked than in any other, and in which it is proportionately difficult to move the people in the morning. There is a Chinese proverb to the effect that an opium-pipe is found in every house in the province of Kwei-Chou, but one in every room in Yün-Nan—which means that man and woman smoke opium universally.

At length it was proclaimed that all was finished, and we thought we were really about to start, when some one discovered that the men wanted their breakfast. Who the men were it was impossible to say. I had noticed Huang-Fu for the last hour, alternately behind his pipe and a bowl of food. My Ma-Fu had been so busy with tsanba that he had left all the horses out in the rain. An enormous pan of rice that had been in the kitchen early in the morning was now all finished, and still the people wanted to eat. 'Everything comes to those who know how to wait,' and we had by this time been sufficiently exercised in the virtue of patience to observe with some amount of philosophy the steady progress of the hands of our watches, although it was with some misgivings that we saw those uncompromising machines indicate the hour of nine as we emerged from the doorway of the house into the chilly rain. As for the rain and fog, except for five minutes when the sun made believe he was going to 'please again to be himself by breaking through the foul and ugly mist of vapour that did seem to strangle him,' rain fell and fog enveloped us incessantly the whole day—and so let us have done with that subject, as the worthy Marco would say.

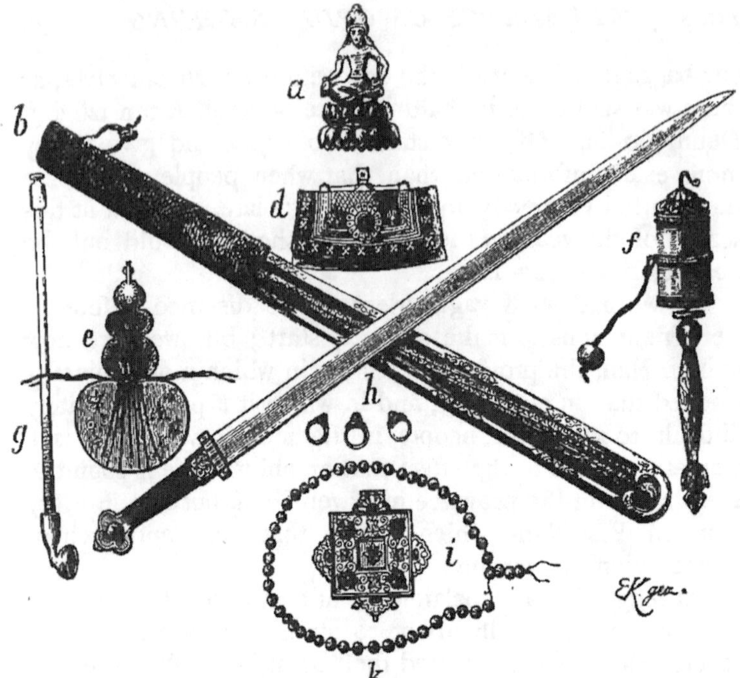

Tibetan Objects.

a, Brass image of Buddha; *b*, Scabbard; *c*, Sword; *d*, tinder box with steel edge; *e*, Tobacco-pouch; *f*, Prayer-cylinder; *g*, Tobacco-pipe; *h*, Finger rings; *i*. Amulet set with precious stones; *k*, Rosary.

CHAPTER XIII.

REGION OF THE RIVER OF GOLDEN SAND.

2. *Sha-Lu to Ta-Li-Fu.*

Sha-Lu—Big Tibetan Dog—City of Chien-Ch'uan-Chou—A Henpecked Warrior—Fair Words of the Chou—Road through Populous Rice-lands—Lake Basins—Opium-smoking—Damp and Dreary Aspects—The Erh-Hai, or Lake of Ta-Li—Road along the Lake Shore—Arrival at Ta-Li-Fu—Père Leguilcher—The Plain of Ta-Li—The Mahometans—Visits—General Yang—Departure from Ta-Li.

TRAVELLING in heavy rain through the same region of forests, passes, grassy plains, and deep ravines, we reached Sha-Lu on the 11th. The chief of the place had a huge dog, kept in a cage on the top of the wall at the entrance. It was a very heavily built black-and-tan, the tan of a very good colour; his coat was rather long, but smooth; he had a bushy tail, smooth tan legs, and an enormous head that seemed out of proportion to the body, very much like that of a bloodhound in shape, with overhanging lips. His blood-shot eyes were very deep-set, and his ears were flat and drooping. He had tan spots over the eyes, and a tan spot on the breast. He measured four feet from the point of the nose to the root of the tail, and two feet ten inches in height at the shoulder. He was three years old, and was of the true Tibetan breed.

From this village, ten days' march, during which two more high passes had to be surmounted, brought us fairly into the midst of the familiar rice-fields and a Chinese population at Chien-Ch'uan-Chou, the first walled city we had seen for months.

The walls of the city and the gates were in good repair, and, if they suffered much, have been entirely restored since the Mahometan rebellion; but the streets through which we passed were poor and wretched, with miserable houses. Here the old familiar Chinese sights again appeared—fruit stalls, eating-stalls, with the favourite bean-curd cake; stalls where hats, bits of ribbon, and other little articles, dear to the housewife, were displayed in as tempting a manner as possible, and the usual crowd of inquisitive Chinese that soon gathered round us.

The house we lodged in stood all by itself just beyond the east gate of the city, and was the sole remaining building outside the walls on any side.

There was a great deal of fighting here during the Mahometan rebellion, and the city was taken and retaken several times. We asked the landlord what he did when the rebels were here.

'Oh,' he said, 'I kept quiet, and did nothing.'

'Don't you believe it,' said his wife, who was standing at the top of the stairs. 'He went over to the white flag; like a fool, he was always fighting, and got wounded all over his body for his pains.'

Of course there was no contradicting a lady, and the worthy fellow beat a retreat rather sheepishly, like many another brave man, more afraid of his wife's temper than of swords or bullets.

Coolies were not wanting, as there was a whole army waiting in the courtyard. When everything had been packed some time, we asked why they did not take their loads and go. They seemed as much amused at the idea as it was possible for such miserable-looking people to be, and replied that they were waiting for the head-men, without whom they said they could do nothing. The head-men used to indulge in the abominable Yün-Nan habits of opium-smoking all night and sleeping all the morning. When they eventually arrived, they looked at the luggage in a stupid sort of way, and then seemed to think they had done enough for that day; the coolies in the mean while sitting placidly in the mud, in the listless manner of people too oppressed to care for anything.

On the 24th we set off through the city, which confirmed our previous impression of poverty and general misery. We saw potatoes in the market for sale, but nothing else that attracted any attention.

Mesny had hired a pony with four white stockings. Curiously enough the Chinese have a rhyme about horses with white stockings something similar to the old English one; but although according to our theory one is harmless, two are doubtful, three suspicious, and four certainly bad, the Chinese say that with one or three the horse is all right, but that if he has two or four white stockings he is sure to be weak.

Our road to-day was a most irritating one; it was over a perfectly flat plain, but twisted and zigzagged about amongst the paddy-fields, first one way, then another, and it was impossible to say where it was going to for ten yards ahead. It had at one time been paved with blocks of stone, which, now all displaced, were lying about in a sea of mud and slush in a state of frightful confusion. But if the road was irritating, the ponies were far more so—they floundered about, and put their feet into every possible hole; just when they were wanted to move a little faster, on a bit of comparatively good road, they would almost stop ; whenever I took out my note-book, mine invariably began to trot, would jump, put its foot with a splash into a mud hole, rush into the edge, if there was one, threaten to tear out my eyes with the thorns, and play any and every trick whereby it could spoil my writing, or bring my note-book to a greater state of decay than had already been caused by rough usage and the weather.

We marched for eight miles over the plain, which supports an enormous population, for we passed villages at almost every quarter of a mile, many of them very large. The crop was nearly altogether rice ; but besides this there was a good deal of buckwheat, some beans, and a grain called by the Chinese *Paidza* ; it is something like rice, and, like it, grows in water.

At the eastern side of the plain there is an extensive lake, into which the river runs. The geographical notions of the people were somewhat vague : they said that one stream that had a name came into the lake, and that another without a name flowed out, and they would not for a moment admit that they were the same river.

The plain of Chien-Ch'uan-Chou is similar in structure to the Ch'êng-Tu basin, and the plains of Ta-Li-Fu and Lang-Ch'iung-Hsien. Surrounded on all sides by high hills, the central basin is fed by numerous streams, and drained by one river that rushes out through a narrow gorge. The city is now some distance from the shores of the lake ; but, as the geological formation is entirely a soft sandstone, it is evident that the outflowing river must continually deepen its channel, that the lake must formerly have stood at a much higher level, and that it will in course of time be altogether dry.

We gained at length the plain of Lan-Ch'ung-Hsien, in its aspect and formation similar to the plain of Chien-Ch'uan-Chou. The road was, like the latitude and longitude of the amateur sailor, 'as before,' and remained so until we reached Niu-Chieh, where we found Huang-Fu smoking his pipe in the doorway of a deserted and tumble-down-looking place, which proved to be the excise office. We mounted by a rickety staircase from the shed below to the upper floor. One long room, where a couple of wooden pillars indicated the imaginary lines that divided it into three equal portions, was furnished with a crazy bedstead, and ornamented with some big stones that were lying casually about amongst the usual dirt and filth. Here we took up our quarters, as the inhabitants of the only eligible house declined to admit us.

It was no wonder, poor creatures ; they were accustomed to the visits of hungry officials, who take up their quarters uninvited, eat their food, destroy their furniture, and enforce their labour without payment ; and it was only natural for them to think that we should come and do likewise.

Some of our baggage arrived in good time, and as the head-men had a favourite trick of driving away the unfortunate carriers directly they had deposited their loads, in order that they might the more easily retain the whole of the wages of these miserable people, we ordered two or three of the coolies to remain in our room with the things they had brought.

The people below us now formed numerous little camps, where they lighted fires on the ground, and our room was soon filled with the pungent smoke of the damp wood that came up in dense volumes through the yawning cracks between the floor boards.

Later in the evening, when I walked to the other end of the room, I discovered that the two or three coolies we had ordered to remain had now become about fifty. They were crowded together, lying in heaps one on top of the other, and when the time came to make a clearance, it was with amazement that I watched them disentangle themselves and file off one by one. Amongst others there was a woman with a baby on her back, which she had been carrying all day besides the load allotted to her. Descending into the place beneath was a matter of no small difficulty ; people were all huddled together, even on the stairs, and for a moment I could not help thinking of a London ball—but what a piteous travesty ! on the ground, men, women, children, and babies in arms, were so numerous that it was almost impossible to walk without treading on them. Some were sleeping; others smoking, or trying to dry their soaking clothes over the wood fires. The occasional flare of some dry splinter in the reeking atmosphere served but to make darkness visible, for the walls and ceiling were black with dirt and the smoke of years. It was one of the saddest scenes I ever saw. The poverty and misery of the people, and the hopeless state of almost brutishness in which they live, were painfully visible in the listless, expressionless faces, which were now and then lit up by some fitful flash that burst for a moment through the heavy smoke. I returned again to the upper room, and the trifling discomforts to myself were forgotten in the recollection of the grievous scene below.

Some of our luggage did not arrive till the morning; and from the window we watched the lazy Yün-Nan people coming into market, for this was market-day in Niu-Chieh.

The people bring all the materials necessary for erecting their booths with them—four pegs to drive into the ground, four upright bamboos, to which four others are attached round the top, a light bamboo mat for the roof, and small bamboos strung together for the table on which their wares are exposed. All this weighs scarcely a pound, and the shed is complete in a very few minutes. We were told that out of the ten thousand families living in the plain, ten thousand people came to the market here; and although, as is usual in dealing with Chinese estimates, a divisor is certainly necessary, yet the very great number of large villages we passed on the road and saw on the plain, the people met at every step with baskets of pears, small red chilies, vegetables, and other things, showed that the population was enormous.

As we penetrated further into Yün-Nan, we did not find the lazy habits of the opium-smoking people improve, and the long and weary watching for coolies became a part of the day's proceedings. Then when the last odds and ends had been packed up in the last box, when even the cooking pots had been finally stowed away, and when the servants, all ready, were sitting listlessly cracking sunflower seeds or gazing vacantly into space, I used to find the hours very tedious. I was much diverted one morning by our host, who, standing on his doorstep, discoursed to an admiring audience on all the wonderful things the foreigners had and did. Amongst other things he told the people that each of us had a pen that we could carry in our pockets, and that we also had knives by which we filled them with ink. This was his way of describing the simple operation of cutting a lead-pencil. After paying our hotel bill, I presented him with an empty wine bottle. I really think that of all I gave him he liked the empty bottle best; he looked at it as fondly as a blue-china maniac would at an old bit of his crockery; he handed it round, took out the cork, examined the label, and even held it up to his baby for admiration; and the last that I saw of him, as I went out at the door, he was still toying with this precious gift.

The rainfall this year had been unusually great, the country was frightfully wet, and the landscape as we splashed over the wet roads was dull and cheerless. Villages standing in the swamps, or surrounded by water, with two or three ruined houses in the outskirts; people poling about in punts, or cormorant fishing; a huge pelican flapping its great wings or floating motionless on the water; the hills all shrouded in mists and rain clouds; the road by the river-side bordered with trees, and stretching out straight to the front across the marsh until lost to view in the distant haze; and the continual drop-drop of the rain from a leaden sky, all combined to make the scene a very dreary one.

In the upper parts of all these plains a good many trees of different kinds grow at the foot of the hills; but the plains themselves, and the villages, are nearly altogether bare. Here the only trees were growing by the edge of the river, and marked its course amongst the rice-fields that covered the flat surface. Rice is the only crop, and this is grown wherever the water is not too deep.

On the 27th the road, as well as the country, was nearly altogether under water, but the mud was less, and we could get on a little faster than usual; and, passing over the lower end of a spur, the lake of Ta-Li lay spread before us. In fine weather it may be very beautiful, but its beauties were not apparent through the mists that shrouded everything.

The lake of Ta-Li, or Erh-Hai, is about thirty miles long, and varies in width from about four to twelve miles; its eastern shores seemed to be bounded by mountains, which run straight down to the edge of the water. On the western side, down which we marched, a wide and very flat plain extends from the margin of the lake to the foot of the western mountains. This plain is almost entirely covered with rice; but, owing to the late continual rains, the crop was entirely lost, and I subsequently saw the young rice, on which the ear had hardly formed, being sold in the streets of Ta-Li as fodder for cattle. It was sad, indeed, in this frightfully poverty-stricken land, to think that so large a population would lose nearly all they had to depend upon until the next crop. The poverty was awful, the result of the terrible ravages during the Mahometan rebellion. At almost every step the ruins of some cottage were passed, where, in the place of a peaceful family happily living under a comfortable roof, wild thorns, briars, and huge rank weeds flourished between the remains of the walls, on the tops of which great prickly pears flung up their spiny foliage. What a contrast to smiling Ssŭ-Ch'uan, where, as Richthofen remarks, everything betokens peace!

At this northern end of the lake stands Shang-Kuan (the Upper Barrier), a small village, but occupying a strong military position, fortified with a double wall.[1] The direct road to Ta-Li-Fu runs along, or very near, the borders of the lake; but, as this was altogether under water, we were obliged to follow an upper road. As I looked again upon the familiar junk, I could not help wishing for a comfortable steam launch, in which the journey to the other end could be done in little more than a couple of hours. The day will come, no doubt, not only for steamers, but also for railways; and, judging from the crowds of coolies, mules,

[1] This is the Hiang-Kouan of Lieutenant Garnier's narrative; passing which, with notable boldness and adroitness, he escaped from the grasp of the Mahometan King of Ta-Li. (See *Voyage d'Exploration, &c.*, i. 515-516.)—*Y.*

and horses travelling in both directions, there can be little question that either one or the other would be a paying concern.

Numbers of military students were flocking to the examinations at Ta-Li-Fu, and I laughed to myself as I passed them by twos and threes, all carrying bows and arrows. The highest military officers have no more difficult subject than the stretching of a bow, or the lifting of a heavy weight, on which to satisfy the stern examiner. This in the days of breech-loaders, hundred-ton guns, and staff colleges!

Round some of the villages a good many of the people, men, women, and children, were engaged in stretching the cotton before weaving it. Two strong pegs are driven into the ground, about fifty feet apart; between these, a double row of thin sticks, two or two and a half feet long, are driven upright into the ground, about three feet apart, the rows being separated by about a foot. In each hand the operator carries a stick about two feet long; at the lower end of each of these is a reel of cotton. He or she walks up and down quickly, passing both reels inside two of the sticks, outside the two next, inside the next, and so on to the end, where the cotton on both reels is passed round the strong peg. In all this process the hands are never crossed; and, at a little distance, ten or twenty people, all walking backwards and forwards, separating and bringing together what look like little white balls, have a most comical appearance. In one village the people were preparing indigo, but I saw none growing in the fields. I saw also here the first large bamboo; there was but one, growing by itself, and it was only large in comparison with the little wild bamboo of the mountains, which is hardly larger than grass.

The great pagoda that stands on a projecting spur outside the city of Ta-Li-Fu is visible from a great distance, and long before the city is gained its height deceives the traveller into the belief that he has reached his journey's end. The longest lane, however, has a turning, and, dreary as were the last few miles of march in the pouring rain, over the poverty-stricken and half-ruined country, we at length rode up to the north gate of Ta-Li-Fu.

It was closely barred, for the spirit of the waters is supposed to flee at the sight of the north gate shut against him.

We entered at the east gate, and the interior of the city presented a sadder scene of desolation than the country round. The streets were wide, but half in ruins, and bore the same aspect of poverty that was everywhere apparent.

Ta-Li-Fu is an ancient city, and was formerly a place of great importance, though now it is little better than a ruin. It is the Carajan of Marco Polo.

It stands at the southern end of a basin, about thirty miles long, entirely enclosed by high mountains. This basin is similar in structure to the plains of Lang-Ch'iung-Hsien and Chien-Ch'uan-Chou, and, like them, is nearly altogether occupied by an extensive lake.

Marco's description of the lake of Yün-Nan may be perfectly well applied to the lake of Ta-Li: 'There is a lake in this country of a good hundred miles in compass, in which are found great quantities of the best fish in the world.'

The fish were particularly commended to our notice, though we were told that there were no oysters in this lake, as there are said to be in that of Yün-Nan. If the latter statement be true, it would illustrate Polo's account of another lake somewhere in these regions 'in which are found pearls (which are white but not round).'

Before the Mahometan rebellion the plain used to be well wooded, the villages were embowered amongst noble trees, and the landscape must have been as beautiful as any in China; but now there is not a tree left standing in the length and breadth of the plain.

The appellation of 'Snowy Mountains' has popularly been given to the summits around Ta-Li-Fu; but snow lies on them for only six or seven months in the year, and the altitude of the highest peak is in all probability not more than twelve or thirteen thousand feet. The line of perpetual snow in this latitude cannot be lower than between eighteen and nineteen thousand feet.

Ta-Li-Fu lies at an altitude of 6,666 feet above the sea, and the climate is always pleasant; but at the time of our visit a most unusual amount of rain had fallen, so much that that irrepressible person the oldest inhabitant had never recollected so wet a season. In the city we constantly heard the sound of falling houses, and Monsieur Leguilcher, the Provicaire, living at Ta-Li-Fu,[2] told us that a fortnight previously, in the plain of Têng-Ch'uan-Chou, he had been going about in a boat over roads on which he had always previously travelled on horseback.

The people and officials were now all praying for fine weather ; and one morning during our stay, the Tao-Tai, in all the glory of official robes, headed a procession, which proceeded solemnly to the city walls, where they fired a gun at the sky, as a sign of anger and displeasure, by which they seriously believed they would frighten the rain god into a more kindly frame of mind.

It was rather a remarkable fact that at the city of Yün-Nan-Fu, only twelve days distant, there was a severe drought ; a fast was proclaimed, the south gates shut, and all the solemn rites, such as we had seen as we were leaving Ssŭ-Ch'uan, were being performed to obtain that rain which here had produced such disastrous effects.

There are some quarries in the neighbourhood of Ta-Li-Fu, where very beautiful marbles are found, so curiously marked, and stained by nature with such diverse colours that, when cut into flat slabs, a landscape of mountains and trees appears on the face. Monsieur Leguilcher made me a present of a very rare specimen framed, and when hung up it might at a little distance easily be mistaken for a painting.

There are now about three hundred villages in the plain of Ta-Li-Fu, the largest of which does not contain more than two or three hundred families, while before the rebellion the population of the villages averaged seven or eight hundred families. In Ta-Li-Fu itself there are from two thousand five hundred to three thousand Chinese families, and one thousand five hundred to two thousand native families—for the Chinese are strangers here, though they outnumber the natives ; the latter have a great dislike to foreigners, amongst whom they include the Chinese.

[2] It was Père Leguilcher who joined the late Lieutenant Garnier in his daring journey to Ta-Li-Fu in 1868.—*Y.*

Over all the neighbourhood the ruin of the country occasioned by the rebellion of the Hui-Hui, or, as Europeans call them, Mahometans, is grievously apparent. This rebellion lasted over many years, during which the most desperate fighting took place in almost every town within fifty miles of Ta-Li-Fu, the great centre of the movement, and the seat of Tu-Wên-Hsiu, the so-called Sultan Suliman.[3] Towns and cities were taken and retaken by each side alternately, acts of frightful cruelty were perpetrated, and retaliations still more cruel followed.

During all these scenes of war and bloodshed M. Leguilcher remained in the province, and his life during this time would form a thrilling narrative of hardship and adven-

[3] 'The word Panthay has received such complete recognition as the national name of the Mahometan revolutionaries in Yün-Nan that I fear it will be almost useless to assert that the term is utterly unknown in the country which was temporarily under the domination of Sultan Suliman, otherwise Tu-Wên-Hsiu. The rebels were and are known to themselves and to the Imperialists by the name of the Hui-Hui, or Hui-Tzu (Mahometans), the latter expression being slightly derogatory.

'The name of "Sultan," utterly foreign to the ordinary Chinese, was never applied to their ruler, except perhaps by the two or three hajjis among them.

'The name "Suliman" is equally unknown. The Mahometans of Yün-Nan are precisely the same race as their Confucian or Buddhist countrymen; and it is even doubtful if they were Mahometans, except so far as they professed an abhorrence for pork. They did not practise circumcision, though I am not sure if that rite is indispensable; they did not observe the Sabbath, were unacquainted with the language of Islam, did not turn to Mecca in prayer, and professed none of the fire-and-sword spirit of propagandism.

'That they were intelligent, courageous, honest, and liberal to strangers, is as certain as their ignorance of the Law and the Prophets. All honour to their good qualities, but let us cease to cite their short-lived rule as an instance of the "Great Mahometan Revival."'—*Mr. Baber's Report—China*, No. 3—1878.

The term *Panthé* is that recently applied by the *Burmese* to the Yün-Nan Mahometans. No one interested in the subject ever supposed it to be 'a national name' in use by the people themselves. Its origin is very uncertain; Sir A. Phayre thinks it has nothing to do with *Pa-thi*, the old Burmese word for Mahometans, which is probably a corruption of *Parsi*, Persian. The name *Suliman* was probably merely a formal style known only to the hajjis; but it is used in the Arabic proclamation which was circulated in neighbouring states, and is mentioned by Dr. Anderson, who appears to have heard it at Momien. (*Report on Expedition to Western Yunan*, 1871, p. 150.)—*Y.*

ture. Once he took refuge in a wood, where he built himself a hut of small trees; after a time he discovered they were cinnamon trees, and he used to vary his diet by eating his house.

At another time he had taken refuge in the mountains, with fifty or sixty Christian families. After a battle, a band of the defeated party came his way, and would have robbed or murdered them, but he bought the good-will of the chief with an old pistol and ten percussion-caps.

The Chinese always maintained that there were a number of Europeans with the rebels; but M. Leguilcher told us that, beyond a few people who came from Rangoon, and knew no words of any European language save *Padre* and *Capitan*, there were no foreigners whatever with them.

During the rebellion a horrible epidemic like the plague appeared, that first of all attacked the rats. These animals used to die about the houses for a few days, and then they would migrate in vast numbers from the towns into the fields. After this, the disease seized upon the miserable population, and carried off an enormous proportion of the people.

Another fact worth recording noticed by M. Leguilcher was that, during the rebellion, when every one was in a state of anxiety, never knowing at any moment whether he might not have to fly for his life, the births amongst the Christians were not more than four or five per annum amongst one hundred and twenty families, the normal number being fifty or sixty.

The Mahometan rebellion has been crushed; but large numbers of Mahometans, who may be known by the white turbans which they wear, but who are as ignorant of the Koran as they are of the Talmud, still remain in the province. They are not less discontented than they were before the rebellion; all the elements of discord still exist, and a very small spark might rekindle a flame that would again cast its ghastly glare over all the horrors of a civil war.

We had scarcely established ourselves after our dreary march at the wretched inn in Ta-Li-Fu, when M. Leguilcher sent us a present of some beef. This was very acceptable, for the magistrates forbade beef to be killed, partly because the number of oxen in the district was so small that it barely sufficed for the agricultural necessities, and partly because there is almost universally amongst the Chinese a superstitious dislike to killing this animal. But in Ta-Li-Fu the pork-hating Mahometans found a way to provide themselves with meat, and M. Leguilcher was able now and then to obtain some portion of a slaughtered ox. Soon afterwards he came himself to welcome us to Ta-Li-Fu, and his friendliness and geniality were more like those of an old friend than the first words of a stranger.

The next day we moved into our new abode, a sumptuous apartment in an upper story, with a good reception-room on the ground floor, where we could receive official visits. When we were fairly settled down in our new hotel, we opened all our baggage, some of which had been shut for many days. The sight was awful; some of the boxes were absolutely rotting, and the things inside them wet and mouldy. We set pans of charcoal about, and soon gave our room the appearance of a laundry, with all our clothes hanging from strings stretched from the walls. The state of confusion became chaotic, and when Monsieur Leguilcher came in to visit us, he had to pick his way amongst the damp clothes, boxes, and masses of wet and mouldering paper that were scattered pell-mell over the floor and on the tables, beds, and chairs.

During our stay in Ta-Li-Fu it rained incessantly night and day, and we scarcely left the house, except to pay the necessary official visits. We found that, notwithstanding the crowds brought into the city for the examinations, we excited but little curiosity, scarcely any one following us in the streets. These, though wide, are very miserable in appearance, and the shops wretched; but the city is very interesting, for people of every type are seen, and the women certainly are better looking than the generality of Chinese and aboriginal women. Some of those walking about in the mud in Ta-Li-Fu were quite fair, a great contrast to the very dark mountaineers amongst whom we had been travelling.

We had omitted to study the Chinese almanac before starting on our round of calls, and found on arrival at the yamên of the Tao-Tai that it was one of those remarkable festivals on which the front gates are kept shut, and visitors are only received by the side door, and in unofficial costume; we therefore deferred our visits until a more auspicious occasion, when we were received by his excellency in all the dignity of full dress. We were regaled with cakes and sweets, wine that tasted like vinegar, and Havannah cigars.

General Yang, the Ti-T'ai, is perhaps one of the most remarkable men in China. He is almost a hunchback, but so active that the people call him the 'Monkey.' In the war, unlike most Chinese generals, who sit in their chairs in the rear, he was always on horseback under fire at the head of his men. One day when he came to visit us he walked over from his yamên, a course of action that would shock the sensitive minds of most Chinese officials. He has made himself so powerful and rich that he keeps two hundred soldiers at his own expense, and is more dreaded than loved by the Chinese Government, to whom, nevertheless, he is an excellent servant.

Baber credits him with the reputation of a Barabbas and a Bluebeard. He is, undoubtedly, a man of very violent temper, but his faults have probably been exaggerated, for those who knew him best used to say that they did not think he would be likely to chop off the head of a legitimate wife, if he could get one. At the time of our visit to Ta-Li-Fu he was very anxious to get a well-educated wife from a good family; he had a great mass of correspondence to conduct, and, afraid of treachery on the part of private secretaries, thought that a wife who could write his confidential despatches would be very useful. The good families, however, did not quite see it in the same light, and, notwithstanding the attractions of rank and fortune, Yang had not succeeded in forming a matrimonial alliance.

We sent all our servants home from Ta-Li-Fu, except the Peking boys. Ting-Ko, who had followed us unasked, was very sorry to leave, and begged to be taken on; but there would have been no possibility of sending him back to Ta-Chien-Lu from Bhamo, and so he went with Huang-Fu and his pipe to Ch'êng-Tu. The Ma-Fus returned to Bat'ang, and I had the satisfaction of hearing many months afterwards that all had arrived in safety.

During our stay at Ta-Li-Fu the rain had fallen without ceasing, and it was with much satisfaction that when I looked out of window (on the morning of the 4th of October, the date of our departure), I could see for the first time the lake of Ta-Li lying at the feet of the mountains, on which the first sprinkling of snow had fallen during the last few days. The sun shone in a clear sky, flecked here and there with fleecy clouds; the deep blue water of the lake sparkled as its surface was rippled by a gentle breeze; the morning was beautiful, and all nature seemed to rejoice in the pleasant change of weather. Out of all that remained of our stud, my grey was the only animal that was fit to take any further. I at first rode a hired pony, and my new Ma-Fu walked on in front leading the grey. Much impressed with his own importance as keeper of the stables to their 'foreign excellencies,' he swelled with pride as he ordered every one we met to move aside; if people were sitting harmlessly by the road, he made them stand up and salute; and he was not satisfied unless all riders dismounted from their horses and paid proper respects. At last, as he was making us a perfect nuisance to all the passers-by, I was obliged to make him fall to the rear.

At the end of the suburb we halted. It was time for Monsieur Leguilcher, who had ridden thus far with us, to return to his solitary abode. Those who have never travelled in distant lands can little understand the feeling with which one stranger meets a fellow wanderer from home—'A fellow feeling makes us wondrous kind;' and it was with no light heart that I bid adieu to our kind friend, for I could hardly venture to say '*Au revoir*!'

Western Chinese Brave.

CHAPTER XIV.

IN THE FOOTSTEPS OF MARCO POLO AND OF AUGUSTUS MARGARY.

1. '*The Land of the Gold Teeth.*'

Marco Polo's Cakes of Salt—Paucity of Present Traffic on Road—Devastated Country—Yang-Pi River—Chain Suspension-bridge—Perversities of the Path—T'ai-P'ing-P'u—Lofty Hamlet of Tou-P'o-Shao—Dearth of Population—Traces of War—Chestnut and Oak Woods—Descent to Plain of Yung-P'ing-Hsien—The Town destroyed—View of the Mekong or Lan-T'sang River—Chain Bridge across it—Desperate Ascent—Ta-Li-Shao—Pan-Ch'iao—Rice Macaroni—Polo's Salt Loaves Again—His 'Vochan' and the 'Parlous Fight' there—Yung-Chang-Fu—A General on the March—A Quarrel Imminent, but the General is Drawn off—Stones and Beads Brought for Sale—Recent Plague on the Road.

HSIA-KUAN is situated at the southern end of the lake, at the entrance to the gorge through which the river escapes, and through which the road from Burmah reaches Ta-Li-Fu.

It is a poor place, half in ruins. The arch and brickwork of the southern gate had tumbled down with a good portion of the wall. These, however, formed a rather rough ramp, over which we rode to our inn, where we dined off some mutton given us by General Yang, which was so good that we both declared the general's name should be Mutton, and not Willow. (The sound of the Chinese word Yang, which means Willow, is the same as the sound of another word Yang, meaning Sheep, though the written characters are quite different.)

Before turning into bed we saw, as we believed, all the animals in the inn-yard, and comforted ourselves with the thought of an early start ; but even yet we had not fathomed the depth of the cunning of these wily people, for when it became light we discovered that, though all the baggage mules were safely in the place, there was not a single riding animal, and we came to the conclusion that even if we should lock them up with us in our room they would somehow disappear before the morning.

The morning was beautifully fine, and as we stood at the window watching the sleepy people turn out and gradually open their shops, I remarked to Mesny that the salt, instead of being in the usual great flat cakes about two or two and a half feet in diameter, was made in cylinders eight inches in diameter and nine inches high.

'Yes,' he said, 'they make them here in a sort of loaves,' unconsciously using almost the words of old Polo, who said the salt in Yün-Nan was in pieces 'as big as a twopenny loaf.' [1]

We followed the left bank of the river which drains the lake of Ta-Li. On the right bank a wall extended from the town of Hsia-Kuan to the entrance of the defile, where it ended in a blockhouse ; but the interior of the work, as well as the greater part of the length of the wall, is so thoroughly exposed to enfilade and plunging fire from the road on the opposite side, that it would be of very little use against a force led by a commander possessed of the average amount of common sense.

[1] Ramusio's version ; see Yule's *Marco Polo*, 2nd ed. vol. ii. p. 48.

It was market day in Hsia-Kuan, and we met great numbers of coolies and people coming in, nearly all laden with walnuts and sticks for firewood. The people met during the hour from ten to eleven were counted, and out of a hundred and sixty-five foot-passengers, seventy-three were loaded with walnuts, forty-four carried sticks, and fourteen were bringing sacks, the contents of which were unknown, but which were probably walnuts. This hour was the most active, for afterwards we met but few people, and not more than fifty or sixty mules laden with opium and cotton. These last may be considered as representing the through traffic, and they came from Yung-Ch'ang.

Most of the trade comes from Ava. One of our muleteers, a black-moustached and whiskered Mahometan, had often traded thither, but had only once been to Bhamo. He said that there were forty marches from Ta-Li to Ava. Judging from what we saw, the through traffic on the road must be very small; but good government at Ta-Li, and the abolition of all Lekin and other oppressive taxation, would no doubt open up the trade.

The road generally was from a hundred to two hundred feet above the river, and very bad to boot. The river was a roaring, rushing torrent, falling 1,400 feet in ten miles, with here and there a waterfall about ten or twelve feet high. The valley of the stream was very narrow, the hills generally running sheer down to the water; but the lower slopes were well cultivated with buckwheat, rice, and a crop noticed before, called paidza. The valley in its palmy days must have been well populated; but the towns and villages were now nearly all in ruins, and could contain but few inhabitants. A little below the very small village of Shih-Ch'uan-P'u, a very unpleasant descent began, ending in a bridge made by laying long slabs of stone from the banks to a rock in the middle; whilst, just below, the opening of a narrow glen gave a passing glimpse of a fine cascade, brimful after the recent rains. Here the walnut trees again appeared, but they now looked very autumnal; the leaves were very brown, and the nuts all plucked; there were a few persimmon trees, with fruit nearly ripe. Much of the rice was nearly ready for cutting, and there were a few very fine large bamboos.

The road was very bad, in one place altogether washed away, and we were obliged to make a cross-country expedition over a field of buckwheat. Here, though the whole of the traffic was diverted through this field, scarcely any damage was done, all the animals following exactly in the same track. The Chinese, whether boys or men, never do wanton mischief, and in enlightened England a road suddenly taken through a field of corn would hardly leave the farmer so unscathed as here. At this point we overtook Chin-Tai, who had been sent on ahead, and who had been taken down the other side of the river to a bridge, now washed away, and we went on together to the little village of Ho-Chiang-P'u, where we found comfortable, though rather rough, accommodation.

We crossed the Yang-Pi river by an iron chain suspension-bridge, of about forty yards span, with nine chains, which was remarkably stiff and steady for one of these constructions; and, leaving the river, we at once commenced a very steep and rather difficult ascent of about two thousand feet; the road then improved. Another thousand feet brought us to the summit of Ch'ing-Shui-Shao, 8,233 feet above the sea, and we then descended one of the very worst bits of road we had encountered in our journey. It had once been paved with very large stones, now all misplaced, and the interstices filled with deep, stiff, sticky mud. Slippery banks at the sides, and holes hidden by mud and slush, made walking necessary for about a couple of miles from the top, after which a certain amount of improvement became apparent, and for the next few miles it was possible to ride.

On the 7th there was no mountain on our way from T'ai-P'ing-P'u (the Peaceful Village), but the road, apparently out of very wantonness, went up about nine hundred feet.

The stream of T'ai-P'ing-P'u, which is bounded on its right bank by a spur from the mountain Ch'ing-Shui-Shao, runs into the Shun-Pi river at a distance of about eight miles from T'ai-P'ing-P'u, and the Shun-Pi river is crossed about a quarter of a mile above the junction of the streams. Any ordinary person would imagine that the road would be taken somewhere near the edge of the water; but he would be quite wrong. This eccentric path rises steadily nine hundred feet to the crest of the spur, and then by a very nasty zigzag goes back to the stream. At first we were unable to suggest any other reason for this monstrous behaviour than that the road-makers were afraid that, by leaving a few level miles, men and animals travelling would get out of training for the succession of mountain ranges that must be crossed. At the top, however, we discovered an unexpected village, Tou-P'o-Shao, and it is for the sake of the two or three huts that compose it that all travellers have to march up the hill and down again. The morning was beautifully bright, and the scenery charming: fine rolling mountains in every direction, whose sides, by no means steep, were well wooded by small pines; there were many open spaces, some cultivated and some covered with rich fine grass, which, after the recent rains, was of the brightest green; and a huge range of mountains ahead promised us a hard day's work for the morrow. The sides of the valley were little cultivated, and we did not pass a single hut until we reached the very crest of the ridge where Tou-P'o-Shao is perched. Whence the half-dozen people inhabiting it draw their supply of water it is difficult to say; but there it is, situated in as lovely a spot as can well be conceived, and, from a point a short distance beyond, the Shun-Pi river can be seen flowing from the north.

The next village of three or four houses, amongst the ruins of thirty or forty others, is three miles further on, at the bottom of a heartbreaking zigzag, and here a couple of caravans were resting, one before undertaking the arduous ascent, and the other after having reached the level ground. The former was a train of fifty-six mules bringing cotton from Yung-Ch'ang, and the latter consisted of twenty-six mules laden with salt. Besides these we met no one during the whole day, except a travelling official and ten or a dozen other people, although this was one of the favourable seasons for travelling on the great highroad from Bhamo to Ta-Li.

The country is scarcely inhabited. Besides the two miserable villages already mentioned, there are but two solitary huts between T'ai-P'ing-P'u and Huang-Lien-P'u, a distance of ten miles, and these two villages themselves contain but few inhabitants.

Huang-Lien-P'u is situated about a quarter of a mile up a small stream tributary to the Shun-Pi river. Here an unexpected treat awaited us, for one of our men-servants, whose permanent employment was that of chief baker to Monsieur Leguilcher, said that he could buy some leaven, and that, if we liked, he could bake us some bread. We did like very much ; but even the thoughts of this luxury in store for us were not sufficient to reconcile us to the smoky atmosphere of the room, which was not rendered more pleasant by the fumes that came in at the window from a house next door, where the family were roasting their annual supply of chilies. Savages have been smoked out of caves with a few grains of red pepper on a fire, and our experience of the chilies led us to sympathise with the savages. Even the Chinese cannot stand this, and they can stand most things ; in fact, it was so impossible, that our request to our next-door neighbours to desist was considered by no means an unreasonable one.

On the 8th of October the road led us across the range of mountains that divides the basin of the Shun-Pi river from that of the river of Yung-P'ing. Both these streams and the range of mountains between them run nearly north and south.

We ascended a very remarkable spur thrown out from this range, some seven miles long and scarcely a mile in breadth, with a deep gully on either side, in each of which a torrent was rushing down to the river of Shun-Pi. The formation was still the same red clay and sandstone ; but after the dry weather the road was good enough, except just at the end of the ascent of Mount T'ien-Ching-P'u, where there was the usual stiff zigzag. It is worthy of remark that in the sandstone districts the roads generally follow the crests of the ridges ; while in those countries where the geological formation is of the harder limestone or granite the roads invariably clamber up the bed of some torrent. The reason is obvious. In the sandstone the tops of the spurs are always more or less level, and offer an easy route, though the ascent to them is often very difficult. But amongst the limestone mountains the crests are torn into wild and ragged pinnacles ; they are sometimes almost as sharp as the edge of a knife, and, as routes, are utterly impracticable.

The country was still almost uninhabited, and bore on its face sad traces of devastation. Long extents of slopes, laid out in terraces, once used for rice cultivation, but where now grasses and reeds were the only crops ; and ruined villages, where rank weeds and prickly pears usurped the place of smiling vegetable gardens, bore pitiful witness to the havoc of the 'dogs of war.' At a distance of two miles from Huang-Lien-P'u a single hut with a patch of cultivation was the only sign of inhabitants, until a ruined village, Pai-T'u-P'u, was reached after another two and a half miles. Here, in the ruins that marked the site of a once flourishing village, where coarse grass and weeds grew amongst the few stones which indicated the positions of the houses burnt or sacked by one if not both parties during the rebellion, two or three huts had been rebuilt, and the busy Chinese occupants were hard at work reclaiming the soil from the weeds that overran it.

The hill-sides were mostly covered with long but rather coarse grass, and woods of pines, oaks, and chestnuts, where pheasants were heard calling. In these regions, where the oaks and chestnuts grow close to and amongst one another, they seem to run into one another, and all sorts of varieties are seen that appear as if they were a cross between the two trees. First there is the *bonâ fide* and unmistakable chestnut, with the real chestnut leaf, and the nut encased in a thick husk covered with prickles ; then we see trees with a leaf almost the same but slightly approaching that of the oak, and with some few leaves more like an oak than a chestnut, till we arrive at the real and true oak with an acorn and cup without any prickles. The fruit also varies from the chestnut to the acorn, some of the varieties being almost like the chestnut covered with prickles, and with only a little bit of the fruit appearing through the husk, while others bear fruit nearly like the acorn.

The next hut was two miles further on, by a temple where there had at one time been two presiding deities or dignitaries, one at each side of the entrance; one of these, however, had shared the fate of Dagon, and its place now knew it no more.

After a long but not difficult ascent of eight miles, we found ourselves at length on the summit of the T'ien-Ching range, 8,140 feet above the sea, where a few wretched huts boast themselves a village, and glory in the name of T'ien-Ching-P'u.

Here a man joined our party, who told us that some time ago both his father and mother had died, and that, finding himself without money to bury them with, he had sold himself to a firm of traders at Ava—for to a Chinaman there could hardly happen a more fearful evil than to be unable to give father or mother a proper interment. He had been to Ava once, but as the firm had now given up business, or become bankrupt, he was free, and he offered himself to us as a travelling companion.

We passed a village of a few huts two miles further, but nothing else until we reached the fine plain of Yung-P'ing. The city of Yung-P'ing-Hsien was, we had understood, to have been our halting-place, but now the muleteers said that it was a little off the road, so we did not go there.

We descended another spur from the western side of the same range, and soon the plain lay extended at our feet.

We asked a man with us if the city was on a river, or a little off it. His reply was eminently characteristic of a Chinaman: 'Oh,' he said, 'the city wall is destroyed, and now there are only houses.'

After a long conversation we prevailed upon him to say that the city was not on the river. Under these circumstances we were not surprised to see it built on both banks of the stream.

The road down-hill was very fair; but when we reached the plain it was awful—in fact there was no road at all, and in rainy weather it would hardly be possible to cross either river or plain. There is little cultivation but rice, and here we saw the first rice harvest; but again there were wide spaces of terraces which had not yet been recovered. The carcass of an old buffalo cow with a good many wounds in her body lay by the road-side, and near her were the remains of a calf; and as Chin-Tai had seen a panther near the temple we had passed in the morning, there were probably a good many wild beasts about.

The city of Yung-P'ing was entirely destroyed by the Mahometans during the rebellion, and not a single house was left standing. Now, although it still remains the prefectoral city, Ch'ü-Tung, which is on the high road, seems gradually to be ousting it from its position of commercial importance. There are already about two hundred families in Ch'ü-Tung, while Yung-P'ing itself can now boast of no more than three hundred. There are a great number of Mahometans at Ch'ü-Tung—as, indeed, there are all over the country; they are easily recognised by their white turbans. They certainly seem sufficiently numerous to render possible another outbreak of the deplorable rebellion that desolated this province. It would be a wise policy on this account for the Chinese Government to assist emigration from Ssŭ-Ch'uan to Yün-Nan. It would not only relieve the already over-populated province, and supply labour for the now waste lands in Yün-Nan which cry out for hands to till them, but, by gradually increasing the number of orthodox Chinese, the population of the so-called Mahometans would be lessened, and the fear of future outbreaks be by degrees reduced to a mininum.

From Ch'ü-Tung we ascended two thousand seven hundred feet to the summit of another mountain, called T'ien-Ching-P'u; and the fact that we went up three thousand feet and down again the other side, was becoming almost as monotonous to write about as the perpetual ascents and descents were wearisome to perform.

I found Chin-Tai at a poor inn, where he repeated his

favourite phrase '*all have got nothing*,' by which he meant that the kitchen arrangements were defective. So, while he went to find a better place, I sat down, and was able to note how the inquisitive Chinese were being gradually left behind. Here, in a large market town, although a good many people collected at the entrance to the inn, no one, not even a boy, passed the threshold, though I was sitting in a room some ten or fifteen yards back; and as I walked to the next place I seemed to excite but little curiosity. There are so many foreigners here, border tribes, wandering Burmese, &c., that as we all, including Englishmen, pass current under the one term *barbarian*, little notice is taken of a fresh specimen of the genus.

The people here called us foreign Mahometans, as we never touched pork. The presence of a large Mahometan population always rendered it comparatively easy to buy beef; and there were plenty of fat geese, so that we were never in any difficulty about food.

We were now in the basin of the Lan-Ts'ang-Chiang, known lower down as the Mekong river; but before reaching it we crossed a ridge about three hundred feet high. The ascent was not very steep, but it was greasy enough to give our animals hard work. Here we met a train of forty-six mules carrying calico made in Yung-Ch'ang. When the summit was gained, we at length saw the much-thought-of and long-talked-about Lan-Ts'ang-Chiang rolling at our feet; for the river seems to maintain the character Cooper gives of it higher up, and though there is not here another 'Hogg's Gorge,' yet the stream flows through desperately steep hills; and down the side of one of these a zigzag led to the river, 1,400 feet below the crest. It was a frightful bit of road, and had this been written at the bottom it would have been apostrophised in no measured terms; but what followed was so much worse that there is no bad language to spare for this descent.

The river, the bed of which is here 3,953 feet above the sea, is crossed by an excellent iron chain suspension-bridge, in very good repair, and very steady. The bridge, from the edge of one pier to that of the opposite one, is about fifty yards long, supported on twelve chains below, and two above for hand-rails. The links are about one foot long of three-quarter-inch iron, and the chains are fastened at the ends with shackles.

Now commenced our day's work, and a hard one it was. The road at first led along the side of the hill; it had once been paved with great round stones, which now, half misplaced, lay about, leaving great muddy chasms. At the end of this was a village; and here the path left the river and went straight up a gorge, which, with a little poetic licence, might be said to be like the wall of a house. The muleteers had told us that we could never conceive the badness of the road, and they can hardly be accused of exaggeration. It was enough to break the heart of a millstone, not to speak of the unfortunate little ponies that carried our baggage or ourselves. We had to face it somehow, zigzag after zigzag, mile after mile of steps, sometimes a foot high, of round and slippery stones, and muddy bogs, into which the feet of the unfortunate animals would slip with a bang and splash the mire in all directions. But still, right overhead, the interminable track appeared; and when at length an ascent of 2,300 feet brought us to the end of this desperate gorge, men and animals 'knocked their heads' each after his own fashion.

From here the road ascended easily in a valley well cultivated with rice, which at this altitude, 6,270 feet, was not yet ready for harvesting. In itself the track was still tolerably bad, but as the gradient was easy, and there was none of those abominable staircases, it seemed like Macadam compared with what we had passed, and after a march of about four hours Chin-Tai's mule at the door of a house was a pleasant sight to men and animals; and, notwithstanding the porridge, soldiers, servants, and Ma-Fu did full justice to sundry bowls of rice all ready for them. After this every one was in a good humour, and although our muleteers had made up their minds to stop here, as the people told us of a village five miles further on, we determined to take that bit off the morrow's journey.

The country now improved in appearance very much.

There was much more cultivation on the slopes, chiefly Indian corn and buckwheat. The valleys between the hill-sides were covered, where possible, with rice; there were no traces of former cultivation fallen into disuse, there were not the same number of ruins about the country, and the villages were far more numerous, not only in the valleys but on the mountains. The ranges of mountains that we had marched across had hitherto been almost unpopulated and uncultivated, and it was only in the valleys of the rivers that people, villages, and crops had been seen. But now it was a pleasant sight to see some snug houses nestled on the hill-side, or to watch a wreath of smoke curling up from the midst of some small wood high up above the road, showing that here at last everything was not given over to nature and wild beasts.

On our way to Ta-Li-Shao, we passed a train of forty-seven animals laden with salt for Yung-Ch'ang. The ascent was gradual, and the road very fair. We found Ta-Li-Shao, a group of about half a dozen cottages, to be 7,412 feet above the sea. A loft in one of them was free from smoke, and civil and obliging people did their best to make us comfortable, after one of the most severe marches on this road of difficult ascents.

It was raining again in the morning of the 11th, and the appearance of the clouds promised us a wet day. Before starting, a man, from whom we were endeavouring to extract some scraps of information, told us that the road to Pan-Ch'iao was 'a good and level one down hill,' a remark that made us inclined to ask if he had any relations in Ireland.

We continued our ascent of the mountain, which was now very easy, only rising about four hundred feet in the couple of miles that took us to the final summit (7,795 feet above the sea), whence we overlooked the fine plain of Yung-Ch'ang. The road was amongst fine, rolling, wooded mountains, with open cultivated spaces, and a fair sprinkling of villages; and then commenced the descent of '*the level road down hill.*' The first part was rather bad and steep, over exceedingly slippery stones, but after about two miles from the top it became really very good, descending easily, and not being particularly sticky.

Pan-Ch'iao, where we halted for breakfast, is a large market town 5,692 feet above the sea, situated in the plain of Yung-Ch'ang, about a mile beyond the edge of the mountains.

A new dish was set before us at this place, macaroni made of rice instead of wheaten flower; it was round, and looked very much like our European macaroni, but thinner, and instead of being tubular was solid. The salt here was in moulds about six inches high, for which there can be no better simile than old Polo's twopenny loaves. The shape was something like the figure 8. Each was stamped, though in this case it was not the 'Prince's mark' that 'was printed,' but a very ancient character, of which the signification is 'happiness,' a way of wishing welfare to the purchaser. This salt comes from Min-Ching, in the magistracy of Yu-Lung-Chou.

Pan-Ch'iao lies close to the left of the river which waters the valley of Yung-Ch'ang, a perfectly flat plain, about five or six miles wide, entirely devoted to rice cultivation. Here again we came across the traces of the war: ruins around the villages and towns, remains of fortified towers, and on the lower slopes of the mountains some terraces fallen into disuse. This part of the country, however, seems to be recovering itself rapidly, for all the small valleys where the streams ran into the plain were well cultivated. The position of this river was contested for three years by the two parties: the Mahometan rebels on the right bank, and the Imperialists on the other, being all this time separated only by the width of the stream—about twenty or twenty-five yards. The Mahometans built strong towers on their bank of the river, and with the aid of these prevented the Imperial troops from crossing. It is very interesting to find that this plain, the scene of that 'great medley' and 'dire and parlous fight,'[2] described by Polo, should in recent years again have

[2] The old Venetian tells us that in this dire and parlous fight, the King of Mien, like a wise king as he was, caused all the castles that were on the elephants to be ordered for battle, and that the horses of

been a position so hotly contested. But how the valiant Nescradin ever managed to get two hundred elephants into China, unless there was some much better road than the one we had followed, must remain a mystery.

The soldier in whom we fancied we had discovered some Celtic blood was a wag in his way, for he volunteered the information that the next bit of road to Yung-Ch'ang was a '*twenty-cash bit*;' for he said it was so bad that it wore out two pairs of straw sandals, each of which costs ten cash, and is supposed to see the wearer through the worst day's march. The same man told us that, in the year 1873, eight or nine foreigners had visited T'êng-Yüeh. He said that they bought all kinds of things, birds, insects, no matter what, and were in the habit of giving one rupee for a single specimen. The Chen-Tai of T'êng-Yüeh, hearing of this, imagined that they were simple folk being imposed upon by his wily countrymen, and he forbade his people to sell any more birds. No doubt the naturalists, whoever they may have been, would now be much amused if they could know why the supply suddenly stopped.[3]

The city of Yung-Ch'ang is a sad spectacle of ruin and desolation. It appeared as if the greater part of the space within the walls had once been well covered with buildings; but now three quarters of it were vacant or under cultivation, for in many places crops of Indian corn were growing where there had formerly been houses. Notwithstanding this, the portion that had been rebuilt seemed very prosperous, and there was an amount of elegance, if such a word may be applied, about the shops that had not been seen since leaving Ssŭ-Ch'uan; the streets were very wide, and were full of well-dressed people, looking comfortable and well-to-do. Stalls at the side of the road were apparently driving a thriving business, and altogether there was an air of pros-

the Tartars took such fright at the sight of the elephants that they could not be got to face the foe. Herodotus mentions that Cyrus in one of his battles used his camels to terrify the cavalry of the enemy, but with better fortune than waited on the wise King of Mien (*Herod.* i. 80).

[3] This was, no doubt, a vague reminiscence of the Sladen Mission of 1868.

perity about it that was quite surprising. The restored portion was very small, but what there was in appearance far surpassed Ta-Li-Fu.

We were lodged in a real and very good hotel, where we had a comfortable upper room free from smoke. The landlord said that it cost him 3,000 taels to build; and the fact that a man could find it worth while to lay out so large a sum shows that the place must be reviving. Indeed we found traders here from nearly every province.

Some general on the march arrived in the town in the morning of the 12th. One of his officers in advance came to the hotel we occupied, and, finding us in the best rooms, cursed the landlord in a tone of voice that reverberated through our apartment. Not daring to attempt any ejection of ourselves, he made great but unsuccessful efforts to take possession of the rooms occupied by our servants and baggage. The general had by this time arrived himself, and sat in the yard of the inn in his sedan-chair.

The news of the turmoil soon reached the ears of the magistrate, who sent a polite message to the general, asking him to find a lodging for himself elsewhere; to which he gruffly made reply, that the magistrate had better find him a place if he expected him to leave the hotel where he was; and his minions thereupon commenced to turn out the occupants of all the minor apartments.

This was not very pleasant for us, for his soldiers, sharing the wrath of their commander, would in all probability have picked some quarrel with our servants, or have contrived to rob us of something. Our apprehensions were shared by the magistrate, who reminded the general that he would be responsible if anything of that sort occurred.

The general paid little heed to this warning, and ordered his goods to be unpacked, sitting, nevertheless, all the while in his sedan-chair, as he no doubt anticipated that the officials of the place would arrange matters somehow without the loss of dignity which he would have suffered by consenting to move to another hotel.

Many varieties of precious stones are found in the mountains in the neighbourhood of Yung-Ch'ang, and, besides this, the sacking of Ta-Li-Fu had thrown great quantities of jewellery into the hands of all sorts of people, some of whom had not the faintest idea of their value; and continual visits were paid to us, and stones of every description offered for sale. A great deal of jade was brought in, some of it probably native. This stone is very highly prized among Chinese of all classes, and officials usually wear a great thumb-ring made of it. One man brought a pair of earrings made of malachite, for which he asked a price that would have bought a table in Russia, where that stone is plentiful.

Another brought some necklaces made of amber, something like the Roumanian black amber, but more opaque, and of a lighter colour; it looked something like brown agate, and we were offered 108 beads for 40*l.* We offered 13*l.*, and if we had remained a few more days would doubtless have compounded for 20*l.*, but in China no satisfactory bargain can be struck in a short time. This was a good necklace; all the beads were more or less similarly marked, and it would have been worth about 40*l.*, or perhaps more, in Peking, where officials give high prices for good necklaces. One hundred and eight is the regulation number, no one venturing to wear a necklace with one bead more or less.[4]

A man brought in a stone about the size of a small nut, perfectly clear, without a flaw, and of a faint amethyst tinge; this, no doubt, was crystal, or something even more valuable, and the man said that he had another much larger and better. We bade him fetch it, which he did; he returned with a stopper of an old scent-bottle, and the drop from a European chandelier, both of which were valued at comparatively high prices. Our ventures in stones were not very extensive, for as the Chinese, like all Orientals, leave their gems uncut, it is impossible for any one but an expert to judge of their value.

There are two roads from Yung-Ch'ang to Fang-Ma-Ch'ang. The main road, which does not pass over a mountain, is better than the other, but some miles longer.

[4] See *Marco Polo*, 2nd ed. ii. 330–331.

The main road, we were told, passes through the plain of Fu-Piau (P'u-P'iao of Baber), which had been entirely depopulated by an extraordinary disease, of which the symptoms were like those of the plague, and which had, during the months of August and September, carried off upwards of a thousand people. Our informant added that now there was no one left except a few poverty-stricken wretches, who could not afford to move. A traveller who was stopping at the same inn with us at Yung-Ch'ang, and who left with us for T'êng-Yüeh, said that he had passed through the place in July; that at that time there were scarcely any inhabitants left, and that the dead bodies were lying about unburied. Now he said that the disease had ceased at that place, and had moved in a southerly direction to Niu-Wa, where it was raging. To a Chinaman, the idea of leaving a body unburied is very dreadful, and it would only be the most dire necessity that would permit such an atrocity. This disease is said to attack people passing through the country as well as the residents.

In describing the symptoms, the people said that a lump like a boil, about the size of half a small walnut, suddenly appeared on almost any part of the body; there was absolutely no attendant pain, and twenty-four hours was the outside that a person could live after the appearance of this lump.

Boccaccio thus describes some of the symptoms of the plague at Florence in 1348:—

'Here there appeared certain tumours in the groin or under the arm-pits, some as big as a small apple, others as an egg; but they generally died the third day from the first appearance of the symptoms, without a fever or other bad circumstance attending.'

From Defoe also may be gathered that the plague of London was somewhat similar; but he was not himself an eye-witness of this terrible calamity, nor does he anywhere give a distinct account of the symptoms.

The city of Yung-Ch'ang itself, about 5,645 feet above the sea, is healthy enough, although there is at certain times a little fever.

'Sanga Bridge,' common in Western China.

CHAPTER XV.

IN THE FOOTSTEPS OF MARCO POLO AND OF AUGUSTUS MARGARY.

2. *The Marches of the Kingdom of Mien.*

Departure from Yung-Ch'ang—Fang-Ma-Ch'ang—Pestiferous Valley of the Lu-Ch'iang or Salwen River—Passage by Chain Bridge—Steep Ascent to Ho-Mu-Shu—Old Custom of 'Wappenshaw' and Military Tests—The Lung-Chiang or Shwé-li River—Salutes by the Way—A Celt for Sale—The City of T'êng-Yüeh, or Momein—Things better managed in Ssŭ-Ch'uan—The Chi-Fu Convention—Nan-Tien—Reception by a Shan Lady—Her Costume—First Burmese Priests—Change of Scenery—Passage of the Ta-ping River—First Burmese Pagoda—Lovely Scene near Chan-Ta—Chan-Ta (Sanda), and the Chief there—Oppressions of Chinese—Festival at Chan-Ta—Shan Pictures by the Way—Shan and Kakyen Figures—Road-side Scenes in Ta-ping Valley—Bamboos and Birds by the Way—Lying Litigants — T'ai-P'ing-Chieh, or Kara-hokah — Reach Chinese Frontier.—Town of Man-Yün ('Manwyne')—Visit from Notorious Li-Sieh-Tai—Treatment at Man-Yün—The Pa-I People—English Goods in Bazar—Letter of Welcome from Mr. Cooper—Scene of the Murder of Augustus Margary—The Kakyen Country—A Shot at the Party; only tentative—Kakyen Huts—Meddling with the Spirits' Corner—Fire got by Air-compression—Buffalo Beef—

Grand Forest Scenery—Bamboos and Potatoes—An Imprudent Halt to Cook—A Venture in the Forest—Perils from Ants and from Bullies—Would-be Leviers of Blackmail—Benighted—A Welcome Rencontre—Cooper's Messengers and Stores—A Burmese Po-é or Ballet—Embark on Bhamo River—The Irawadi Disappointing—Kindly Welcome from English Agent at Bhamo—Alas, poor Cooper!—Bhamo to Dover—The Journey Ended.

THE little market town of Fang-Ma-Ch'ang is one day's journey beyond Yung-Ch'ang, and lies at the head of the descent to the pestiferous valley of the Salwen, or Lu-Chiang. Our muleteers were anxious to cross the dreaded river before the sun was hot; and every one was, for once, ready at an early hour. We started amongst rounded undulating hills, but soon entered a valley, which we descended by an easy gradient until we could see the mysterious river at our feet. A few low clouds hung over the valley, and, as we stayed a few moments, we could not but be impressed with a scene connected with so many weird associations.

Centuries had rolled by since Marco Polo spoke of the country 'impossible to pass, the air in summer is so impure and bad; and any foreigner attempting it would die for certain.' Already at Ta-Chien-Lu Monseigneur Chauveau, who had passed many years of his life in Yün-Nan, had warned us of this pestiferous place, and had told us that, before the rebellion had destroyed every organisation in the province, it had been customary to keep a guard at certain places on the road to prevent any one from attempting the passage during the unhealthy season. As we approached nearer and nearer, though the warnings were more frequent, the details of the story varied but little, and, incomprehensible though they appeared, we could not but give credence to the tales so oft repeated of the 'valley of the shadow of death.'

As it lay at our feet all nature seemed to smile, and invite the tired traveller to stay and rest. But it was the smile of the siren, for should a stranger venture there to pass the night, it would be with fever-stricken limbs that, when the morning broke, he would attempt the escalade of the surrounding heights.

Even in autumn, the most healthy season, it is with bated breath that passengers hurry across at a favourable moment; and when the fiery rays of summer are darted on that low-lying valley, even the acclimatised inhabitants flee the 'infections that the sun sucks up,' and for months no living thing may venture there.

It is during an alternation of rain and sun that the poison is most rife, and then they say a lurid copper-coloured vapour gradually folds the valley in its deadly embrace.

But as we looked the sun rose higher and gradually dispersed the clouds, and we were assured that the moment could not be more favourable for crossing.

The reasons for the extraordinary unhealthiness of the valley are not apparent; for although it is 1,300 feet lower than the Lan-Ts'ang, and nearly 2,000 feet lower than the Lung-Chiang or Shwé-li river, yet it is still 2,600 feet above the sea.

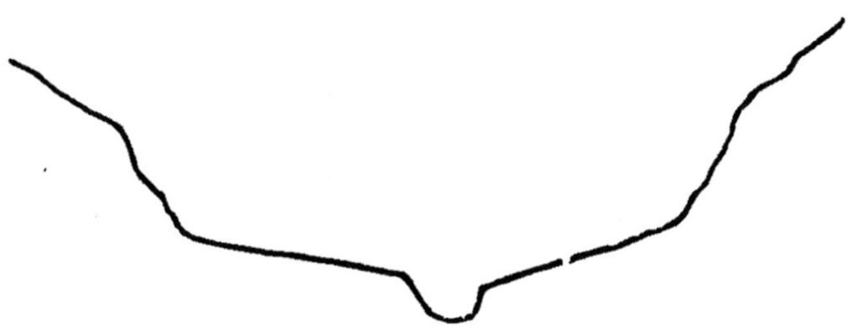

It was the finest-looking valley we had passed; instead of being perfectly flat, like so many others, the ground slopes gently on both sides from the foot of the hills.

This formation is very favourable for the terrace cultivation, and here the rice harvest was well forward.

There are a few small undulating hills in the bottom of the valley, which is bounded by mountains well wooded or covered with long grass. There are plenty of villages, with a good many trees round them, and the landscape is more varied than any we had seen for some time.

From the rapidity of the river, and the undulating nature

of the ground, it might have been supposed that this district would be healthy enough ; but the secrets of the red miasma must remain hidden yet awhile in the recesses of the beautiful, but deadly, vale.

The river is crossed by a chain suspension-bridge of two spans, the second span in a line parallel to the continuation of the first, but about four yards from it on the same level. This system is probably adopted for the greater facility given for tightening up the chains ; but it makes a mis-shapen affair of what would otherwise be a well-constructed bridge. The eastern span was about seventy-three and the western fifty-two yards long ; each span is supported on twelve or fourteen chains underneath, and two above, the links being of three-quarter-inch iron, one foot long. At the time of our visit it was in excellent repair, but the eastern span, destroyed by the Mahometans during the rebellion, had only recently been rebuilt. At the time of Baber's visit it was 'in a dangerous state of dilapidation.' The stream was running rapidly below the eastern span, but the western was quite dry.

We halted at Lu-Chiang-Pa, a little village about a quarter of a mile beyond the end of the bridge, and here, at 10.30 A.M., the thermometer marked 80° Fahr. Baber noticed the sultriness of this place, for on the 29th of April his thermometer registered 96° Fahr.

On leaving this we went straight up the mountain by a very fairly paved but exceedingly steep road to Ho-Mu-Shu, 2,800 feet above the river, and 5,486 above the sea.

Our lodging was a shed made of split bamboos, over which mud had been thrown in some places to fill up the interstices, and so exclude the wind and rain sufficiently to enable people to smoke their opium-pipes, without having their lamps put out by either one element or the other. There was a good thatched roof, and the hut was divided into three compartments by partitions of split bamboos, reaching not more than half-way up. My pony was lodged in one, we occupied the other two, and, as it was easy to see through the partitions, I could watch over my animal whilst sitting writing. The weather, fortunately, was fine, sunshiny, and without wind, so we did not find our airy apartment in any way uncomfortable.

The little village of Ho-Mu-Shu was more than crowded when we arrived. We occupied as much room as twenty or thirty Chinamen, and it appeared as if our fellow-travellers were obliged to take it in turns to go to bed, and cook their provisions for the morrow; for we were kept awake all night by their lively conversations and culinary operations, everything that was going on being seen and heard quite plainly through the wickerwork partitions of the rooms. The other guests were mostly candidates on their way to the military examinations at Yung-Ch'ang. Upwards of one thousand present themselves for examination every year from the T'êng-Yüeh district. If they pass they gain a certain social position in their town or village, and are eligible to serve in the capacity of petty municipal officers. Few of them have any idea of becoming soldiers, but pass the examination for the sake of the importance they thereby obtain. It seems at first somewhat inconsistent that the Chinese, who usually hold all military officers more or less in contempt, should offer advantages to the men who pass military examinations, which are tests of physical strength only. But it is the old custom handed down from generations. In days of yore, and of much hard fighting, when the sword, bow and arrow, and the spear were the ordinary weapons, it required stout, skilful, lusty fellows to wield them well; so the Government established these athletic sports, as they might well be called, at which the prizes were social positions amongst the people, and were well worth striving for. So everywhere military exercises became common, nearly every one practised them, and thus the State had always ready-made soldiers that they could call on when required. The old custom still survives, though the reason, in its full force, no longer exists.

The Lung-Chiang[1] is crossed by another very good iron chain suspension-bridge in one span of about fifty yards,

[1] Lung-Chiang is the Chinese name of the Irawadi's tributary, called by the Burmese Shwé-li.—*Y.*

supported on eleven chains below, with two more above. Both this river and the Lu-Chiang were very low, but when they are full a vast body of water must flow down them. The Lung-Chiang is the more rapid of the two, but its bed is much higher above the sea level—4,502 feet.

The road from the bridge ascended gently through rice-fields to Kan-Lan-Chan, where we were saluted for the third time by three soldiers in charge of a Pah-Tsung, who sent and apologised for not heading his army, as he did not expect us so soon, and was not dressed. The number of times that we were saluted during the day must have been a serious expense to his Celestial Majesty, who pays for the powder. At Tai-P'ing-P'u I was some distance ahead, and as I approached the village three soldiers fired off a musket apiece, went down on their knees to the 'Imperial Commissioners,' as they were pleased to call us, and repeated the formula usual on these occasions :—

'Welcome, Great Excellency! The men of Tai-P'ing-P'u have come out to salute you.'

This they did in a droning, chanting way, that sounded like the 'responses' in a church where the parson is short of a congregation.

Mesny arrived about half an hour afterwards, but his salute was reduced by one gun, for one of the dirty old matchlocks spluttered for a minute or so, like an indifferent squib of amateur manufacture, and gradually burnt itself out without any report. But in these parts a few guns more or less in a salute are not of much moment.

In the afternoon some soldiers at a village, and some more at the Lung-Chiang Bridge, burnt gunpowder for us. One lot were rather put out because a little boy who had brought up a matchlock from the last place arrived too late to have it loaded ready, and there was an awkward pause between the second and third guns. As far as I was concerned, the dignity of the thing was quite spoiled by the behaviour of the pony I was riding, who always shied away from the soldiers at the critical moment. My other mischievous grey, too, would insist on contributing to my discomfiture by intruding himself between me and the army—

rushing up against me, and knocking me completely out of time, or breaking through the ranks (a single rank of three), with a snort and a toss of the heels. The white pony was always in mischief, if he could find any to get into. If he could leave the road and wander away into the forest, he would—especially if he saw another horse or two likely to follow him. Nothing pleased him better than to jump violently into a mud-hole just when some one was in a position to be splashed all over. If he saw the pony I was riding balancing itself on some narrow or slippery stone, where there was barely room for one foot, that was the moment of all others that he chose for running me down and knocking me, with perhaps a drop of a couple of feet or so, into the bog.

A man came up in the evening with a 'celt,' which may or may not have been genuine. It looked to me quite new, though we wondered who the antiquarians could be who made it worth while for any one in these parts to fabricate relics of the stone age;[2] but, since a certain occasion on which I was astonished by the offer of sham Roman coins near Damghan in Persia, I have always been prepared to find false antiquities in the most unlikely spots.

On the 17th the road was very good for a change, and there was a generally easy ascent amongst undulating hills with but little wood on them. Now and then we passed through a deep lane cut in the soft sandstone, the banks at each side covered with ferns, grass, creepers, and shrubs or small trees, that brought to mind many a lane in Surrey or Kent. Then the road would emerge into a downy country, where in a hollow the margin of some small pond would be lined with rushes, reeds, and ferns, now turning yellow and red—the very place for a duck, if the whole country had not

[2] Baber explains the discovery of a copper knife and a 'celt' at the fair in Ta-Li-Fu. He says: 'The knife is undoubtedly genuine; the celt—called locally, and, indeed, all the world over, "thunder stone" (lei-ta-shih)—bears traces of sharpening on the axe-edge, and is well adapted for use; but as these objects are now employed as charms, on account of their supposed supernatural origin and properties, and as there is a brisk demand for them, it is difficult to satisfy oneself of their authenticity.'—(*F. O. Report, China*, No. 3, 1878.)

been disturbed by a train of eighty or a hundred mules laden with salt, which had passed just before, on their way, like ourselves, to T'êng-Yüeh.

We wound along, now up and now down, but steadily rising, till we reached Ch'in-T'sai-T'ang, where soldiers turned out as usual to salute. I was walking on ahead, alone, but just at this moment Chung-Erh galloped up and passed me, anxious to be ready to receive me in proper style at the door of the hut. The soldiers, never for a moment imagining that either of their excellencies would be on foot, mistook Chung-Erh for one of them, and as he passed bent one knee, and, much to our diversion, gravely informed him that 'the men of Ch'in-Ts'ai-T'ang had come out to salute him.'

We had already mounted about two thousand feet from Kan-Lan-Chan, and another five hundred feet brought us to the summit of Mount Urh-T'ai-P'o, whence we descended two thousand feet by a very fair road to the city of T'êng-Yüeh, or Momein, situated at the head waters of the Ta-Ying river, in a perfectly flat and treeless plain, some five miles broad and long. This was entirely covered with rice-fields, where the crop was being harvested, and was bounded on all sides by uncultivated grassy slopes, from which every trace of trees had disappeared.

The Chen-Tai paid us a visit in the morning of the 18th, apparently for the purpose of frightening us. He told us that in the year 1876 the King of Burmah had asked the Chinese Government to send some troops across the frontier, and put down some tribes who were giving trouble. Our visitor had been in command, and had not succeeded in his mission without much hard fighting and a great deal of sickness—for the campaign had been carried out during the unhealthy season. The King of Burmah had paid the whole expenses of the expedition, and had asked for and obtained a loan of three hundred soldiers after the main body had returned to China.

The Chen-Tai told us that this body of men had just been disbanded, on the demand of the British Government;[3]

[3] The British Government, of course, had had nothing to do with the matter.

that they were roving over the country in lawless bands; that travelling was very dangerous; and that he could not be responsible for our safety unless we would give him time to recall these men, and get them out of the way. He also said that the governor-general of Yün-Nan intended to raise three million taels to work the mines in the province, under the superintendence of Europeans.

The mines of Yün-Nan no doubt are exceedingly rich; but before they can be made to pay, communications must be improved, and the country better governed. It struck us very forcibly that the government of Ssŭ-Ch'uan was far better than that of Yün-Nan. In Ssŭ-Ch'uan the officials were invariably more than attentive, and it was easy to see that their orders were promptly and efficiently carried out. The difference was apparent the very day we crossed the boundary into Yün-Nan. The Margary proclamation, which had been universally posted in Ssŭ-Ch'uan, was rarely seen; and although the officials were almost always civil and polite, there was a marked difference in our treatment in the two provinces. It must be said that the higher magistrates seemed to pay us most attention; but their orders were not carried out by the petty officials with the alacrity and regularity always observed in Ssŭ-Ch'uan. It happened on more than one occasion that despatches sent on from the prefectoral city before our departure did not reach their destination until after our arrival; and although these are trivial matters they serve to compare the government of the two provinces.

On the whole, there can be little doubt that the central Government of Peking wields a potent sway even in these distant provinces; it is due to the Chi-Fu Convention that Englishmen may travel in comfort throughout the vast empire; and this one fact alone will stamp the term of office of Sir Thomas Wade as one memorable in the annals of our dealings with the Chinese Government; and it is to be hoped and expected that it will do much to bring about that intercourse with foreigners which is the one and only means by which cordial and comprehensible relations can be established between the Chinese and European nations.

The civil official of Man-Yün, who was also staying in the hotel, paid us a visit, and told us the Chen-Tai's story with considerable variations. He said that thirty soldiers, not three hundred, had been lent to the King of Burmah, but that the officer in command was of so bad a character that the king had disbanded the company; that the officer had been disgraced by the Chinese Government; that he now did not dare to return to Chinese territory, and was roving the country, committing depredations, and robbing whomsoever fell in his way.

The Man-Yün magistrate and another military officer came again in the evening to endeavour to induce us to wait a few days; and now the former said that the disbanded soldiers numbered one hundred; that they were very dangerous; that in any case we should be compelled to wait at Man-Yün until he could join us; and that we had much better remain at T'êng-Yüeh-T'ing, where the quarters were comfortable. To all these blandishments we lent a deaf ear; and, ultimately, the magistrate sent his steward and a lot of people with us, amongst them two Cantonese, to help us on the road, and placed his residence at Man-Yün at our disposal.

The road down the long valley was good and level, but the inhabitants have a most eccentric custom of using it, not only as an aqueduct, but as a reservoir.

The numerous streams that flow out from the mountains are turned on to the road wherever it is hollowed out between banks; little dams, about a foot or eighteen inches high, are made across the track to keep in the water; and thus the adjacent rice-fields can be flooded when required.

We met thirty loads of cotton, but, besides these, there were few people about. We saw some men thrashing with flails made of bamboo, one in each hand; but everything was still thoroughly Chinese, and there were no signs of the manners and customs of the Burmese, or of the wild mountain tribes between Man-Yün and Bhamo, except the turbans of the women, which were built up like towers on their heads.

We passed through the walled town of Nan-Tien, and

about two miles further found the house of the native chief, or Tu-Sze, in the small village of Che-Tao-Ch'êng. There appeared not to be enough soldiers to fire a salute with matchlocks; but, instead of this, three iron guns, about eight inches long and with a calibre of about an inch, were planted upright in the ground, and were touched off by a man with a bit of lighted paper at the end of a bamboo, quite in the style of a professed pyrotechnist; and what they wanted in dignity was made up for by the loudness of the report.

The native chief has the rank of a Yu-Chi, and wears the clear blue button, as the English always call it, though a more inappropriate term could hardly have been devised. The French call it *globule*, just what it is—a globule a little more than an inch in diameter, which is worn on the official hat. Strangely enough, there is no regulation size for this, though for almost every part of a Chinaman's dress there are stern rules and regulations; and every man, official or non-official, must shave his head and wear a plait, for if he leaves his hair it is a sign that he is a rebel.

The 'Ugly Chief of Homely Virtues,' who entertained Margary, had died of grief for the loss of all his fortune during the rebellion; the boy of whom Margary speaks was not yet of age, and the honours of the house were done by an old relative holding the Chinese rank of Pa-Tsung.

The circular about us sent from T'êng-Yüeh-T'ing five days before, arrived about an hour after us; but it was not wanted, as the family of the chief were quite ready to dispense their hospitality without it. The way in which these despatches used always to arrive just in time to be too late was both amusing and instructive; and I thought with the 'Sentimental Traveller' that 'they manage these things better in' Ssŭ-Ch'uan.

The mother of the former chief, and the grandmother of the children (two sons—the eldest fifteen—and three girls), looked after the house, and invited us into her rooms after dinner to drink tea.

She wore a white jacket, with sleeves turned up, and a

good deal of embroidery in gold on the cuffs; this was fastened at the throat by a brooch with twelve (or fifteen, I am not certain which) different coloured stones, set in three rows, like the pictures of the breast-plate of the Jewish high priests. Silver bracelets adorned her wrists, and she wore white trousers with some red stripes; but the room was so dark it was impossible to make out the details of her costume. A majestic turban rose to a height of eighteen inches above her head, and bulged out about half-way up, as though swelling with honest pride at its exalted position.

She introduced her two sons, and told us that their territory stretched for a length of thirty miles by the river-side, and extended back from it for a distance of sixty miles.

She evidently entertained a sincere regard for Margary, and told us that he had given a sword and a microscope to the late chief; but she did not mention the 'fine pair of scissors' which he gave to the 'amiable spouse.' What has become of her we did not learn. The language of these people is alphabetic, with nineteen letters, and they write as we do from left to right.

On the morning of the 21st, as we rode out of the gates, where a couple of Burmese priests were standing about in their yellow garments—the first signs of a change of country—three more terrific explosions startled our animals. The old Pa-Tsung had promised us sixty soldiers as a guard of honour, but only two sorry-looking fellows turned up. The morning was fine, but it came on to rain at about nine o'clock, and rained all day; a perfect deluge falling in the afternoon.

As we advanced, the scenery changed. Hitherto the hills had been grass-covered; now trees appeared, many of them of a kind not seen before, and the vegetation was almost tropical in appearance; creepers with huge leaves trailing up the trees, plantains growing here and there, and an occasional banyan, all indicated a change of climate.

The road again was bad: sometimes at the river level, and strewn with huge stones; then it went up a ravine and down again; here it was feet deep in mud, or, as before, turned into a series of reservoirs. We found some sheds of matting by the road-side, where we sat down to discuss our sandwiches; but presently some people from a neighbouring village appeared and took possession. These proved to be the proprietors; they had brought with them great baskets of hot cooked rice, and some of the little dishes that always accompany it, and soon they were doing a fine trade. Their shanties are midway between two towns, and there is hardly any other halting-place on the road. People going backwards and forwards generally start much about the same time, so the owners of these huts know pretty well when to expect the 'up and down trains,' and come from their village to feed the hungry passengers. The natives here are very fond of tattooing their legs with all sorts of figures, and they wear on each leg, just below the knee, a number of very fine rings of rattan-cane painted black. They chew a mixture of lime and very coarse tobacco, as well as betel-nut. In this they are unlike the Chinese, who never chew tobacco or lime, though they sometimes make use of the betel.

We stayed here about an hour, to let somebody get ahead. Both my Peking boys were now in a deadly fright that we, and they with us, would share Margary's fate; so not only would they not go in front, but they always remained at a safe distance behind, looking particularly mean; but once they found themselves inside the walls of a house, all the old northern bluster came out, and they were tremendous fire-eaters, especially Chin-Tai, who was the greater coward of the two. On the road we met a chair, in which the mother of Li-Sieh-Tai was travelling; she was supposed to be a sister of the King of Burmah, though this was disputed by most of the Chinese. Some of the coolies and people with her were heard to say:—

'What! Here they are again; are they not frightened yet?'

These sort of remarks from people about had been rather frequent lately, and they had not contributed to raise the courage of my two servants.

It was now astounding to note the manner in which the river (Ta-Ying-Ho or Ta-Ho) had grown since T'êng-Yüeh, where it was but a stream a few yards wide. Here the bed was nearly a mile across; at this season it was not, of course, full, but we were seven minutes fording the main branch, the water being above the horse's belly, and flowing two to three miles an hour. Besides this there were four other channels twenty yards wide, and several smaller ones, and I began to understand, what had hitherto appeared almost incredible, that the sources of the majestic Irawadi might be as far south as they are represented on all maps.

On the 22nd, after the heavy rain of the previous day, all nature was fresh and green; there was a delicious feeling in the air, and the sun was shining in a clear sky, as a salute of three guns announced our departure, with an escort that reached the respectable number of thirty.

The direct road to Chan-Ta[4] is on the right bank of the river; but a portion of it was so bad and muddy that it was deemed advisable to cross and recross the stream; we crossed in the dug-out trunk of a tree, our animals swimming over. This was an amusing performance, chiefly on account of my grey, who was a pony of remarkable force of character; the other animals always submitted to the authority he established over them, and here the half dozen, with whom he had only been acquainted a couple of hours, obeyed him with the utmost docility. Being driven into the river, he led as long as he could find the bottom; but, unaccustomed to swimming, he did not like the deep water, and as soon as he was nearly out of his depth he wandered about in a purposeless manner, leading the rest to follow his example. Our canoe then made for the group; we drove them on, and they swam until they reached a shoal, where the grey, always ready for mischief, anchored himself, the other beasts doing the same with admirable regularity. And now all the persuasive eloquence of the Ma-Fu on the opposite bank was powerless to induce them to move, until they were driven on by another canoe that passed that way. Once started there was no other halting-place until they reached the land; and here it was really delightful to see how thoroughly they all enjoyed a good roll in a fine bed of bright, clean sand, which seemed

[4] *Sanda* of Anderson and others —*Y.*

as if it had been laid there expressly for that purpose. For the last month my grey had been covered with mud, which had never been removed, and now that at length his coat was really clean, it was scarcely possible to recognise him.

This business had been a somewhat lengthy one, and although Chin-Tai and Chung-Erh had taken very good care to start long after everybody else, they had by this time overtaken us, and might have been observed standing about on the opposite bank in a nonchalant sort of way, trying to look as if they had no connection whatever with any one else.

As we proceeded, fresh sights continually presented themselves. Here there were some ricks of unthrashed rice, in shape like English hayricks, and standing in fields of rice-stubble ; and, notwithstanding their un-English surroundings, they could not fail to bring recollections of many an English country scene. In a hamlet hard by we saw the first Burmese pagoda, with a high steeple ; and the huge leaf of the plantain and the delicate bamboo sheltered the mud walls and thatched roofs of every village. Yellow wild ducks, that apparently knew no fear of man, paddled lazily in the broad reaches of the river ; but these, they say, are sacred—the Lamas, or Phoongyees, as the priests ought now to be called, throwing over them their protecting ægis of sanctity, chiefly on account of their colour.

Leaving the river, we ascended a spur, the end of a ridge dividing the Taping from a small tributary called by Anderson the Nam-Sanda,[5] and from the crest, about two hundred feet above the river, there was a glorious view to the south-west, over the magnificent valley. It was a lovely scene : the plain was covered with rice-fields, the crop now nearly or quite ripe, and as yellow as a September corn-field at home ; dotted over it were numerous villages, all enclosed, and the houses nearly hidden, by fine bamboo or banyan trees. Here and there would be a noble old banyan, placed by nature on the summit of some grassy knoll that rose up from the midst of the golden meadows ; in other

[5] *I.e.* the 'Sanda (or Chan-Ta) River.'—*Y.*

places these trees might be standing up amongst the rice on an artificial mound, and often some young sapling just planted would be protected by a fence of split bamboo. On both sides rose a fine range of mountains, their slopes diversified with woods, patches of cultivation, and stretches of fine grass; and, winding through the plain, the fine river rolled smoothly down to join the Irawadi.

An excellent road took us to Chan-Ta, the residence of another Shan chief, who holds the Chinese rank of Yu-Chi. This was probably the little boy who became the adopted heir of Sladen in 1868, for he was now fifteen years of age, his affairs being conducted by a relative. He seemed miserably poor, and was dreadfully ill at ease during the ceremonious reception. He wanted to learn English, and asked us whether any one would teach him if he went to Rangoon. He talked Chinese very slightly, and complained that it was a very difficult language. The whole house was half tumbling down, and very dirty—a remarkable contrast to the 'handsome structure of blue gneiss on a large and handsome scale' described by Anderson.[6] We had the usual suite of a building to ourselves: one room in the centre quite open in front, and another at each side. There was a wretched old table with one leg missing, and the other three tied up with bamboo strips. The beds were made of doors on trestles, and everything betokened poverty and ruin. The people complained bitterly of Chinese oppression; they said that nothing was left to them, even their very tables and chairs being taken if they had any. One man standing about had been to Rangoon; he loudly praised the English rule, declared that their own government was abominable, and, though he did not say so, evidently wished from the bottom of his heart that England would walk in and annex this country. We were not saluted on arrival, but the affairs of this chief seemed so badly managed that it was no matter for surprise. A fowl and a duck were brought in and flung under a bench; we afterwards learnt that these were meant as a present; but we had no idea of it

[6] *Mandalay and Momein*, p 169.

at the time, as the presentation of a gift of this kind ought to be, and almost invariably is, attended with considerable ceremony.

The conduct of the two Cantonese men who were with us was abominable. The rank of the native chief was higher than that of their master; but amongst the Chinese that counts for nothing, a Chinese coolie thinking himself as good as, if not better than, the highest native chief. Directly we arrived, the Cantonese wanted their opium and a place to smoke it in; they called for this and for that, and spoke to the people as if they were so much dirt. One place was too draughty for the lamps, another not comfortable, and they grumbled and cursed and made themselves generally disagreeable. In the hearing of all they told us in a loud voice that these natives did not understand common politeness, that no guns had been fired for us on our arrival, and that it would be a good thing when they were all killed. The native chiefs must put up with all this, as they dare not say a word even to the servants of a Chinese official. The exactions they have to support, too, are terrible. Chinese officials passing and repassing take lodging, food, coolies, horses, and everything without payment, and grind down the people till they can scarcely live. Some time previously, in the territory of Kan-^{Ng}ai, some of the wild mountaineers, subject to no one, made a descent, attacked a party of traders, and stole some bales of cotton. The chief was called on to pay, not only the full value, but double the amount over again in squeezes to the various Chinese officials, though he was quite powerless to have prevented the attack. No wonder all these people who live so close to our good rule wish that we would come and govern their country.

The 23rd of October was a day on which a great festival of some sort was held at Chan-Ta, and nearly two hundred retainers had been brought into the house to accompany the chief to a temple. The people are not much earlier in their habits here than generally in Yün-Nan. I enjoyed a quiet hour's writing before any one else was astir, and then watched the people get up one by one and perform their scanty ablutions in the courtyard, after rubbing the sleep out of their eyes.

As the Shan chief went off to his devotions, he passed through a double line of men, who were attired in most picturesque costumes. All were armed with swords or guns, some had both, and after the sober dresses of the Chinese, the contrast of the brilliant colours in which these people love to deck themselves was very striking. The Chinese almost invariably wear the dark blue cotton in winter, and in summer they dress in white; the Tibetans, too, indulge in little bright colouring, for the clothes of the Lamas are but a dull red; but here, all of a sudden, there were people wearing green, red, yellow, or purple cummerbunds and turbans.

The Shan chief rode in his chair, carried by some very ragged and clumsy chair-coolies; his official red umbrella, seal of office, and diploma, all done up in red or yellow, went before him. There were two or three big muskets, like punt-guns, carried by two men apiece, the rest of the retainers being armed with matchlocks or old percussion-guns. The chief was away at this business a little more than an hour, and as soon as he returned the people began to stir themselves about getting mules, and as all the men and women for miles round came in to pay a state visit to he chief, every one was very glad to get us out of the way, and as much haste as possible was made to find us what we wanted.

The consumption of pork in the house on this festive occasion was enormous; half the pigs in the village must have been killed for the purpose. Every two or three minutes a man passed through the door leading to the private apartments, carrying a huge lump of pork. Up to this point, as far as eating is concerned, the people had been exactly like the Chinese: at all the little stalls, under the trees, the usual Chinese dishes had been invariably found, and here the regular Chinese love of pork was most evident. As we started, and rode off through the village, where numbers of a small, but particularly repulsive-looking, breed of pigs, with unusually long snouts, were wallowing in the mire, and where, as a contrast, there were some very handsome ducks and geese, we met all the people dressed in their best clothes coming in—and really it was a very pretty sight. The women mostly wore tight black cotton garments, which were folded many times round their hips, giving to this part of the body the appearance of great breadth. Some, instead of black bodies to their dresses, wore them of blue, green, or almost any bright colour except red, and some wore white. The people looked very much cleaner than the Chinese, their white clothing, whether on men or women, always being clean and fresh. Their sleeves were generally ornamented with red cuffs. They wore loose black trousers reaching a little below the knee, the rest of their legs and feet being quite bare. Round their waists there were brilliant cummerbunds, mostly of cotton, but some of silk. These were of every hue, red being the favourite tint, and there was a bunch of bits of cloth of all sorts of bright colours, like a large tassel, tucked in behind. Their turbans, swelling as they rose high above their heads, were black, and decorated with pins, from which hung large ornaments of beads, with very large and bright-coloured tassels, generally red. A narrow slip of black cloth formed a necktie, and was fastened at the throat with a large brooch of silver, sometimes set with fifteen stones in three horizontal rows.

Round their necks they wore two or three heavy silver hoops, eighteen inches in diameter; earrings, with bright red tassels, played against their cheeks; their wrists were weighted with three or four massive silver bracelets, and their fingers were tricked with a quantity of heavy silver rings, set with stones of a very inferior description. The ears of some of the women were pierced with holes about half an inch in diameter, in which silver tubes, two or three inches long, were inserted; and a bunch of the delicate black rings of rattan-cane encircled the legs of all. They were very fond of flowers, nearly all having a brilliant yellow flower in their turban, or somewhere else about their dress.

It was very amusing, too, to see that at least half the men wore buttons from England, made in imitation of half-rupees, with the head of her Most Gracious Majesty embossed upon them. We met also a few women from the wild mountain tribes. They were dressed quite differently, with bare heads, and their hair cut in a horizontal fringe across the forehead, and with a skirt to their dresses, embroidered in front;[7] and here and there a good many Lamas or Phoongyees stood lazily about in bright yellow dresses and flat yellow turbans, their lips and mouths all red with the betel-nut that they chew. It was altogether very interesting watching these people, and the first hour of the journey passed very quickly.

Our road generally led through rice-fields. Most of the rice was now cut, and the fields were quite dry; but a good deal was still standing, and the horses we were riding could hardly be prevented enjoying an occasional mouthful of this delicious food, for the path was but a track, with the crops growing close on both sides. In some cases a little fence of split bamboo was erected at the edge; and every now and then, where the road became wider, running between banks or hedges of cactus, there would be fences across the track with gates, the first gates I had seen since leaving Europe. Now there would be a little undulating stretch of beautiful turf; and at another time we rode for nearly a quarter of a mile under a fine grove of banyan trees. Here, under a gigantic banyan, would be an old man or woman seated with a little refreshment stall, where a picturesque group of people, horses, or mules would be collected, resting and taking a dish of rice, blancmange, pickled quince, or a piece from a gigantic cucumber, the size and shape of a melon.

Presently up came an old man, riding a fine chestnut pony; he smiled when he saw us, made a European salute, and, very pleased, stopped to say a word or two. He had lived twelve years in Ava, and loudly sang the praises of the English, who, he said, had treated him, though only a poor trader, like a prince. He wanted us to buy his pony. He said that our honourable countrymen always liked to

[7] These must have been Kakyens (or Kach'yens).--*Y.*

buy good horses, and his was just the thing to suit them. We did not make the purchase, but wishing him good-bye, we rode on. It was very pleasant to find that those who had been amongst the English in Burmah were always glad to see us, and spoke of our people and our rule as so good and just. Here the villages were almost hidden by very fine trees and bamboos, but I never saw a bamboo of the extraordinary dimensions of which I have heard. All the way from Ch'êng-Tu I examined every bamboo grove that I passed, and I never saw one more than six inches in diameter.

The road was generally very good and level, about a mile or so from the river, but now and then coming close down by the edge, where we could see people fishing or poling about in their dug-out canoes. Great numbers of white paddy-birds flapped about; there were a few cormorants, and a yellow wild duck or two; the magpie was as much a part of the landscape as ever, and in the banyan trees a kind of black and white chattering bird was generally in flocks of ten or a dozen. The day was very fine, the temperature just pleasant, and the ride would have been perfect but for the unpleasant habit the people have of purposely keeping their roads under water. Once we came to a drop of about two feet into a bog, where one of our ponies literally sank up to his nose in the mud, and it was all the poor beast could do to extricate himself.

To our great surprise Chin-Tai galloped on ahead with one of the Cantonese, and we wondered what had caused this sudden access of courage; the natural suggestion would have been 'cash'—and so it was.

Shortly before we arrived at the market-place of T'ai-P'ing-Chieh (or Kara-hokah of Anderson), he returned, and, scarcely intelligible with rage, poured out a torrent of words, explaining as well as his excitement would permit how, as his pony was unable to travel fast, he had said to the Cantonese:—

'Dear sir, would you be so good as to go on first, and kindly find a house for their excellencies to breakfast in; and if, honourable sir, you could make it convenient to command rice for the little ones, I should esteem it a very high favour.'

'Whereat,' said Chin-Tai, 'the Cantonese began to curse and swear, and said that he was no servant of the foreigners, and would do nothing for them.' Such in effect was Chin-Tai's tale, and now the Cantonese, who had by this time rejoined us, gave us his version.

He said that no sooner was he a long way ahead with Chin-Tai, than the latter had accused him of extracting eight taels from the native chief to pay for our horses and mules, and that Chin-Tai had demanded half of this sum, which existed only in the imagination of our follower; and that he had said to Chin-Tai:—

'Dear Chin-Tai, you are quite mistaken, for I have received nothing. I am but a poor Cantonese, and really have no money, while you come from the noble city of Peking. If I had a few cash, I would willingly share it with so honourable a person; but I have nothing, really nothing.'

'Then,' said the Cantonese, 'Chin-Tai drew his sword and beat me twice, and as I was unwilling to be on anything but the most friendly terms with your excellencies' servants, rather than defend myself I ran away.'

That both tales were a string of lies went without saying; for if King David had only lived a little further east, his verdict, delivered as he confesses in haste, might safely have been pronounced in his moments of leisure after the most mature deliberation. Not that the Chinese are worse than other Eastern nations, in fact they are not so bad as many. A Chinaman will always tell the truth for choice, if there is no conflicting interest; but it would be of course too much to expect that he would sacrifice either his pocket or his convenience to the exigencies of veracity; on the other hand, I have noticed that some Orientals will always lie merely for the pleasure of doing so.

We poured very cold water on the complaints of both the disputants with most discriminating impartiality, and so contrived to extinguish the flames of their wrath.

When we arrived at Tai-P'ing-Chieh, which consisted of one very broad street between low huts of bamboo wickerwork, splashed with mud, with thatched roofs, Chin-Tai proposed one house and the Cantonese another. Anxious to retain the credit we had acquired for holding the scales of justice even-handed, we went first to the house of the Cantonese selection, and then, finding no rice cooked, moved across the road to Chin-Tai's choice, thus hurting the feelings of neither party.

The weather was hot, and the room was small, but it was soon densely packed with inquisitive Chinese, who settled themselves down comfortably to enjoy the show, until we expressed our regret that we could not invite all of them to breakfast, for what was one bowl of rice amongst so many? This shamed the greater part of them into a retreat, and we were allowed to finish our meal in peace.

We had a pleasant afternoon's march through the same magnificent and fertile valley; the trees, with which all the villages were surrounded, giving the plain the appearance of being well wooded. The ground was nearly covered with yellow rice, with here and there a small patch of beans, cotton, tobacco, or cabbages; and we arrived at Man-Yün,[8] the frontier town of China, at about six o'clock in the evening.

We were conducted to the residence of the civil magistrate, of which that officer had spoken in such unctuous terms at T'êng-Yüeh. He, however, had no house, but lived at the back of a temple, the eaves of which projected about nine feet; the space underneath, for a length of twenty feet, had been walled in by a straw mat, and divided into two compartments by another. One of the rooms so formed was the house of the Chinese magistrate; the other was the mansion of one of his subordinates; and an open cesspit was just outside. The poor fellow in giving us his house had certainly done the best he could for us, and, as it is never wise to be critical with regard to a gift horse, we settled ourselves down as well as circumstances would admit.

The march from the Chinese frontier to Ma-Mou or Sicaw is a difficult one, and long and frequent were the legends told

[8] This is Manwyne (Manwain), known by the treacherous murder of Augustus Margary there.—*Y.*

us of the fearsome nature of the path itself, and the savage conduct of the 'wildmen,' as the Chinese called the mountaineer inhabitants of the border-land between Cathay and Amien.

It is customary for travellers to pay tribute to the heads of all the places passed through. If this is not done they have a pleasing habit of cutting down trees and putting them in the way; then the traveller must make a detour to some other village, where he may find more trees across the road, if he has not been robbed before arrival. In this way the journey, if performed at all, naturally occupies some days; but sometimes traders will band themselves together, to the number of seventy or eighty, and pass through in one march, regardless of the 'wildmen.' There was no native chief here; he being dead, a woman, his widow, reigned in his stead. She was a stout little woman of already fifty summers at the time of Sladen's visit, and ten years had probably not added to her activity; but we did not see her. Her affairs were conducted by some deputy, and were, as a consequence, all more or less 'east and west;' but he promised to find us mules and coolies, and a 'wildman' to take a letter to Bhamo.

We had already sent a letter from Ta-Li-Fu, which the Tao-Tai had informed us would travel at the rate of fifty miles a day. At T'êng-Yüeh I had written another, and had entrusted it to the officials, but it had been returned to me the same evening with the excuse that it had been opened by some one in mistake; and although it is probable that this was true I did not deem it worth while to make another attempt. But Li-Sieh-Tai, who called on us, told us that my letter despatched from Ta-Li-Fu on the 30th of September, had only reached Man-Yün on the 20th of October; and as the 'wildmen' demanded 5*l.* for taking a letter to Sicaw, and there seemed much uncertainty of its getting beyond that place, we abandoned the idea.

Li rather made light of the difficulties of the road, but said he did not think we could reach Sicaw in one day.

We naturally looked with peculiar interest at this man, whose career had been so remarkable, and on whom so much suspicion hung with regard to the deplorable death of our countryman Mr. Margary.

A Burmese officer called on us, who astonished us by shaking hands in European fashion. He wore a bright yellow embroidered silk handkerchief on his head, and a Chinese jacket, with the regulation five buttons, and lined with fur, though the thermometer was between 70° and 80°. A long piece of silk, about a yard broad, striped yellow, green, red, and white—yellow being the predominating colour—was wound round his waist, forming a skirt; and the end, folded three or four times into a sash, hung down in front. His legs were bare, and his feet were encased in a pair of wooden sandals turned up in front. He was in some way connected with the place, held a Chinese official rank, and talked Chinese very well.

Our meals at Man-Yün put me in mind of the Zoological Gardens. We used to take them in the chief part of the temple, which was open to the front, except for some large wooden gates with vertical bars about nine feet high. Here the inquisitive crowd used to collect and stare through at us. It only wanted a placard outside—'Animals feed at 11 and 7'—to make the resemblance complete.

The Chinese civil magistrate, whose house we were occupying, arrived in the evening; but he would not let us turn out, and he found a small garret adjacent. He told us that he would make all the arrangements with the chiefs of the districts, and that we should find twenty native soldiers sufficient as an escort.

He advised us to take some opium as a present for the heads of the villages. He added that the mountaineers had a superstition that if people rode through their villages, ill-luck would follow, and he counselled us to dismount and walk through them. We asked if the officers of the British force that marched through dismounted at the villages. He said he thought not, but that they were a strong body, and could do as they pleased. The number of disbanded soldiers had again risen, and according to the latest intelligence there were three bands, of two hundred or three hundred each; and, instead of being between Man-Yün and T'êng-Yüeh, it was now stated that they were at Ma-Mou, or between that place and Man-Yün.

A steady rain kept us indoors during our stay at Man-Yün, but we managed to visit the market between the showers. Some of the Pa-I people were seen about. The customs of the Pa-I in south-eastern Yün-Nan, as related by Garnier, seem similar to those of all the tribes in this district, especially the delight in silver ornaments; but none of the dresses in Garnier's picture are much like those of the natives here. The Pa-I women in Man-Yün were certainly very good-looking as compared with the Chinese.[9]

There were quantities of English goods in the market—needles, buttons, balls of thread, and English cotton—and a long train of two hundred or three hundred mules came in from Bhamo laden with salt from England. The caravan had been attacked on the road, and had lost twenty mules. The salt reaches Nan-Tien, although it has no business to go even as far as that; for Nan-Tien, though under a native chief, is ruled by, and is a part of, China, where salt is a Government monopoly, and where the importation is forbidden by law.

As far as T'êng-Yüeh, we passed trains of salt going the same way as ourselves, and beyond Nan-Tien we saw it coming up from the other direction.

At the time of our visit to Man-Yün there was a head-man with one of the most villainous faces that it had ever been my lot to see, but he appeared all-powerful, and even the Chinese magistrate seemed more or less in his hands. He seemed to have had a guilty conscience about something, for when the Grosvenor expedition was here he cleared out and ran away. The Chinese magistrate was, of course, determined to make as much out of us as possible. He averred that he had no authority whatever over the people between Man-Yün and Bhamo; but although we completely failed to get mules without his assistance, directly he made sure that he could gain a large profit the mules were arranged

[9] Pa-I is the Chinese name of a Shan race widely diffused in Yün-Nan, or rather is the synonym of *Shan*. See *Marco Polo*, 2nd ed. ii. 51.—*Y*.

for. He professed to be very much annoyed when the people asked us five taels per animal for the journey, and assured us that one tael was quite enough. He, however, made arrangements with a chief to conduct us for 2·2 taels. He told us that we must pay a further sum of ten taels to this chief as a kind of tribute, and also give him one hundred taels weight of opium to distribute along the road. He said that we ought to pay the money and opium through him, and he wanted us to give the whole in advance. This we refused, but paid him half the opium, the whole of the ten taels tribute, and half the mule hire.

This sum of 2·2 taels was very high; but Sladen's expedition, Margary, and subsequently the Grosvenor expedition, all paid more, and it was consequently very difficult to make arrangements even at this rate; but we were determined, as far as possible, to consider those who might follow us; otherwise, as it was the last stage, we would willingly have paid whatever was asked, to avoid the haggling.

Whilst at Man-Yün we received a warm letter of welcome from the late Mr. T. T. Cooper, and after all our wanderings it was a pleasant thing to feel ourselves once again so nearly under the shadow of the British flag.

Before leaving Man-Yün I instituted a gun-bearer, for during the journey to Ma-Mou we should be more or less liable to an attack of some sort, and the coolie was given strict injunctions never, under any circumstances, to leave my stirrup.

The muleteers kept us a long time waiting, so we started in advance early on the 29th and sat down under a banyan tree until our caravan should catch us up; the air was pleasant, and we were well amused watching the people pass. The men—even the agriculturists—without a single exception, were armed with swords, and sometimes with guns as well, and were tattooed from the waist to the knee. This tattooing is commenced at the age of puberty, and it must be a long time before it is complete, for no man could stand the pain and inflammation on so large a surface of the body at one time.

The wild Kakyen women from the mountains were

coming in to Man-Yün, all with their hair cut in a fringe across the forehead.

When at last we moved off together we were an imposing force, with twenty native soldiers carrying swords and guns.

Just beyond a stream we came to a hot-spring. We asked the chief if this was the scene of poor Margary's death. No, he said, but just by the edge of the water where we had crossed it.

Standing thus at the scene of his cruel murder, I could not but feel what a loss the country had sustained in that brilliant young officer, who, through sickness and the difficulties attending a pioneer in new and untravelled districts, had carried out with singular tact the delicate duties entrusted to him, and may, in the words of Dr. Anderson, be said 'to have bequeathed it as a public duty—made more imperative by its being the most fitting tribute to his worth,—to establish in those border-lands the right of Englishmen to travel unmolested.'

'The name of AUGUSTUS RAYMOND MARGARY will be most fitly honoured by a party of his countrymen formally asserting the right to traverse, in honour and safety, the route between Burmah and China which he was the first Englishman to explore, and which should be maintained as his most durable monument.'

It was our fortune to be the humble instruments of thus honouring his name, but any feeling of gratification was lost in the thoughts of the rueful scene that had been enacted on that fatal shore. We had claimed the legacy bequeathed by him, but it was in sorrow that I felt that we had redeemed the right his life had purchased. For a moment I thought of sketching a spot which will ever be a hallowed one to Englishmen; but it might have raised suspicions in the superstitious minds of our companions; and long after such a paltry record would have perished his name will stand bright and clear in the recollection of his regretful countrymen. I uncovered my head as the only tribute of respect that I could pay to the memory of one who will ever be dear to the hearts, not only of those who knew him, but of all who value the noble qualities of uprightness, courage, and determination.

There are three roads between Man-Yün and Ma-Mou,[1] and the one we followed does not keep close to the river, but winds about amongst spurs thrown out from a high wooded range of mountains that bounds the valley, and separates it from that of the Nampoung river. There is but little cultivation, the country being entirely inhabited by Kakyens, who mostly live in small huts by themselves, though at about every ten or twelve miles there is a collection of perhaps half a dozen, forming a village. These solitary huts generally have no walls, but simply consist of a gabled roof of thatch supported on bamboo stakes, with a raised floor, rather higher than the lower edge of the roof, underneath a portion of it. The floor is made of thin strips of split bamboo, and the supports, like almost everything in these parts, are of bamboo. The thatch is made from the long grass that grows to a height of seven or eight feet, and through which the narrow track, which cannot be called a road, passes.

There were no rocky places, nor steep gradients, the great difficulties we had to contend with being the frequent bogs, one of which was so deep that we were obliged to cut branches of trees and grass, and make a path, before the animals could cross. We passed through a regular jungle of thorns, very long grass, and trees, but as yet did not enter the forest of magnificent trees of which I had heard so much. The country is very undulating, and admirably adapted for robbers' purposes: even a couple of men, hidden away amongst the grass on the top of a hill, could easily throw a caravan into confusion; and our chief showed us a place where, as the grass was much trampled down some yards off the track, he considered there must have been a robbery during the last day or two.

We had been informed that our chief was going to conduct us to his house, a march of only ten miles; but

[1] Ma-Mou is apparently 'Old Bhamo' of our maps, at which (according to Dalrymple) the East India Company had a factory in the middle of the seventeenth century.—*Y.*

after having ridden about seven miles, in answer to my inquiries he said that he had taken a different road, as there were a good many troublesome people on the other, and that now we had come about half-way to our halting-place.

As it was now about two o'clock, I determined to eat my breakfast without dismounting, and soon afterwards became so absorbed in the interesting occupation of peeling a hard-boiled egg, that I failed to notice a group of some twenty or thirty people in a clearing at a little distance.

The sound of a shot caused me to look up; but it did not strike me as anything more serious than a man frightening birds, until Mesny called out—

'Won't you load your rifle? they are firing at us!'

The *bolt* that I made of that egg would even have astonished '*Pip*,' as I sprang down and clapped a couple of cartridges into a heavy double express. The bullet had struck a bamboo just in front of the chief, who was riding first.

And now how our old friend Marco would have revelled in the telling of how the mules turned tail and fled, and nothing on earth would have induced them to turn. How off they sped with such a noise and uproar that you would have trowed the world was coming to an end! And how, too, they plunged into the wood, and rushed this way and that, dashing their burdens against the trees, bursting their harness, and smashing and destroying everything that was on them! How the battle raged furiously; how you might see swashing blows dealt and taken! How the din and uproar were so great, from this side and from that, that God might have thundered and no man would have heard it!

The necessities of a truthful tale, however, compel me to admit that the above animated description, adapted from that of the battle of Vochan, is in no way applicable to the attack at Pung-Shi. No one seemed either excited or alarmed; the animals, when they were stopped, began quietly to nibble the grass; even the Peking braves shared the general apathy, and scarcely turned their heads. The native chief put a fresh quid of betel into his mouth, as he assured us that it was nothing, and begged us to move on.

Not another shot was fired; and the scene was far more ludicrous than thrilling, as one of our party, with an old sixteen-bore muzzle-loader, the best lock of which had a useful knack of tumbling off at critical moments, and which was charged with No. 7 shot, stood at the *ready* behind a hedge so thick that he could not have seen the whole Russian army if it had been at the other side.

The excitement soon 'dwindled to a calm,' and we quietly marched away from our assailants, who were some of the people living in these solitary huts, and who, notwithstanding the patch of rice with which they surround their dwellings, are more robbers than agriculturists. If they see a small train of twenty or thirty animals, they fire a shot, when, if the travellers are Chinese, they generally take fright, stop, or run away. The wildman then takes tribute, or helps himself, seldom killing anybody. In this case the assailants, in all probability, had not the faintest idea that there were foreigners, and when they saw that we were prepared to fight they made no further attempt to interfere with us.

We passed on, and presently came to the outskirts of a small village, where all sorts of wonderful things had been put up to frighten away the spirits. Two posts were driven into the ground, sloping at an angle of about 60°, on which curious cabalistic signs were painted in black and white; little square or triangular platforms were erected on bamboo stakes for the spirits to sit on; these were decorated with dried branches of leaves and tufts of grass; and there were long rows of bamboo stakes, to each of which a bit of small bamboo, about a foot long, was fastened. The history and meaning of each and all we could not learn. The people would only tell us that they were a protection against the spirits, or 'Nats.'

Immediately after this we arrived at the village of Pung-Shi,[2] consisting of about half a dozen bamboo huts. These are all exactly alike. A level platform is first cut out on the slope of the hill, leaving a steep bank on the upper side

[2] Pung-Shi is the 'Ponsee' of Anderson and Sladen.—*Y.*

against which the hut is erected, the thatched roof coming down to the top of the bank, which thus forms a sort of wall. Three feet above the level platform there is a flooring, extending over about half the covered area, the other half having no floor. The upper portion is divided into compartments by bamboo matting; the flooring is of split

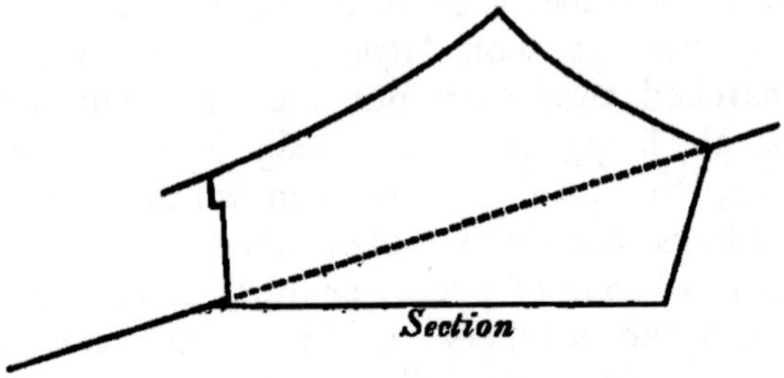

bamboo, supported on bamboos resting on piles; and it is reached by a sloping log of wood, in which there may, or may not, be notches for the feet. The gable at the upper end is closed by matting, with a door leading out. This is a private door, for the use of the family only; the other gable is either half or altogether open.

We were shown into the largest compartment, in the

middle of which some sticks were burning on some earth that had been plastered over the flooring to make a hearth.

On entering, I saw a nice little square wicker shelf in the corner—the very place for my hat, I thought, and put it down there. Straightway a man leapt up from the ground on which he was seated, and, with anxiety pictured on his face, snatched it away. At the same moment Chung-Erh deposited my saddle-bags underneath this shelf, but hardly were they there when another of the men hastily removed them. This was the spirit's corner; for in every house there is a portion set apart for the spirit, so that he may not intrude himself elsewhere, and if people put anything or sit down in the spirit's corner the consequences that ensue are terrible.

We had a long conversation with this chief, who told us that he had not received one cash of the ten taels paid for safe conduct, nor one little piece of the opium, all of which had been retained by the Chinese magistrate, who probably divided the spoil with the head-man with the villainous face.

The natives have an apparatus by which they strike a light by compressed air. The apparatus consists of a wooden cylinder, two and a half inches long by three quarters of an inch diameter. This is closed at one end, the bore being about the size of a stout quill-pen; an air-tight piston fits into this, with a large flat knob at the top. The other end of the piston is slightly hollowed out, and a very small piece of tinder is placed in the cup thus formed. The cylinder is held in one hand, the piston inserted, and pushed about half-way down; a very sharp blow is then delivered with the palm of the hand on to the top of the knob; the hand must at the same time close on the knob, and instantly withdraw the piston, when the tinder will be found alight. The compression of the air produces heat enough to light the tinder; but this will go out again unless the piston is withdrawn very sharply. I tried a great many times, but covered myself with confusion in fruitless efforts to get a light, for the natives themselves never miss it. Altogether, however, I thought that Bryant & May were preferable, whose matches are sold at Man-Yün for twenty-five cash a box (less than a penny farthing), though the lowness of the price seems incredible. We dined off some beef of the buffalo. When it first came in hot, the odour seemed strangely familiar, and suddenly the dining-hall of the Royal Military Academy flashed upon me. I again saw it as it used to be, the tables and forms, with many long-forgotten details. For there was a peculiar smell appertaining to the beef supplied at this institution that I never met with before or since. It is curious how a smell will sometimes call to memory scenes of long ago. This buffalo beef was exceedingly coarse, but it was eatable, and not particularly tough. I tried to believe that the animal had not died a natural death, but wisely asked no questions on the subject.

The muleteers would not start before daylight next morning, but left soon after six ; they all took cold rice with them wrapped up in plantain leaves ; everything betokened a long march, and we thought we should sleep at Ma-Mou that night.

It was a lovely morning, and soon we plunged into a forest of mighty teak trees with a dense undergrowth of long grass, brambles, and bushes, the large forest trees growing widely apart. It was magnificent forest scenery, and might well have originated some of the wildest fancies of Gustave Doré : creepers growing to a huge size and twisting round the limb of some tree like a gigantic python, the resemblance being all the more complete, as the creeper in its growth gradually crushes the life out of the limb that has supported it. The dead limb then rots away, and the cruel creeper, like some monstrous corkscrew, stretched across the path, supports itself with difficulty for a while, and then shares the fate of its victim. Sometimes after reaching the top of a tree a creeper drops down to the ground, so perpendicularly, and so straight, that it is difficult to believe that it is not a stout rope suspended from a branch. One very remarkable fact about these creepers is that they all train, without exception, from right to left (against the hands of a watch). Then there are trees, with weird-looking roots above the ground, grasping an unyielding rock, that fancy might conjure into the form of some antediluvian cuttlefish, which, in its dying agony, was clutching at and striving to crush the rock. Butterflies of marvellously brilliant and varied hues flutter about amongst the glossy fronds of great tree-ferns, and bamboos of a length almost incredible shoot up, till, often unable to bear their own weight, they fall across the road. The bamboos do not attain any great thickness, the largest I measured being five and a half inches, and the largest I saw being certainly not more than seven inches in diameter; but their height is extraordinary, as is the number of them; they grow in clumps of twenty or thirty together, and, as the road is traversed, there are always two, if not three, of these fine groups in sight. They are used for nearly every purpose, even that of water buckets; lengths of about three feet are taken for this, and in the houses there are always some half-dozen of them in a corner.

We had rather a tiring march, a great deal of up-and-down hill over a somewhat indifferent road, rocky and very steep; but the mules kept up a steady pace until mid-day, when, after fording the Nampoung river, we came to a little opening. Here the packs were taken off, and the animals let loose to graze and roll themselves after their six hours' march. All the people had brought cold rice with them, and even the chief himself sat down to his cold meal. This looked as if they were determined to push on till night, and, as some rice had also been put up for the animals, we thought the halt would not be long. These people partook very contentedly of their uninteresting food; no Chinaman would eat cold rice unless he were driven to very hard straits, for he would at least pour some hot or warm water over it, and my boys even preferred cold potatoes, some of which they fortunately had with them. Potatoes grow in the hills here, so that all the way from Ta-Chien-Lu this valuable root is found, and, notwithstanding the contempt in which the Chinese hold it, the culture has spread with wonderful rapidity.

A wood fire is easily lighted, and so tea was ordered. Chin-Tai then came up, and asked if we would like some poached eggs. We were hungry—a portion of a stale loaf, and hard-boiled eggs, one of which was bad, was not a tempting meal even in the forest. Chin-Tai's proposal was most seductive ; everything appeared handy—still we did not quite like the idea of commencing cooking operations ; but he who hesitates is lost. We hesitated, finally acquiesced, and, as the sequel shows, were lost.

The chief and all the muleteers, though they had clearly made up their minds to start soon, had done so sorely against their will, and only on account of the tremendous presents that had been promised should a Ma-Mou roof shelter us this night. When they saw us making cooking preparations, the temptation was too strong : numerous fires were lighted, men sent off to cut grass for the animals, and the unthrashed rice prepared for them was reserved for another occasion. The despatch of the grass-cutters we did not notice until it was too late ; but after our breakfast and a cigar, when we mooted the question of moving, the chief quietly replied we would move to-morrow morning, and reach Ma-Mou in plenty of time. Threats, persuasions, and offers of egregious reward were alike useless ; the chief and the muleteers sat stolidly smoking or cooking their rice, and simply took not the slightest notice of anything we said. We determined, however, to go off, hoping the rest would follow ; and, ordering the Ma-Fu to get the ponies, we packed up the few things we had out, amongst others the thermometer. This instrument had much exercised the chief, and he asked if it was the machine by which we found out whether there were thieves on the road. 'No,' we answered. 'We can't show you that affair—this is to see whether it is hot or cold.' 'Why, you needn't trouble yourself to do that, you have only to ask me and I can tell you—without using anything like that,' was the rather obvious retort.

The people were all very lazy, and even the Ma-Fu, who was generally most active and willing, seemed to share the general lethargy. Mesny's boy had gone off to cut wood to make a bed with, and Chin-Tai and Chung-Erh would not catch their animals, and expected the muleteers to do it for them, who looked on with a grin. Seeing we were in earnest, the muleteers gave our riding animals some rice ; and cowardice prevailing over laziness, my two boys, all at once becoming very humble, captured their erring beasts, and saddled them without more ado. The chief, though clearly more or less uneasy in his mind, made no motion of stirring, and we started alone, our party being Mesny, Chin-Tai, my Ma-Fu, my gun coolie, Mesny's boy, and myself. Chung-Erh was not quite ready, but he followed as fast as he could, fear now keeping him close to our heels.

Of course none of us knew anything of the road, but we recklessly plunged again into the forest, trusting to good luck and the chances of war. We had not gone far before a guide sent by the chief overtook us, for, having undertaken to conduct us in safety, he did not like the idea of our wandering about by ourselves in the dense forest. We rode on steadily, and as fast as we could, but after a little more than an hour our guide remarked—

'It will be dark before we get to Ma-Mou.'

'Will it?' we answered; 'then we shall not get to Ma-Mou before dark.'

This reply, though it ought to have satisfied anyone, did not seem to please him, for immediately afterwards he stopped at a stream to drink, fell behind us, and at a village a hundred yards further on he disappeared, and we saw him no more.

In about half an hour we came to a bifurcation of the trail, a halt was called to consider the momentous question, and we decided to wait six minutes for the guide. That period having expired, the gun-coolie, who coming out quite in a new light displayed the instinct of a Mohican chief, now examined one path, then the other, and gave it as a deliberate opinion that the left hand or upper road was the right one. We consulted a little, and all voting for the motion of the gun-coolie, we again went off.

Mesny was hopefully of the opinion that '*Tout chemin mène à Rome.*' I could only give a doubtful assent to this pleasing theory. We were riding through a very narrow track, our faces being continually brushed by the grass or leaves, when, all of a sudden, I felt as if there were a necklace of thorns on me. I fancied that a bramble stretching across the road must have caught me, and thinking that I should get sadly torn I tried to bring my pony up abruptly ; this animal however, accustomed to follow in a string, stop if the beast in front of him stops, and go on when his leader moves, would not come to a halt as quickly as I wished ; and then I found that though there was no feeling of scratching, the pain was becoming every second more intense, as if my necklace of thorns was being gradually tightened. In a very few moments I could bear it no longer, and, nearly frantic with wonder as to what had occurred, and the sharp, stinging pain, I shouted out to Mesny in front. He looked back, and called out—'Get down, get down ! you are covered with ants.' I jumped off the pony, and found that thousands of huge red ants nearly a quarter of an inch long were in my hair, under my shirt, all over my clothes, and viciously biting with one accord ; I was simply covered with them. I took off my clothes, and though the Ma-Fu and both my boys came to my aid, it was a long time before I was altogether free.

Mesny had gone on a few yards with the gun-coolie, and now I suddenly heard his voice in loud altercation with some one. I was behind a hedge, was completely hidden from everything in front, and could not see what was going on. I hurried up, and saw Mesny pointing his revolver at a man, who, at that moment, disappeared into a hut about twenty yards off the road, and the gun-coolie squatting down and struggling with the buckle of my rifle-case.

Chinamen are never able to manage a buckle ; indeed, I have often thought a buckle almost as good as a padlock. I quickly extracted and loaded my rifle, and asked Mesny what was up.

'Oh, he says we may not ride past his house, but must walk.'

'Does he ?' I answered ; and we both jumped quickly on our ponies, and, revolver in hand, rode on till the bushes and trees hid him from view.

Mesny now told me that, as he went on, the gun-coolie just in front sat down to brush off the ants, some of which had attacked him also, when a man armed with a sword ran towards Mesny, who he thought was alone, as owing to the bushes he could see no one else, and whom he evidently mistook for a Chinaman.

The native called out that no one was to ride past. Mesny shouted to the coolie to bring the foreign gun, but the latter was so busy with the ants that he did not understand what was happening. The man then went into his hut, and came back with a gun, followed by another man, or woman, unarmed; he knelt down, and, resting his gun against a post, aimed at Mesny, who, pointing his revolver at the native, called out—

'If you shoot, you are a dead man.'

'Oh,' he cried, 'I'm not shooting your way.'

'I don't care where you shoot; if you fire, I shall hit you,' said Mesny; whereat the man put away his gun, again said that no one must ride past, but retired into his hut.

This was the work of a few seconds, and it was at this point that I came up. Nothing more came of this adventure; but we gave orders to our people not to make any noise when there were any huts about, for we did not want any more of these occurrences.

This is the way these natives always treat passers-by; the Chinese are afraid, they give way, and then when the wild-man has gained the first point and made them walk, he calls his neighbours, and all demand blackmail—tobacco, opium, and silver—so that the wretched trader has altogether a mean time of it. But these people, like all bullies, are regular cowards, and the smallest show of resistance brings them down from their tall trees.

We rode on, and as it began to get dark we wondered where we should pass the night. Though there was no moon, the stars were very brilliant, but here and there not a ray of light could penetrate the thick and heavy foliage. At last the darkness became so pitchy that we might have been knocked out of our saddles by some overhanging bough before we could have seen it, and, not deeming it safe to ride, we dismounted. We stepped into a regular quagmire, and, up to our knees in mud, groped and stumbled about amongst great rocks and stones for fifty yards or so, until, the trees being a little more open, it was again safe to mount. We saw a hut or two, but, doubtful as to what sort of a reception we should meet with, we passed them by; but, at last, getting very uneasy as to whether or not we were on the right track, we called out to a man sitting over a fire. He would give us, however, no reply of any sort, and we passed on. At seven o'clock we came across a deserted hut ; here we halted, lit a fire, and began to prepare some torches ; but while this was going on we held a consultation. We did not even know whether we were on the right road ; we could see nothing ; we did not know how far Ma-Mou might be, nor what sort of a place it was ; it might have walls and gates, and, if so, the latter might be shut, if we ever arrived there. From what we had seen of the plain before it became dark it looked as if there was a great deal of water about. Here was, at least, a shelter for the night. It was true that Ma-Mou, if we had kept the right road, could not be far off ; but, even if thus far we had not gone wrong, we might possibly stray in the next few miles. At length the final verdict was given to stop, and then everyone was more or less glad. I had some bread still in my saddle-bags, my servants had the remains of a few potatoes, and a kind of root like a turnip was discovered by some eyes that could see in the dark. There was also a pinch of tea and a small brass wash-hand-basin to make it in; so, after a meal that was rather simple than plentiful, I smoked one cigar, wrapped myself in a blanket, and defied the mosquitoes until dawn.

The mosquitoes annoyed Mesny sadly, but they let me alone somehow, although I dreamt I was under mosquito-curtains engaged in hunting some dozen of venomous brutes the size of dragon-flies ; but it was after all only a dream, and I managed to get through a considerable number of hours of sleep before the first grey streak of dawn.

There had, as usual, been a very heavy dew, and, riding through the jungle, we were soon all wet enough to welcome the sun when at last he topped the hills and began to dry us as well as the bushes. There had been nothing for us to eat or drink before starting, but the thoughts that now we really were at the end of our land journey, quite drove away unpleasant feelings of any kind. A very short ride brought us to a village at the foot of the hills; but before reaching it we passed a stream over some planks which would most effectually have stopped us in the dark. At the village, the promise of a rupee procured us a guide, who, soon after turning abruptly to the left, showed us that even if we had passed the bridge we should most certainly and inevitably have taken the wrong road at this point, and it was comforting to think that we had after all done right in stopping.

Presently we met a man carrying a couple of mallards and a double-barrelled breechloader. While I was wondering who he might be he made a military salute, and, in a language of which no one of us understood one single word, explained that a letter had arrived somewhere; he then turned back with us. We now dismissed the guide with a rupee borrowed from the gun-coolie, and, much elated, continued our ride, discussing meanwhile our new companion, who continually shouted to an invisible person somewhere away in the jungle on our right. We, however, could make nothing of him, and soon Ma-Mou was pointed out. We were taken straight to a house, where a Bengali met us, and, making a salute, told us that Cooper had sent him, his boat, and a number of men to meet us, and that he had been waiting for us eight days. This my almost forgotten Hindustani enabled me to gather; but I must confess in shame that I was not long in discovering that he spoke English very much better than I did his language. A house had been prepared for us; here was a pile of newspapers, a letter from Cooper, two huge boxes of eatables and drinkables, pipes, tobacco, cigars, candles, candlesticks, matches, and everything one thoughtful and experienced traveller could send to comfort the heart and mind of another.

Though the news was not very recent it was the latest Cooper had, and no one who has not gone through the anxiety that I had felt during the last two months can form the slightest conception of the feeling that came over me—one that I utterly failed to comprehend even myself, a feeling of peace, ease, and contentment quite indescribable, and so apparent that Mesny told me afterwards that I appeared to be quite a different person. Chin-Tai was set to work at once to cook rice for our unfortunate and starving crew. Much to our delight the mules arrived before the rice-eating was finished. A bath, clean clothes, and breakfast was followed by one of Cooper's Havannah cigars, and I exclaimed with Pangloss, 'All is for the best in the best of worlds possible.'

The corporal, for such he was who spoke the English, told us that the steamer would not be at Bhamo for two or three days, and would not start for two or three more, so we determined to take it easy, remain at Ma-Mou till the next morning, and then drop quietly down the river. The corporal added that a letter that we had sent from Pung-Shi arrived the previous afternoon, and that he had found a means to forward it to Cooper.

The house we were in was of bamboo, raised about five feet above the ground on piles of teak; the roof was of thatch, and the walls and floor of split bamboos, and here we looked on to the river of T'êng-Yüeh, now grown to a fine large rolling stream.

In the afternoon the corporal came to tell us that the Burmese officer had arranged that 'Burmese woman should make ball this evening,' if we liked, by which we eventually understood that a dance had been arranged outside our house, for our edification after dinner.

The dance eventually took place by the light of a quantity of crude petroleum in a large broken earthen jar, in which there was a long branch of a live tree. There were three women performers, their hair done neatly and quietly up in a knot on their heads; they had small earrings, a white jacket, and a red skirt reaching down to the ankles; each had a yellow silk handkerchief laid over one shoulder, but which was continually used during the dance, and they all wore heavy silver bracelets. There were four or five men, one or two naked to the waist, and with broad cloths of different colours and patterns wound round their hips. Music and drumming was kept up all the time; first the women danced for half an hour a very slow quiet measure, simply moving their feet and hands very gently, and with infinitely more grace than the hideous, impossible, and unnatural postures that our most admired European opera-dancers fling themselves into. Then it was the turn of the men; and after some time one who must have been the recognised favourite of the troupe appeared, for his entrance was greeted with a burst of laughter, though there did not appear to be anything particularly amusing about it. That he did the low comedy business was subsequently quite clear, by the continual laughter that was showered on his words and actions; for besides dancing there was a sort of play, in which all the men and women joined, and in which the picking of leaves off the branch of the tree seemed to take an important part. What it was all about I never had the faintest idea, and had it not been for Cooper's packet of cigars, which I finished, I might have wearied of the performance; but, sitting outside the house on a large platform in the lovely cool starlight night, and looking down on the play by the fitful light of the petroleum, which sometimes flared up and at others nearly died away, casting wonderful lights and shadows over the performers and a great number of people collected to see the theatricals, some leaning against the posts of the next house, some lying or sitting on the ground, others on great logs of wood, but all in graceful attitudes, there was a pleasant feeling of ease and comfort, which lasted as long as the cigars. When these were done, I gave the corporal some silver for the actors and retired to bed.

Cooper had sent up his boat for us, a fast and comfortable one, with a little covered-in house at the stern, where we could just lie down or sit. Another native boat was hired for luggage, servants, and the horse, and we started easily at nine o'clock on the 1st of November.

It was rather warm on the way down. The river winds between low and uninteresting banks of high grass jungle with trees; hills are away in the background; a porpoise rolls here and there, kingfishers dart about amongst the reeds, huge pelicans drop into the water with a splash that seems to threaten destruction to their breast-bones; a few native boats are passed made on Dicey's plan—two dug-out canoes, separated by three or four feet, with a deck across, and a house at the stern; single canoes also are paddled about; but the scenery did not vary sufficiently to raise excitement, and, after reading the last word of the last newspaper, I slept during the greater part of the journey.

The T'êng-Yüeh river enters the Irawadi about a mile above Bhamo, and in the Irawadi I was much disappointed. I had expected an immense and gigantic river, like the Yang-Tzŭ at Chin-Kiang. It is true that the river even now is very wide—a quarter of a mile perhaps—but it is shallow, and the current is slow. Now that I had seen the marvellous way in which the T'êng-Yüeh river increases in a few miles, had also seen how much less water passes Bhamo than I had thought, and when I considered the almost continual rain that falls over the basin of this river, the Irawadi ceased to be a mystery.

We reached Bhamo before three, the distance being about twenty miles, and here was Cooper to shake our hands. Oh, the pleasure of a hearty British shake of the hand! who shall measure it after the everlasting ceremonies of the Chinese! I know of strange people in England who object to shaking hands as an ungraceful, rough, and barbarous salutation. It may be so, but I know that that one hearty grasp meant more than ten thousand Chinese flowery expressions about my honourable self, and did me more good and put me in better spirits than anything that had happened for many a long and weary day. The attempt to convey an idea of the kindness Cooper showered upon me would be vain, nor can I describe the delightful feeling of being once again in a clean house, where I could walk without tucking my trousers inside my socks, of seeing a damask tablecloth, and the thousand and one things never noticed at home, but which seem such luxuries after long separation. We had something to eat immediately, and to drink. We passed the afternoon and evening in talking over our travels, and went to bed early.

We were generously and hospitably entertained by the late Mr. T. T. Cooper until the 6th of November, when pack-animals were left behind, and we were swiftly borne down the broad bosom of the Irawadi towards home and civilisation.

How quickly those first hours of idleness sped by, though the past had already begun to assume the misty outlines of a dream when the day of our departure arrived. One warm shake of the hand, and, as we stepped into the boat and left our host alone to his solitary life, with cheery wishes that we soon might meet again, it was well that the future was hidden from us.

Death, alas! has made sad havoc amongst those to whose kindness in distant lands I owe so much; and there is something of irony in the fate that permitted Mr. Cooper, in his desperate attempt to pass from China to Burmah through the rebel camp during the Mahometan insurrection, to live so long with his life in his hands, and to escape to tell the tale, and that yet, whilst in comparative security, and with the British flag floating above him, gave him over to the bullet of an assassin.

The boat pushed off into the swirling stream; in a few minutes we stood on board the 'Ta-Pa-Ing,' the last rope was cast loose, and, as Bhamo disappeared from our view, a veil seemed as it were to pass over the recollections of the old travelling life, and it almost appeared as if a new phase of existence had been entered on, as we swept past the wooded shores, with here and there a town, where high-sterned boats would be drawn up in tiers, and where, in the early morning, we might hear the musical swell and fall of the Phoongyee's bell.[3]

On by New Mandalay, with its temples, whose gilded roofs bring to mind the gold and silver towers of Mien;[4] by Prome, and at last to Rangoon. A few days' steaming on a sea of glass, and the City of Palaces was reached; a few weeks amongst many Indian friends, and everywhere the kindness and hospitality surrounding me helped to banish

[3] In Burmah the priests, or Phoongyees, go round from house to house collecting rice from the well-disposed; as they walk slowly round the village or town they strike from time to time a silver-toned piece of gun-metal.

[4] *Marco Polo*, vol. ii. chap. liv.

from my recollection the fatigues and discomforts of travel; never can I sufficiently thank those amongst whom I passed those first few weeks of civilisation, and of enjoyment such as I can hardly hope for again.

Westward again ; and it was with mingled feelings that my glances first lighted on the European continent ; soon the white cliffs of Dover rose on the horizon, and after twenty months of travel I was home at last.

INDEX.

CHINA
M O N G O L I A
Y E L L O W
S E A
C H I N A
S E A